D1452882

Citizens
of Zion

Citizens of Zion

THE SOCIAL ORIGINS OF
CAMP MEETING REVIVALISM

Ellen Eslinger

THE UNIVERSITY OF TENNESSEE PRESS / KNOXVILLE

Library of Congress Cataloging-in-Publication Data

Eslinger, Ellen, 1956-
   Citizens of Zion : the social origins of camp meeting
revivalism / Ellen Eslinger. — 1st ed.
      p. cm.
   Includes bibliographical references and index.
   ISBN 1-57233-033-3 (cl.: alk. paper)

   1. Revivals—Kentucky—History—18th century. 2. Camp
meetings—Kentucky—History—18th century. 3. Christianity and
culture—Kentucky—History—18th century. 4. Revivals—Kentucky—
History—19th century. 5. Camp meetings—Kentucky—History—
19th century. 6. Christianity and culture—Kentucky—History—
19th century. I. Title.
   BV3798 .E75 1999
   269'.24'09769—ddc21   98-25485

For Nancy,
who saw this through

CONTENTS

Illustrations

Figures

Maps

Table

ACKNOWLEDGMENTS

After so many years of working on this book, it is my very great pleasure to acknowledge the numerous people who helped along the way. My first thanks belong to the University of Chicago for giving an aspiring advertising copywriter the chance to make a meaningful contribution to society. Ted Cook played a pivotal role by bringing the university's Reuben T. Durrett manuscript collection to my attention and encouraging me to take on the study of early Kentucky settlement. I would also like to thank Jerald C. Brauer because it was in his University of Chicago Divinity School seminar that I first encountered new ways to understand religious revivalism. Kathy Conzen forced me to reconceptualize the role of Kentucky in western expansion and to stop avoiding the larger implications of my research. In this work, and in my teaching as well, I owe a lot to these three fine people.

I was also fortunate to have the warm support of fellow graduate students, especially Susan Gray, Kay Carr, Robin Einhorn, Susan Rugh, and Winstanley Briggs. I would also like to remember my good friends Nathan Sugarman, Karolla Wielgoz, and Anthony Turkevich.

The early encouragement has meant all the more because this project has enjoyed few friends. Those it has gained, however, have been extraordinary in their loyal support. First and foremost is Robert M. Calhoon, who read the dissertation and many years later served as a reader for the manuscript. Robert's comments and suggestions were—I search for words—invaluable. I would also like to thank the members of the Shenandoah Regional Studies Seminar, especially Ken Koons, Warren Hofstra, and Ann McCleary. Their intellectual comradeship provided sustenance through four difficult years early in my career. Their thorough knowledge of the eighteenth-century backcountry prompted me to consider the settlement of Kentucky in broader regional terms. It is therefore with great fondness that I recognize them here.

Several other people also read portions of this work in draft and, while their reactions have varied, all have made valuable contributions to the final outcome. These include Gail Terry, Randy Sparks, Gregory Nobles, Randy Roth, Cathy Matson, Daniel Jones, Thomas Wermuth,

Timothy Silver, and Beth Kelly. Stephen Aron took time while still working on his own study of early Kentucky to serve as reader for another press. Despite his mild enthusiasm, I am gratified to see from his book that Steve was persuaded on at least a few points, particularly concerning the Great Revival. I hope that he will understand why I've chosen to hold my course.

Researching this book took me to archives and libraries in seven states, where I relied on the expertise of numerous library professionals. Much of the work was done in Kentucky. I well remember my first trip to Kentucky, in a ten-year-old Volkswagen Beetle, when the occasional researcher in the manuscript room of the Filson Club Historical Society worked at a folding card table in a dusty rear room. Back then, the Kentucky Historical Society in Frankfort was open seven days a week, almost entirely oriented toward genealogy. In the Bourbon County courthouse, the tables in the records room were all provided with ashtrays. I feel old beyond my years in recalling these early research experiences, but modern historians of Kentucky owe the state's archivists and recordkeepers an enormous debt for the work they have done to catalog, preserve, and make available the state's rich heritage.

Also deserving special mention for help with this project is the staff in the Manuscripts Division at the Library of Congress. I remember with much warmth their enthusiastic assistance during several months I spent on a J. Franklin Jameson Fellowship, sponsored by the Library of Congress and the American Historical Association.

I would also like to thank the Newberry Library for research support, as well as DePaul University for an academic leave that allowed me to finish this project.

Sections of this book previously appeared as articles in the *Filson Club History Quarterly* and the *Register of the Kentucky Historical Society*, and I appreciate the permission to reproduce some of that material here.

I am also pleased to acknowledge a debt to my good colleague and friend Alex Papadopoulos for his valuable expertise, technical assistance, and artistry in preparing the maps.

Thanks also to the numerous friends and family members, especially my mother, who enriched me and refreshed me through the many long years of labor. It is impossible for me to adequately express my appreciation except to say that, in writing about the crisis of community in early Kentucky, I have many times reflected on my own good fortune.

This book would not exist without the contributions of all these people, plus many others who must remain unnamed, but the remaining flaws are mine alone.

INTRODUCTION

Revivalism is nearly as old as religion itself, but historically it has found various forms of expression. After a long period of declining religious interest, American churches made a noticeable recovery around 1800. The revival of religion occurred with particular force in the recently settled regions of Kentucky and Tennessee, where it was accompanied by a new form of evangelical outreach later known as the camp meeting. This Western Revival or Great Revival culminated with a massive gathering of some ten or fifteen thousand people at Cane Ridge Presbyterian Meetinghouse in Bourbon County, Kentucky, in early August 1801. Meetings in the "Kentucky style" soon appeared in other parts of the country. Camp meeting revivalism eventually became one of nineteenth-century America's most important forms of public worship.

As its name suggests, what most distinguished camp meeting revivalism from other types of outdoor evangelical events was that participants arrived prepared to camp. This simple innovation produced an extraordinary religious experience. Perhaps most obvious was the way that camping dramatically expanded the scale of outdoor evangelicalism. "For more than a half mile, I could see people on their knees before God in humble prayer," wrote one participant at Cane Ridge. Removed from the cares of daily life, participants often experienced intense emotions. Individuals, suddenly struck by their spiritual plight, began falling to the ground "as if dead." At times the effect was awesome, with several hundred people "swept down like the trees of the forest under the blast of the wild tornado." Later, this seemingly involuntary behavior evolved into shrieking, rolling on the ground, barking, and a notorious convulsive movement that contemporaries called "the jerks." The camp meeting formed a world unto itself as rich and poor, man and woman, black and white, joined to worship together. The evangelical proceedings continued without interruption, day and night, for days on end. The result was not only spectacular but, in terms of church growth, also spectacularly effective.

I

Whereas contemporaries understood the camp meeting phenomenon in supernatural terms, as either modern miracle or satanic hoax, scholars have tended to regard it as a product of earthly forces. By far, the foremost explanations have been tied to the frontier environment. Among the first historians to explain camp meeting revivalism as a reflection of a frontier context were Catherine Cleveland and Peter Mode. Both were inspired by Frederick Jackson Turner's famous thesis, "The Significance of the Frontier in American History," originally presented in 1893.[1] Turner himself made only the briefest reference to religion, but his suggestion that the frontier contributed to a more individualistic national culture seemed generally congruent with the personal, decentralized nature of camp meeting revivalism. According to Cleveland, the trans-Appalachian pioneers endured lives filled with "hardships and privation, loneliness and solemnity characteristic of sparsely settled regions." The frontiersman had to be strong and self-reliant. Western society was yet in an infant state, hampered by isolation and high rates of population turnover. Social norms were still vague and weak. Government institutions were usually distant and unresponsive. A comfortable livelihood, moreover, was far from assured. Until land could be cleared for agriculture, the frontier remained an economically marginal region. Many people had moved west full of hope for personal advancement, only to find those hopes dashed by the realities of wilderness life. These experiences presumably created an acute need for emotional solace. Western ministers responded by softening the harsher tenets of Calvinism or abandoning them altogether, thereby rendering Christianity more relevant to the individualistic and democratic frontier setting. Far removed from established religious communities, without the benefits of church institutions, they preached in Nature's wooded groves. The result was the boisterous, chaotic, and emotional camp meeting revival. Over time, religion tamed the wild pioneer character, and the accompanying church structures played an instrumental role in organizing western society.[2]

The scholarship of recent years has tended to emphasize other concerns. John B. Boles stands out as the first to consider the Great Kentucky Revival as something other than a product of frontier conditions, placing it instead within the broad development of southern culture. More recently, Leigh Eric Schmidt traced the Great Revival's influences across the Atlantic, to a major wave of revivalism among Scots-Irish Presbyterians in the early eighteenth century. Paul Conkin expanded on these insights in a more detailed examination of the Great Revival in Kentucky and Tennessee. By demonstrating earlier influences, these studies correct one of the most serious flaws in frontier explanations for the Great Revival. Yet they also verge on reducing it to merely another episode in the waxing and waning of Christianity. Indeed, Conkin has gone so far as to state that "little if anything that happened in this great revival was new."[3] As is sometimes the case in historical revision, the pendulum has perhaps swung back a little too hard. These works nonetheless make an important point in connecting camp meeting revivalism to its larger religious context.

Despite the implicit criticism by these scholars, and a frontal assault by others on the whole portrayal of frontier expansion as set forth by Turner, the simplest glance at textbook treatments of camp meeting revivalism will show that frontier explanations still prevail.[4] In large part, this is because no one has offered a persuasive alternative explanation for why camp meeting revivalism began where it did, when it did, and then went on to become a virtually national phenomenon. This book, which began in 1988 as a dissertation, rests on two fundamental insights.[5] One is that, by the time of the Great Revival in 1800, Kentucky no longer bore much resemblance to its frontier beginnings, particularly not according to Turnerian criteria. The other is that early camp meeting revivalism differed in significant ways not only from earlier evangelical forms but also from its later manifestations. Tightening the temporal scale of analysis and carefully reconstructing both the setting and the phenomenon itself suggest that camp meeting revivalism owed its phenomenal popularity to the ability to reintegrate a society rent by economic hardship, political partisanship, and cultural conflict.

II

Although Turner's "Frontier Thesis" offers more hindrance than help, the process of Euro-American expansion is nonetheless important for understanding the beginnings of camp meeting revivalism. My interpretation of early trans-Appalachian settlement has been guided by a new interpretive framework oriented around early American expansion into the region west of the Blue Ridge Mountains, primarily in Pennsylvania, Virginia, and North Carolina. This region, known as the "backcountry," was settled in the eighteenth century. It has attracted a thriving scholarship in recent years, "blazing an academic Appalachian Trail from the backwoods of Maine to the upcountry of Georgia." The long stretch of interior settlements shared certain traits that historian Gregory Nobles has summarized as "independence and integration." Whereas Turner looked at the frontier as a fresh departure, studies of the colonial backcountry have tended to emphasize the connection with established cultures.[6] And, in contrast to Turner and other historians of his generation, recent scholars have recognized that these established cultures were both white and red. What Turnerians would call a frontier, or border, is instead seen as a "middle ground" or regional zone with a mixture of traits creating a distinctive subculture.[7] The geographic dimensions of the backcountry, never really finite, were defined as much by conflict as by anything else. On one hand was the tension produced by an insatiable appetite for native land while on the other stood a desire for autonomy from control by seaboard centers of power. As settlement developed, of course, the backcountry found itself absorbed by the seaboard centers into the emerging national culture. Thus, as a recently settled region, Kentucky at the time of the Great Revival in 1800 had been going through a period of stressful reorientation.

Also important in how I have approached the secular context of camp meeting beginnings is a growing appreciation among historians for the late eighteenth century as an era of profound social transition. Two themes have especially engaged scholars of the period. One concerns America's capitalist transformation. Increasing involvement in commercial markets was, many historians believe, beginning to erode older notions of society as interdependent. Competition was replacing cooperation as the reigning ethic, causing a widespread but still incompletely understood sense of social malaise.[8] Social disintegration was also part of changes taking place in the political realm. Most late-eighteenth-century Americans still accepted a civic humanist tradition of a virtuous citizenry that subordinated personal interest for the common good. The partisanship and division produced in the wake of the American Revolution was therefore extremely disturbing, often interpreted as a moral crisis threatening to the country's survival. Moreover, as liberalism gained ground, the pursuit of self-interest seemed to acquire a legitimacy it had not enjoyed earlier. Intertwined in the popular mind with Christian morality, these concerns acquired a special seriousness.[9] In other ways as well, the late eighteenth century was widely experienced as an era of unusual and troubling change. The late eighteenth and early nineteenth centuries saw the organic, cohesive, cooperative ideal of age-old tradition being supplanted by a new liberal, plural, and competitive reality. Several recent historical studies have revealed the ambivalence with which many early Americans regarded this transformation.[10] The experience in newly settled areas such as Kentucky, where the institutional framework was not yet capable of lending much guidance and stability, was often more difficult.

The first seven chapters of this book accordingly trace Kentucky development from the beginnings of settlement in 1775 to the eve of the Great Revival in 1800. Several themes rise to the surface. One is trans-Appalachia's extraordinarily violent frontier beginnings, covered primarily in chapter 1 and designated as Part I in order to emphasize how different conditions were compared with the more peaceful and prosperous decade that directly preceded the Great Revival. Coinciding with the rebellion against

Great Britain, Kentucky's frontier phase was severe by any standard. Unlike later episodes of expansion, no protective national government had extinguished Native American claims or made even basic provisions for justice and public order. Rather, the war with Britain contributed directly to formidable Native resistance, which lessened after the 1783 Treaty of Paris but did not completely subside until 1794. The constant presence of danger during this initial settlement period discouraged additional migration and forced western settlers to organize into fortified settlements called stations, where they often remained for several years. Although the Indian threat ended years before the Great Revival, Kentucky's bloody beginnings left a deep imprint. Two major areas of public concern, the difficulty of gaining sound title to land and the undermining of traditional leadership structures, caused particular trouble. Kentucky settlement thus began in the face of vigorous resistance and at a very high social cost.

Another theme, covered in Part II, is the rapidity with which Kentucky developed as times became safer. The decade preceding the Great Kentucky Revival was one of phenomenal growth, particularly in the Bluegrass region where the Great Revival was to reach its greatest strength. Population surged following the Revolution, and settlement spilled outward from the core area around Lexington. The pent-up ambitions that had fueled the dangerous and expensive trans-Appalachian migration finally burst forth. Kentucky soon hosted a thriving agricultural economy and ambitious enterprises of every variety. Impediments to western development, be they a timid national Indian policy, the excise on domestic distilled spirits, or the failure to obtain navigation rights through Spanish New Orleans, received little toleration and indeed nearly sparked treason. In politics as well, Kentucky made tremendous progress during these years, going from being a trans-Appalachian extension of Virginia to becoming an independent state. Particularly noteworthy was the emergence of a new political culture, confirmed with the second state constitution in 1799. Local government institutions, initially weak and distant, multiplied and grew in strength. Religious institutions saw similar growth. Though plagued by problems of interdenominational competition, doctrinal orthodoxy, and internal division over slavery, most Kentuckians enjoyed reasonable access to public worship by the time of the Great Revival. Any comparison of conditions in 1800 with those of a decade earlier reveals impressive improvement. By 1800, Kentucky bore a greater resemblance to the rest of rural America than to its frontier beginnings.

A parallel theme that surfaces in Part II is that much of the economic, political, and social turmoil experienced by Kentuckians in the late eighteenth century was not unique to the western settlements but was found in varying degrees throughout the new nation. The problem of recovery from a lengthy war for independence from Britain put fresh pressure on the accumulation of wealth, accelerating the transition to capitalism. Traditional ideals of competency and cooperation survived, but a more acquisitive and competitive ethic seemed increasingly more evident. At the same time, the process of establishing republican institutions challenged old ideals of representation and leadership. The traditional emphasis on disinterested officials working for the common welfare of all was giving way to factions and parties working directly for the benefit of particular constituencies. Naturally, these developments entailed much personal uncertainty and anxiety, but perhaps even more troubling were their social implications. The age-old notion of society being an interdependent, organic whole seemed well on the way toward being supplanted by narrow self-interest. The task of establishing a new nation certainly accelerated and accentuated these changes. No "imagined community" yet existed to psychologically unite the citizenry.[11] The new language of liberty seemed to have released people to pursue their own interests, creating what to all appearances was a frightening moral crisis. The problem was probably more serious in the trans-Appalachian settlements and other places having weak institutional structures, but it was still widespread. This partially explains why so many parts of the new nation experienced religious revival during this era. Kentucky's Great Revival went one step further, creating a new form of worship, but once created, many other parts of the country were receptive to it.

Camp meeting revivalism, then, was the product of a particular social context. Although the aftermath of a very violent settlement process had created unusual stress, the problems facing Kentuckians in 1800 were no longer those of isolation, deprivation, and danger but rather of social disorganization, economic competition, and political partisanship. As in many other sections of the country, long-standing beliefs concerning the individual's relationship to the rest of society were undergoing painful renegotiation, involving nearly every facet of daily life. And, as is often the case in such situations, contemporaries tended to view these adjustments in moral terms. Religious clarification and confirmation therefore seemed necessary. Nowhere was the social pressure greater, nor were the religious institutions more flexible, than in the trans-Appalachian settlements. The result was not only a revival of religion but also a new form of evangelical worship.

III

By positing a connection between the frontier environment and camp meeting revivalism, historians of the Great Kentucky Revival have been influenced as much by Émile Durkheim as by Frederick Jackson Turner. Durkheim, one of the very first scholars to explore the connection between religion and society, viewed religion as "primarily a system of ideas with which the individuals represent to themselves the society of which they are members, and the obscure but intimate relations they have with it." By analyzing how the sacred is collectively conceptualized, a society itself can be better understood. Yet Durkheim believed religion to be more than simply a reflection of social reality. He contended that religion also affected that social reality by exerting an integrative force among participants.[12] This was accomplished particularly through ritual, the aspect of religion based on action. Through ritual, "collective beliefs and ideals are simultaneously generated, experienced, and affirmed as real by the community."[13] Unfortunately, the theological emphasis of traditional church history has meant that studies of religious change usually devote more attention to belief than to ritual. This has begun to change in recent years.

Previous scholarship on camp meeting revivalism has not ignored ritual, but most attention has focused on only one aspect of ritual, the personal conversion from an unregenerate to a regenerate condition. This genre of ritual is known as a rite of passage. As was originally elaborated by Arnold Van Gennep in the early twentieth century, rites of passage involve a basic three-stage process of individual transformation.[14] The first stage brings separation from the initial status or condition, followed by what has become known as a liminal status, followed by reaggregation to the new status or condition. The liminal stage, derived from the term *limen*, or threshold, defies ordinary categories of social existence. It has been described as a state of being "*both* this *and* that," a position "betwixt-and-between" established or normal statuses. The individual has abandoned one identity and not yet assumed a new one. The liminal stage of transformation is one of indeterminacy or chaos, devoid of standard organizing structures such as class, race, or creed. It is the inverse of normal social reality: unstable and ambiguous. Although usually a brief phenomenon, it is a painful, dramatic, and unpredictable contrast to ordinary personal existence.

The attention given to rites of passage is understandable because the camp meeting format was always remarkably successful at eliciting spiritual transformations. Most explanations for this success have tended to emphasize the direct evangelical appeals delivered by ardent preachers, but some scholars have also recognized, sometimes only instinctually, that the event's structure also played a role. Even some participating clergymen realized that drawing people away from the distractions and obligations of daily life and immersing them day and night in a religious environment made evangelical appeals more effective. Yet the organizational structure also operated in less obvious ways. Not only were people jolted from familiar settings; the primitive camp meeting setting also accentuated the fundamentally universal condition of all humanity. Differences of wealth, religion, and politics took on reduced significance as strangers slept side by side on the ground, in the early years, accommodating themselves as best they could. Also worth noting, camp meetings were often massive in scale, in large measure because they were more inclusive than regular Sunday worship, with people from every age, race, denomination, and rank. Camp meeting revivalism thus situated the rite of passage within what might well be described as a more general liminal condition.

Anthropologist Victor Turner identified such undifferentiated collective events as a distinct category of ritual, characterized by a quality he termed "antistructure." Like the liminal stage of personal transformation, this more general condition of antistructure is marked by the temporary absence of social distinctions or categories. One result is an acute sense of human connectedness, termed "communitas." When all the categories, statuses, and other structures normal and necessary for daily life are removed, all that is left is "full, unmediated, communication, even communion."[15] Pure communitas is found rarely because it almost inevitably inspires efforts to preserve and regularize the experience through the creation of institutional support structures. By its very nature, however, institutional structure diminishes or tempers the sense of communitas. Complete communitas therefore exists only for the brief time when structure is absent. This quality of nearly pure communitas, more than anything else, distinguished early camp meeting revivalism from other forms of religious worship. All participants encountered it, even those—the majority—who did not undergo spiritual transformation and rite of passage.

Camp meeting communitas played an important role in making participants more receptive to a spiritual transformation, a role which has not been fully appreciated by scholars. But perhaps even more interesting is a rich body of theoretical literature suggesting that the experience of camp meeting communitas held significance beyond simply providing support for rites of passage. Three themes in this literature seem particularly striking. The first is the idea that ritual involves a developmental process. Religion and society proceed through a continuous, though sometimes barely perceptible, cycle of adjustment. Anthony F. C. Wallace has argued that because, among other functions, religion serves to inculcate values and to relieve tensions generated by structural contradictions in society, rituals and beliefs undergo a continual process of readjustment. Religious institutions consequently pass gradually and more or less regularly through a cycle of revitalization, stabilization, and deterioration.[16] Victor Turner has advanced a four-stage model of change he termed "social drama." A breach of norm sets off a second stage, crisis, which in turn requires redressive action. This leads to one of two outcomes, either reintegration or the recognition of irreparable schism.[17] Other developmental models have also been posed, none of which have been previously applied to camp meeting revivalism. Yet contemporary records make it quite clear that the camp meeting as it existed in Kentucky in 1800 was different from that observed, say, in New York's "Burned-Over District" a generation later.[18]

The second theme follows from the first, for several theorists of ritual have asserted not only that religious rituals offer an insight into a society's culture but that this is especially so during periods of innovation and change. Max Weber observed that, in ordinary existence, congruence between religion and society operates imprecisely and is difficult to detect, masked by internal contradictions, tensions, and variations. The congruity is usually most direct and apparent during moments of change, often experienced as a crisis or malaise.[19] Wallace said almost as much when he suggested that the revitalization phase of religion is often characterized by an effort to make religious practice more "closely and consciously relevant to the real functional needs of the society as these are perceived by the reformers."[20] Turner believed that social dramas "make clear the deepest values of a culture." They provide a "limited area of transparency in the otherwise opaque surface of regular, uneventful social life." Clifford Geertz likewise speaks of the "window of ritual."[21] Limiting analysis of camp meeting revivalism to its formative Kentucky phase may thus offer special insight into contemporary values, anxieties, and relationships.

Third, and most intriguing, is the notion that ritual not only reflects reigning social reality but actually shapes it. This idea has its genesis with Durkheim's understanding of religion as a vehicle for creating social solidarity. For Max Weber, the idea that religion and society exist in a dialectical relationship suggested that alterations in one, when of sufficient magnitude, inevitably evoke changes in the other. For Victor Turner, the redressive phase of the social drama often evoked a reflexive response of distancing oneself from subjective experience in order to objectify, detach, and reflect. Turner also discerned a collective level of response, or "plural reflexivity," but exactly how rituals of social drama promoted reflexivity remained largely mysterious. He thought that reflexivity generally carried over into secular life, but with a strength that varied considerably. Clifford Geertz dealt with a similar problem in his distinction between "deep play" and "shallow play."[22]

A few scholars have been more explicit in arguing for the power of ritual. Sally Falk Moore and Barbara G. Myerhoff boldly claim, "Ritual may do much more than mirror existing social arrangements and existing modes of thought. It can act to reorganize them or even help create them."[23] Similarly, Catherine Bell states that ritualization "defines, empowers, and constrains."[24] At the very minimum, ritual provides shape. It is a "vessel that holds something," giving form to its contents. The very fact that it exists makes a difference. Unfortunately, demonstrating that difference is far from easy. Participants themselves are often unable to explain the effect of their experience—or even to adequately describe the experience itself. Historians, of course, work with additional challenges. Moore and Myerhoff at least propose a five-part typology for understanding the various effects of ritual, only one of which corresponds to the decision to undergo the rite of passage for spiritual rebirth. Other anthropologists have offered their own models, and more will likely be proposed in the future. Regardless of the relative virtues of these models, all rest on the assumption that ritual exerts a varying effect on participants. Evaluating camp meeting revivalism simply in terms of the rite of passage and subsequent church growth is therefore not enough. The camp meeting experience also held meaning for those who did not undergo personal transformation. Just because this meaning is virtually impossible for historians to measure or assess does not mean that it did not exist.

These ideas inform the analysis of the Great Kentucky Revival presented here. Part III follows camp meeting revivalism through its formative period, from its creation in 1800 to just past the massive assembly held at Cane Ridge in Bourbon County in late summer of 1801. Camp meeting revivalism evolved from the Presbyterian sacramental occasion as a result of evangelical efforts by a young Presbyterian minister named James McGready in southern Kentucky. People experiencing a spiritual transformation began to fall to the ground as if dead, struck down by a powerful sense of their sinful nature. The seemingly involuntary nature of the falling suggested supernatural causes, attracting widespread curiosity, not only among Presbyterians but with the public at large. Camping at the site became a practical necessity, adding further religious intensity. Although still discernibly a sacramental occasion, these structural changes made for a very different type of religious experience. The result was a broad wave of religious interest that culminated in August 1801 at Cane Ridge, an event commonly estimated to have attracted between ten and twenty thousand participants. Cane Ridge proved to be a pivotal event. It demonstrated beyond question the effectiveness and popularity of the camp meeting format. It also demonstrated to church leaders the need to organize and control future meetings. Shortly after Cane Ridge, camp meeting revivalism assumed an altered character, becoming markedly more organized and structured.

A close consideration of camp meeting revivalism's brief and fluid formative phase challenges reigning impressions that camp meeting revivalism succeeded because it offered people a form of religious worship more directly congruent with the emerging national culture. The extraordinary chaos and size of the Kentucky camp meetings were evidence not of a new individualism born of spiritual wildness and frontier culture but of the unmediated communitas typical during early stages of a new ritual. Far from endorsing an unrestricted individualism, the rite of passage often occurred in connection with the activities of surrounding participants. The communitas was also a product of the evangelical imperative, or universal character of camp meeting revivalism. People were drawn not only from other faiths but from a much wider range of the western population than usually attended church. Camping at the meeting site brought all these people into close and sustained contact, which the primitive accommodations compounded. The early camp meetings created a society in microcosm. The only government was the gospel call to live in harmony, unity, and equality. At a time when people had been suffering prolonged political, economic, and social change—compounded for Kentuckians by a costly and distant relocation—the communitas of the camp meeting posed a startling and impressive contrast. Huge segments of the population found it irresistible.

This book, then, attempts to do more than simply explain a particular instance of religious revivalism. It explores the creation and widespread adoption of a new form of evangelical worship. It contends that the primary significance of camp meeting revivalism was not that it offered people a form of worship more reflective of the emerging liberal culture but rather that it served as an integrating mechanism that enabled great masses of people to more comfortably relate to that new culture. The camp meeting assembly countered the general sense of apprehension and social breakdown with an intense collective experience. This is especially apparent in terms of the camp meeting's formative phase, and it helps explain why camp meeting revivalism first appeared where it did, when it did, and quickly thereafter found national popularity.

Part I.
SETTLEMENT

The violence that accompanied the Anglo-American settlement of Kentucky set this episode of United States expansion apart from most others. It produced a society oriented totally toward military defense. A unique settlement form, the station, enabled westerners to survive, but little that was accomplished during these years was suited to normal, peaceful conditions. Although the origins of camp meeting revivalism have often been attributed to a frontier setting, early Kentucky was under such duress that it could not possibly have hosted a massive revival. Nonetheless, it is appropriate to note that camp meeting revivalism began within a society which had an extraordinarily stressful settlement experience in its recent past.

1

THE REVOLUTIONARY
FRONTIER IN KENTUCKY

The trek to Kentucky loomed large in the eighteenth-century imagination. It marked the first significant breach of contiguous Anglo-American settlement. Yet what made Kentucky a daunting place was not so
much the distance and challenge of travel as the danger upon arrival, for
the beginnings of Anglo-American settlement in Kentucky coincided with
the war for independence from Great Britain.

While the seaboard states confronted the main British army, British
garrisons around the Great Lakes, particularly at Detroit, mounted major
assaults on the interior rebel settlements, including the new ones in Kentucky. Western British forces were small, but they were allied with native
opponents in Ohio who recognized the ominous significance of previous
colonial expansion. The Shawnees figured most prominently among
Britain's native allies, but joining them were members of the Wyandot,
Miami, Delaware, Piankashaws, Potawatomi, and Mingos.[1] For arms, ammunition, and trade goods, these natives fought for their own cause as
well as that of Britain. Several large offensives against the cluster of rebel
settlements south of the Ohio River were personally led by British officers. But even more destructive and demoralizing to the Kentucky settlements were the countless small sorties of natives, who struck without
warning. At times it seemed that the trans-Appalachian settlements could
not possibly survive. Many western venturers prudently withdrew to await
safer conditions. A few held on tenaciously, but they faced some of the
strongest and most prolonged native resistance in the history of Euro-
American expansion, the impact of which left a deep imprint on Kentucky's
subsequent development.

Virginia's Western War Front

The first permanent Euro-American settlements in Kentucky began
in 1775. Although Kentucky figured as an important Indian hunting ground,
it was not actually a homeland at that time. No native occupant had to be
expelled for American settlement to occur.[2] While this did not diminish

Indian rights to Kentucky, it did diminish the practical challenges of Euro-American occupation. The strongest claims belonged to the Shawnees, but they had been forced to cede their rights to the territory south of the Ohio River as a result of Lord Dunmore's War in 1774. The cession did not have full Shawnee support, but the British colonists who had already begun establishing speculative land claims in Kentucky chose to ignore this fact. The boldest undertaking was that of the Transylvania Company, an organization of speculators headed by Richard Henderson, who side-stepped Shawnee claims in Kentucky by obtaining a land cession from more cooperative Cherokee claimants. The result of Henderson's enterprise was the founding of Boonesborough in 1775, intended to be the capital of a fourteenth British mainland colony, the first interior to the Atlantic Ocean. What Henderson, Daniel Boone, and the other Transylvania colonists did not know was that this same region was already attracting attention from other colonial quarters. A settlement located west of the Kentucky River known as Harrodsburg had been founded recently by a rival group of land speculators who had come down the Ohio River from western Pennsylvania. Several other parties from Pennsylvania, as well as Virginia, were also attempting to begin Kentucky settlements, often quite unaware of parallel undertakings. By the end of 1775, several hundred thousand acres had been reserved either by purchase from the Transylvania Company, by warrants for military service in the French and Indian War, or by invoking the Virginia tradition of settlement preemption.[3] The Kentucky land rush was on.

All this western activity had occurred despite official sanction rather than because of it. Britain had tried to contain colonial expansion with the Proclamation Line drawn in 1763, only to be thwarted almost immediately by North American speculators and squatters. The breach with Great Britain in 1776 eliminated royal impediments to western expansion, but provincial leaders were no less cool to trans-Appalachian settlement once rebellion had broken out. Facing a war with Europe's strongest power, they could not support—much less protect—a tiny population separated by several hundred miles of rugged wilderness. The activities of the Transylvania Company, however, left little choice because they conflicted with the royal charter granted Virginia. In 1776, therefore, the Virginia Assembly countered Henderson and all other rival claimants by extending local government across the Appalachian Mountains in the form of Kentucky County. Although the territory of Virginia's new westernmost county encompassed roughly the same contours as the later state of Kentucky, nearly all settlement was concentrated in the lush central region now known as the Bluegrass. The following year the Virginia Assembly enacted a western land policy confirming the "ancient cultivation law," which granted a personal preemption on the basis of an improvement, usually a crude cabin or patch of corn, indicating an intention to settle. Each Kentucky settler who had done this before June 1, 1776, was allowed up to four hundred acres of land. In 1779, the qualifying period was extended to January 1, 1778.[4] Grappling for independence from Europe's strongest power, Virginia could offer her westernmost citizens little more, forcing them to fill the void as best they might.

The first year or so of Kentucky settlement had been fairly quiet, but once the Ohio Indians discovered the western white presence, violent encounters became a regular occurrence. Anglo-Americans quickly retreated from their land claims to the protection of larger settlements. Some abandoned Kentucky altogether. According to a surveyor writing in mid-1776, "I think more than 300 men have left the country since I came out, and not one has arrived—except a few cabbiners down the Ohio."[5] Several outlying settlements were completely abandoned. At Boonesborough, work resumed on the timber stockade, creating what was known as a station. Stockades soon enclosed the cabins at Harrodsburg as well as John McClellend's settlement north of the Kentucky River at Royal Spring. McClellend's Station was evacuated in early 1777, following an Indian attack in which its leader was killed. By the end of the winter, a new fortification had been built by Benjamin Logan at an old camp known as St. Asaph's Station but soon known better for its connection with Logan. These three remaining settlements included some 120 able-bodied defenders and a total population of about 280.[6] Their survival, several hundred miles removed from the coastal settlements, would depend on Virginia's willingness to divert military resources from the Atlantic warfront.

George Rogers Clark quickly emerged as the key figure in defending the Kentucky settlements. Aided by his family's political connections, Clark persuaded the Virginia Assembly in 1776 to supply the trans-Appalachian settlements with five hundred pounds of powder. He also saw to its successful shipment down the Ohio River. But Clark understood that more was necessary if Virginia's westernmost citizens were to survive. He therefore returned to Williamsburg in late 1777 and presented Governor Patrick Henry with plans for an audacious offensive campaign across the Ohio River. Virginia's Executive Council authorized Clark to recruit seven companies of men and proceed to Kentucky. These men were ostensibly to help defend the Kentucky settlements, but a secret directive ordered Clark to lead them in an attack against the British post of Kaskaskia in the Illinois country. After considerable difficulty recruiting the authorized troops, Clark finally left western Pennsylvania in May 1778 with approximately 150 men, and in July he led this force in a successful surprise attack on Kaskaskia. By exploiting the ambivalent loyalties of the French inhabitants, Clark was also able to secure British posts at Cahokia and Vincennes.[7]

The British meanwhile were not inactive. Lieutenant Governor

Hamilton set out from Detroit with a force of nearly two hundred whites supplemented by approximately three hundred Indians. Although Hamilton recaptured Vincennes without a struggle in December, he could not proceed against Clark at Kaskaskia because the intervening countryside was swampy and virtually impassable. Hamilton therefore prepared to winter at Vincennes, demobilizing most of his army until the return of better weather. For Clark, whose army was several times smaller, the choice was clear: "We must either quit the country or attack Mr. Hamilton." The consequences of defeat were equally clear: "This country as well as Kentucky I believe is lost."[8] In February Clark and his small force crossed a chilly land saturated with melting snow. The British, who assumed that Clark must be at the head of a great army if he was able to undertake such action in winter, were caught by surprise. From his new stronghold, Clark desperately wished to proceed against the British posts at Sandusky, Mackinac, and especially Detroit, but an offensive of that scale lay beyond Virginia's wartime means. Instead, Vincennes, Kaskaskia, and Cahokia were secured with small garrisons under the command of a civil governor from Virginia. Clark was ordered back to his old headquarters at the falls of the Ohio, from which point he was to supervise the construction of a line of forts at key points along the Ohio River intended to buffer the civilians in Kentucky.

The Ohio campaigns proved politically significant, providing the basis for later American territorial claims to the Old Northwest, but their immediate purpose was to take pressure off the civilian population trapped in Kentucky stations. For most of the Revolution, the survival of these small, isolated outposts remained uncertain. Not only were they the target of numerous small forays that rendered daily life miserable and often fatal, but on several occasions the British launched sizable invasions aimed at their utter destruction. The only way for a station to survive a more numerous force of British, Canadians, and allied Natives was to trust in the timber walls of the stockade and wait out the siege.[9] The experience was inevitably terrifying. Boonesborough had only forty or fifty able-bodied defenders in 1778 when it was besieged for thirteen days by a British-led force estimated at four hundred. When the settlers rejected demands for surrender, the enemy attempted tunneling under the stockade from a nearby embankment. At night as they lay in their beds, the inhabitants of Boonesborough could actually hear the shovels at work. Fortunately for them, the tunnel collapsed.

Station inhabitants elsewhere were not always so fortunate. In June 1780, the British crossed the Ohio River with approximately 150 Canadians and Loyalists plus several hundred Indians. They had dragged two small pieces of artillery across the whole of Ohio. Though the British were eager to attack the falls of the Ohio and engage Clark, the Indian

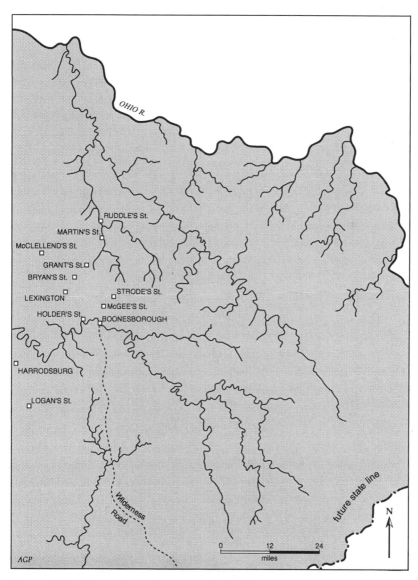

Map 1. Major Kentucky stations, c. 1780–1783.

desire for civilian booty prevailed. Moving up the Licking River, the British forces were able to advance rapidly upon two fortified settlements on the south fork, those of Isaac Ruddle and John Martin. Located some five miles closer to the Ohio River, Ruddle's Station was attacked first. Knowing that Indian modes of warfare were not geared for prolonged sieges, the forty-nine men inside Ruddle's Station prepared to hold out against the superior force outside. After a brief demonstration of the two field pieces, however, Ruddle decided to surrender and negotiated terms with the British officers. But contrary to their promise, the British made little effort to intervene when the gates were opened and several hundred Indians rushed in killing, plundering, and capturing. The invaders then proceeded on to John Martin's Station. Better order prevailed at this surrender. Burdened by loads of booty and several hundred captives, the invaders quickly withdrew to Detroit.[10]

The most devastating American military defeat in Kentucky occurred two years later, in August 1782, when a British-led force of Indians attacked Bryan's Station, at that time the northernmost settlement in eastern Kentucky. The attackers made every effort to breach the stockade, but also knew better than to risk a prolonged siege. After two days, the Indians retreated northeasterly, along a major buffalo trace, crossing the Licking River at a salt spring known as the Lower Blue Licks. Their route was obvious, and the Kentucky militia pursued closely behind. Eager for revenge, the Kentuckians chose not to wait for reinforcements but charged across the river. Once across, though, the Indian forces sprang out in ambush. The Lower Blue Licks was by far the bloodiest defeat of the war for the western Americans, with approximately seventy dead, a dozen wounded, and additional men unaccounted for. The Kentucky settlements reeled under the impact of the numerous casualties.[11] The American disaster at the Lower Blue Licks was shortly followed by the usual retaliatory campaign, led by George Rogers Clark and resulting in the destruction of winter food stores at the Indian town located at Sandusky. This was the last major campaign of the Revolution.

The constant demands of war during these early years reduced the western settlements to a miserable condition. When the Collins family arrived at Boonesborough in 1778, for example, "we found a poor, distressed, 1/2 naked, 1/2 starved, people; daily surrounded by the savage, which made it so dangerous, the hunters were afraid to go out to get Buffalo meat." Casualties occurred frequently. "We are all obliged to live in Forts in this Country, and notwithstanding all the Caution that we use, forty seven of the Inhabitants have been killed & taken by the Savages, Besides a number wounded since Jany. last," reported John Floyd in early 1781. People risked annihilation any time they moved between stations. "Whole families are destroyed, without regard to Age or Sex—Infants are torn from their mothers Arms & their Brains dashed out against Trees . . . . Not a week passes & some weeks scarcely a day without some of our distressed inhabitants feeling the fatal effects of the infernal rage and fury of those Execrable Hell hounds." The guerrilla style of Native American warfare kept the Kentucky settlements in a fairly constant state of siege. Even at Lexington, a place less exposed to Indian danger than Floyd's location, casualties took a serious toll. "There is scarce one fort in the country but once a month seems upon the eve of breaking [up] for want of men to defend it," wrote Col. John Todd Jr. Those inhabitants who still had horses had moved to the safety of Lincoln County, back from the raids coming from Ohio, and Todd believed that the remaining inhabitants would have left, too, had they possessed the means. As Floyd reiterated a few months later, "The most distressed widows & orphans perhaps in the World make up a great part of our Inhabitants."[12] The minuscule military force Virginia had sent to help defend the Kentuckians was in the same destitute condition. From the ramshackle garrison near Louisville, Col. George Slaughter reported to the governor in 1781, "The situation of my little Corps at this place at present, is truely deplorable; destitute of clothing, victuals & money, the Commissaries have furnish'd them with little or no provisions these three months past . . . and unless unexpected & immediate supplies of clothing & provisions are obtain'd, I shall evacuate this Post." Local purchases were impossible; government credit was threadbare.[13]

Unfortunately, the Treaty of Paris in 1783 confirming American independence brought little peace or security to Kentucky. "The settlement of Kentucke appears to be in a perfect state of war," observed one visitor in 1786. "The Indians [are] constantly stealing horses and frequently killing individuals."[14] Well-armed Indian armies several hundred strong no longer descended from across the Ohio, but small raiding parties maintained a level of danger sufficient to keep most settlers in stations for several more years, particularly in outlying areas. Kentucky would not be fully secure for another decade. Nonetheless, the time was past when the Shawnees and their allies could hope to expel the white settlers now pouring into Kentucky. Freed from military service, overwhelmed by taxes for war debts, thousands of Americans fled toward a fresh start in the west. Native raids could still be shockingly bold and bloody at times, but no longer were they able to evoke the levels of despair and panic experienced during the 1770s.

The Station Settlement, 1776–1786

The hostile conditions surrounding American occupation of Kentucky, during and after the Revolution, required a fortified form of settlement known as the station. The idea of enclosing cabins with a protective timber stockade was not original, but in Kentucky the extraordinary and prolonged danger made station settlements much more important.[15] Whereas previous stations had served local civilians mainly as a temporary refuge, left unoccupied except in moments of alarm, hardly anyone arriving in Kentucky before the mid-1780s avoided the station experience. In some instances, residence in a station involved only a brief period of adjustment, but often people remained for years before conditions became safe enough to move on to a farm of their own. Consequently, in Kentucky and other areas settled during the Revolutionary era, the significance of the station form of settlement extended well beyond its defensive functions.[16]

The most famous of the Kentucky stations is probably Boonesborough, located near the end of the Wilderness Road in the lush Bluegrass region of modern Madison County. Life at Boonesborough, however, was not the typical station experience. Boonesborough's first years of existence were extremely tenuous, but after 1778 this station served less as a military outpost and more as a western entrepôt. Newly arriving settlers often paused at Boonesborough or one of the several other prominent stations near the terminus of the Wilderness Road until they had recovered from their arduous journey and could decide on a final destination. Particularly in spring and fall, Boonesborough's transient population swelled into the hundreds. Except during periods of extreme danger, most newcomers moved as quickly as possible to a more permanent and spacious location.

The typical station was a relatively small and intimate grouping of between one and two dozen families, plus a number of rather mobile young bachelors. The primary purpose of the station was mutual protection. In times of attack every adult inhabitant, man and woman, white and black, had a role to play in the common defense. Yet survival required more than just the ability to repulse an enemy. Securing a reliable food supply was just as essential and required just as much cooperation. The hunters always worked in groups, and those who were fortunate felt an obligation to share with those who were not. Similarly, the people who worked in the cornfield took turns guarding the others. The stations were not communal ventures, but they did rely on a very strong sense of mutual assistance. Isolated by miles of dangerous woodland, these fortified civilian communities constituted the basic unit of settlement in Kentucky through the first decade of occupation. In outlying areas, station settlements dominated longer.

Strode's Station, located about twenty miles east of Lexington in modern Clark County, offers a fairly representative example of the early Kentucky station arrangement. In late 1779, Colonel John Strode led a party from his neighborhood in Berkeley County, Virginia, to his land claim some ten miles north of Boonesborough. They began constructing cabins, and in late November a second party from Berkeley County arrived. Most were bachelors or men who intended to bring their families to Kentucky later, but the station founders included at least a few families. This small group built shelter, hunted, and explored the country until winter set in.[17]

That year it set in before Christmas and lasted until March. The winter of 1779–80 became known throughout Kentucky as the "Hard Winter," with snow "garter deep." One of the men at Strode's Station recalled seeing "cattle laying with their heads to their side, as if they were asleep; just literally froze to death. Great many lost their cattle." Corn prices soared far beyond the reach of most people, forcing them to subsist all but entirely on game, sometimes for weeks on end. They tried mental tricks, calling turkey "bread" because it was dry and lean, and calling bear "meat" because it was fatty and tough. At some stations the malnutrition was so prolonged and so severe that women lost their ability to conceive. The limited diet increased vulnerability to disease and a depressed mental outlook. A time of acute privation and misery throughout all the infant settlements in Kentucky, the Hard Winter lodged permanently in local memory.[18]

The winter conditions deterred Indian attacks, but in spring the settlers at Strode's Station proceeded to build a protective stockade and establish a reliable food supply. When spring finally arrived, the women "would follow their cows to see what they ate, that they might know what greens to get." The men renewed their efforts to find wild game. In addition, with still no grain in their diet, starting a crop of corn was vital. The easiest method for clearing land was by burning, but the growth at Strode's and many other parts of the Bluegrass region was unfortunately too thick and damp. The need for protection also hindered the clearing of land. Recalled one early station inhabitant, "Some had to stand guard while others wrought." Fortunately, the exceedingly high quality of the soil meant that only two or three acres per worker was enough to provide a subsistence, and one acre could usually be "grubbed" in a matter of days. By the station's second summer, following the arrival of additional settlers, the northern cornfield extended for nearly half a mile. It remained, however, a common field during these early years. According to William Clinkenbeard, one of the original inhabitants, there were "as high as 100 acres in that corn field. No fensing of parts off." The cornfield also extended to the western side of the station. The gardens on that side and on the south side lay directly along the stockade wall, separated from the cornfield with a crude fence. "Every fellow had a garden round the fort that wanted one. It was all in one field with no fencing between. . . . One-fourth of an acre was allowed to each farm yard and staked off." This arrangement was in keeping with that of most other stations.[19] With cleared ground at a premium, livestock was left to forage in the underbrush, relying particularly on the thick stands of wild cane. Game constituted the main part of the daily diet, particularly before the first corn harvest. Pioneers generally acknowledged that "Kentucky never could have been settled in the way it was had it not been for the cane and game." Both, however, were very quickly exhausted.[20]

The inhabitants of Strode's Station were technically tenants of the site's owner, Colonel John Strode. According to William Clinkenbeard, "Strode gave us all a chance to clear what we pleased and we were to have it rent free until the end of the war." This arrangement was the standard at most other stations as well. Later, as the vicinity of the station gradually became safer, the original inhabitants moved out to where they had claimed land. Their places were usually filled by second and third waves of western settlers. The latecomers had to go further beyond the edges of settlement in order to find unclaimed land. Until these outlying areas became safe enough to inhabit, which could take several years, the informal rental system at the station or on land near a station offered distinct advantages. As one pioneer, John Hedge, pointed out, "It was for some time a prevalent custom for persons to take a lease on lands in the more central parts, free from probable incursions of the Indians, till they could either go out to lands of their own in safety, or have opportunity and the means of getting land of their own." The arrangement carried a mutual advantage: "The lease was to secure their privileges, and the lessor got his lands cleared." Hedge observed, "Most of the people when I came here [in 1789] were on leased lands, till times became more safe."[21] A phase of tenancy was a common experience during the early years of settlement. Reflective more of danger than of economic failure, it carried no social stigma.

However practical, station life involved much unpleasantness if not misery. The stations were generally cramped and dirty. Personal memoirs tend to overlook this aspect of pioneer life, but contemporary records offer a less idealized picture. Col. William Fleming, a physician, visited Boonesborough in late 1779 and described it in his journal as "a dirty place in winter like every other Station." In the stockade at Harrodsburg, however, Dr. Fleming found sanitary conditions utterly appalling. "The Spring at this place is below the Fort and fed by ponds above the Fort so that the whole dirt and filth of the Fort, putrefied flesh, dead dogs, horse, cow, hog excrements and human odour all wash into the spring which with the Ashes and sweepings of filthy Cabbins" made a "most filthy nauseous potation." As Kentuckians soon realized, an internal water source was more a hazard than an advantage. Most other stations were located adjacent to, rather than around, the primary water supply.[22]

The station's design was such that it could be defended—and was— with as few as a dozen men. At Strode's Station, the stockade measured approximately one hundred by three hundred yards in size. The three gates were located so that no matter from which direction an attack came, settlers had a reasonable chance to retreat inside to safety. The two large entries were fitted with heavy puncheons hung on a horizontal pivot. Each corner had a blockhouse protecting the gates. From the second floor of the blockhouses, which protruded out about two feet, any assault up near the stockade wall could be countered. The two main blockhouses faced west, overlooking the fields that sloped upward from the creek, where people would be busy working on their crops. The east side was sufficiently protected by a steeply banked creek; Indians storming from that side would be slow-moving targets as they waded through the water. Further advantage was gained by constructing the cabin roofs so that they sloped inward, with the high side facing out. The station form of settlement functioned remarkably well. Any assault on the walls would entail considerable loss of life, and Indian modes of warfare were not oriented toward lengthy sieges.[23]

The station walls served not only as a physical barrier to danger but also as a psychological barrier. Nothing illustrates this so well as does the treatment accorded Indian prisoners. As the Indians soon learned, Kentuckians took few prisoners. When on occasion they did, usually for use in exchange for white captives, they faced a serious moral dilemma. On the one hand, surrender obligated the victor to offer protection. On the other hand, keeping an Indian captive within the station was very disturbing. In an incident that occurred in 1788, several men from Strode's Station captured an Indian leader named Blue Jacket. A fellow pioneer recalled that Stephen Boyle let the captive escape, explaining, "It would be better than to take him up and show him how weak they were at Strode's Station, and then let him go back [in exchange for white prisoners] . . . and tell it." William Clinkenbeard remembered the incident as well, stating that the men "Didn't want to save him" because they "Never wanted any [Indian] to see our fort or our situation."[24] This seems at first glance merely a wise policy in terms of security. However, any information gleaned by an escaped Indian captive regarding station arrangement and armed strength could easily have been obtained through a little basic reconnaissance. Stations were simply not that complicated or mysterious. Rather, the reluctance to have Indians inside the station probably served a more subtle function. Pioneers subjected for a prolonged period to a hostile wilderness, where catastrophe often struck without warning, may have psychologically needed a small preserve of absolute safety. An Indian, even as a captive, threatened not only actual security but also—and perhaps more importantly—violated the inhabitants' sense of security. Feelings of revenge and racism also contributed toward taking few Indian captives. "The white Americans also have the most rancorous antipathy to the whole race of Indians," observed an early visitor from Britain, "and nothing is more common than to hear them talk of extirpating them totally from the face of the earth, men, women, and children." Several pioneer memoirs recount instances where Indians, including noncombatants, were needlessly killed instead of captured. One settler recalled years later a horrific incident at Harrodsburg, where "they fed three Indians to the dogs to make them fierce." Most Indians, however, were saved and exchanged for the return of white captives.[25]

The defenses at Strode's Station were put to the test in the summer of 1780 after the fall of Ruddle's and Martin's Stations, "frontier stations" on the northern edge of settlement. With their fall, Strode's Station to the south and Grant's Station to the west suddenly formed the new frontier. Inhabitants at both places viewed the situation as one of true crisis. According to William Clinkenbeard, Strode's Station "was very near breaking up at that time. Heap of people packed up their plunder to move off." Only the arrival of a small guard from the militia convinced them to stay. Although Strode's Station survived the turmoil, Grant's Station had to be abandoned as untenable. The northeastern frontier of Kentucky thus contracted to McClellend's, Bryan's, and Strode's Stations. Tension remained high. A few weeks after the destruction of Ruddle's Station, some of the Strode's Station men were hunting and happened upon the ruins. The bodies had been buried in a shallow mass grave. In the silence the hunters walked among the ruins, observing "Little wheels, plough irons, blacksmith's tools, feather beds ripped open, etc., scattered about there."[26] It was a chilling sight, and they had little idea but that it might be a glimpse of their own future.

The panic subsided once snow fell, and the ease of following a track reduced the probability of Indian attack. As a frontier station, however, Strode's now received little warning of danger. The settlement was caught by surprise on March 1, 1781. Indians rarely struck so early in the season. Nearly half of the station's men were away that day, as a militia escort for a party of settlers who wished to return to the protection of Boonesborough.[27]

All seemed normal that morning as the women finished the milking just outside the western wall. On this particular morning Jacob Spahr was lending a hand by driving the milked cows past the corn field and into the underbrush to browse. He was followed by his daughter Rebecca and her friend Polly Donaldson, "little girls," who had "skipped out to follow Mr. S. and see him drive the cows away." But when Spahr passed by the garden fence, he was shot dead by several Indians who laid in wait. "The indns. chased the little girls to within 20 steps of the fort, & wo'd have gotten them, but the dogs broke out on them." Terror-stricken, Polly Donaldson forgot to duck as she ran through the small gate and smacked herself so hard on the low overhead beam that she carried a scar for the rest of her life.

The early morning gunfire drew a confused response. Most people inside Strode's Station had been preparing breakfast. Patrick Donaldson sought the source of trouble and climbed up between two of the cabins, bracing himself against the logs. As he peered over the wall, perhaps anxiously looking for his daughter Polly, a bullet struck him in the forehead. Made of soft lead and fired from a distance, "The bullet didn't go in, but knocked the bones in. The brains seeped out in the day, & he didn't die till night."[28] Young John Judy, who had been across the creek on the opposite side of the station, was wounded in the side as he fled toward the east gate. A female slave may have been captured before she could reach the station, although firsthand accounts conflict on this point. Once alerted, people inside the stockade mobilized quickly. Though caught while inadequately garrisoned, some of the women may have been able to handle guns, and others knew how to prepare the lead and powder.[29]

Instead of pointlessly storming the stockade walls of Strode's Station, the Indians chased some of the cattle and sheep up into the center of the cornfield. There, within plain sight of the station but beyond the range of guns, they methodically slew the animals. Taunting the station people to come rescue their precious livestock, "they wo'd ha! ha! ha! as loud as to be heard all thro' the fort." Any attempt to do so, however, would have been a mistake. The settlers were relatively safe as long as they remained within the stockade. They worried, however, that the returning militia escort might get ambushed as it approached the station clearing. Fortunately, the Indians had left by the time the eight men did return, but evidence of their visit was all around. Said William Clinkenbeard, a member of the escort, "When we got in there we saw what we didn't want to see."[30]

What could possibly have prepared people for such travails? Many of them came from the backcountry of Pennsylvania, Virginia, and North Carolina. These regions had recent experience with Indian conflict and the various other problems common to new settlements. Moreover, some men had served in Revolutionary units, so the care and use of firearms was generally familiar. Yet a war in the wilderness demanded special abilities. Indian tactics were capricious, and attacks occurred in isolation from other settlements. Many of the early settlers were not prepared for this. The move west often entailed a brutal if not fatal adjustment for those lacking the necessary skills. The majority of people at Strode's Station came from Berkeley County, Virginia, an area that had been settled in the face of serious Indian conflict in the 1730s. There, too, the early settlers had initially organized stations, but the lessons of that experience had faded from memory as conditions improved. A generation later, the Berkeley people who settled Strode's Station possessed limited wilderness skills. Thus, when Indians first began harassing Strode's Station, the inhabitants made little effort to track them down. According to William Clinkenbeard, a young man at the station, "We never followed an Indian till Major Hood came, that I recollect of; all raw hands[, we] knew nothing about it."[31] But they soon learned.

Perhaps the most important lesson was that of bravery. Ironically, the most cowardly man at Strode's Station was probably its founder, Colonel John Strode. Young William Clinkenbeard thought so, because after going to Kentucky in 1776 to claim land and making a second trip in 1779 to organize the station, Strode returned to the safety of Berkeley County and stayed there for the next three years. Clinkenbeard probably believed that Strode was shirking his responsibility to the station, which after all protected and cleared his land. Clinkenbeard substantiated his opinion by relating a small incident that occurred sometime after Strode's return. Strode, his son-in-law James Duncan, and others from the station had been out hunting. When one of the men a short distance from the group shot a buffalo, "Strode took the alarm." Thinking the gunfire had come from Indians, Strode "rushed through the prickly ash that grew very thick on Green Creek at that time, and never stopped until he got into Strode's Station." Such reactions received fierce social condemnation because cowardice jeopardized the entire group. As one western pioneer explained, the men "mutually confided in the bravery of each other for their own safety, & the protection of the frontier."[32]

Fear of ridicule rivaled, if not surpassed, fear of Indians. At times it drove men to unnecessary recklessness, as illustrated by an incident involving William Clinkenbeard and a fellow inhabitant of Strode's Station named Joshua Stamper. The two were coon hunting one night, and Clinkenbeard, being younger, had climbed a tree to shake down their prey when footsteps sounded in the dry leaves somewhere very nearby. Clinkenbeard belatedly realized that the noise was being made by Indians, hearing "one make water on the leaves, as plain as I ever heard myself." Stupidly, to prove that he was unafraid, Clinkenbeard kept talking to Stamper, who was waiting alone at the foot of the tree. Meanwhile, the Indians attempted to capture Clinkenbeard's profile against the moonlit sky and shoot him down. "Old Daddy" Stamper finally declared that he had had enough and commanded Clinkenbeard to descend, but instead of spreading the alarm when they returned to Strode's Station, Clinkenbeard and Stamper kept quiet because "so many tricks were played by men of the Station, going out and hiding round to scare others." Although in this instance the alarm was genuine, practical jokes were common and provided tests or rehearsals for facing actual dangers.[33]

Throughout the early period of settlement, "Indian wars, midnight butcheries, captivities, and horse-stealings, were the daily topics of conversation." The result was a distinctive calmness in the face of physical danger, later immortalized in frontier legends, but acknowledged even by the people who experienced it firsthand. James B. Finley, who came as a youth to Kentucky, echoed hundreds of pioneer narratives when he wrote, "This constant warfare made the settlers so familiar with scenes of blood and carnage, that they became, in a measure, indifferent spectators, and at the same time reckless and fearless of all danger."[34] Pioneer William Sudduth made a similar observation when he recalled an incident that had occurred at dusk one day at Hood's Station when several Indians were seen lurking nearby. Although there were only three men and three boys at the station, "we went in, shut the gates, went to bed & slept soundly without placing out a cingle centinal." Sudduth concluded, "It shows how well the people of them perilous times were prepared to bear such alarms."[35] Sudduth's romantic idea of frontier character aside, the chronic violence accompanying early Kentucky settlement created a special set of rules and obligations, the learning of which involved much pain. Though essential for survival in a violent setting, the eventual arrival of peace would render them largely obsolete, material for myth and legend rather than normal life.

The Station Community

The same conditions that kept people huddled in stations rather than moving directly to their own land also kept western society in a simple condition and prevented normal functioning. The station existed for only one purpose: mutual protection. Although people might live in a station for several years, they always did so reluctantly and regarded it as but a temporary home. The possibility of settling their own farms, often located miles away from the station, always seemed right around the corner even when it was not. Their commitment to the station and its future development therefore had definite limitations.

One result was that western society remained practically devoid of any social institutions. People still worried about the afterlife, they still desired education for their children, and some needed legal protection. But organizing churches, schools, or government to meet these needs was difficult. Even had more people been interested, most stations lacked enough people to adequately support formal institutions, and the miles of dangerous wilderness between stations effectively prevented them from combining resources. As a result, those few churches, schools, and government institutions which did appear during the station era were few in number and generally distant and weak. Yet, despite being left practically on their own, most stations appear to have been orderly and cohesive. A private structure of friendship and kinship effectively stabilized these tiny, isolated communities. Though less obvious, this informal structure was as essential to survival as the station's timber walls.

Although the American frontier has been popularly characterized as a place of "rugged individualism," numerous preexisting relationships were a key element in structuring station society. Because migration to Kentucky involved great distance and much danger, it was virtually never a single-family undertaking. The trip was usually done with at least two or three families and often in a much larger group. For example, John McKinney's wife left Augusta County, Virginia, in 1785 to join her husband in a company of about three hundred persons.[36] This party was perhaps larger than most but by no means extraordinary. Some personal ties thus survived the trip west and affected the choice of final destinations. At Strode's Station, for instance, at least thirty of the fifty-two men present by 1781 were from Berkeley County. Several more came from neighboring parts of Frederick County or the area of Maryland just across the Potomac River. Said William Clinkenbeard, "All came out from one neighborhood in Virginia, and as we knew each other there, we worked together here."[37]

The number of people hailing from a single source area may have been unusually high at Strode's, but similar patterns prevailed at several other early settlements. Many of the people at John Martin's Station, for example, were from Botetourt and Rockbridge Counties in Virginia. A few miles north of Martin's, Isaac Ruddle had built a station, "with several families, with him from Virginia," primarily Frederick County.[38] Bryan's Station, the next station west of Ruddle's, had a concentration of Baptists from Spottsylvania County, Virginia. In addition to the obvious material advantages derived from joining stations with familiar people, the old connections sometimes also offered less tangible benefits. The Stevenson family, for example, settled initially at Lexington but soon relocated to McConnell's Station specifically because they worried about the moral effect Lexington society might have on their children. Having formerly lived near the McConnells, the Stevensons knew them to be decent, upright people and, like themselves, good Presbyterians.[39] The specific factors that created settlement clusters in Kentucky clearly varied, but the effect was general. Drawing persons already known to one another and of similar background greatly enhanced the station's ability to sustain order and harmony.

Stations were bound not only by shared origins but in many cases by kinship as well. At this distance, of course, such ties are evident only through close genealogical research. For example, of the fifty-two men known to have been in residence at Strode's Station during the first two years of its existence, the overwhelming majority were related in some way to at least one other adult station inhabitant. This network is all the

more impressive considering that single young men constituted a significant segment of the population at most stations. It grew tighter, of course,
as some of the single inhabitants married. Tracing these connections is
not easy. The genealogical literature is generally biased in favor of the
more prominent lineages. At John Strode's Station, the Strodes,
Swearingens, Bedingers, and Morgans were part of the Berkeley County
elite and therefore well documented families. Fewer family genealogies
exist for people of modest means, a problem aggravated by imperfect
county records in both Virginia and Kentucky. Thus, additional links between the individuals probably remain concealed.[40]

If Strode's Station was at all representative of early Kentucky settlement, then many pioneers lived near a relative, just as in older settlements. On the frontier this was especially important. Of the fifty-two men
at Strode's Station by 1781, at least six would be dead, three would be
seriously wounded, and two would be captured by 1785. Fortunately, the
wives and children could usually turn to other relatives in the station. For
example, "Jimmy" Beathe, the father of five young children, was wounded
and captured by Indians while hunting. Beathe was kept a prisoner in
Detroit for three years. His wife, fearing the worst and burdened with
responsibility, would have liked to remarry. She was not thrown back on
her own resources, however. Also at Strode's Station was Mrs. Beathe's
sister, a widow with three children; her husband had died in a battle with
Indians in the summer of 1782. Both families were assisted during this
difficult time by the husband of a third sister. Family ties thus proved
critical for survival. And, as this particular tragic sequence illustrates, the
kinship bonds between women, while much more difficult to uncover,
also tied the station together.[41]

Old friends were another important source of support in times of
trouble. The experiences of the Allen family at Stephen Boyle's Station,
located less than a mile from Strode's Station, illustrate this well. James
Webb, a single young man from Berkeley County, Virginia, had been residing at Boyle's Station when he was drafted in 1790 for Harmar's disastrous campaign against Indians in the Northwest Territory. As he prepared
to go, Webb had a gloomy but accurate premonition that he would die on
the campaign. Deciding at the last minute to make a will, Webb turned to
Stephen Boyle for assistance.[42] Webb's beneficiaries were two adolescent
boys, Benjamin and Thomas Allen. Their father had recently been killed
by Indians, only a few months after bringing his wife and six children to
Kentucky. In Benjamin's words, they were left with "nothing to begin life
with—horse, dog, cat, nor even a mouse." Fortunately, old friends were
present to lend assistance. Stephen Boyle knew the Allens well, and in
letters he had encouraged Mr. Allen to bring his family to Kentucky. Webb
was surely aware of this connection between the Boyles and the Allens

when he made Boyle the executor of his will. Webb wanted Benjamin Allen to have his clothes and the younger brother Thomas to inherit his stallion named Brutus, an unusually fine animal. No evidence indicates that the Allens or Boyle were related to Webb. In relating Webb's largess many years later, Benjamin Allen referred to him either formally as "James Webb" or impersonally as "This Webb."[43] Webb's bequest probably stemmed from nothing more than sympathy and concern.

The Allens also received aid from other long-standing friends. Joshua and John Baker were nephews of Mrs. Boyle. They too had known the Allens in Virginia, and the Allens had attended John Baker's wedding back in Berkeley County. Although the Bakers were not related to the Allens, and they no longer lived at Strode's Station, they came forth as true friends after Mr. Allen's death. Joshua Baker went to considerable trouble to rescue young Benjamin (who had been captured at the time his father was killed), care for him, and deliver him safely home to his mother. John Baker, his brother, also responded to the Allen family's plight. The following winter when young Benjamin visited John Baker at his farm, Baker sent him home with a present. According to Benjamin, "Having lost my father, he gave me a hog, suppose it weighed a hundred pounds, and I brought it all the way, about thirty miles, to Bile's [sic] on my horse, [driving it] before me."[44] Such acts of friendship enabled the Allens to get by. Their experience was unusually tragic, but the general importance of station connections is also apparent in local court records. When people needed bondsmen, guardians, or executors, they turned first to fellow station inhabitants.[45]

On another level, these tight networks of kinship and affinal ties enabled the station community to exert an unusually high level of social pressure that, combined with the station's isolation and the external threats to survival, was generally forceful enough to fill the institutional void and maintain order. An excellent example of how strongly it could operate is illustrated in an incident related by William Clinkenbeard and Benjamin Allen of Strode's Station concerning the death of a young man named Peter Harper whose mother had been an Indian captive. According to Clinkenbeard, Peter Harper "looked as much like an Indian as could be; black hair and straight walk." Benjamin Allen, who was just a boy at the time, described him as "a sort of yellow man." Despite his mixed ancestry, Harper was well liked at Strode's Station, and his friends there were upset when they learned that he had been killed while out hunting alone. Strong circumstantial evidence suggested that he had been mistaken for an Indian by James McMillan, who had served as a delegate to the Virginia Assembly. McMillan admitted having killed an Indian near where Harper had been last seen alive, but he insisted that it had not been Harper. Few people, however, were convinced. First, they knew that Indian warriors never traveled alone, and McMillan had admitted shooting a lone Indian. Second, the coincidence of time and place seemed just too great. Third, McMillan claimed that the Indian he shot had shot at him, but the pattern of bullet holes in McMillan's coat suggested that he had balled it up and shot holes in it himself. People at Strode's Station believed that "if it was a white man, through a mistake, he ought to have told it." McMillan was never convicted, but the doubt cast on his character irreparably undermined his standing in the community. Clinkenbeard claimed that McMillan "never seemed to do well after this," and Allen said that he "took to drink before long." Though it could not be legally proven, in the eyes of people at Strode's Station, McMillan was guilty.[46]

As long as the station remained small in size, isolated, and pressed by an external foe, this informal system worked sufficiently well. Station life may have been boring, filthy, and poor, but it did afford security. Religious and governmental institutions, had they been more readily available, would have been almost superfluous in terms of enforcing social norms. Nonetheless, the delay in establishing these institutions carried serious consequences for later development. As the Indian danger lessened and westward migration increased, the tight, intimate, and interdependent station community would give way to a much more competitive, culturally diverse, and geographically fluid set of inhabitants. Until an adequate institutional framework was in place to help order the burgeoning number of western inhabitants, Kentucky society would experience much conflict and instability. Thus the extreme nature of the Revolutionary frontier era exerted a lingering effect.

The Station Network

The close of the Revolutionary War signaled important changes for Kentucky settlement. The British ceased supplying and encouraging their Indian allies to harass the western American settlements. No more "Indian armies" descended from Detroit, although smaller Indian raids for horses or other property continued for another decade. Settlers began migrating westward in greater number; Kentucky's federal census in 1790 counted 73,677 inhabitants, black and white.[47] This influx of population bolstered frontier settlement tremendously, securing the old stations and encouraging the founding of new ones further out. In a few short years, the area of American presence in Kentucky expanded dramatically. The new settlements formed a protective band around the older ones in the central Bluegrass region, where people were now able to proceed toward their final goal—eagerly abandoning the stations for their own farmland. The decade following the Revolutionary War in Kentucky was thus characterized by a dual settlement system—a secure interior region increasingly marked by family farmsteads surrounded by a protective band of station settlements on the expanding frontier.[48]

As westward migration swelled during the 1780s, outlying stations proliferated. At Strode's Station, John Constant began the process of branching off as early as 1781. Constant's example was followed by Andrew Hood, Stephen Boyle, Ralph Morgan, George Stockton, Michael Cassidy, John Fleming, Joshua Baker, John Baker, and other early inhabitants. The surviving records are far from complete in identifying everyone who resided at these stations—or their dates of residence, for some people are known to have moved several times. Nonetheless, a mixed pattern of old Strode's Station people combined with newcomers can be detected. Daniel Deron, Andrew Swearingen, John Wade, and his brother James Wade moved from Strode's to Morgan's Station. William Sudduth was initially at Strode's Station and later at McGee's and Hood's Stations. Thomas Jones left Strode's Station for John Fleming's Station.[49]

Although the branching out of Strode's Station inhabitants is fairly evident, the result was not necessarily more numerous but smaller and exclusive clusters. Original station inhabitants usually moved on to a branch station only if their land was in an outlying area. Many of the original inhabitants at Strode's Station had claimed land relatively nearby, so they simply stayed there until it was safe enough to move directly to their farms. The founder of an outlying station therefore needed to recruit widely, among both old station members and newcomers. Few former Strode's Station people can be identified among lists of settlers at Montgomery's Station (a branch of Morgan's Station), John Baker's Station, and Boyle's Station. One of the few complete lists is for Morgan's Station in 1789, where only two of the eight men can be traced back to the Strode's Station neighborhood. Some of the new stations, such as that of Elijah Crosswaite, drew their inhabitants from stations other than Strode's, then forged ties with Strode's because it was closer.[50] The reverse might also occur. The stations founded by John Fleming and Michael Cassidy, for example, were so distant from Strode's that they soon forged stronger ties with the settlements at Limestone and Washington.

As the other early stations became more secure, they entered a second phase of development. For example, Strode's Station took on the role of support base for new stations, just as during the early war years it had once been supported by Boonesborough. By 1783, Strode's was no longer the vulnerable outpost that it had been two years earlier, "facing the danger," and was generally regarded as a secure place. By the end of the decade, Strode's was unmistakably "inside."[51] Newly arriving settlers could rest and reconnoiter at Strode's before continuing to a final destination in the area. The Allen family, for example, had paused at Strode's in 1789 on their way to Stephen Boyle's Station. Similarly, the Rogers family stayed

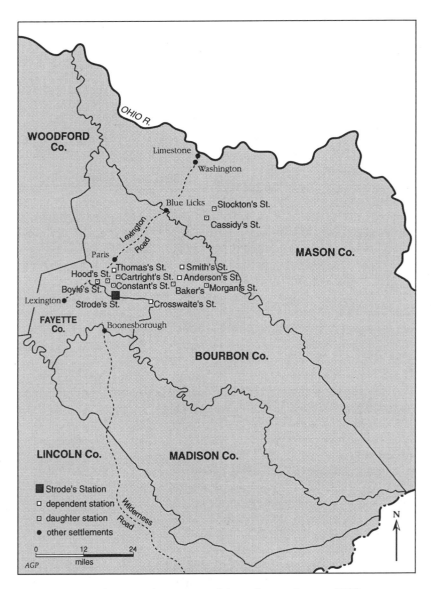

Map 2. Strode's Station and its system of dependent stations, c. 1790.

at Strode's Station while their cabin was being built near Cane Ridge.[52] Strode's Station also figured economically as a base of supply. When a flock of wild turkeys destroyed the young field of corn at Morgan's Station, for example, the people there sought replacement seed from Strode's Station.[53] Other stations were closer, but only an older station possessed the resources for this kind of assistance. The school and the Baptist worship at Strode's also contributed to its local prominence. In 1792, when Clark County was created from sections of Bourbon and Fayette Counties, it seemed natural to make Strode's Station the site for the county court's first meeting.

The stations that branched off from Strode's and the other established settlements in the postwar decade differed from them in several ways. First, these stations tended to be smaller, usually involving between two and six cabins. John Constant's Station, the first station to branch out from Strode's, consisted of three families. Constant's brother-in-law, Andrew Hood, also had three families at his station, two and a half miles east of Strode's. John Baker founded a station in 1790 with two other families. Ralph Morgan's Station was a little larger, having been founded in 1789 with eight men, although three of them were unmarried. Thomas Montgomery began his station with three families from Morgan's Station. Stephen Boyle's Station, "a short mile" from Strode's, comprised four cabins.[54] Stations in other parts of Kentucky that were founded during this period followed basically the same pattern of smaller size.[55]

The layout of these smaller stations was well suited for mutual protection. One visitor recalled, "Five or six cabins are often put together in a court with the doors opposite or at right angles, so that in case of an attack, you may fire through the holes of one door at the enemy before the other." The cabins were built closely together. At Boyle's Station there was "a yard, about twenty or thirty steps sq., a house at every corner, and a family in each house." Morgan's Station was originally three cabins, "in the shape of a 3-footed stool as it were; with the doors all facing one another, and [around them] about 40 acres of land planted in corn."[56] Other variations existed, but all followed the same concept of providing mutual support in time of attack.

The smaller stations multiplied rapidly during the 1780s and were not nearly so self-sufficient and isolated as their predecessors. In late June 1790, for instance, Hood's Station received word of trouble at John Baker's Station. Major Hood immediately gathered a relief party, leaving William Sudduth alone at the station to guard. At dusk the following day, a messenger rode in with news of an Indian siege at Morgan's Station, continuing on to Strode's Station and elsewhere. Alarmed, the women at Hood's Station insisted that Sudduth wait until daybreak before leaving them. When Sudduth finally set out, he encountered the Hood party returning home. Hood and his men immediately turned around and went to Baker's Station and Enoch Smith's Station for reinforcements. A total of between fifty and one hundred men showed up to save Morgan's Station, drawn from a distance of at least thirty miles.[57] Strode's Station and the other stations established during the war had sought to be as self-sufficient as possible because external sources of help were unreliable; the stations built after the war sought just the opposite. Minor points in an ever more complicated and extensive network, their survival depended on outside assistance.

Perhaps the most obvious difference between these smaller stations and the older ones was that many of them were not stockaded, particularly in later years. Rogers' Station in western Bourbon County was described by a settler as "6 or 8 cabins in a square—but needed no picketing, so close together." In any case, "A few hours would have picketed them if needed—if troublesome times had come." Another settler said of Irish Station, located in the eastern part of the county, "They laid out 5 acres to a lot, each side of the road, and that made the station. It was not picketed." In the Strode's Station neighborhood, neither Andrew Hood, John Constant, nor Enoch Smith raised a stockade at their respective stations. The unpicketed clusters of cabins were referred to as stations because the primary purpose for the arrangement was mutual protection.[58] Nevertheless, the term was becoming less accurate over time. The transition could be seen at Wilmot's Station in southwestern Bourbon County. The settlers there were "settled pretty much in [a] little neighborhood. The neighborhood retaining the name Wilmot's Station." The arrangement of settlements continued to relax in this manner, so that by the late 1780s it was becoming common throughout central Kentucky to "see a dozen little cabins, say, at a time."[59]

These small stations usually operated under a type of tenancy similar to before, usually a four- or five-year period of free rent in exchange for clearing the land. Their small size, however, rendered the common field arrangement more or less a thing of the past. As early as 1785 at Constant's Station, a surprise Indian attack found John Constant and Joshua Stamper at opposite sides of the station, each working in his own field. The members of neighboring Irish Station each received five-acre plots. Near May's Lick in Mason County, Daniel Drake recalled years later how his parents participated with other family members in a joint land purchase, subdividing the tract and then building their family cabins where the lot corners converged. This plan offered security as well as the opportunity to immediately begin improving individual farmsteads.[60]

As the example of the Drake family suggests, kinship ties continued to be an important organizing principle in the new stations. William Sudduth moved from Strode's Station to a new one built by his father-in-law, Andrew Hood; James Lane joined the station of his uncle, Enoch Smith. Of the four families at Constant's Station, John Constant was related by marriage to two and had lived with the other two at Strode's Station.[61] Of course, other connections also influenced settlement decisions. The Clinkenbeards had been previously employed at Thomas Swearingen's mill back in Berkeley County. The Allen family had known the Boyles and the Bakers back in Virginia. Several men had performed military service together during the Revolution. In a world of strangers, people sought the familiar.

Thus, the 1780s marked a transitional phase of development in Kentucky, between the extreme danger of the Revolutionary frontier and the security of full peace. The process began first in Kentucky's protected central area, in the lush Bluegrass country surrounding Lexington, then expanded outward. By the end of the decade, most of the wartime stations were half empty and falling into disrepair. More common was the modified station form, which allowed some economic independence. Although the Bluegrass settlements were now fairly secure, protected by a surrounding buffer of expansion, outlying locations remained vulnerable. Security remained a lingering public concern.

The next step for Kentucky settlement would be the gradual disappearance of the stations altogether. The timing varied according to location; the protected interior region began in the early 1780s, while outlying neighborhoods were not really secure until General Wayne's victory at Fallen Timbers in 1794. At Strode's Station most of the original inhabitants occupied individual farmsteads by 1790. Their places at the station were filled by more recently arrived settlers, who would themselves depart as soon as practicable. By this time, Strode's Station was more important as a central place than for its protective but decaying stockade. After 1794, when Strode's Station lost the contest for the Clark County seat to the town of Winchester, three miles away, the old settlement deteriorated and shrank. Other stations survived the transition better and evolved into towns. More importantly, whatever the fate of a particular station, Kentuckians could at long last proceed toward a more normal way of life.

The beginnings of Kentucky settlement were exceedingly violent due to the convergence of two extraordinary circumstances. On the one hand was the incredibly lush quality of the Kentucky Bluegrass, which lured speculators and settlers not only across a mountain barrier and a distance of several hundred miles but also beyond the bounds of authorized occupation and contrary to the policy of both Great Britain and the Commonwealth of Virginia. On the other hand was the outbreak of the war for independence from Great Britain. This conflict provided Kentucky's native claimants with a powerful ally. As a result, hardly any participants in

Kentucky's first decade of settlement escaped a fearful, if not sorrowful, ordeal. Few other American frontiers, before or later, faced such strong and persistent native opposition.

The violence that accompanied Kentucky settlement rendered the replication of society as it existed in Virginia and elsewhere impossible. Instead, the trans-Appalachian settlements were pressed into a special kind of social organization, the station, oriented around the primary purpose of mutual defense. The intimate station community followed a different set of rules than did normal civilian society, enforced more through direct social pressure than governmental institutions. Although settlers viewed their commitment to the station as only a temporary and unfortunate necessity, the tight nucleus of personal relationships forged within the stockade survived into the next stage of settlement.

Historians who attribute camp meeting revivalism to frontier social conditions have generally overlooked the station phase of settlement, when those conditions were most extreme. Had they considered it more carefully, they would have discovered that Kentucky was utterly incapable of supporting any sizable religious revival because of the effects of border warfare. Not only did few religious institutions exist, but even the briefest venture from the station was fraught with risk. This is not to say, however, that Kentucky's difficult frontier period was irrelevant to the Great Revival and the beginnings of the camp meeting format. Rather, the story of Kentucky settlement needs to be understood as a distinctly two-phase process. Until the early 1780s (later in outlying areas), Kentucky settlement was oriented almost entirely toward survival. Only later did it begin to resemble the ways of life found in older Anglo-American settlements. The decade preceding the Great Kentucky Revival would see tremendous strides in this direction, but one result was a special sort of social strain, caused not so much by harsh frontier conditions as by the task of recovering from them.

Part II.
DEVELOPMENT

*T*he decade preceding the Great
Revival was one of recovery and
development. Kentuckians worked ag-
gressively, as if trying to make up for the
delays and destruction caused by border
warfare. The compressed process of
replicating American society was of itself
enough to cause unusual social strain.
Also important, the closing years of the
eighteenth century brought a special set
of political and economic concerns.
Although not unique to Kentucky, they
were more acutely felt there. The overall
result was a society marked by severe
instability and division.

2

THE RURAL ECONOMY OF
THE EARLY NATIONAL WEST

As Kentuckians "settled out" from the stations and private farmsteads became the norm, agricultural production increased dramatically and with it came a proliferation of facilities for processing produce and minerals. The energy behind these undertakings was striking. All the aspirations that had been pent up behind the stockade walls of the station for so long seemed to suddenly burst forth. As one visitor exclaimed, "Never before have I heard so much talk of agriculture and commercial projects; never before have I seen the spirit and taste for enterprise developed in so many different shapes." The striving commercial spirit was represented by nail factories, salt works, distilleries, iron forges, ropewalks, and even vineyards. Every possible stream was dammed to build mills to make gunpowder, full cloth, saw timber, and grind grain. A marvelous transformation of the wilderness was under way: "No one speakes, no one dreams of anything here save the sites of cities, of ferries, of bridges, of mills, of roads, of new communication, of efforts in agriculture, of the construction of houses."[1] The grander schemes failed to materialize until well into the nineteenth century, but the decade preceding the Great Revival still witnessed a phenomenal transformation. Within a few short years, Kentucky went from a dangerous and isolated outpost to a thriving agricultural region. Those historians of the Great Revival who attribute the suddenly heightened religious interest to deprivation and hardship have greatly underestimated the achievements of the 1790s. By 1800, western life generally resembled that found in other parts of the rural United States.

Family Farming in the
Eighteenth-Century Bluegrass

Material well-being improved tremendously once people could safely leave the stations and settle out on independent farmsteads. Station agriculture had not aimed at much beyond a basic subsistence. Although the continued migration of new settlers provided a ready market for foodstuffs, the station presented little incentive to enlarge production. As one prominent Kentuckian explained in a letter to Virginia's governor, "While they are shut up in Forts & Stations, on other men's Lands, they are extremely unwilling to bestow much labour on Improvements, which they Know they are not to long enjoy."[2] Even people who remained at a station for several years did not enlarge their planting space. When times were dangerous, no one wanted to be cut off from safety by large fields, and when times improved, people optimistically expected that their stay at the station would soon end.

People were exceedingly anxious to inhabit their own land and willing to undertake considerable risk in order to do so. Tales of premature "settling out" abound, often with tragic consequences. Bourbon County pioneer William McClelland had constructed a fine stone house, yet was forced by danger to flee to the neighborhood station four times. People whose land was adjacent to the station or immediately nearby could take such risks much sooner than could those whose land was more distant. In the interior or central parts of Kentucky, people began to settle out as early as 1782 or 1783. By the end of the decade, settling out was in full motion everywhere. Strode's and many other older stations were now functioning less as forts and more as rest stops for the continuing stream of newly arrived settlers. By the time Kentucky became a state in 1792, only the outlying frontier districts were dominated by station settlements, and even there the length of time spent at a station was becoming ever briefer. The rush was on to open farms.

In "settling out," certain forms of the station were initially retained. One arrangement, already referred to, was building the cabin within range of a neighbor so that if one cabin were attacked, shots could be fired from the other. Defensive features were also incorporated into the cabin design. Presbyterian minister Robert W. Finley built a log cabin for his family near the modern town of Flemingsburg, at that time on the northeastern frontier of settlement around 1790. His son recalled, "The first story [was] made of the largest [logs] we were able to put up; the second story of smaller ones, which jutted out over two or three feet, to prevent anyone from climbing up to the top of the house." The door was six inches thick, securely barred on the inside. "In the upper part of the house were portholes, out of which we could shoot as occasion might require; and, as no windows were allowed, they also answered for the purpose of light and ventilation."[3] Like the stations, early domestic structures were designed for security because defense remained an ever-present concern. Daniel Drake recalled that the family's ax and scythe were kept in the cabin at night in case of attack. And, come morning, "the first duty was to ascend . . . to the loft, and look out through the cracks for Indians, lest they might have planted themselves near the door, to rush in when the strong cross-bar should be removed." Another settler recalled that his father always primed the guns before retiring for the night.[4]

In addition to influencing architectural forms, the station experience provided valuable lessons in frontier farming. As people settled out, farming practices continued along much the same pattern as at the station. Now, however, farmers were anxious to expand their cleared acreage. With one man able to clear about three acres over the course of a winter, it took between five and ten years before the average Kentucky farm began to resemble its counterpart elsewhere in the United States. Meanwhile, Kentucky farms continued to follow the same basic agricultural pattern as at the station: a primary emphasis upon corn, a "patch" of hemp or flax, a garden plot, with livestock left to forage in the wild. Every winter, man and boy worked to prepare additional ground, and previously cleared land required further improvement. A new settler writing home in 1792 declared, "The countrey In General looks as if it just jumpt out of the bushes[,] all Stumps and Dead trees."[5]

The heavy emphasis on corn that characterized station agriculture continued—and for good reason. Corn provided a much higher yield than other grain crops. Furthermore, it was less labor-intensive. It could be sown in fields only roughly cleared, and the plants did not require nearly as much attention as did other types of grain. One pioneer explained, "Deep plowing was not as necessary as in soils long cultivated, and if demanded would have been impracticable, as the ground was full of roots."[6] A poor man using only a hoe could still expect a yield of at least twenty-five bushels. For fields in better shape, it was reasonable to expect yields in the range of fifty to sixty bushels per acre.[7] This was roughly twice the yields found on eastern farms. Nor were such estimates only the stuff of promotional literature. In a private letter written in 1797, a settler insisted, "Industry will produce a great plenty; . . . 5 acres will produce between 3 & 4 hundred bushels of Corn."[8] Another advantage for the frontier farmer was that the harvest time for corn extended over a longer period than for small grain crops, enabling a single worker to cultivate as much as eight or nine acres.[9] The usual practice was to plant the corn "in check," rather than in rows. The field was plowed in furrows about four feet apart and then cross-plowed with the furrows again four feet apart. The seed was planted at the intersection along with beans, melons, pumpkins, and other climbing crops. Methods of corn cultivation had not yet diverged very far from that of Native Americans.

Although corn was the mainstay in the western diet, Americans retained a dietary preference for wheat flour. Western farms initially included only small amounts of wheat because the extraordinary fertility of virgin soil ironically produced wheat with stems that were too long to support the grain. Successful wheat cultivation usually required depleting the soil for several years with corn. Normal wheat yields in eighteenth-century Kentucky ranged between twenty-five and thirty bushels per acre, considerably less than for corn but carrying a higher market value per bushel.[10] Probate records show that early Kentucky farmers began growing wheat as soon as it became feasible, although usually not in commercial quantities. By the beginning of the nineteenth century, wheat and flour would constitute major Kentucky exports.

In addition to the main crop of corn, nearly every farmer also attended to small quantities of fiber crops for clothmaking. Contrary to popular images of early Kentuckians proudly attired in coonskin caps and buckskin suits, probate inventories and travelers' accounts show a decided preference for fabric. Homespun manufacture of cloth could be delayed until the second year and involved three types of fiber: flax, hemp, and wool.[11] A few pioneers experimented with growing cotton, but Kentucky's growing season was really too short. Pioneer memoirs almost ritualistically boast, "Every family had to wear their own make."[12] Probate inventories confirm that most households engaged in clothmaking or at least some phase of the process. For example, of twenty-nine Bourbon County probate inventories covering the five-year period from 1786 to 1791, 24 (83 percent) listed equipment used in clothmaking. During the remainder of the eighteenth century, this proportion hovered around two-thirds of all probated households. Flax wheels and hackles are mentioned in approximately half of the early Bourbon County probate inventories, supporting the observation by an early traveler that it was "very common for all linen which is used in the family to be made at home." According to a newspaper essayist writing in 1797, Kentucky households were actually producing surplus quantities of linen.[13]

People also made a strong, low-quality cloth out of hemp, although as time went on, hemp became more important for the manufacture of rope. A large proportion of early Kentuckians came from the Shenandoah Valley, the leading hemp region in eighteenth-century America, and they were familiar with methods of cultivation and processing.[14] Breaking hemp was extremely laborious, but because this task usually transpired during the late winter months, hemp fit easily into seasonal work patterns. A traveler in 1793 described Kentucky farmland as "Indian corn forever, except what is appropriated to hemp."[15] As Tennessee emerged as a cotton region requiring bale rope and bagging, and as naval demand for rope increased in response to uncertain foreign suppliers, Kentucky hemp production expanded. Late-eighteenth-century newspaper essayists publicly hailed hemp as "the most certain crop and most valuable commodity." Ropewalks were among the earliest manufacturing facilities in Lexington, with five in operation by 1800. Rope making became a major regional industry that contributed greatly to the growth of slavery.[16]

The other fiber that Kentuckians used for homespun clothing, wool, was generally less available during the early years of settlement because of the protection that sheep required from the elements and from predators. The latter was a widespread problem. The annual number of wolf bounties paid out by the county courts usually ranged between one and three dozen during the eighteenth century. Loss from predators or other causes was high enough to make some people doubt the profitability of sheep. Nonetheless, the production of woolen cloth gradually increased. Probate inventories indicate that by the late 1790s, nearly every rural household included sheep, wool, or equipment for processing wool.[17]

Household clothmaking, however, signified neither self-sufficiency nor a western preference for homespun fabric.[18] While many households included flax breaks, wool cards, or spinning wheels, only a few commanded all the equipment necessary for producing finished cloth. Second, merchant account books and probate inventories list enough imported fabric to indicate that the production of homespun cloth had more to do with economic necessity than with personal preference. Despite the high cost of imported products, westerners turned to manufactured cloth as soon as possible. As one Kentucky visitor commented disapprovingly, "Here as elsewhere they have the mania for buying imported cloth."[19] Early merchant account books reveal that approximately 75 percent of all Kentuckians, from all ranks of society, purchased cloth.[20] The quality of local homemade cloth was good, but "none but the inferior inhabitants use them." Enoch Smith of Clark County complained in a letter, "Insted of our appearing in our own make as we aught to do nothing is to be seen in publick company but imported cloathing." Similarly, in 1790 a Lincoln County settler named James Davis complained in a letter, "If we wished to manufacture our own wear, Money would be plenty . . . now the Stores takes it all that is in circulation."[21] Despite frequent public calls for Kentuckians to wear more homespun, the taste for imported fabric was too entrenched. Just how much clothing was made at home is also questionable. "There is about thirty taylors in town," reported a Lexington tailor in 1792. Despite the many competitors, "we never was in such a Way of bisaness in our lives."[22] In a society of strangers such as that of Kentucky during this time, concern with appearance and other signs of status may have been stronger than in more settled sections of the country.

The cloth, butter, maple sugar, and other products made by women nonetheless constituted an important source of buying power in many households. Western merchants who could not sell for cash wanted the labor-intensive goods that could be most easily rendered into cash. The preference for household manufactures over field produce is readily evident in numerous mercantile advertisements. Lexington merchants Dennis McCarthy and John Moylan, for instance, advertised an extensive stock of imported goods, "Which will be disposed of for Cash, Country made linen, and [maple] Sugar, Whiskey and Bacon." Similarly, a merchant in the town of Paris advertised that he would accept in payment whiskey, country linen, maple sugar, bacon hams, cheese, green hides, flax, or seven hundred thread. Soon after his arrival in 1790, settler James Davis reported a "ready market" for butter, cheese, tallow, and lard.[23] Transactions recorded in merchant account books indicate that women were often directly involved in the marketing of the products they made. "Many of the inhabitants cultivate flax," noted a traveler in 1802. "The women manufacture linen of it for their families, and exchange the surplus with the trades-people for articles imported from Europe."[24] For a frontier family struggling to establish itself, household manufactures played an important role. Whether the increased importance of women's economic contribution translated into a larger role in household decisions nonetheless seems doubtful.[25]

Many early farms also included a small patch of tobacco.[26] Few westerners were initially in a position to produce tobacco on a commercial scale, and even if they had been, the mouth of the Mississippi River was controlled by Spanish authorities at New Orleans until 1795. All American goods passing through that port were subject to a prohibitively high export duty. The expectation remained, however, that Kentucky was destined to become an important tobacco region. As early as 1783, the inhabitants were pursuing this goal by petitioning the Virginia Assembly to authorize local inspection warehouses.[27] More than a dozen additional warehouses were in place by century's end, primarily in the Bluegrass region where soil conditions were the most encouraging. Tobacco deposited at public warehouses was inspected for quality and stored until being sent on to market. Leaf meeting specifications of weight, condition, and packing was stamped, and the owner was issued a receipt. In an economy chronically short of cash, these receipts, or notes, helped lubricate local exchange. Western merchants generally favored tobacco or tobacco notes over other farm produce. Tobacco received added encouragement from a Virginia law enacted in 1787 that accepted tobacco in payment of taxes. Every tithable in Bourbon County, for instance, was assessed forty-eight pounds of tobacco that year, pro-rated at twelve shillings and sixpence per hundredweight.[28] Likewise were the county's creditors paid. The clerk and sheriff, for instance, each received 1,248 pounds of tobacco annually. Wolf bounties were paid with one hundred pounds of tobacco, and court witnesses received twenty-five pounds for each day's appearance. Despite tobacco's special utility as a substitute for specie, the acreage grown was probably modest during this early period. With the estimated yield per acre ranging between 1,000 and 1,500 pounds, a mere fraction of an acre was sufficient to meet all obligations.[29] Production on a commercial scale

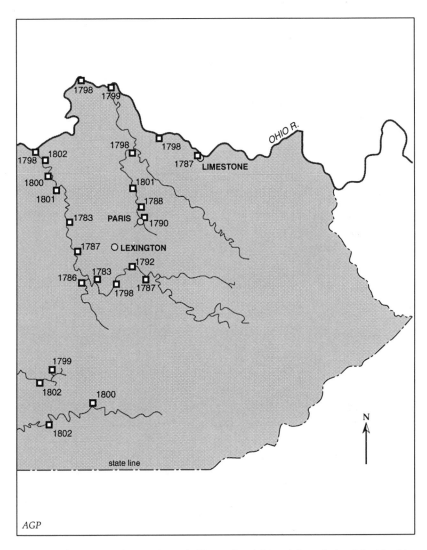

AGP

Map 3. Tobacco warehouses in early Kentucky. Adapted from Leland Smith, "A History of the Tobacco Industry in Kentucky, 1783–1860," M.A. thesis, Univ. of Kentucky, 1950, 30.

would have to wait until Kentucky enjoyed easier access to international markets.

Livestock formed the other main component of early Kentucky agriculture. Contrary to modern impressions, wild game played only a supplementary part in the western diet. The bison, bear, and other large animals disappeared almost immediately following human occupation, either overhunted or scared away. Within a few months of Boonesborough's founding in 1775, hunters had found it necessary to travel fifteen or twenty miles after game. "When we came to this county in 1787, the buffalo were gone," stated Jesse Graddy of Woodford County. "Never saw a wild one." The same was true for most other settlers. Although turkeys and other small game could still be found, even they quickly became unreliable. Domestic livestock, especially hogs, became the main source of meat.[30]

During station times and the early years of opening individual farmsteads, little provision could be made for domestic livestock. Every cleared acre of land went to crops, with virtually none to spare for pasturage. Fortunately, the Bluegrass habitat supported thick stands of a native plant resembling bamboo, commonly called cane. Growing to heights of ten to fifteen feet, often so thick that a person could not see through it for more than a few feet, the cane provided excellent forage for cattle, particularly since it remained green through winter. Observers all agreed that livestock thrived on the stuff.[31] "It was common at that day to take the cattle out to the fresh cane region and bore holes in the trees and logs and fill them with salt," recalled one old settler. "This would 'hant' the cattle to this place and the owner would visit . . . once a week and call them."[32] The transition to domestic grasses began fairly soon, however, since cane marked some of the lushest soils and was therefore quickly cleared. Very little cane survived the 1790s. Kentucky farmers soon began setting aside land for clover, timothy, and other fodder crops. Some farmers tried to stretch their limited pasturage by herding cattle to "range land" in summer, but this became less feasible as the area of settlement expanded. By late winter, shortages of fodder were a common problem. Swine, the primary source of meat in the early American diet, were hardier than cattle and could survive on forest mast. Horses and sheep received somewhat better care, but on the whole western livestock had to fend for themselves during the settlement period.[33]

The most important factor affecting a farmer's productive capability was the amount of labor available at his disposal. Farmers found field hands scarce and expensive. In the early 1790s an unskilled laborer might earn about three shillings per day, plus provisions. Another estimate for these years calculated annual earnings at approximately fifteen pounds, plus room and board. This was better than what a worker could earn in other regions, but most settlers without money for land preferred to farm as tenants because it offered more independence than did working for wages.[34] Members of the gentry trying to develop plantations found it exceedingly difficult to hire a good laborer, and when successful they complained that one "must humor him a good deal, and make him sit at the same table with him." Some gentlemen claimed that the small farmer was better able to secure hired help because payment through exchange of labor or bartering some desired item did not raise the delicate issue of social status.[35] Perhaps the most common way that western farmers obtained agricultural labor was through informal exchanges such as log rollings, barn raisings, and corn huskings. The festivities that usually accompanied these events did not obscure their economic importance. Beneficiaries were under an obligation to return the favor. As pioneer Daniel Drake candidly described preparations for a corn husking, "When the crop was drawn in, the ears were heaped into a long pile or rick, a night fixed on, and the neighbors notified, rather than invited, for it was an affair of mutual assistance."[36]

Slave labor presented an alternative solution to the labor shortage and figured significantly in Kentucky farming from the very beginnings of settlement.[37] Daniel Boone himself owned slaves, and so did many other early settlers who knew how difficult it was to secure agricultural laborers in newly settled areas. Scattered evidence suggests that most stations included at least a few slaves. For example, John Cowan at Harrodsburg in early 1777 counted eighty-one men, plus four unable to bear arms, twenty-four women, twelve children above age ten, and fifty-eight younger children. The black inhabitants included twelve slaves above age ten and seven younger children.[38] By the time of the first federal census in 1790, nearly thirteen thousand slaves lived in Kentucky. Slavery was also widely dispersed, with nearly one out of every four Kentucky households owning at least one slave. Slavery continued to grow rapidly throughout the next decade. By 1800, the number of Kentucky slaves had reached 40,343, which was 18.25 percent of the total population. More than 32,000 Kentuckians owned slaves in 1800, roughly one-quarter of all householders, a level comparable with much of the seaboard South. The greatest concentration of slaves was in the Bluegrass region, where in some counties nearly 40 percent of the households included slaves. The number of free blacks was very small throughout this period: the 1790 census included only 114 free people of color, increasing to 739 by 1800.[39]

Early Kentucky offered slavery a fertile field. Although slavery is usually associated with staple crops, clearing land was just as backbreaking and tedious. When a prime field hand could clear three acres in the course of the winter, just one or two slaves made a tremendous difference in the productive capability of a new farm. The strong western demand boosted slave prices beyond their normal value in the east. According to one estimate, a male adult who might sell for seventy pounds in Virginia went for one hundred pounds in Kentucky. Those westerners who desired slaves could usually only afford one or two. In Madison County where Boonesborough was located, for example, 42 or 44 percent of the slave-owning households included only one slave in 1787; 83 percent numbered five or fewer. By the end of the century, the emergence of staple crop agriculture, particularly hemp and tobacco, was beginning to have a noticeable effect in some areas, but western slavery remained comparatively dispersed. The average slaveholding unit measured only 4.39 statewide in 1800. Approximately one-fifth of Kentucky masters owned only a single slave.[40] The use of slave labor in Kentucky settlement, it should be noted, extended beyond what ownership figures convey. Those westerners who could not afford to buy a slave, or objected to slavery, might hire their labor on a short-term basis. The intense demand for field laborers made the trans-Appalachian West conducive to slavery.[41]

Some evidence suggests the operation of a small-scale slave trade.[42] Most western slaves had migrated with their owners rather than a professional trader, but a surprising number soon found themselves with new owners once in Kentucky. For example, Madison County tax lists show that 13.4 percent of the slaveowners in 1792 had had no slaves five years earlier. Others had apparently bought additional slaves. Of the 247 Madison County slaveowners in 1792, 101 had also been resident five years earlier, of whom 47.5 percent had gained additional slaves in patterns impossible through natural increase. For example, William Miller Sr. had

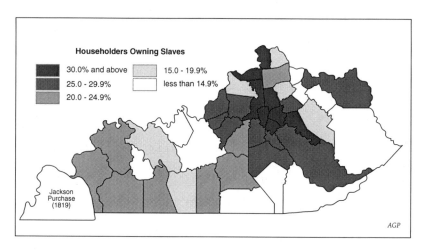

Map 4. Kentucky slaveholding in 1800. Based on data from Joan Wells Coward, *Kentucky in the New Republic: The Process of Constitution Making* (Lexington: Univ. Press of Kentucky, 1979), 63.

owned one adult in 1787, and in 1792 owned three adults and one slave below age sixteen.[43] At least some people appear to have brought slaves to Kentucky with the intention of selling them. John Breckinridge advised an eastern friend in 1794, "Negroes would exchange well for lands, or sell for cash."[44]

With small numbers of slaves distributed across numerous white households, the races lived in close regular contact, but nothing indicates that this in any way resulted in better living conditions or treatment. People still in the process of opening new farms had little to share, and slaves were the least likely to partake in what was available. A slave put to the laborious task of pounding corn in a mortar and pestle stole mouthfuls of the precious meal as he worked. The food supply was so meager that this slave had become "so weak, he could hardly carry a bucket of water." Slaves also routinely experienced exposure to danger, perhaps even more than did white settlers. Settler John Bruce, for example, left a slave man and woman to work his land claim, until one day the man was found tomahawked and scalped and the woman was missing and probably taken prisoner.[45]

The majority of western farmers did not have slaves. Instead, they relied on the labor of family members. Farming without a family was virtually impossible. Females did not work in the fields except under extreme circumstances, but boys labored from an early age.[46] At least one early traveler thought too many Kentucky youth were working in the fields when they should have been in school.

Daniel Drake, who spent his early years at May's Lick in Mason County, began working in the fields at age eight. Drake's father wanted a better life for his children, but one day when the work seemed too much he marched into the schoolhouse and brought his eldest son home to help in the field. Young Daniel performed numerous tasks. He helped with the plowing by riding and guiding the horse while his father struggled behind holding down the plow. He also helped plant, dropping the seeds as his father followed along covering the seeds with a hoe. Other responsibilities included helping to care for the livestock, hunting the cows and sheep out of the woods, and hauling water. Although milking was strictly women's work, Drake helped his mother by controlling the cows for her. Boys could also churn without risking their masculinity. Drake helped his mother by husking corn for the breakfast mush, hauling water for laundry, and assisting in the annual maple sugar harvest. He also helped when she made cheese and soap. Drake's parents depended on their oldest child a great deal and at times called on him to perform work beyond his strength. In his memoirs Drake recounted an episode when he had to take corn to the mill, but was too small to load the bag onto the horse. The trip home was a very anxious one: "Had my bag at any time fallen off, I could have done nothing but cry over it." Child labor involved more than just a few daily chores. By age fourteen Drake could split seventy-five rails of Blue Ash logs in a single day.[47]

Thus, the transition to family farmsteads commenced in earnest once station settlements were no longer necessary. By the time of the Great Revival, the transition was virtually complete. Buoyed by the fantastic yields of virgin Bluegrass soil, western farming quickly resembled rural districts in more established parts of the country. The main difference was the acute shortage of field labor. Practices that were labor-extensive, most notably a reliance on corn and the foraging of livestock, therefore tended to be more prevalent. While the level of self-sufficiency is impossible to gauge with the firmness that would allow comparison, it was probably higher than in other sections of the United States at this time. Like Americans elsewhere, though, Kentuckians did not follow principles of self-sufficiency in order to live independently of the market. Rather, subsistence farming offered the best use of resources for people of limited wealth. Evidence of the western appetite for manufactured cloth and other imported amenities could be found in even modest households, town and country alike.

Pursuit of a Western Staple

Developing agrarian settlements involved not only clearing farms but also establishing facilities for processing their produce. The most obvious need was for gristmills to grind grain, as well as other sorts of water-powered processing. In Kentucky, distilleries and points for the inspection and warehousing of major staple goods also played a key role. No one wanted to be far from these services.

Although corn was a major element in the western diet, very few water-powered gristmills were constructed during the first years of settlement. Fortunately, corn intended for household consumption could be prepared by other means. "Roasting ears" were ready in August. Later, as the kernels began to harden, a tin grater was used to render a sort of pulp. When fully hardened, the corn could be beaten or pounded with an improvised mortar and pestle. A superior alternative at this stage was the handmill, with thirty-pound grinding stones. Only some families had their own handmill, but it was common for neighbors to share. The practical capacity of a handmill, however, was quite limited. A few enterprising pioneers constructed horse-powered mills, or "horse hells" as one pioneer described them, with the horse slowly walking in endless circles. Horse mills could handle a much greater volume of grain than a handmill, but they were fragile devices. Most went out of service when water-powered mills became more numerous.

Such operations, however, were slow to appear in Kentucky. One reason was the danger posed by hostile Indians, because mill seats were generally exposed sites and difficult to defend. Mill construction was also an expensive undertaking, since millstones had to be imported from abroad and then transported down the Ohio River. A third problem was the scarcity of good natural mill seats. Although Kentucky had plenty of streams, the larger and more reliable sections were often lined for great stretches with limestone bluffs, which left little room for a mill. Smaller streams gushed with water in winter and spring but slowed to a trickle by late summer and fall, just when demand was greatest. Thus, building a water-powered gristmill that could operate profitably was not an easy matter.

Because milldams interfered with riparian rights held by the community, long-standing English common law tradition required that anyone who believed they owned a likely location for a mill had to petition first for a writ of *ad quod damnum* from the county court, which also regulated milling fees and standards of measure. The court usually responded by appointing a committee of neighboring citizens to inspect the proposed site and ascertain the dam's probable impact. If the dam stood to flood a neighbor's land, for example, the committee would determine the damages to be paid. It also assessed the probable effect on navigation and the seasonal migration of fish, when relevant. After hearing the committee's report, the court decided whether to issue the writ. Occasionally a problem arose, but most prospective millers did not bother the court without being reasonably sure of a favorable finding.

Milling facilities in Kentucky multiplied rapidly in the post-station decade, but local grain production increased even faster with the steady stream of new immigrants. In 1790 western farmers complained in a petition to the Virginia Assembly that travel to the nearest water-powered gristmill commonly entailed one-way distances of eighteen to twenty-five miles. A Bourbon County resident claimed, "The water-mills or horse-mills were so far off, that it was like going on a pilgrimage to get a grist." Even under favorable conditions, the seasonality of the business meant that customers usually had to wait their turn. Nine times out of ten, or so people claimed, the corn had to be left at the mill and returned for later or on the following day. The fluctuating nature of Kentucky's water courses exacerbated the situation. Combined with the fees paid to millers, these problems meant that while grain intended for market might be milled commercially, that for family consumption was often still prepared at home.[48]

Mill access, however, soon improved. The buoyant economic atmosphere of the early 1790s, combined with rapidly increasing agricultural production, encouraged all sorts of enterprises, especially gristmills. A general boom of mill construction seems to have been under way during this time. At Limestone, the main port of entry on the Ohio River for all of eastern Kentucky, a traveler in June 1792 remarked that he saw "56 large millstones lying around on the banks ready to be taken away by the owners."[49] Court records for Bourbon County indicate that, of sixty-four requests to build milldams, forty-four mills had been authorized by the end of 1795. By the end of the century, mill construction fell off, but it is difficult to discern whether this was because all the good mill seats already had been taken or because the economy had slowed. The rate of construction earlier nonetheless indicates that local access to milling facilities improved rapidly during the 1790s. Elsewhere in Kentucky, the number of water-powered gristmills also seems to have greatly increased after 1790. Newcomer Harry Toulmin found that Fayette County had ten gristmills in operation by 1793, even though it was thought not particularly "well situated for mills." Jefferson County, dominated by Louisville, had eight, as well as three fulling mills and eight sawmills. By the close of the century, access to milling facilities had markedly improved throughout central Kentucky.[50]

Indeed, some western mills were already becoming sophisticated, highly capitalized operations. A traveler en route to Lexington in 1794 was very impressed with a business he passed at Millersburg: "There is a dam; and on one side of it there is a grist and saw mill, and on the other side right opposite, there is a grist and fulling mill; . . . one dam answering the whole."[51] Water-powered gristmills with auxiliary functions, usually sawing plank or fulling cloth, became quite common. In Scott County one man erected a paper mill, the only such operation in Kentucky. Yet the business most commonly associated with mills, distilling, actually did not require water-powered equipment, although it did require good water. Many early millers engaged in distilling because grinding fees were usually paid in grain and liquor was a good way to market the surplus.

The beginning of Kentucky distilling remains lost among numerous early references to whiskey consumption and sale. A daily morning dram was customary in many households, "and when company come the bottle was always set out with the sugar bowl," explained one Kentuckian. "Such was the fashion of the day every where." Hosts suffered genuine mortification if they were out of whiskey when a guest dropped in, for it was justly feared that a reputation would be gained for inhospitality. And for guests, to refuse a drink was like refusing to shake hands. At funerals, auctions, elections—indeed, at any social gathering—"the green glass quart bottle, stopped with a cob, was handed to everyone, man and boy, as they arrived, to take drink." Abstainers were regarded with suspicion.[52]

The distilling business emerged early throughout Kentucky. Corn, being so plentiful, was the most commonly used grain. "Indian Corn must long remain a drug in Kentucky, as every farmer makes a large surplus of it," reported planter David Meade in 1797. Because Kentuckians could not ship produce through Spanish-held New Orleans, "the great quantities made must necessarily be consumed amongst us."[53] Some rye was distilled as well during this period. Wheat, on the other hand, generally had more market value in the form of flour. As western orchards matured, distillers also produced increasing quantities of brandy. "Every man who is settled on land leased for a long time is paying attention to the raising of orchards," reported settler Harry Toulmin.[54] Some of the largest orchards in Kentucky belonged to the region's distillers. In 1799, for example, Bourbon County miller and distiller Laban Shipp advertised a five-hundred-acre farm for sale that included "Between 4 and 5 hundred bearing peach trees . . . a good still house, with two good stills, one containing 118 and the other 96 gallons, thirty mash tubs &c. a tolerable grist mill on the same."[55] Peaches prevailed over apples during this early period, largely because peach trees matured more quickly.

Although profitable and easy, distilling required too much of an investment for it to be a common household operation. The western settlements had very few coppersmiths, and stills generally had to be imported, chiefly from Philadelphia. Moreover, the ingredients had to be distilled twice in order to obtain a palatable product. This could be done with a single still, but commercial production really required a second, smaller still called a "doubler." The two stills plus iron and pewter connecting apparatus, all told, required a considerable capital outlay. Each still ranged in capacity from 40 to 120 gallons, its price determined according to capacity at a rate of about seven shillings per gallon. Distilling thus involved considerable expense and consequently operated as a business rather than as a household manufacture. "A few only of the inhabitants have a still," recorded one of Kentucky's early visitors. "The others carry their peaches to them, and bring back a quantity of brandy proportionate to the number of peaches they carried, except a part that is left for the expense of distilling."[56]

In addition to lively levels of local consumption, Kentucky liquor was also enjoyed by more distant consumers. Descriptions of early trading with new settlements along the Mississippi, Wabash, and Illinois Rivers routinely include references to quantities of distilled liquors. Harry Toulmin, for example, was told in 1793 that Kentucky whiskey sold "tolerably well" among American settlers along the Mississippi River and Gulf of Mexico.[57] These markets were modest during the eighteenth century, but bourbon enjoyed a growing reputation. Meanwhile, even without significant external markets, Kentucky's distilling industry helped consume surplus grain.

Although corn dominated the western landscape, tobacco dominated the western imagination. American settlers quickly recognized that Kentucky's climate and fertility were perfect for tobacco cultivation. Its emergence as a tobacco center, however, proceeded slowly due to the isolation from external markets. The only way that Kentuckians could efficiently market the bulky hogsheads pressed full of cured leaf was by shipping it down the Mississippi River and through the Spanish-controlled port of New Orleans. The customs duties on American goods, however, were prohibitively expensive. Perceiving American settlement west of the Appalachians as a potential threat to her poorly guarded North American dominions, Spain was not eager to encourage additional migration by giving the interior United States ready access to foreign markets. Tobacco cultivation on a commercial scale therefore had to wait. As one western settler explained in 1785, "The want of the Navigation of the Mississippi has hither to prevented the cultivation of Tobacco, except by way of experime[nt]."[58] Probate inventories and similar sources confirm that early Kentucky agriculture included very little tobacco.

Prospects for tobacco culture surged forward in the late 1780s in the wake of a private trading mission led by one of Kentucky's leading characters, General James Wilkinson. He left for New Orleans in early 1787 with several flatboats loaded with Kentucky produce, including some tobacco. "Loudly exclaiming . . . against restraints on the rights, of navigation and free trade," Wilkinson set forth down the river, "leaving his countrymen enraptured with his spirit of enterprise, and liberality: no less than with his unbounded patriotism." The fanfare surrounding Wilkinson's departure—and his triumphant return nearly a year later—rekindled western ambitions. Tobacco sold for only two dollars per hundredweight in Kentucky, but for nine dollars in New Orleans. No other agricultural commodity seemed to offer a greater margin of profit. According to a letter written in November 1788 shortly after Wilkinson's return, "If a man owes Tob[acc]o the Merchants will not except Cash in Liew of it, so there is a great demand for Tobo."[59] Eventually the public would discover that the trade concessions gained by Wilkinson were not granted to all Kentuckians but restricted to him personally. The immediate result of Wilkinson's triumphant return, however, was a general excitement for tobacco cultivation.

The eagerness with which Kentuckians pursued tobacco cultivation is strong testimony to the early presence of a commercial orientation and is dramatically illustrated in a controversy concerning the impact of milldams on local navigation in Bourbon County. Although new settlers passing along the Lexington Road provided Bourbon County farmers with an excellent local market for foodstuffs, Wilkinson's success at New Orleans convinced many to pursue tobacco. They were prepared to sacrifice an immediate but limited market for a potential one offering better opportunities for acquiring wealth. In a petition to the Virginia Assembly dated July 1788, 119 Bourbon County inhabitants successfully requested a warehouse facility to be located at Ruddle's Mill, a central site where Hinkston Creek and Stoner Creek joined to form the south fork of the Licking River. There, locally grown leaf could be inspected for quality and await export.[60]

The first indication of trouble surfaced even before the warehouse was constructed, in September 1788, when a prominent local man named Alvin Mountjoy applied to the county court (where he was a magistrate) for a writ of ad quod damnum for a mill seat on his land along Stoner Creek. Mountjoy's site was only about ten miles upstream from the proposed warehouse, so his application prompted considerable consternation among inhabitants located further away. Perhaps because Mountjoy was a fellow justice, the county court made repeated efforts to accommodate him. Yet when the court finally issued Mountjoy the necessary writ in May 1789, it was on the condition that the dam allow the passage of boats twenty feet wide by forty feet long, requiring costly locks.[61]

Meanwhile, a more serious confrontation was taking shape. The trouble began when a prominent neighboring inhabitant named Laban Shipp set out, like Mountjoy, to overcome the problem posed by erratic water levels with a strong, high milldam on Stoner Creek. In December 1789, Shipp had requested a writ of ad quod damnum from the Bourbon County Court for a site a short distance downstream from Mountjoy. Keeping with standard procedure, the court ordered the sheriff to summon a committee of twelve neighbors to meet, examine the proposed site, and estimate the flood damages that might ensue from the dam. At the court's next session, on January 15, 1790, the committee reported that "the Navigation of the Creek above Said proposed mill will not be of any considerable advantage And the obstruction made by the dam immaterial."[62] The court accordingly granted Shipp a writ for the dam. The only hint of trouble was the dissenting judgment of Justice Edward Waller.

A formal protest surfaced in late March when eight prominent residents, including Waller, sent the Virginia Assembly a petition protesting the dam. This petition contended that Stoner Creek was "navigable a very considerable Distance" above the tobacco warehouse at Ruddle's Mill. Stoner Creek was the only available water route from central Bourbon County, and overland transport of the large tobacco hogsheads was impractical for more than a short distance.[63]

In a petition of his own, Shipp countered that the navigability of Stoner Creek was questionable even in winter when water levels were highest and that the distance from the dam to the warehouse was so short that it hardly justified the risk of navigating a wild creek. Not only was the navigability of Stoner Creek doubtful, but also that of the Licking River below Ruddle's Mill. Boats leaving the county had not met with much success. On the other hand, Shipp argued, the growing pioneer community desperately needed more gristmills.[64]

The conflict escalated, and the Virginia Assembly received five petitions that autumn concerning Shipp's dam. An additional petition requested a second warehouse to be located in the town of Paris, upstream from Shipp. The petitions reveal a sharp division in local opinion. At a time when parts of the county were still subject to occasional Indian dangers, signatures were collected from roughly two-thirds of the white adult male inhabitants. Shipp and 165 men supported the milldam while 366 men opposed it. Geographical location presumably played a big role in determining alignments. Opposition was to be expected from the majority of inhabitants who lived upstream. On the other hand, those who lived downstream from Shipp did not have their access to the tobacco warehouse obstructed, and they stood to benefit from a new mill in their neighborhood. Unfortunately, poor land records and high tenancy levels obscure neighborhood patterns.[65]

The most striking aspect of the Shipp controversy is how many local farmers were prepared to downplay their immediate need to process grain for the future possibilities offered by tobacco. Much of the opposition to Shipp's milldam came from poorer farmers who, realistically speaking, probably did not possess the resources necessary for pursuing tobacco cultivation on a commercial scale.[66] Their optimism was perhaps naïve, but people recently arrived in Kentucky or recently released from the confines of station life probably did not dwell much on the negative aspects of reality. Rather, inspired by Kentucky's extraordinary soil fertility, and no doubt also anxious to recoup the cost of a distant migration, rich and poor farmers during this early period shared high aspirations for future prosperity. Despite the ready market for grain created by the heavy influx of western immigrants, past experience indicated that the most direct route to prosperity was through the cultivation of staple crops for export. The enthusiasm for tobacco among poorer farmers elsewhere in Kentucky is also apparent in the efforts of Nelson County inhabitants to obtain a warehouse. Between 1787 and 1789, more than four hundred individuals signed five legislative petitions, although nearly one-quarter did not even own land.[67] For the moment, western agriculture remained subsistence-oriented, but rich or poor, Kentuckians shared strong aspirations for achieving something better.

Unfortunately, nature could be uncooperative. The millers along Stoner Creek had to provide their dams with locks, but the waters still proved barely navigable. Boats departing from central Bourbon County for the

Ohio River proceeded at great risk. "No great quantity of Tobo. was made this year," reported a planter located upstream in neighboring Clark County in 1793. "The discouragement for two years past ocation [*sic*] but little attention to the Cultivation of that Article."[68] After Kentucky achieved statehood in 1792, several statutes were passed to improve this route, but little benefit came from these efforts. Whether to one of the warehouses on the Kentucky River or to Limestone on the Ohio River, overland remained the most reliable way for Bourbon County farmers to market tobacco. Even for farmers who were more advantageously situated, low international market prices during the 1790s offered little encouragement. Consequently, one settler later recalled, "After a few years, the culture of Tobacco was relinquished in a great measure."[69] The search for a staple crop nonetheless continued, settling eventually upon hemp. International embargoes in the early nineteenth century created a domestic market for rope, and Kentucky entered a golden age of prosperity as the nation's leading hemp producer.

A Boom Economy Comes and Moves On

Shortly after moving to Kentucky in 1790, a settler named James Davis wrote back to friends in Virginia concerning the most important question of every prospective settler: "You wish to Know what the industrious man can Do with the Surplus of his Labour." Davis cited recent prices for pork, bacon, whiskey, wheat, corn, and tobacco. Household manufactures—butter, cheese, tallow, and lard were "ready market." He concluded, "But it depends altogether on the Encouragement to trade Down the River whether the prices will rise or fall."[70] The Mississippi River, as Davis and every western farmer knew, was crucial to Kentucky's future prosperity. Unfortunately, the Spanish authorities at New Orleans obstructed American commerce through their territory, a situation which did not improve until 1795.

Although farmers were denied direct access to export markets, the western economy was not mired in idleness and poverty. The early 1790s was actually a time of considerable prosperity as a result of the wealth introduced by the heavy influx of settlers. These newcomers bought foodstuffs, livestock, and other items, and many of them paid with cash. Every year, thousands of immigrants descended the Ohio River, which soon superseded the Wilderness Road as the principal route westward. Most people disembarked at Limestone (modern Maysville), the next port being several days further downstream at Louisville. As one western traveler said of Limestone, "This place is in a manner the entrance to Kentucky."[71] Few people remained at Limestone who had money to move on; the land was poor and prices were inflated. Most proceeded toward the interior via the Lexington Road, a former buffalo trace that at some points measured two hundred yards wide and brought travelers directly into the heart of the settlements. The distance from Limestone to Lexington measured approximately sixty-five miles and took two or three days to cover.

This ancient route, Lexington's main connection with the Ohio River, was more important during the eighteenth century for what it brought into Kentucky than for what it allowed out. New immigrants could bring only part of the provisions needed to carry them through to their first harvest; they counted on getting the rest once in Kentucky. Some supplemented their supplies immediately, pushing prices in Limestone and Mason County way above normal. A traveler who stopped there wrote that the inhabitants of Limestone "live in idleness and poverty & for support depend upon what they can lay hold of from travellers." The immigrant market was so good that the military, restricted by government budget allowances, competed for provisions with difficulty. Newly arriving immigrants tried to avoid the inflated prices at Limestone by buying what they needed later.[72] Farmers across a much larger region thereby shared in the benefits of the immigrant market. In 1789 settler Peyton Short reported, "Every production of our Land sells for as high a price as the Cultivator could in reason ask owing to the astonishing migrations to the Western Country." Robert McAfee recalled that in Mercer County his father "raised an abundant crop [which] he sold to new settlers which poured into Kentucky every year." Kentucky farmers still eyed the Mississippi impatiently, anxious for the lucrative possibilities of staple agriculture, but for the present a good market for farm produce came walking down the main road.[73]

Kentucky's other source of prosperity in the early 1790s was the U.S. army. A series of campaigns against Indians in the Northwest Territory used Kentucky as a major base of supply. According to one inhabitant years later, "Money was plenty then; Kentucky [was] furnishing the supplies for the war." Especially nice was that the government made its purchases in cash. Although most of the U.S. army's flour and whiskey provisions were purchased in western Pennsylvania and shipped down the Ohio River, Kentuckians supplied cavalry mounts, pack horses, beef cattle, pork, and great quantities of corn.[74] This happy situation lasted throughout the early 1790s, until General Wayne's victory at Fallen Timbers in 1794, after which military activity lessened and then shifted to more distant regions.

Unfortunately, just as military purchases began decreasing, so too did the immigrant market. Ohio and other areas opening for settlement drew an ever greater proportion of western settlers. In Lexington and the town of Washington near Limestone, two of the areas most affected, local leaders organized societies to promote emigration. Both groups produced newspaper articles in 1797 praising Kentucky as a land for personal betterment. Nonetheless, as a visitor to Kentucky observed, "the emigration of the eastern states, having taken a different direction, incline very feebly toward Kentucky." Farmers everywhere, but especially along the commercial corridor to Lexington, suffered the decline of an important market for their produce. Bad crop years in 1795 and 1797 added further strain.[75]

The economic downturn of the late 1790s had a measurable effect. One of the most sensitive lines of business was retailing. Dependent upon extensive lines of credit, stores were usually among the first businesses to fold in hard times. Most retail stores in early Kentucky were small and basic, but still involved a considerable capital commitment, starting with a twenty-five-dollar retail license. The annual number of retail licenses, which were issued by the county court, provides a crude indicator of economic conditions. In Bourbon County, for example, the number of retailers multiplied impressively through the mid–1790s, but only about half survived to the end of the decade. In Harrison County, created from the northern section of Bourbon County in 1794, the pattern was much the same, though briefly delayed by unrealistic ambitions for the new county

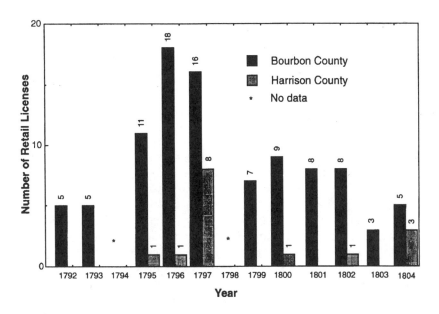

Fig. 1. Retail store licenses for the Bourbon County area, 1792–1804. (Harrison County was created from northern Bourbon County in 1794.) The data was culled from county tax lists.

seat of Cynthiana.[76] Local conditions were aggravated by an alarming rate of inflation. In mid-1796, the Bourbon County Court discovered that the construction of a bridge at Paris was seriously over budget because prices had risen at least one-third over the twelve months since the bridge had been contracted.[77] In the rest of Kentucky as well, the closing years of the century marked hard times, serious enough for attention in Governor James Garrard's annual address to the legislature in 1799. The exuberant economic spirit that had opened the decade was gone. Forced to adjust their expectations, inhabitants now stridently protested the "great scarcity of money."

Most responses to the economic malaise centered around the regional outflow of cash payments for manufactured goods imported from eastern merchants. One after another, essayists in the Kentucky newspapers decried the "consumption habit" that Kentuckians had developed during more prosperous times. Every consumer purchase drained the region of cash as Kentucky merchants conveyed it back to their creditors in Philadelphia and other Atlantic ports. According to a newspaper essayist who signed himself "Merlin," "Pack-horses, and even wagons, loaded with dollars destined for Philadelphia remittances, have been latterly no uncommon sight on the high roads of this country." Another commented, "For as long as these drains continue open, they must as certainly and effectually impoverish and exhaust the political body as the same numbers would the human body." The *Kentucky Gazette*'s editor reprinted an essay by "An American Farmer," who lamented the passing of a time in the recent past when Americans had been self-sufficient and not "enslaved" by an insatiable hunger for consumer goods.[78] In Bourbon County, where the economic depression perhaps hit with particular force because of local reliance on the declining immigrant market, the unhappiness came to a head in February 1800 when a mass assembly protested the "ruinous intercourse between the People and the Merchants." The meeting adopted and submitted for publication a set of resolutions calling for the nonconsumption of imported goods and a revival of home manufactures, urging other Kentuckians to follow suit.[79]

These calls for self-sufficiency were reacting to economic recession, but they tapped long-existing anxieties about dependence on seductive commercial markets. Warnings had surfaced regularly in public discourse, even in times of relative prosperity. Many contain a sharp moral rebuke. In 1788, for example, the *Kentucky Gazette* printed an essay decrying the "fatal consequences of luxury." It warned readers, "There is no greater calamity can befall any people, than when luxury is introduced among them, especially where it becomes general and is carried to so great a height, that every individual is under some necessity of living beyond his fortune, or incurring the censure of being avaricious." Once addicted to foreign imports, a man not only risked his family's well-being, but was vulnerable to actions that might "sacrifice his honour, country, conscience, and every other consideration." The basic truth was this: "However amiable virtue and integrity may appear in our eyes human nature will find it difficult to withstand the threatening misery of immediate want." Such a man "is no longer master of himself." The lesson was clear: love of luxury might lead to "poverty, to shame, villainy, dependency, and disgrace, and, at length, to sell one's country, to support an idle extravagance." Excessive indulgence threatened not only personal welfare but ultimately also the virtuous underpinnings of republican society and public morality in general.[80]

These fears were widely shared, yet not strongly enough to inspire self-sufficiency on any significant scale, and they were increasingly supplanted by other solutions to economic malaise. In 1798, for example, the *Kentucky Gazette* reprinted a list of methods for "a country's growing rich." Fertile soil led the list, followed by manufactures and reliable commercial centers. Closing the list at twelfth place, finally, was a caution against excessive indulgence in consumer luxuries. The essayist "Merlin" tried to convince Kentuckians to adopt a more viable strategy, proclaiming, "Exportation, not importation, is your *Way to Wealth*." Similarly, "A Worn-Out Merchant," tired of taking blame for the region's economic troubles, proposed in 1798 that government help promote western commerce through New Orleans by building warehouses and similar sorts of infrastructure.[81] The issue surfaced again in a series of lengthy economic essays published in 1803. Condemning the prevailing pattern in which western cash left the region in exchange for imported consumer luxuries, "Aristides" urged that Kentucky exporters of agricultural produce receive better encouragement. "A more liberal commerce is the only thing that can give us the greatest possible share of the goods of life."[82] These commentators belonged to a growing number of western citizens who rejected nonconsumption for the prudent enjoyment of commercial goods, financed through regional economic output.

The overall development and growth of the western economy is perhaps best demonstrated in the rise of urban places. As early as 1786, a military officer traveling through Kentucky observed that Lexington already had close to a hundred houses, Bardstown and Louisville about half that number, and Danville and Washington about forty houses each. Bryan's Station had taken on the appearance of a small village with fifteen or twenty houses. About a dozen houses had been built at Limestone.[83] Other prominent towns in the eighteenth century included Paris, Georgetown, and Frankfort, the state capital. At the end of the century, Lexington still topped Kentucky's urban hierarchy. With nearly eighteen hundred inhabitants, it was about three times the size of Kentucky's next largest town,

Frankfort. Louisville, unable to fully utilize its river location until American traders gained navigational privileges through New Orleans, ranked fifth with 359 inhabitants.[84]

The 1790s witnessed substantial urban growth. François-André Michaux visited Kentucky for a second time in 1802 and happened to pass through Paris, the county seat of Bourbon. "This small town in the year 1796, consisted of no more than eighteen houses, and now contains more than a hundred and fifty, half of which are brick," he marveled. "Everything seems to announce the comfort of its inhabitants." Another visitor, returning to Lexington in 1807, remarked, "We were struck by the fine roomy scale on which everything appeared to be planned. Spacious streets, and large houses chiefly of brick, which since the year 1795, have been rapidly taking the place of the original wooden ones, several of which however remain."[85]

Lexington's early prominence resulted from its location in the heart of the main settlement region. One-quarter of all Kentuckians lived within forty miles of Lexington. Incorporated in 1782, commerce was the mainstay of its economy. At a time when the town's timber stockade was still in use, the local stores offered foreign cloth, coffee, tea, window glass, and hair ribbons. Few people could afford many of these luxuries, but the cash brought into the region by the steady stream of new settlers who needed to stock new farms kept business lively. By the time Kentucky became a state in 1792, the burgeoning town boasted around thirty stores. Exclaimed a man passing through in 1794, "Lexington is a fine stirring town, containing about 350 houses, thoroughly inhabited, and is the greatest place for dealing I ever saw." Another visitor described it as the "Philadelphia of Kentucky." Artisans were already numerous in town. Lexington had about four saddlers, six blacksmiths, a coppersmith and a tinsmith, a clockmaker, a printer, and several joiners. More sophisticated sorts of manufacturing were also becoming more common, such as a mechanized cotton spinning operation that opened in 1796.[86] By the time of the Great Revival, most visiting businessmen did not bother to count the numerous general stores or the variety of common artisans. They did, however, usually note Lexington's two printing offices, two large ropewalks, spacious market house, two silversmiths, the first powder mills, and the new brick courthouse. A visitor in 1804 described Lexington as a "handsome" town, with a number of "elegant two story buildings, [of] brick & stone, many stores & Mechanicks of every branch."[87]

Culture followed prosperity. In 1793, a recently arrived Virginia planter reassured his wife, who apparently harbored doubts about the quality of western society, that she would find Lexington "populous, gay & extravagant beyond your imagination."[88] The state's first newspaper, the *Kentucky Gazette*, had been founded in 1786 by John Bradford. Transylvania

University, really only an academy when it started, relocated to Lexington in 1788 and added law and medical departments in 1799. The Grand Lodge of Virginia chartered the first Kentucky chapter of Masons in 1788. The first subscription library was organized in 1795 with four hundred books. Theater troops performed in the courthouse by 1798. Dancing and singing schools flourished. Inhabitants of Scots-Irish descent, among whom were many early settlers, organized St. Andrew's Society in 1798. Horse races, long a favorite public pastime, had been held regularly since 1789 at Lexington, and in 1797 races were organized by the Lexington Jockey Club. Urban services also improved. Most notable in this regard were the volunteer fire company organized in 1790 and the stretch of Main Street paved a few years later. A few frontier vestiges still remained, but by the close of the eighteenth century, Lexington resembled many other medium-sized American cities.

Although the Kentucky origins of camp meeting revivalism have often been attributed in part to the hardships of a frontier economy, when westerners were reduced to a bare subsistence and daily life was fraught with danger, the Great Revival was actually preceded by a period of phenomenal growth and development. Outlying settlements lagged behind, but in the Bluegrass region, where the Revival exerted its greatest strength, subsistence farming was fairly ensured, and many farmers stood on the brink of staple production. Indeed, the Bluegrass inhabitants may have been drawn to religion in 1800 not because of poverty but because of prosperity. The eagerness to justify the migration to Kentucky created an extremely competitive, acquisitive, and volatile economy. And, while few wished to return to the more traditional cooperative arrangement of economic relations geared around competency and independence, many people were unhappy at the toll on society. The ambivalence to changing economic values was evident throughout America during this period, of course, and may help explain why the religious crisis encountered in 1800 was not unique to Kentucky.[89]

Nowhere in the United States, however, was the new economic ethic stronger than among the self-selected body of westerners who had risked their lives and property for better land. Despite some lingering nostalgia for a more cooperative, contented past, Kentuckians emerged from their stations with a burst of commercial activity. By 1800, the landscape had been literally transformed. Even the depressed economy did not eradicate the many achievements. Local businesses were threatened, and farmers felt victimized as Kentucky's economy faltered and fumbled to find a new footing, but the contrast with material conditions from a decade earlier was tremendous. As one observer exclaimed, "Such has been the progress of the settlement of this country, from dirty stations or forts, and smoky huts, that it has expanded into fertile fields, blushing orchards, pleasant gardens, luxuriant [maple] sugar groves, neat and commodious houses, rising villages, and trading towns." In little more than a decade, the material condition of central Kentucky had undergone a remarkable transformation. Daniel Drake summarized it in a single sentence: "Kentucky was no longer a promise but a possession."[90]

3

A BEST POOR MAN'S COUNTRY?

B y the late eighteenth century, wilderness regions in America were almost routinely hailed as "a best poor man's country," where people
willing to "live low and work hard" might have a better chance of one
day obtaining a freehold title to enough good land to support a family
comfortably and even settle adult children nearby. Such claims were not
without foundation. Land on the edges of Anglo-American settlement was
often much cheaper than in older-occupied areas. Nonetheless, attaining
landowner status seldom proved as easy as migrants had been led to believe.[1] In Kentucky, the process was particularly fraught with difficulty
and uncertainty, and remained so even after the Indian danger receded.
The problem was not that the quality of Kentucky land had been exaggerated or misrepresented but, ironically, rather the opposite. The lavish praises
for Kentucky land led many prospective settlers to underestimate the task
that lay before them. Equally troublesome was that eastern governments,
distracted by the Revolution and other immediate problems, were unable
to properly direct the settlement process through such means as an efficient land policy. Whether the industry and determination of the pioneer
generation would prove sufficient against these daunting obstacles was
far from certain. Thus, although historians looking for economic preconditions for the Great Revival have tended to emphasize the raw material
suffering of frontier life, failing to appreciate the rapid advances of the
1790s, their emphasis on disillusionment may still hold some relevance.

The Potential for Success

By the time Kentucky became a state in 1792, thousands of Americans
had already responded to enticing descriptions, in personal letters and
published accounts, that hailed it as a land of unsurpassed bounty. One
early venturer described Kentucky as "a garden where there is no forbidden fruit." Another stated that it was "delightful beyond conception."
One visitor claimed that Kentucky soil was so exceedingly fertile that it
provided "all the necessities of life spontaneously." Another claimed with
enthusiasm, "The luxuriance of the soil exceeds everything to be met with

in eastern America." George Rogers Clark declared, "A richer and more Beautifull Cuntry than this I believe has never been seen in America yet." Virtually every account agreed that Kentucky was a "new found Paradise."[2] To many people struggling with the postwar American economy, it seemed like the only obstacle to financial recovery was that posed by the geographical distance separating them from Kentucky.

One of the most influential accounts of Kentucky was a series of glowing letters written by Gilbert Imlay, a native of North America, to a friend in London. Published in 1792, the collected letters quickly went through several American and European editions and spread even further through serialization in newspapers and cheap periodical publications. At the heart of Imlay's great popularity was his optimistic agenda for opening a new farm in Kentucky. Imlay showed in seductive detail how a man could start with nearly nothing yet rapidly progress to security and prosperity. Even individuals who were aware that Imlay's main interest in Kentucky settlement was as a land speculator found his hypothetical account of western farming compelling.[3]

The words of Imlay and other western promoters enticed many poor families to make the big move across two hundred miles of wilderness. Pressley Anderson and his wife came to Strode's Station on foot, he barefooted and she carrying their child. When William Clinkenbeard married at Strode's Station, he and his bride "had neither a spoon, dish, knife or anything to do with." Daniel Drake's father had only a dollar left in his pocket after the expenses of bringing his small family to Kentucky.[4] How much truth could these settlers and others like them find in the words of promoters such as Imlay?

According to Imlay, an industrious man needed only enough wealth to obtain a few essential agricultural tools, build a cabin, and procure some fowls, a cow, and a sow. The sow, with two or three litters of eight to ten pigs per year, would quickly make the family self-sufficient in pork and provide a surplus of it in the second year. Assuming this industrious man too poor to own a horse and plow, cultivation with merely a hoe could still result in a corn crop of approximately thirty bushels per acre. With three acres cleared and planted the first year, and allowing a half-acre for a vegetable garden, Imlay figured the first year's corn crop to total seventy-five bushels. Assuming a wife and two children, Imlay allowed half of the crop for the family's subsistence. The remaining thirty-seven bushels of corn presented a surplus to be marketed in exchange for household necessities such as salt, iron, lead, buttons, and so forth. The second year would bring two new acres into cultivation, plus the original three acres into better condition. One of the latter would be sown with hemp or flax. The second year's corn crop was to yield a minimum total of 125 bushels. Proceeds from the sale of the surplus, approximately double that of the previous year, was to be put toward a plow and horse. This debt would be completely paid during the third year, by which time the industrious man might be ready to consider the purchase of some land of his own.

Imlay's optimistic agenda relied on two basic assumptions. The first of these was the quality of Kentucky soil, which was already legendary. Imlay's estimates of expected crop yields, twenty-five bushels of corn on roughly cleared ground and fifty bushels on improved ground, are consistent with other statements. Harry Toulmin estimated between forty and seventy bushels of corn per acre. The Lexington Emigration Society figured a yield of sixty bushels. For the less fertile soil in Mason County, the Washington Emigration Society estimated fifty bushels. Even allowing for exaggeration, the fertility of Kentucky soil did create agricultural surpluses almost immediately, at least in the Bluegrass region. As a new settler in Mercer County, Harry Innes boasted to a friend in Virginia that fully half of his first crop was surplus. When farmers in Pennsylvania were getting as little as fifteen bushels of corn per acre, the high praise for Kentucky becomes perfectly understandable.[5]

The second assumption underlying Imlay's enthusiasm was that settlers would refrain from indulging their desires for manufactured goods. The American Revolution reinforced an ideal of self-sufficiency—of being economically independent of the market—and diminished its association with poverty. On the frontier as well, self-sufficiency was portrayed in positive terms, as a practical strategy for upward mobility. Promoters of western settlement depicted a region where a man could start with nothing yet realize his material aspirations through personal discipline. According to one enthusiast for Kentucky, "A cultivator is obliged to purchase salt and iron; everything besides depends upon a man's habit and his industry." The western pioneer probably did not have a great deal of choice. High prices and limited credit imposed a high degree of self-sufficiency upon almost everyone. Cash was scarce throughout the West and consumer goods, when available, were commonly marked up "cent for cent" and even higher for items difficult to transport, such as crockery.[6]

Self-sufficiency was necessarily high, but even under the primitive conditions of station life people carried on a lively exchange of goods. William Clinkenbeard and his bride, for example, had as their first dishes a set of wooden trenchers made by a fellow resident of Strode's Station named Enos Terry. According to Clinkenbeard, "He turned dishes and bowls, and being no hunter exchanged them for meat and tallow to us hunters." Barter probably dominated over transactions involving cash, but does not necessarily indicate the absence of a more sophisticated understanding of commercial exchange. Clinkenbeard and his fellow pioneers appear to have been equally comprehending in money matters, as demonstrated by their experience with Continental currency. When the settlers around Boonesborough, at the terminus of the Wilderness Road, learned of the drastic deflation of Continental money, some of them hurried to Strode's Station and other outlying settlements to get it off their hands, before the news spread further. Clinkenbeard initially thought he had gotten a fair deal when he accepted one hundred dollars of the paper money for a load of buffalo meat. He got stuck with two thousand paper dollars before discovering that they had lost nearly all their value. Another man at Strode's, Van Swearingen, was returning to Virginia soon and thought he might be able to redeem the notes for at least something. He gave Clinkenbeard a cow for the notes, which proved worthless after all.[7]

Like Americans elsewhere by the late eighteenth century, Kentucky's pioneer generation possessed a taste for commercial goods. People, as one individual observed, "are seldom contented with the mere necessaries of life. There are certain luxuries which the progress of society has taught us to consider as necessary. Sugar, coffee, and tea, belong to this class; as do sundry articles of foreign dress."[8] Probate inventories filed in early Bourbon County reveal that a majority of western households included manufactured dishes (in contrast to turned wooden trenchers or crude earthenware), as well as books and flatware. Coffee mills, teapots and cups, pepper mills, and mustard pots were present less frequently but still not uncommon. These small luxuries had probably been carried west rather than purchased at a frontier store, for such items were present from the very beginnings of settlement but became more plentiful only very slowly. The proportion of households with chairs, time pieces, and lighting devices increased more rapidly. Although probate records are somewhat biased toward wealthier individuals, they suggest that by the early nineteenth century domestic life in Kentucky encompassed measurably more comfort and convenience.[9]

Virtually none of Bourbon County's early probate inventories refer to furniture other than bedsteads and sometimes to chests, probably because the pieces people began with were simple homemade things of minimal value. Small three-legged stools were widely used instead of chairs. According to one settler, who probably furnished a cabin at the time of his marriage in 1791, "Tables were made of hackberry, split & the heart taken out so that it could be adzed, and then set on 4 legs. Bedsteads were made by resting one end of a rail on the side of the cabin; the other end on a fork." Another common piece of cabin furniture was known as the dresser: "The dresser was a board on which the pewter plates were; pretty, shining, polished. . . . Another little board, notched and placed above, received the spoons, so as to come in the spaces, and hang down between the plates." By the end of the eighteenth century most households included at least a table and chairs. Other types of furniture became more common, too. Crafted furniture, however, remained expensive because of the higher western wage rates. Even prosperous households seldom contained more than one or two good pieces.[10]

It appears, then, that Imlay was reasonable in his two assumptions. First, at least within the Bluegrass region, an unusually fertile soil yielded immediate surpluses. And second, people were not prepared for total self-sufficiency but would temporarily endure a restricted standard of living for the higher goal of building a farm and attaining long-term economic security. Many Kentuckians probably shared the view of settler Alexander Martin, a man of sober judgment who wrote home to Virginia, "I must Confess I think it is a good Country, for any poor man who has his living to earn by hard industry."[11] Nonetheless, on the eve of the Great Revival, numerous settlers had not realized their goals. Many factors were involved, but the main reason probably lies with a third underlying assumption. Imlay made no allowance for setbacks and misfortunes. As farmers have always been painfully aware, a number of things could go wrong with little warning.

Daniel Drake's memoirs of his youth in Kentucky illustrate many of the ways in which unexpected turns of fate could complicate the task of opening a farm. Daniel's father brought his young wife and son to Kentucky in 1788, migrating from New Jersey in company with his older brothers and their families. Shortly before disembarking at Limestone on the Ohio River, the elder Drake seriously sprained his ankle. He had only one dollar in cash, and by the time the ankle healed it was June and too late to begin a crop. Mr. Drake found work hauling goods from the landing at Limestone to Lexington, a sixty-five-mile distance still dangerous along certain sections. Drake began farming the next spring on thirty-seven acres of land at May's Lick on the Lexington Road, his portion of a joint purchase with his brothers. Unfortunately, an unusually early frost destroyed the entire crop of corn. According to Daniel Drake, who was about three years old at this time, the family had only game to eat for the entire winter. "My parents often told me afterwards that I would cry and beg for bread, when we were seated around the table, till they would have to leave it, and cry themselves."[12]

The family's afflictions were not yet over. Just a few years later Mr. Drake was the subject of a lawsuit because a rented horse had died while in his possession. On the day of the hearing young Daniel and his mother remained at home, anxiously "speculating on the result and its consequences." Had Drake been found liable for the dead horse, the consequences would have been quite costly. A horse of average quality cost between twelve and fifteen pounds (Virginia currency) in the mid-1790s, while farmers received only about six shillings per bushel of corn.[13] Another crisis arose when Mr. Drake was drafted for militia service. Nearly every summer Kentuckians were drafted for patrol duty on the frontier or to augment federal troops fighting Indians in the Northwest Territory. Militia service might easily keep a man away from his farm for two or three months of summer. And nearly everyone was drafted sooner or later. "For a poor man who by his Industry has his family to support, to spend the Months of May & June in a block house on the frontier," explained one officer, "some would prefer the decision of a Court Martial & abi[de the] consequences." Others turned to subterfuge. Pressley Anderson of Strode's Station made himself sick by swallowing a chew of tobacco in order to avoid a military campaign.[14] Mr. Drake chose instead to incur the expense of hiring a substitute. Work accidents posed yet another type of labor problem. While struggling to hack out tree roots one day, Mr. Drake's mattock caught fast and then suddenly broke free, causing a gash in his forehead down to the skull. Drake hints that work accidents were not unusual. In fact, some wounds were even a badge of honor; "The maxim of the harvest field was, that no boy becomes a good reaper till he cuts his left hand." Even when not serious enough to result in medical expenses, injury and illness could cripple a family's well-being.[15]

Crop damage from natural pests was likewise common and difficult to avoid. In 1795, the Kentucky legislature passed a law requiring each male over the age of sixteen to kill a certain number of squirrels and crows each year. Although crows and squirrels caused the worst damage to young corn, raccoons, opossums, and hedgehogs also exacted their toll. One report calculated that wild pests accounted for the destruction of two or three acres out of twenty-five. Domestic animals were also guilty, "The horses and sheep would jump over the fence, the cows would throw it down with their horns, and the hogs would creep between the rails." Keeping the marauders, wild and domestic, out of the crop was a common childhood chore. Neighborhood squirrel hunts helped, too, the competitive spirit often producing several hundred dead squirrels in a matter of one or two days. Permanent solutions, however, remained elusive.[16]

Except for horses, livestock received such minimal attention that losses occurred frequently. Continuing the old station practice, animals were left to forage in the brush, where they were vulnerable to natural predators. The county courts paid out dozens of bounties on wolves every year. Ranging livestock were also more likely to stray off. Straying was a relatively minor problem with cows, which returned daily to be milked. Other cattle could be retained by making a salt lick. Swine, notorious for their ability to survive in the wild, were customarily fed corn once or twice a week purposely to keep them in the general vicinity of the cabin.[17] Horses were more likely to stray afar and posed a serious loss, difficult to guard against and difficult to recover from. Sometimes the animals were turned in at the county stray pen. If the value of the animal warranted, a notice could be placed in the newspaper. Lost and found notices were a regular feature in newspapers of the period. Unfortunately, little more could be done.

Any of these problems might constitute a serious economic setback for a family trying to get ahead, but without question the worst nightmare was to lose one's land in court through a faulty land title. The confusion and resentment generated by conflicting land titles can hardly be overestimated. An army officer in 1786 declared, "There is scarce a tenth man in Kentucky who has land with clear title." A traveler in 1802 commented, "I never stopped at a house of a single inhabitant, who did not appear convinced of the validity of his own title, while he doubted that of his neighbor." The problem was ubiquitous. One new settler reported back to Virginia, "The Rights of Land is so hard to Assertain that it is almost impossible for a Man to deal Safely." Even careful land purchasers found it difficult to avoid problems. People throughout Kentucky readily acknowledged, "The greatest difficulty in the Country is the uncertainty of title."[18]

The problem stemmed from the character of Kentucky's land system and the conditions under which it had been originally implemented. By the time the Virginia legislature finally asserted its authority over Kentucky, hundreds of settlers had already staked claims, trying to preempt a prime location in the expectation that Virginia would soon extend its old policy of granting bona fide settlers land on easy terms. Finally, in 1779, the Virginia legislature took action and established a policy for western land, but the delay had ruined any chance of an orderly settlement process. Central Kentucky was already criss-crossed by thousands of over-lapping claims of every shape and size. Not only was it too late to correct this, but the cumbersome provisions of Virginia's western land system did little to prevent future problems. The legislature's concern was primarily to get Kentucky settlement on a legal footing and raise revenue through land sales for the war with Britain while involving the government as little as possible.

Virginia gave early settlers a much-deserved advantage. The military surveys conducted under the old royal government were confirmed and granted precedence against all other types of claims. These surveys were few in number and belonged mainly to politically connected members of the gentry. Bona fide settlers who had resided in Kentucky for one year or had demonstrated a commitment by raising a crop of corn before January 1, 1778, were allowed a settlement claim of four hundred acres for the price of two pounds, plus the requisite fees for registration. Such settlers were also entitled to preempt an additional one thousand acres for two hundred pounds, plus fees. Settlers arriving after that date, but before the passage of the new land legislation, could preempt four hundred acres for eighty pounds. A special commission was appointed to receive evidence that the necessary conditions had been met and, if so, to issue a certificate to that effect. The Virginia land commissioners convened as ordered in late 1779, and that winter they visited each of the major settlements in turn, where they recorded entries and determined whether the claimant qualified. By the time it finished, 1,327 claims had received certificates for 1,340,850 acres. Settlement claims held a slight precedence over preemption claims in that they could be entered before April 26, 1780, whereas the latter could only be entered between that date and May 1, 1780.[19] No attempt was made to check whether any of these claims interfered with one another. That was left to the claimant, who also had to commission and pay for an official survey and then to register the survey with the government land office before receiving the patent.

Only a small number of people, however, qualified for these homestead provisions. The rest, nonresident speculators and settlers who arrived after 1778, could obtain unclaimed land by two means. One was by earning a military warrant or purchasing one from its recipient, heirs, or assignees (Virginia designated a vast portion of southern Kentucky as a military reserve for the state's Revolutionary War veterans). The far more common method of obtaining land in Kentucky was by purchasing a Virginia treasury warrant, available in any amount, at a rate of four shillings per acre. Locating unencumbered land was left to the warrant holder, who usually relied upon the services of a local guide. A number of expert woodsmen, including Daniel Boone, made a regular income in this manner. The land then had to be surveyed, again at the owner's expense, and then entered with the county surveyor. The procedure was not simple, it was not cheap, and it had to be completed by certain deadlines that were often not easy to meet.

The cumbersome system combined with frontier conditions to make conflicting claims almost impossible to avoid. Initials carved into trees became obscured over time, creeks changed their course, landmarks went by various names. Sometimes survey errors were introduced deliberately. Surveyor John Severns, who marked a number of military surveys in 1775, later testified that "it was common in the making those military surveys . . . to make large allowances in the measure." As another surveyor explained, "In dangerous times the chainman walked fast, and even in the act of staking moved on so that with the long sticks they always took in more land than the survey called for."[20] Such practices protected the interests of the private party who had commissioned the survey, but it practically guaranteed eventual conflict with neighbors. Who would win that conflict was hard to predict, but by the 1790s two things were becoming clear. One was that many early settlers stood to lose some or all of their land. The other was that a good deal of money would be spent in the course of determining the winners. Kentucky land cost a lot more than the rates charged by the land office.

The overall effect, everyone agreed, was a "complicated calamity." Throughout Kentucky but especially in the Bluegrass counties where the early surveys were concentrated, land entries were strewn across the countryside "as autumn distributes its falling leaves."[21] Scarcely a landowner in the entire state escaped unscathed. Kentucky's surveyor general reported in 1797 that while "there has been Lands granted to sundries in the State above 24 Millions of Acres, . . . all the Counties contain but 12,476,116 Acres, so that some persons will fall short."[22] Those claimants who could afford to do so bought out the challenging party, but this often proved insufficient. For example, Thomas Rogers's father bought land in Bourbon County and worked several years at transforming it into a good farm. When a man appeared one day claiming to have a superior title to the land, "my father knew little about law and would not venture a lawsuit. He would rather pay for his farm over again than run the risk of a suit [and lose it all]." But then a third party appeared claiming to be the true owner. This time Rogers refused to buy out the claim to his farm. Instead he took a loss, selling his interest to a neighbor for the value of the cabin and cleared acreage, and leaving the neighbor to oppose the third claimant as best he might.[23] Most early settlers were probably like Rogers, either too unsophisticated or too poor to put up a legal defense.

Numerous other Kentuckians became mired in lengthy litigation. A settler named Michael Cogan wrote to the Virginia speculator from whom he had bought his land in Fayette County, "When I purchased the Land of you thirteen years ago I hoped to spend the ballance of my days in peace with out any Law, or dispute with any man, But I find myself more involved in Law and disputes in the close of life then I ever was before."[24] Many settlers did not discover the fault in their title until many years had passed and they attempted to sell. Then neighbors on every side suddenly filed lawsuits. If lucky, only part of the land was lost, but an unfortunate number of Kentuckians had "paid every farthing they had for land; had encountered all the dangers of an Indian warfare in settling it, and had spent the vigor of their strength in clearing and bringing it under cultivation; and just when they found themselves beginning to live comfortably, some other claimant would come and dispossess them of their land." And even victory, when it occurred, came at a high price. In 1798, a public meeting of Fayette County farmers protested that for lawyers to charge half of the land to save the other half was unjustly expensive.[25]

A superior title alone was often not enough. A claim's validity relied on the ability to gather convincing evidence about events that had occurred as much as two decades earlier in a dangerous wilderness. Often there had been only one or two witnesses, and these had subsequently relocated elsewhere—some even to other states. Others had died, suffered infirmities that prevented travel to court, or no longer had sufficient recall of the particular survey in question. In many cases, the defendant had bought the land from the original claimant, and it was this former owner's associates who had to be identified and located. Given the circumstances, many settlers could offer only minimal evidence in support of their land title.

In October 1795, for example, James Beathe requested that the local county court appoint a commission to establish the improvement made by Jesse Hodges on Strode's Creek, the basis for Beathe's claim. Both Beathe and Hodges had resided at Strode's Station during the early 1780s. In January 1796, Hodges testified that he made the improvement (which was required for all preemption claims) in late 1779 in the presence of Thomas Brooks. In his deposition, Brooks confirmed that in late December 1779 he saw Hodges initial a tree to mark the beginning of his survey. Brooks's own claim was made across the creek. Hodges said that he gave Ralph Morgan 800 acres of the 1,400-acre preemption "to clear out on the shares." Hodges soon sold his remaining 600-acre tract to Christopher Irwin and John South. Although the improvement qualified Hodges for the 1,400-acre preemption claim, he had the patent issued in Morgan's name, and Morgan "gave his bond to said Irwin and South." Having thus clarified the early transference of Beathe's tract, the beginning of the survey was reestablished. The tree marked by Hodges was gone, so the commissioners initialed a new one in the presence of two impartial witnesses, as directed by law.[26] As this testimony suggests, defending a land title could become extremely complicated; even the successful resolution of a land title could be expensive and prolonged. Beathe, who had been in Kentucky since 1779 and had spent three of those years as an Indian captive, became so entangled in defending his various titles that he finally sold out and bitterly took his family to Ohio, where he died about a year later.[27]

Not only did people lose a life's work to legal technicalities, but they were also liable for retroactive rent. Never mind that they had built cabins and barns and cleared acres of land—any credit for this labor required a separate suit in chancery. Unfortunately, further litigation was usually beyond the means of ordinary victims. The winning claimant, on the other hand, might gain a ready-made farm at relatively low cost. The popular sense of justice soon demanded some redress. In 1792 the Kentucky legislature received a petition from residents of Bourbon County requesting that a law be passed providing persons who lost their court battle and faced eviction with compensation for their labor in clearing and building a farm. Petitions from other counties followed, but a law providing the needed relief was slow in appearing. Popular House bills repeatedly succumbed to opposition in the state Senate, a body dominated by creditor interests. A law finally passed in 1796, after a fresh election of state senators, but with an amendment explicitly making evicted persons liable for any accrued back rent.[28] Meanwhile, occupants could only bring suit in chancery for the value of their cabin, fence, and other improvements and obtain an injunction against being evicted by the true owner. This strategy, however, was "circuitous, dilatory, expensive, and troublesome."[29]

Though experienced as a personal tragedy, the tangle of land claims also exacted a more general price on society. Humphrey Marshall declared that the lack of confidence in Kentucky land titles had "retarded her population—obstructed her improvement—distracted her people—impaired her morals—and depreciated the value of her rich soil."[30] Setting neighbor against neighbor, title conflicts hindered the development of community feeling. No one knew when a trusted neighbor might suddenly file a lawsuit. The problem also deterred westerners from fully developing their farms. After seeing men like James Beathe expend their prime years building a farm only to lose it, some Kentuckians tried to minimize potential losses by postponing major improvements such as a new house or barn. Moreover, many claims took decades to resolve, prolonging the effect upon the community. Title conflicts were still a major problem at the time of the Great Revival. As a visitor reported in 1802, "This incertitude in the right of property is an inexhaustible source of tedious and expensive lawsuits. Likewise, in a letter dated 1804, settler John McKinney admitted, "No man is sure of his lands in this country."[31]

Thus, opportunity did exist in Kentucky, but progress was slower, less comfortable, and much less certain than suggested in the writings of Imlay and other promoters of western settlement. How many people were crushed by conflicting land claims or by some other tragedy is impossible to determine. But clearly Kentucky offered opportunities for success, too. As the story of the Drake family suggests, people could start with nothing and achieve landowning status. The Drakes certainly experienced their share of obstacles, but ultimately they succeeded. Moreover, they did it with very little to begin with and without resort to credit or loans. In 1794, after six years in Kentucky, Mr. Drake swapped his thirty-seven-acre farm of second-rate land on the Lexington Road for two hundred acres of more remote and uncleared land. The struggle to open a farm was to begin all over, though this time with a nine-year-old son available to help. With considerable effort and sacrifice, the Drakes eventually succeeded in reaching a secure and comfortable standard of living and providing their children with a better start.[32]

Landownership

Historians of the Great Revival have often attributed the western interest in religion to poverty and disillusionment, and the primary measure of economic well-being has always been land. Land ownership constituted the single most important distinction among free white males in the rural world of early America. The difference between a man who owned no land and another who owned just one hundred acres was much greater than the difference between a man who owned one thousand acres and another who owned two thousand. Regardless of the quantity, men who owned land were what eighteenth-century Americans considered independent. Though often dependent on trade with the outside world for a wide range of goods and services, the man who farmed his own land enjoyed an unmistakable autonomy. He decided for himself how to spend his hours and what crops to plant. A tenant or wage laborer, on the other hand, worked ultimately at the bidding of another man. Their ability to earn their daily bread depended directly on another person. The distinction was enormous to early Americans, and it surfaced in countless ways throughout the culture. Cheap land on the edge of settlement therefore exerted a strong pull on landless citizens and small property owners who worried about providing land for their children.[33]

The great majority of immigrants to Kentucky had been drawn there by the prospect of obtaining land of the best quality, but obtaining some of this fine land proved far from easy. Except for holders of military warrants, a small class of individuals, Kentucky land after 1779 cost money. Americans in the seaboard states heard extraordinary tales of price gouging by ruthless land jobbers, but the cost of a farm actually varied quite widely according to location, soil quality, and improvements. In the early 1790s, Harry Toulmin advised immigrants that an acre of good Kentucky land typically sold for just under fifteen shillings Virginia currency or seven to nine shillings British Sterling. A farmstead of one hundred acres without improvements sold for about ten shillings per acre (Virginia currency). With fifteen acres cleared and fenced with a cabin, the price rose to about twenty shillings per acre. The high wages paid western laborers helped offset these prices; a common laborer earned about three shillings per day and outlying land might cost between twelve to twenty shillings per acre, but of course cash was very scarce. One poor settler in 1790 indentured his time for nine months in exchange for a hundred acres of land in Montgomery County, priced at a dollar an acre.[34] Prospective settlers were told that a hundred acres in more remote neighborhoods could be had for ten to thirty pounds in Virginia currency. Outlying land could be an excellent bargain, for the population was expanding rapidly during the 1790s and "what is out of the settlements in one year may be in the heart of them the next."[35]

Patterns of landownership show that accumulating the necessary money and finding a suitable tract of land, with sound title, was not easy. In 1792, the year Kentucky was admitted as the fifteenth state, 65 percent of the heads of households did not own land. By 1800, after nearly a generation of settlement, the situation had improved, but half of all householders still remained landless. In some parts of Kentucky, the proportion of landless was as high as two-thirds.[36] Historian Frederick Jackson Turner posited many years ago that the frontier contributed in a major way to American democracy because the "free" or inexpensive land helped reduce extreme differences of wealth. For Kentucky, the excited descriptions of the Bluegrass land had just the opposite effect. Land speculators and early settlers quickly engrossed all the prime areas and later settlers stood little chance of obtaining any unless they could pay the price. At the close of the eighteenth century, Kentucky ranked as one of the most unequal states in the union in terms of freeholding.[37]

The slowness or inability of so great a proportion of the first generation of American settlers to achieve landowning status has often been attributed to the rapid emergence of plantation agriculture, which squeezed out the small farmer.[38] Kentucky was well suited for tobacco and soon attracted Virginia planters with enough money to purchase many thousands of acres of land, driving prices beyond the reach of poorer settlers. A closer look at patterns of ownership for slaves and land, however, suggests that plantation agriculture had only a minor effect on the general availability of land for settlement.

First, none of the five counties where slavery was strongest during this period exhibited particularly poor rates of landholding. Indeed, Jessamine County, where 40.7 percent of the household heads owned slaves in 1800, ranked among the top ten counties in terms of the percentage of householders who owned land. The situation in Scott County was almost identical. The other three counties with high proportions of slave-owning households (Woodford, Franklin, and Boone) fell within the middle range of landholding rates. Only for Fayette and Jefferson Counties does evidence seem to support the idea that plantation agriculture made it more difficult to achieve landowner status. Although neither county had an unusually high percentage of households owning slaves, these two counties led the rest of the state in the number of slaves per owner. Tax lists for 1800 reveal that in both counties the average slave-owning household exceeded six slaves, compared to a statewide average of 4.39 slaves. Fayette and Jefferson also stood out for their many large landowners. In 1800 the percentage of small landowners under two hundred acres was only 56.5 percent in Fayette and 55.6 percent in Jefferson, compared with a state average of 69.4 percent. Elsewhere in Kentucky, plantation agriculture had yet to make much of an impact.[39]

Second, in some Bluegrass counties supposedly dominated by plantation agriculture, rates of landownership actually improved over time. In Woodford County, 54.7 percent of the heads of households listed on tax lists in 1792, the year Kentucky became a state, owned no land. A decade later the rate had decreased to 51.5 percent. In Bourbon County, a landless

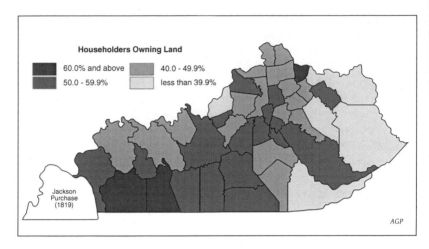

Map 5. Kentucky landownership in 1800. Based on data from Coward, *Kentucky in the New Republic*, 55.

rate of 83.8 percent in 1792 had decreased to 49.7 percent by 1802. Of those Kentuckians who owned land in these counties, the proportion of individuals with more than five hundred acres was decreasing, while that of individuals with less than one hundred acres was increasing. Large tracts of land were apparently being partially broken up and sold. Even in Jefferson County, not in the Bluegrass region but where plantation agriculture appeared early, large landowners fell from 23.8 percent in 1792 to 18.2 percent a decade later. The proportion of small landowners meanwhile increased from 4.8 percent in 1792 to 16.8 percent.[40] To some extent these statistics may merely reflect changing county boundaries as the older counties became more populated and underwent subdivision. But some of the most dramatic differences occurred in older settlement areas, suggesting that early land claimants were selling off undeveloped parcels of their large tracts. In any case, prospects for the small purchaser seem to have improved with time.

Closely related to the problem of plantation agriculture was that of land speculation. Kentucky planters and land jobbers were often one and the same, and both activities might diminish the availability of land for settlement. Rates of landownership in outlying counties were generally better than the state average, a result of lower prices, but a few outlying counties were the worst in the state due to large-scale land speculation. Indeed, the very lowest rates of landownership were in Knox and Montgomery Counties, inferior soil regions on Kentucky's eastern frontier. In Knox, only 31.5 percent of the taxpayers in 1800 were assessed for land,

and in Montgomery County the proportion was 30.1 percent. The rates of landownership were slightly better in Kentucky's western counties and would have been better still but for 200,000 acres granted by Virginia to the Transylvania Company proprietors as compensation for their expenses at Sycamore Shoals and subsequent efforts to attract settlers.[41] The soil in these outlying areas tended to be inferior to that of the Bluegrass region, but few people seemed to care in the aggressive atmosphere of the Kentucky land rush. All that really mattered was their being in Kentucky.

Land speculation was a big business in eighteenth-century Kentucky. Though land jobbing was "a profession scarcely heard of in Virginia," a new settler was amazed to discover that, "here are many—who have no other occuppation, or other means of support, than that of bartering lands and other property." The opportunity to make quick money, moreover, attracted some men of dubious character. In a letter dated 1785, a leading Kentuckian complained about "the Character of our Land-Jobbers," saying that although the business had been accompanied by "much villainy" in other parts of the country, in Kentucky "it is reduced to a System, and to take advantage of the Ignorance or of the Poverty of a neighbour is almost grown into reputation."[42] The potential for amassing a quick fortune was practically unprecedented. George Nicholas, in a letter urging his brother to invest in western land, claimed that "lands generally have risen more than one hundred per cent in a year."[43] Although the opportunity for such dramatic gains diminished rapidly in the closing years of the century, the 1780s and early 1790s witnessed some stupendous profits in western lands. A few individuals wielded truly massive territorial holdings, such as Thomas Marshall, father of the chief justice, who claimed 128,000 acres; David Ross, who claimed 211,417 acres; and Thomas Shore, who claimed 344,783 acres. The landholdings of John May, one of Kentucky's earliest and most intrepid surveyors, at 831,000 acres, dwarfed even these.[44] Perhaps just as significant were the numerous individuals operating on smaller scales, dabbling in the land business as opportunity arose.

Land speculation of such intensity could not help but diminish opportunities for people of modest means, but the problem was not a simple matter of high price.[45] Even with huge amounts of land concentrated in relatively few hands, a competitive market still operated. Indeed, larger speculators were anxious to sell. As early as 1782, John May wrote to his partner in Virginia, "With the abundance of land we claim, if the Titles are confirmed to us, the Taxes, surveying, Patenting &c will ruin us." Therefore, "I prefer much a Sale to holding the Lands, except for a few Valuable tracts."[46] In a letter dated 1785, a prominent Kentuckian named William Christian reported that as a result of land disputes, even "the

Speculators are starving and can sell no Land. Every man is a seller & no purchasers." Only a year later his wife, Ann, observed with worry, "Lands have fallen so low & no purchasers." Similarly, in 1789 George Nicholas wrote of the speculators that "necessity obliges them to offer the best land in very eligible Situations (not yet inhabited) for fifteen dollars a thousand."[47] Writing the same year, John Breckinridge explained, "Tho' lands are cheap; yet money is scarce." A decade later John Breckinridge wrote James Monroe, "There is more Land now for sale, of good quality, than ever there was cash in this Country to purchase."[48] In order to move land, many speculators found it necessary to lower prices and offer credit.

The speculatory dilemma involved considerations of scale as well as price. Land in thousand-acre tracts carried a low price per acre, but settlers seeking land for cultivation rarely wanted more than one or two hundred acres. Furthermore, they often needed credit in order to make the purchase. Modest purchasers were often willing to pay a higher price per acre, but land jobbers usually preferred to maximize scale rather than price—especially when so much land was under uncertain title. No land jobber wished to become mired in countless petty transactions, with payment stretched over a prolonged period of time. Some actually turned away small purchasers. For example, a land agent in Campbell County reported to his client in 1799 that the property he had been authorized to sell remained on the market. "I have had several applications," he wrote, "but it has been from men of low circumstances, who would not incline to purchase more than about 100 Acres." The land agent believed that it was better to keep the land intact and sell it at a flat per-acre price. Still, some people believed that it was harder for a large purchaser than for a small one to locate a good tract.[49]

Because so few Kentuckians were interested in acquiring larger tracts, some western land jobbers turned to wealthy easterners looking for long-term investment opportunities. In an age when banks were few in number and often poorly managed, real estate offered an excellent way to safely harbor surplus wealth. And real estate in newly settled areas offered the best opportunity for gain. In Philadelphia, Richmond and other centers of trade, Kentucky land jobbers jostled each other in their attempts to unload large tracts of land, often sight unseen. To attract these investors, land jobbers deeply discounted the price per acre, but often recouped the difference by misrepresenting the quality of the land or the soundness of the title. Blinded by visions of easy profits and unaware that the main chance in Kentucky land had already passed, few of these absentee speculators fully realized the risk they were taking.[50]

The mania for Kentucky land crested around 1795 and gradually subsided thereafter. One of the most important causes was the implementation of a state revenue act. In addition to taxing land according to its quality, placing a greater burden on citizens owning prime acreage, landowners still delinquent after February 4, 1795, risked forfeiture of their property. Suddenly, holding land off the market became more costly and numerous speculators began intensifying efforts to trim their holdings. As John Breckinridge informed a client in 1794, "There are hundreds of sellers and but few purchasers of back lands in this Country." Besides lingering Indian danger in these areas, "the heavy tax which will soon become due on all lands in this Country, is a great bar to the sale of lands."[51] Speculators who had entered the land market late were especially hard hit. They either had to sell at a loss or wait for prices to perhaps recover and meanwhile pay taxes on land yielding no income. By late 1795, Kentucky land had become hard to sell in Baltimore and Philadelphia. Robert Smith told Breckinridge, "All large speculative purchasers of lands are involved in the greatest embarrassments, and many of them are on the verge of Bankruptcy."[52] And in Kentucky, purchasers with hard cash were never more scarce due to the depressed local economy. As one land broker confessed in 1797, "I cannot sell to the same advantage as we could before." Speculator Leven Powell of Virginia directed his brother to sell off his Kentucky property "without too much sacrifice," if possible, and use the proceeds to buy land in New York.[53]

The opening of new regions for settlement also weakened the position of land speculators. The Green River military tract, for example, provided cheap land just south of the densely populated Bluegrass region. In 1779 Virginia had designated a huge tract in the Green River Valley of Kentucky as a reserve for locating military land warrants given to Virginia's Revolutionary veterans. Early settlers had passed this land by, intent on securing a piece of the lush Bluegrass and perceiving the prairielike "Barrens" of southern Kentucky as inferior soil. It was inferior, but not nearly to the extent Americans initially believed, and as land elsewhere escalated in price, the Green River country began to look increasingly attractive. Virginia lost her rights to this military reserve when Kentucky became a state in 1792, but the Kentucky legislature did not agree on a settlement plan until 1795. In a law passed that year, bona fide settlers already resident were eligible for a preemption of two hundred acres at the rate of thirty dollars per hundred acres.[54] In 1797 a second law allowed any person who had moved into the Green River District before July 1, 1798, a preemption of one to two hundred acres at sixty dollars per hundred acres for first-rate land and forty dollars per hundred acres for second-rate land. Settlers received one year of credit, which the state legislature soon extended to four equal annual installments with interest. In 1800, the legislature bowed again to popular pressure and lowered the price to twenty dollars per hundred acres for those settlers occupying up to four hundred acres.

These generous provisions attracted landless settlers from all over Kentucky and beyond. A gentleman writing from Fayette County in 1796 noted "a prodigious spirit for removing to Green River." The next spring, as the roads dried and the moving season commenced, John Breckinridge reported that "considerable numbers" were embarking for Missouri, so many that he thought Kentucky might see a decrease in total population. In addition, he wrote, "I have no doubt but as many inhabitants will remove to Green River, as the quantity of good land will justify." Breckinridge expected that the price of Bluegrass lands would consequently fall: "There are great quantities at market, & mony [sic] scarce. . . . There seems at present, to be a great rage for new, and frontier places."[55] The Green River District was not really any more immune to speculatory ventures than had been the Bluegrass, but the generous government provisions gave this region some of the best rates of landownership in the state. Logan County ranked highest, with 67 percent of its free adult males owning land in 1800. Rates of landownership in Christian, Barren, and Green Counties were not far behind, ranging from 63 to 59 percent.

Part of the slowness most westerners experienced in realizing their dreams of landownership lay with the settlers themselves. The same ecstatic descriptions of Kentucky as a western paradise that fueled land speculation and drove up prices also generated wildly optimistic expectations of economic opportunity. As a result, many migrants arrived in Kentucky poorly prepared for reality. The settlers streaming into Kentucky "seemed absolutely infatuated by something like the old crusading spirit to the holy land."[56] A Virginia planter named Moses Austin was astonished at the naiveté of migrants he encountered during a trip to Kentucky in 1796. "Ask these Pilgrims what they expect when they git to Kentuckey the Answer is Land. have you any. No, but I expect I can git it. have you any thing to pay for land, No. did you Ever see the Country. No but Every Body says its good land." The idea of Kentucky seemed to have robbed people of their common sense. Here they were, noted Austin in his travel diary, "Travelling hundreds of Miles, they Know not for what Nor whither, except its to Kentucky." Never mind that equally good land was both closer and cheaper: "its not Kentuckey its not the Promis.d land its not the goodly inheratence the Land of Milk and Honey." It struck Austin as nothing short of folly to expend what little wealth one might possess for "this Heaven in Idea." Although Kentucky land was good, ownership lay beyond the reach of people without the necessary resources. Austin predicted that most of these foolish dreamers would ultimately be reduced to nothing more than "hewers of wood and Drawers of water."[57]

The inflated optimism caused some of the state's worst rates of landowning to occur not in the gentrifying Bluegrass region but in counties that served as main ports of entry into the state. Nowhere is this more evident than for Mason County, where Limestone served as the primary port of entry for Lexington and the Kentucky interior. The Ohio River formed a little cove at this point, the only one for a long distance, offering boats protection from the current. Many of the people who debarked there had underfinanced their move west and suddenly found themselves unable to continue further.[58] The local population swelled with such people. By 1800 Mason County was Kentucky's most populous county with nearly two thousand households. Although most of the land in Mason County was of inferior quality and therefore cheaper, only 19 percent of the inhabitants owned land. Furthermore, the underfinanced migration stream affected an extensive area. Those newcomers who could do so escaped the crowded and expensive situation at Limestone and proceeded up the Lexington Road as soon as practicable. As the largest urban place in the state, Lexington offered good possibilities for wage labor. Some newcomers stopped sooner, settling along the route and depressing rates of landownership in Nicholas and Bourbon Counties. In 1800, only 41 percent of the inhabitants in Nicholas County owned land, and only 46 percent of those in Bourbon County, compared with 49.2 percent for the state as a whole. Bourbon County lay almost entirely within the Bluegrass region, and its first-rate land commanded higher prices, but Nicholas and Mason Counties were almost entirely of lesser quality and much more affordable. A similar pocket of landlessness existed at Kentucky's other river port, Louisville. Only 36 percent of the population in Jefferson County owned land in 1800. As with Limestone, some of the newly arriving settlers moved a short distance toward the interior, contributing to the depressed rate of landownership in adjacent Shelby County (41.7 percent).

The generally youthful character of the western population also contributed to Kentucky's high proportion of landless inhabitants. People were most likely to migrate while in early adulthood. According to the first federal census, Kentucky and Tennessee had the youngest populations in the union. At this point in life, most people had not yet accumulated much wealth, and the expense of moving several hundred miles depleted what wealth they did possess. For people starting with limited material resources, the migration to Kentucky might take several years to pay off. This must have been experienced as a deep disappointment, but it is not surprising when so many western adults were young and no more than one-third of the population had been in Kentucky for as long as a decade. In many cases, success would come after further relocation, either to outlying sections of Kentucky or to adjacent federal territory. By 1810, great expanses of the American interior were open for settlement and thousands of Kentuckians had already moved on.[59]

Meanwhile, tenancy presented a common alternative. Even after stations had become things of the past, many if not most new settlers began their lives in Kentucky as tenants. A phase of tenancy could be quite advantageous. "Many people come from Virginia & other States very poor & are strangers, [and] know nothing of the Country," explained an English emigrant in a letter home. "They often take a piece of land to clear & have the income for 4 or 5 years, after that they pay a rent, if they keep it: but ordinarily if prudent they go off on land of their own full stock & provisions." Most renters lacked the means to purchase land, but not always. One pioneer explained, "The land my father had bought lay remote from any settlement, and times being dangerous, we could not go to it: we therefore took a lease of Alexander McConnel." Settler Harry Toulmin, writing in 1793, observed that while perhaps three-quarters of Kentucky's inhabitants were tenants, "many of them have lands of their own on the frontiers." Overall, it appears that during the eighteenth century, Kentuckians viewed tenancy as a temporary condition, a sensible strategy for eventual improvement.[60]

Tenants could usually find favorable rental terms. In outlying areas, where the land was unimproved, the standard arrangement was for a lease of three or four years in exchange for clearing acreage and providing improvements such as fencing. As improved land became more available, leases increasingly called for a specified annual rent, payable in cash or produce but still relatively modest.[61] Landowners found tenants helpful because they helped ward off squatters, they provided added income, and most of all, they offered a cheap way to get land cleared. Even small landowners, such as Daniel Drake's father with a mere thirty-seven acres, could benefit from taking on a tenant.[62] The market for agricultural products also played a role in keeping rents down. "As there is very little sale for produce in this [western] Country," one land agent explained to his employer in 1794, "I am obliged to rent low." In this case, "low" meant eighty acres at a rate of one dollar (or ten bushels of corn) per acre.[63] Harry Toulmin, writing for prospective emigrants in 1793, estimated that a hundred-acre tract with a cabin and fifteen acres already cleared and fenced might rent for ten shillings per acre of cleared land, or for ten bushels of corn (worth fifteen shillings each), or for one-third of the yield. Of these three options, the latter was commonly regarded as the least advantageous for a tenant.[64]

Probably the biggest factor contributing toward low rental rates, as with land prices, was Kentucky's proximity to wilderness land. John Breckinridge's land agent in Fayette County reported in 1791, "Your tenants are not all such men as I could have wished for, I find it hard to get tenants as there is a better chance on the frontier."[65] Similarly, James McDowell's western agent wrote his employer, "I . . . find it impossible to rent your land at the price you have directed it to be rented for the Tenants will move off rather than give ten shillings per acre." The local rate was nine shillings. "You cannot Expect more as it is in their power by moving to Green River to get land at less than a Dollar per Acre, or if they settle on vacant land they get it at the state price of Nine pounds per Hundred."[66] With wilderness priced so low, rental rates could rise only so far, even for prime Bluegrass acreage.

The average prospects for attaining land in Kentucky also look less discouraging in the context of landholding patterns elsewhere. An analysis of landholding in mid-eighteenth-century Augusta County, Virginia, determined that two-thirds of taxable white males owned no land after a quarter-century of residency. Even in a commonly acknowledged "best poor man's country" such as southeastern Pennsylvania, nearly one-third of the inhabitants were landless in 1782. Similarly, a study of tenancy in Washington County, in western Pennsylvania, indicates that approximately 40 percent of the adult white males did not own land in 1776. There too most landless inhabitants viewed tenancy as a temporary status. This study also demonstrated that many were not destitute individuals but owners of other types of productive assets such as livestock.[67] Such was true of many landless Kentuckians as well. In Scott County, for example, a northern Bluegrass region, 55.5 percent of the inhabitants paid taxes on land and personal assets such as horses. Another 38.5 percent were taxed only for personal assets. Less than 1 percent owned no taxable property in 1800. Thus, high tenancy rates alone do not necessarily signify personal failure or impoverishment.

It is easy to cite paradisiacal descriptions of Bluegrass soil on one hand and low rates of land ownership on the other, as historians have sometimes done, and declare Kentucky a fraud.[68] Some people certainly did swallow the bait and go west inadequately prepared; witness the hordes languishing around the Ohio port towns. But the experience of eighteenth-century migrants to Kentucky should not be reduced to a simple comparison of promise to performance. Land prices remained within reasonable reach, the population was young and only recently arrived, and tenancy practices were generous enough to allow some accumulation of wealth. The opening of land for settlement in the Green River country in southern Kentucky and in the Northwest Territory north of the Ohio also helped keep landownership a reachable goal. With time, many still hoped to become freeholders. But it was much harder than many people had foreseen.

Historians have often associated economic distress with religious revivalism, especially historians of the Great Revival. The privation and hardship of a frontier setting supposedly contributed to the emotional intensity of the early camp meetings. The low rates of Kentucky landownership usually offered as evidence of western poverty and despair, however, reflect a more ambivalent situation. While personal disillusionment should not be dismissed too easily, the western adult population was self-selected. Their expectations for Kentucky were inflated. Most discovered that fulfilling their dreams was slow and difficult, but most of all it was risky. Western settlers faced all the usual problems of eighteenth-century American farming. Some, such as crop damage and stray livestock, were slightly more serious than in other parts of the country. But, close on the heels of an expensive long-distance migration, even minor setbacks could be difficult to absorb. More important, Kentuckians were subject to a special problem: gaining clear title to land. Everyone knew at least someone who had lost all or part of their land to a rival claimant. The courts were clogged with such cases, with little sign of improvement any time soon. The psychological toll is incalculable. It was worse than if the speculators had driven land prices beyond reach. Thus, in 1800, on the eve of the Great Revival, the economic weight upon the popular mind was not poverty and deprivation but anxiety and uncertainty. This no one escaped, no matter what their status.

4

ORDERING A
HETEROGENEOUS SOCIETY

The lush reputation of Bluegrass land attracted people from a broad variety of backgrounds, making for a noticeably more diverse society than existed in most other parts of the eighteenth-century United States. Probably only the larger cities at this time had a more diverse population. Like the cities also, Kentucky was overwhelmingly a society of newcomers. Moreover, even after station times western migrants seldom made their first location a permanent home. Developing a sense of community order under these circumstances would take time, all the more so because the social institutions were yet new and lacking in strength.

As long as people had remained in stations, the cultural differences tended to be minor and seldom created much difficulty. The migration process, in many cases a product of previous social contact, produced relatively homogenous stations. A collection of Berkeley County people settled at Strode's Station, Germans settled at the Low Dutch Station, and Regular Baptists from Spottsylvania County settled at Big Crossing Station. The surrounding wilderness insulated these clusters from other people who might be different. But, as people left the stifling confines of the small frontier stations, the social landscape took on a much more complex and fluid character. Now people of different backgrounds often found themselves living in close proximity, increasing the potential for conflict. And even where cultural differences were not a problem, people had to cooperate with strangers in order to achieve basic needs.

A Diverse and Fluid Society of Strangers

As part of the vast trans-montane interior claimed by colonial Virginia, it was predictable that Virginians would figure conspicuously in Kentucky's settlement. At least half and probably many more of the people living in Kentucky at the time of its admission as a state in 1792 had come from Virginia. The predominance of Virginians did not, however, necessarily provide Kentucky with a homogenous society. Late-eighteenth-century Virginia encompassed two distinctly different ethnic subcultures, known as cohees and tuckahoes. Cohees were of Scottish or Scots-Irish Presbyterian heritage; tuckahoes were of English descent and Anglican beliefs.[1] These two Virginia subcultures were divided for the most part by the Blue Ridge Mountains. Settlement to the east had filtered outward from the lower Chesapeake, whereas the Shenandoah Valley had been settled by a later wave of settlers originating from Philadelphia, many of whom were Scots-Irish Presbyterians. The two distinct migration streams led some people to call the eastern part of the state "Old Virginia" and the western part "New Virginia." Similar regional patterns existed in the adjacent states of Pennsylvania and North Carolina and South Carolina, though without as distinct a geographical separator as the Blue Ridge Mountains.[2]

Settlers to Kentucky brought the distinction between cohee and tuckahoe with them. As one early settler explained, the Irish were "mostly from Pennsylvania country and South Carolina. Were called Cohees. Mostly Presbyterians. Virginians were called Tuckahoes." Although only a small proportion of cohees were foreign-born at the time of Kentucky settlement, they nonetheless remained ethnically distinctive. The most glaring difference was in speech, but cohee culture was also visually apparent. Said one settler, "You could tell where a man was from, on first seeing him." Explained another, "We have two sorts of people in this country, one called tuckyahoes, being Generall[y] of the Lowland old Virginians. The other Class is Called cohees, Generally made up of Backwoods Virginians and Northward men, Scotch, Irish, &c,."[3]

Whereas in Virginia cohees formed only a small minority and were relegated mainly beyond the Blue Ridge by lower land prices there, the situation was much different in Kentucky. Cohees formed a sizable minority of the early trans-Appalachian settlers and lived interspersed with people of other backgrounds. And, while in Virginia they were distant and removed from centers of politics and power, such was not the case in Kentucky. An analysis of surnames estimates that a quarter of the men in Kentucky by 1790 were of Scottish or Scots-Irish descent.[4] The analysis of Revolutionary War pension applications for selected Kentucky counties likewise indicates that, whereas tuckahoes predominated in early Kentucky, they had to contend with a substantial population of cohees. The Kentucky pensioners originating from western Virginia, North Carolina, and Pennsylvania—regions that attracted large populations of Scots-Irish settlers—suggest that Kentucky's cohee population may have been as high as 34 percent. Tuckahoes, counted as those pensioners from east of Virginia's Blue Ridge and unspecified locations in the Old Dominion, comprised only about 50 percent. The remaining pensioners came from other states, principally Maryland and New Jersey. The ethnic mix, of course, varied somewhat among counties, but the proportion of cohees was generally substantial.[5]

The tension produced by the cohee and tuckahoe cultures is evident in an episode that transpired in Fayette County in 1786. Prominent citizens informed Governor Patrick Henry that several militia officers had exerted illegal force by impressing supplies for two military expeditions against Indians in the Northwest Territory. The militia contingents from Fayette County were commanded by Colonel Levi Todd and Colonel Robert Patterson, both Presbyterian lay leaders of Scots-Irish heritage. In one incident, a party of seven soldiers under orders from Colonel Todd impressed fourteen head of cattle from a man named Eli Cleveland, "by way of making an example of him, and with further orders to kill him should he resist." Later that month, while collecting provisions for the second expedition, Colonel Patterson impressed salt from a Lexington store. When the young store clerk refused to provide the full quantity of salt that Patterson demanded, Patterson's men broke down the store's doors and seized the salt. Patterson had the clerk arrested and taken away under armed guard, with the store left unsecured for several days afterward. The complainants claimed that the underlying issue was not salt but Patterson's desire to make a show of his authority.[6] As one Fayette County justice explained to Governor Henry, the controversy reflected a power struggle between two rival factions. Kentucky had "two sorts of people," tuckahoes and cohees, "which seems, In some measure, to make Distinctions and Particions amongst us." As this man further explained, local government carefully balanced the two groups, each with an equal number of tuckahoe and cohee justices on the Fayette County bench.[7]

In a more serious incident several years earlier, a man named David Pomeroy had agitated for land reform and petitioned Congress for relief, an action which Kentucky's political establishment feared would invalidate their land titles granted by Virginia. Kentucky's attorney general, Walker Daniel, was uncertain precisely what Pomeroy was guilty of, but he resuscitated an old law from the Restoration era against divulgers of false news. Pomeroy was very probably a cohee, being a Presbyterian elder and having migrated from Pennsylvania. As Christopher Greenup, a prominent westerner, commented in reference to the Pomeroy affair, "The Quo'he's are in general against the Virginia rights & have they strength their will is good to intirely extirpate the Virginians from the Country." Another gentleman, James Speed, remarked, "Many of the Inhabitants of this place, are not natives of Virginia, nor well affected to its Government, and are sowing sedition among the inhabitants as fast as they can."[8] These were exaggerations, but ethnic differences were clearly a source of strain in early Kentucky politics.

Ethnic tension surfaced whenever a cohee sought public office. When

Andrew Steele of Fayette County stood for election to the Virginia Assembly, rival candidates "ran him off (at the election) with Cohea." They circulated a demeaning story that his wife had called him in to eat his mush, saying, "The pegs have been in it, and will be in it again" if he did not come promptly. As the person who related this tale explained, it directly referred to Steele's cohee origins: "Mush was a strictly cohee or western Virginia term while east of the Blue Ridge it was called hominy." Yet Steele was not as backward nor as slovenly as his tuckahoe opponents would have him appear. Letters he wrote to the governor of Virginia reveal a literate, sensible man. Nor was he poor, as tax records demonstrate. When he ran for public office, however, his ethnic background became a reason for ridicule.[9]

In addition to cohees, the backcountry of Pennsylvania and Virginia also contributed German-speaking settlers, often referred to by British-Americans as "Dutchmen."[10] By the late eighteenth century, many of them were American-born and English-speaking but still retained aspects of German ethnic descent. The Kentucky "Dutch" often chose to settle in small clusters, creating identifiable neighborhoods where they might better preserve their heritage. For example, the will of a Bourbon County settler named Peter Smelzer who died in 1795 directed his wife to raise their children "in a Christian Like manner and give them such learning as may be done amongst us Dutch people." When Smelzer needed witnesses for the will, the people he called upon had German surnames. Other records also refer to neighbors of German descent, such as Smelzer's petition to build a mill on a local creek across from the land of John Kizer. The county marriage records reveal that the local German community was large enough for at least some of Smelzer's children to find spouses of German descent. Another early pocket of Germans existed in Jefferson County around the "Low Dutch" Station. According to an individual who grew up nearby, "They lived in their own Areas always."[11] Most of these people probably preferred the German language, domestic customs, and religious culture. Yet only a small proportion of western Germans were of foreign birth, and studies of eighteenth-century ethnicity suggest partial assimilation, particularly in the realm of economics and wealth. Smelzer, for example, understood enough about the American legal system to file a will. An analysis of early Kentucky surnames shows that Germans comprised approximately 5 percent of the Kentucky population in 1790.[12] Although not numerous, Germans nonetheless constituted a distinctive element in Kentucky's social landscape.

British-American opinions of the Germans tended toward ridicule and derision. "It was the amusement of the wits to make fun of the Dutch," recalled Joseph Ficklin. Language barriers did not help matters. To neighbors of British descent, Germans seemed also to follow a baffling set of cultural priorities. "These old Dutch fellows were such fools, they couldn't take care of themselves," remarked Kentuckian Josiah Collins. "Thought if they didn't go out and work, they would starve to death, and never thought of danger." As a result, "most all of the old Dutchmen got killed in those days." Said another English-speaking settler, "They understood nothing of Indian warfare."[13] Thus, for external as well as internal reasons, Kentucky Germans tended to live on the edges of western society, separate and distinct.

Slavery also added to Kentucky's social diversity. Nearly one out of every five Kentucky pioneers was of African descent. Their status was defined by Virginia's legal system, which Kentucky adopted with only minor alterations when it became a state. Unfortunately, very little is known concerning the daily life of black Kentuckians during the eighteenth century. The small size of the typical slaveholding suggests that socializing and especially family formation must have been somewhat more difficult than what they had known before. Throughout the eighteenth century,

---

Slaveholding in Selected Kentucky Counties, 1787–1789

HOUSEHOLDS

County	Total	With Slaves	With 1 Slave	With 2 Slaves
Fayette (1787)	1,299	413 (31.8%)	120 (29.6%)	69 (16.7%)
Bourbon (1787)	376	89 (23.6%)	26 (29.2%)	15 (16.8%)
Madison (1787)	393	98 (24.9%)	43 (43.8%)	11 (11.2%)
Jefferson (1789)	572	85 (14.9%)	29 (34.1%)	14 (16.5%)
Nelson (1787)	420	66 (15.7%)	21 (31.8%)	8 (12.1%)

SOURCE: Netti Schreiner-Yantis and Florene Speakman Love, comps., *The 1787 Census of Virginia, An Accounting of the Name of Every White Male Tithable Over 21 Years; the Number of White Males between 16 & 21 Years; the Number of Slaves Over 16 & Those Under 16 Years; together with a Listing of their Horses, Cattle & Carriages; and also the Names of all Persons to whom Ordinary Licenses and Physician's Licenses were Issued,* 3 vols. (Springfield, Va.: Genealogical Books in Print, 1987).

the great majority of Kentucky slaves lived by themselves or with only one other slave. The crude age structure evident in county tax records nonetheless indicates a healthy rate of natural increase because the migrating slaves tended to be young adults. Kentuckian James Davis, for example, authorized a friend in Virginia to purchase "a young Negroe fellow between Sixteen & twenty & a girl between twelve & Eighteen." In addition, probate inventories reveal a balanced sex ratio. By the close of the century, the Bluegrass region hosted a number of impressive plantations, but the generally dispersed location of Kentucky blacks raises some doubt as to whether they could participate in an African-American subculture such as had recently emerged in Virginia and other established communities.[14] Daily life probably resembled that typically found in the backcountry of Virginia or North Carolina, except for a higher level of physical danger, at least initially, and more primitive material conditions.

The unusual degree of cultural diversity in the trans-Appalachian West was also apparent in religion. Whereas the Anglican legacy still dominated postrevolutionary Virginia, dissenting denominations held sway in Kentucky. Religious institutions were practically nonexistent during the early years, but most of those settlers who did profess a faith were either Baptist, Presbyterian, or Methodist. The result was an evangelical, multidenominational religious culture that set Kentucky apart from her parent state and much of the rest of America as well.

The regional contrast was most dramatic for the Baptists, who had suffered harassment and marginalization in Virginia but whose numbers and early removal to Kentucky soon made them part of the social establishment.Like other dissenting churches, the Baptists followed an evangelical ethos that stood in sharp contrast to that of the more liturgical Anglican Church and its postrevolutionary Episcopal offspring. For these believers, religion meant more than just participating in routine worship. It was a deeply spiritual experience oriented around a single objective: salvation. They rejected the worldly obsession with wealth and prestige and submitted to a strict church discipline. This included most forms of conspicuous personal display, such as dancing and ostentatious attire. Less motivated to acquire wealth, the members of dissenting churches were also more likely to perceive the essential humanity of blacks and thus to oppose slavery. In other ways as well, dissenter piety carried an implicit critique of secular society, something not missed by the solidly Anglican upper classes of Virginia.[15]

Official reactions centered mainly on the Separate Baptists, an especially fervent branch of Baptists that began gaining ground in Virginia during the 1760s and 1770s. Like other Baptists, Separate Baptists believed in adult baptism, but the "Regular" Baptists were Calvinist and subscribed to the Philadelphia Confession of Faith, whereas the Separate Baptists refused to recognize any creed save the Bible. To Virginia authorities, the Separate Baptists therefore seemed dangerous and even seditious, so that when a few of their preachers ignored the Virginia law requiring dissenting ministers to obtain a license from the county court, local magistrates responded with jail sentences. This, however, seemed only to make the preachers into martyrs. Through the tiny, barred windows of the county jails, the defiant Baptist preachers continued their passionate exhortations, often attracting large crowds. Wrote an early church historian, "Magistrates and mobs, priests and sheriffs, courts and prisons all vainly combined to divert them from their object."[16]

Government pressure was mild compared with the treatment handed out by private citizens. Most Virginians were indifferent to the Baptists, but some resented their self-righteousness and zeal. One Virginian complained that Baptists could not meet a man upon the public road "but they must ram a text of Scripture down his throat."[17] Popular feeling ran high enough to produce a number of violent incidents, and few perpetrators bothered to distinguish between defiant Separates or more compliant Regular Baptists. Elijah Baker was pelted with apples and stones in Accomac County. A group of assailants held down James Ireland and urinated on his face in Culpepper County. In separate incidents, Edward Mintz and David Barrow were ducked underwater and nearly drowned in Nansemond County.[18] Public hostility was serious enough to convince many Virginia Baptists that they might be better off elsewhere. Therefore, as western conditions improved following the Revolution, hundreds of Virginia Baptists migrated to Kentucky—including entire congregations. According to one estimate, approximately one-quarter of Virginia's Baptists migrated westward during this period.[19]

Though a vulnerable minority in Virginia, the Separate and Regular Baptists soon formed the largest religious denomination in Kentucky. No longer were they so easily harassed. A small incident that happened to General Charles Scott, one of Virginia's leading Revolutionary heroes, illustrates just how dramatically the Baptist position had changed. Shortly after Scott settled his family in Woodford County in 1783, the local Baptist congregation sent one of their preachers to Scott's place to ask that he remove himself to another neighborhood. Scott had a reputation for drinking and swearing and, as the preacher explained, local Baptists did not want "so profane & wicked a man living so near them." The general probably had never before been addressed in so brazen a manner by a social inferior. Struggling to rein in his temper, Scott pointed out that his presence could benefit the local inhabitants in their defense against Indian attacks. The preacher conceded the truth of this, but insisted that Scott should leave anyway. Finally, letting loose his anger at the Baptist's effrontery, Scott ordered his workers to grab the preacher, declaring, "I'll punch this scoundrel, who has insulted me & wants to drive me from my own home." As Scott's dogs snapped and snarled, the preacher beat a hasty retreat.[20] The preacher failed in his objective, but a confrontation of this sort was almost unthinkable in Virginia. While it would be going too far to claim that Baptists and other dissenters imposed a new moral order on western society (their numbers were too few for that), they did challenge the smooth extension of gentry dominance, adding yet another strain to western society during the era preceding camp meeting revivalism.

By several measures, then, the first generation of Kentuckians constituted an unusually diverse group compared with most other regions of the early republic. Settlers originated "from every state in the Union," observed one traveler, "particularly from North Carolina, Virginia, Maryland, and Pennsylvania."[21] Few other parts of the young United States, except perhaps its few large urban centers, drew inhabitants from so broad an area. The mixture of ethnicity, religion, and race fragmented the western population. Forging these various elements into communities, into a society, would not be easy. The settlers themselves understood this. One reported, "We are as harmonious amongst ourselves as can be expected of a mixture of People from various States & of various Sentiments and Manners not yet assimilated." Attorney George Nicholas wrote in a similar vein, "The peculiar character which belongs to our citizens in general will contribute for a time at least to our unhappiness." Originating from other states, "citizens generally consisting of such men must make a very different mass from one which is composed of men born and raised on the same spot." Nicholas and others believed that Kentucky's political factionalism "might have been expected in a Country, the inhabitants of which have come from almost every part of the World."[22]

Social cohesiveness was further hindered by continued population movement. Migration to Kentucky seldom involved a single trip to a final destination. The problems of relocating across so formidable a distance were simply too great. Rather, the family was preceded when possible by a male representative who scouted for land, began building a cabin, and prepared the way. Sometimes several trips occurred before the actual transfer of residence. Once in Kentucky, families often moved several times before finally settling at a permanent site. John Rubard, for example, came in 1784 from Rowan County, North Carolina, and initially joined Hunter's Station in what later became Jessamine County. Four or five years later, he began a farm in Bourbon County. Not all relocations were voluntary. The 1787 tax lists for Mercer County, to take a particularly dramatic example, indicate that nearly a third of the population had recently retreated to safer interior locations.[23] Other moves occurred as a normal part of the life cycle. Particularly mobile were individuals who had no family or property tying them to one place.

Not everyone kept moving, of course. A small stable core existed, particularly in the counties of central Kentucky that had attracted the earliest settlement. In Bourbon County, of 1,191 households listed in the 1791 tax list, 483 or 40.5 percent of the names appear again a decade later, either for Bourbon County or for the adjacent counties of Harrison and Nicholas, which had split off from Bourbon in the interim. Landowners were more likely than tenants to remain in place. In more recently settled parts of Kentucky, however, this core of persisters was much smaller. In Bourbon County the rate of persistence was 47.6 percent between 1792 and 1797, compared with only 34.4 for Logan County in the more recently settled Green River region of Kentucky.[24]

Permanent settlers contributed a valuable stability to western society, but their influence was countered by two types of population movement not reflected in the persistence rates derived from county records. One was local or internal county movement, such as from the station to a nearby farmstead or from a rented farm either to purchased land or to another rented farm. Because such short-distance moves are practically impossible to detect, they are easy to overlook, but in eighteenth-century Kentucky short-distance relocations were extremely common. Upon arrival in Kentucky, newcomers sought out family or friends, choosing a more permanent location only after gaining more familiarity with their new locale. And, for the thousands who came to Kentucky without money to buy land, tenancy at several locations was a distinct possibility. Compared with the trans-montane experience, of course, local movement involved only minor upheaval. Strong interpersonal ties could survive short-distance relocations, yet still entail a substantial reorientation. Thus, eighteenth-century Kentuckians remained relative strangers to one another, and developing a sense of neighborhood or community was often delayed.

Persistence rates also fail to reflect the instability caused by the phenomenal rate of population growth throughout the postrevolutionary decade. In 1781 the Kentucky militia was only 760 men strong, but by 1788 it was estimated at more than 5,000, and by 1791 the militia numbered 9,278 not counting officers. The first federal population census in 1790 counted 73,677 people in Kentucky. A Virginia newspaper informed readers that between August 1, 1786, and mid-May 1789, 19,889 "souls," 1,067 boats, 8,884 horses, 2,297 cattle, 1,926 sheep, and 627 wagons had passed down the Ohio River bound for Kentucky, "besides those which passed in the night, unnoticed."[25] Kentucky's population increased so rapidly during this period that local officials strained just to keep count. John Edwards, county lieutenant for Bourbon County, wrote the governor of Virginia in 1790 that the arrival of new settlers was so considerable that he was unable to report with any accuracy on the size of the county militia.[26] Kentucky's population grew by about 9 percent annually throughout the

1790s, and by 1800 Kentucky's black and white population totaled 220,955, a threefold increase in only a decade.[27] People marveled at such rapid growth. As an individual visiting Kentucky in 1802 remarked, "Thus, in this state, where there were not ten individuals at the age of twenty-five who were born there, the number of inhabitants is now as considerable as in seven of the old states."[28]

Such extraordinary population increase virtually overwhelmed any stabilizing influence lent by the persisting core of old pioneers. By 1800 the early settlers accounted for but a small and rapidly diminishing portion of the western population. For example, the Cane Ridge tax district, one of four in Bourbon County, had 683 taxpayers in 1800, but only about 13 percent had been there a decade earlier.[29] Other neighborhoods had experienced a similar scale of increase. Thus, the great majority of Kentuckians at the end of the century had been there for less than a decade, and they remained relative strangers to one another. Considering also the cultural mixture of western settlers already described, any sense of commonality or community identity was probably still in its beginning stages at the time of the Great Revival in 1800.

Local Government Institutions

Contrary to the American frontier's reputation as a place of individualism and independence, Kentucky settlers regarded the establishment of government as desirable if not essential because of their need to secure land claims. Kentucky was originally part of Virginia, and extending government institutions to the trans-Appalachian settlements was procedurally a simple matter despite Kentucky's great distance from the Virginia capital at Williamsburg. Virginia had long experience in governing expanding settlement areas. Almost any map of colonial Virginia shows a tier of huge western counties, their boundaries extending off into the vast unoccupied North American interior claimed in Virginia's royal charter. As settlers spread into each successive tier of western counties, the Virginia Assembly subdivided the original county area to form additional counties. Kentucky was no different. Considering western government solely in terms of its institutional structure, however, yields a highly misleading impression. Even after Kentucky achieved statehood in 1792, local government suffered chronic problems of leadership and stability.

Theoretically, Virginia's system of county government encompassed Kentucky even before the arrival of settlers, as part of the westernmost county of Fincastle. Partly to counter the influence of the Transylvania Company, Fincastle was subdivided in 1776, with the entire territory west of the Alleghenies designated as Kentucky County. The boundaries of Kentucky County roughly followed those of the future state. Although huge, the number of inhabitants was modest and concentrated in the lush central region. After slow but steady population increases during the Revolution, the Virginia Assembly in 1780 subdivided Kentucky County into three new counties, named Lincoln, Fayette, and Jefferson. Subsequent divisions followed as postwar migration accelerated. By the time Kentucky became a state in 1792, it comprised nine counties. Most of Kentucky's early inhabitants resided in the fertile central region later known as the Bluegrass, and the process of creating additional counties therefore progressed fastest in that area, with thinly settled outlying counties remaining quite large. The early years of statehood would see the proliferation of additional counties, which numbered forty-two by 1800, a sign that Kentuckians desired more rather than less local government.

Each subdivision of territory brought local government a little closer to the inhabitants. In addition to the right to send representatives to the state legislature, county status brought with it the appointment of justices, constables, a sheriff, a surveyor, a coroner, and militia officers. Most important of all was the establishment of local courts. The county court met monthly and functioned primarily as an administrative body. In addition to being a court of record for registering such things as transfers of property and powers of attorney, the county court regulated riparian rights, tavern rates, the routing and maintenance of public roads, tax collection, and similar local concerns. It also supervised probate matters such as the recording of wills and appointment of appraisers, guardians, and execu-

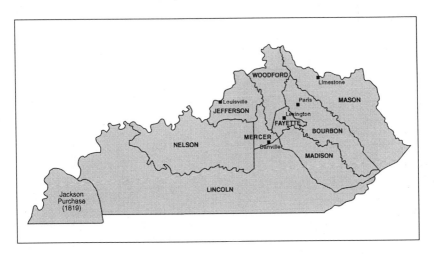

Map 6. Kentucky county boundaries at the time of statehood in 1792.

tors. A second local court, the court of quarter sessions, met on a quarterly basis and held jurisdiction over minor offenses and civil cases involving amounts exceeding twenty-five shillings. (Smaller disputes were decided by an individual justice.) The county court of quarter sessions also examined charges involving more serious offenses, those with penalties involving loss of life or limb, either dismissing the case for insufficient evidence or remanding it to a higher court in Virginia for trial. This was seldom necessary after 1783, when the Virginia Assembly established a supreme court for the District of Kentucky. For slaves, however, the court of quarter sessions exercised total jurisdiction, including capital sentences. The appellate review process still culminated at the Virginia capital, but very few cases reached that level. This decentralized governmental structure was well suited to the needs of frontier communities, and its essential features were retained when Kentucky became a state in 1792.[30]

Kentucky nonetheless suffered weak government during its early years due to the combined effect of distance and wartime conditions. When Kentucky County's first militia officers were announced in early 1777, several of the men named by the governor had not yet moved west. The county magistrates remained unknown until early April, and as late as June only three were actually present in Kentucky. Meanwhile, because the court could not conduct business without a quorum of four justices, Kentucky remained effectively without civil government. Only after an additional round of appointments did the first court finally convene in September 1777. Even then, the continuing pressure from adjacent native groups kept western government weak. The challenge of filling local government offices occurred all over again in 1780 when Kentucky County was subdivided to form three smaller counties for the growing number of settlements. Many of the newly created offices in Fayette, Jefferson, and Lincoln Counties remained vacant, and substitute appointments were again slow in coming. Thus, the creation of smaller counties, which should have improved the quality of local government, initially had the opposite effect.

Meanwhile, mounting numbers of Kentuckians were dying or suffering injury or property loss, with little sign of relief in sight. Neither was it clear that the land these people defended would ever belong to them. "Our Inhabitants are discouraged," stated a petition in 1782. "'Tis now near two years since the division of the County & no Surveyor has ever appeared among us."[31] Without a county surveyor, land claims could not be secured. Under such conditions, it was difficult for some westerners to justify the risk and deprivation of remaining on a dangerous frontier. A number of outlying settlements disbanded or came close to doing so. According to John Todd, a militia officer writing from Lexington in 1781, in

Fayette County and then one of Kentucky's northernmost stations, "Such residents as had most property and Horses to remove their effects, have retreated to Lincoln [County]. One half the remainder are unable to Remove." These poor stranded people and others like them in other countries bore the brunt of defending a wartime frontier. To many of them, the inadequacies of government seemed pathetically irrelevant. As Todd pointed out, "We have no tax Commissioner in the County & almost nothing to tax." Later that year local government in Fayette County came to a virtual standstill when the number of magistrates once again fell below the requirement for a quorum of the county court.[32]

In Jefferson County, surrounding the nucleus of settlement at Louisville, conditions were no better. In January 1781, Colonel John Floyd informed Governor Thomas Jefferson that he had received the set of commissions appointing the first set of officials for Jefferson County, including the one appointing himself as colonel of the county militia. However, only four of the six men appointed as county magistrates actually lived within the bounds of the new county and had actually received their commission. One of these had subsequently been chosen to serve as sheriff, while another was so infirm that he had been unable to attend court until March. And, of greatest immediate significance, the militia officers had been unable to take their oath because, "they being the Justices also," swearing in one of them left the bench without a quorum. Meanwhile, at a time when the county's able-bodied defenders numbered only about 354, some 47 inhabitants had been killed or captured, plus numerous others wounded, bereaved, and impoverished. Colonel John Floyd had promptly written the governor back in January requesting commissions for additional justice appointments and blank militia commissions, but no word came until April 4, when two letters arrived. Unfortunately, both predated Floyd's January request and therefore brought no help. As Floyd wrote in a second appeal in April, the county court's recommendations for additional magistrates were just then being sent to Richmond, making it very unlikely that the governor's commissions would reach Kentucky before late summer.[33] Thus, Jefferson County went through nearly its entire first year without effective local government.

Conditions were safer south of the Kentucky River in Lincoln County, but there, too, local government labored against problems of war and distance. In particular, western militia officers encountered open draft resistance by men who feared leaving their families without protection. In 1781 Virginia passed a new law stipulating that draft resistors were to be turned over to a Continental officer for six months of national service, but in Kentucky this law had little if any effect. In April 1782 Benjamin Logan of St. Asaph's Station wrote to the governor of Virginia, reminding him that the Continental officer as provided in the recent law had never been sent. As a result, Lincoln County suffered a "great neglect of duty" because "it is generally known, by the Militia the[y] can not be brought to Justice in this County according to Law." Logan pointed out in the same letter that an insufficient number of appointed officials crippled the Lincoln County Court. The County had only five magistrates, and these were "seated at a great distance & Hostilities dayly commensing, it is with great difficulty we can have a Court." The situation worsened before it improved. Four months later, Logan reported that the number of magistrates was down to only three due to casualties suffered in the recent American defeat at the Lower Blue Licks. Without a quorum of four justices, government in Lincoln County could not proceed.[34]

Even after the war with Britain, federal inability to make peace with the natives of Ohio left Kentucky government vulnerable. In May 1788, for example, Lieutenant Colonel James Garrard forwarded a report on a court-martial of Captain John Waller. The court had not been a legal one, Garrard explained to the governor of Virginia, because recent Indian attacks had obstructed repeated attempts to convene a proper court-martial. Governmental inadequacy seems doubly apparent, for Waller's main defense was that he had not been properly commissioned in the first place. Explained fellow officer John Edwards, writing in November, "Our officers that compose the Board is so scattered that we never have been able to get them collected since las' Spring so as to make a full Board." According to Garrard, even that meeting had not comprised a full board.[35] Although strict adherence to proper legal procedure worked in this instance for the benefit of Waller, it tended to undermine public security. It therefore became common practice for militia officers nominated by the county courts to assume their duties immediately, before receiving their commission from Richmond. In other instances, the executive sent blank commissions. Local government remained nonetheless fragile, with many justice appointments inadvertently given to men who were either not present, already deceased, or declining to serve.[36]

The frailty of Virginia government over its trans-montane domain is also evident in the electoral process. As Colonel Benjamin Logan reported in 1787, "The Desorders in Defferent Elections for the General Assembly in this District is Alarming."[37] Nothing caused more chaos and contention than did the issue of suffrage qualifications. Although Kentuckians, like most early Americans, believed that suffrage qualifications were necessary to ensure that voters had a true stake in the outcome of an election, thinking varied considerably about how to define that stake. Traditionally, it had been defined in terms of landed wealth. Virginia at this time restricted suffrage to freeholders of twenty-five improved acres or one hundred acres of unimproved land, but for the three counties in the District of Kentucky this standard made little practical sense.[38] If strictly adhered to, most Kentuckians would have been eliminated from voting because so many were yet in the process of becoming freeholders. Furthermore, it seemed to many settlers that any man prepared to risk his life in the common defense possessed as good a stake in society as any landholder. Even Kentucky's political elite had doubts about the freehold requirement. When the Danville Political Club, Kentucky's premier political caucus, debated the problem in early 1787, it came no closer to a resolution. The members generally concurred that suffrage qualifications should be retained, but they were unable to formulate an acceptable standard.[39]

In conducting elections, however, the problem could not be avoided, and finding Virginia's freehold requirements inappropriate to their situation, Kentuckians generally abandoned them. The 1789 election for delegates to the Virginia Assembly from Jefferson County resulted in a major controversy when one of the candidates, Colonel John Campbell, insisted that only freeholders should be admitted to the polls. General confusion ensued on election day, nearly to the point of violence. In the various depositions spawned by this conflict, one of the other candidates attested that since he had been in Kentucky it had been customary for all free males aged twenty-five and older to be admitted their suffrages by consent of the candidates. He knew of no one else in Kentucky except Campbell who still insisted on restricting suffrage to actual freeholders.[40]

A contested election in Bourbon County reveals that there, too, candidates were determining suffrage qualifications independently of the Virginia statutes. Interestingly, the problem in this case arose not from an attempt to restrict suffrage but just the opposite. Before the polls opened in April 1789, the four candidates running for the Virginia Assembly bickered at length before finally resolving that "no nonresident unless he was possess't of a Deed or Patent should vote" and "all Free male Inhabitants of the county above the age of 21 Years Should have that Liberty." Unfortunately, casual arrangements such as these left ample room for voting fraud. One of the candidates, Notley Conn, resided near the boundary with Fayette County, and opponents alleged that the "neighboring part of Fayette was Industriously search'd and that all that could be prevailed on were brought, traviling men were persuaded from the road and Boys were prevail'd on to vote."[41] Thus, in actual practice, universal free manhood suffrage was already a common practice by the time Kentucky attained statehood in 1792. Even conservative politicians did not dare challenge it, at least not in public.

Early Kentuckians operated most independently of formal government in military matters. Under Virginia law, all free adult males between the ages of sixteen and fifty were required to perform duty in the county militia. Although useful for the occasional offensive expeditions across the Ohio, where large bodies of men had to be maneuvered as efficiently as possible, such formal structure was ill-suited to station defense. Most Indian encounters after the Revolution involved small raiding parties that relied on the element of surprise and then quickly retreated across the Ohio River. Mobilizing the militia usually took too long to be effective against this type of attack. Each station therefore managed their own defense independently, turning to militia reinforcements in times of crisis. Facing a common fate should the station fall, the fine points of military rank seemed irrelevant. Every station inhabitant contributed as fully as possible. Even women and slaves might wield a rifle.

Thus, two military structures operated during station times, one hierarchical and the other universal. In fighting Indians, explained one man whose father was one of Virginia's western Indian agents, "military etiquette was but little observed—the great matter was, to get men into the fielde, and when fighting came on, everyone fought for himself; officers and all." According to this individual, frontier militia officers were "leaders rather than commanders." Likewise, a traveler who passed through several Kentucky stations in 1775 commented with disapproval that it was difficult to tell who was in command, "for in fact no person actually did command entirely." The western stations of Virginia suffered a "total want of subordination."[42] At Strode's Station, for example, the ranking militia officer for most of the early period was Captain John Constant, a man well respected for his knowledge of Indian warfare. Constant commanded the militia company from Strode's Station on official campaigns such as that led by Clark in 1780, but in defending the station, Constant's rank meant little. Everyone joined together because they shared a common fate. Once, when the men of Strode's Station pursued a party of Indians who had stolen some horses, the leader was not Constant but William Clinkenbeard, a young man with hardly a dollar to his name. Apparently even this signified little. As Clinkenbeard explained, "We were all heads; every fellow tried his best."[43]

Loyalty to the station often outweighed other obligations, and when direct militia orders conflicted with station welfare, many men preferred to risk a court-martial. In 1782, for example, when George Rogers Clark ordered a draft of one-quarter of the Kentucky militia to help fortify Fort Nelson, he encountered widespread noncompliance. As Colonel John Floyd explained, "From the immediate danger, in which every one conceives his own Family, the authority of militia officers . . . grows every day weaker & weaker."[44] Similarly, when William Sudduth and Andrew Hood were drafted to join Clark's campaign in 1786, both refused to go because, as Sudduth explained, "We were the frontier fort and only five men strong."[45] Though understandable, such defiance undermined Virginia's military effectiveness in the West. Even when local authorities were so inclined, however, they could do little about it.

Thus, Kentucky's early development proceeded largely without the benefits of strong government direction. Although Virginia provided her farthest western settlements with a governmental system that was decentralized, inexpensive, and familiar, its implementation was to a great extent thwarted by wartime conditions and geographical distance. Virginia's lack of power over her trans-Appalachian counties surfaced not in insurrection or overt challenges to authority, likely reactions to oppressive rule, but by improvisation and selective neglect. Fortunately, the same conditions that undermined government also limited the possibility for disunity and conflict. The struggle with Great Britain kept rates of migration low, and the continuing Indian conflict kept the new settlements too vulnerable to indulge internal differences. Public life remained, for the moment, a simple matter. The real questions about government authority were left for the future.

Administering Justice and Public Order

Despite the prolonged difficulties in appointing court officers, once operating, most courts worked adequately. The surviving order books kept by the early Kentucky county courts appear practically indistinguishable from similar records made by county courts elsewhere in eighteenth-century Virginia. Although the presence at court of justices, jurymen, witnesses, and the involved parties often entailed considerable personal risk, by the mid-1780s Kentucky's county courts generally met according to schedule and adhered to proper legal procedure. In Bourbon County during 1787, its first full year of operation and a time when the area was still subject to attack, the court failed to meet in January and was delayed one day in November due to lack of a quorum. The grand jury failed to reach a quorum in March. Otherwise, the county courts convened according to schedule. The regularity of the Bourbon County Court is especially impressive because until the courthouse was completed, sessions convened in private homes. By contrast, in Virginia's Lunenburg County, which was settled earlier in the eighteenth century than Kentucky but with much less violence, the early courts missed roughly half of their stipulated sessions.[46]

The most frequent item on the docket of Kentucky county courts involved the disposition of lawsuits for the recovery of overdue debts. The chronic shortage of cash in newly settled areas compelled people to purchase many things on credit, which practically guaranteed a large number of suits for debt. The mere filing of a lawsuit was often sufficient to motivate repayment because debtors knew that the justices would levy court costs on top of the amount already due. In other instances the defendant acknowledged the debt and found a friend or relative to act as surety, or attempted to obtain the money by in turn suing one of his own debtors. Only a small proportion of such suits ever reached a jury because most debt cases were dispatched promptly. Of 127 suits heard by the Bourbon County Court of Quarter Sessions in 1787, only 55 were continued by the plaintiff, the defendant, or the court. Of the 35 suits decided that August (the Bourbon Court's busiest term), only 20 percent had been continued from the previous session and 6 percent continued from 1786. Nearly one-third of the judgments were dismissals, usually because a settlement had been reached out of court or because one of the parties no longer resided in the county. A slightly smaller proportion of the judgments were settled by default when the defendant failed to appear. This was a common outcome when the debt was legitimately owed but the defendant lacked the means for repayment. Only in rare instances were debtors jailed.[47] The efficient resolution of most lawsuits indicates that Kentucky's county courts performed adequately and held the confidence of the citizenry.

In other economic matters, too, local government performed effectively. The monthly county court supervised the construction of market houses, commissioned public weights and measures, and regulated tavern rates. Of these, none consumed more court attention during this early period than the construction and maintenance of local roads. The process for extending the public road system was fairly straightforward. Persons desiring the establishment of a new road could petition the county court, which then appointed a committee of viewers to determine the most suitable route. It also appointed an overseer to supervise construction and maintenance. The overseer was usually a moderately prominent citizen residing along the particular stretch of road, but the job carried little prestige. Road maintenance was hard work, and making sure that the local inhabitants put in their required time often involved coercive pressure. Overseers who failed to keep their assigned stretch of road in proper condition were indicted by the grand jury and fined if found guilty. Western courts recognized the difficulties facing overseers and therefore dealt with most delinquents leniently, dropping charges when offered a reasonable explanation. The threat of a fine was usually enough for most overseers to promise future reform.

Although the Kentucky courts played an active role in matters pertaining to property and commerce, they were considerably less aggressive about regulating public order and morality.[48] Kentucky quickly gained a reputation in other parts of the country as a haven for felons and tories, but at least during the initial years of settlement, western society was relatively free of serious wrongdoing. Settler Caleb Wallace reported to James Madison soon after moving to Lincoln County in 1785, "In point of Morals, the bulk of the inhabitants are far superior to what I expected to find in any new settled Country. We have not had a single instance of Murder, and but one Criminal for Felony of any kind has yet been before the Supreme Court."[49] Harry Toulmin, gathering information for prospective emigrants in 1793, was told that over the previous four years seven men had been charged with crimes in Nelson County, only one of whom had been remanded to the district court for trial—and this defendant had been acquitted. The seven defendants included two slaves, who were sentenced to whipping. Similarly, the clerk for Jefferson County reported to Toulmin that there had been "Not more than three or four persons imprisoned in the county in the three last years, on criminal accusations, and I think in ten years there has not been more than two persons executed in Kentucky."[50] The number of defendants was greater in Fayette County, where approximately a quarter of all Kentuckians resided. Three were committed to jail in 1791, seven in 1792, and eleven in 1793. According to the county clerk, the crime rate had recently risen in the wake of a wave of army deserters and a ring of horse thieves. From the county's establishment in 1786 until mid-1792 when Kentucky became a state, the Bourbon County Court of Quarter Sessions remanded only three cases to the district court for a felony trial.[51]

Kentuckians were probably no more law-abiding than people living elsewhere, but the western population initially was small and isolated in stations that offered little privacy or possibility for concealment. Most inhabitants had little worth stealing anyway. The surrounding Indian danger and the difficulty of a safe escape no doubt made crime less attractive. According to Humphrey Marshall, an early settler and one of Kentucky's most critical historians, "Such . . . was the pressure of danger, the simplicity of manners, the integrity of the people, and the state of property, that there was but little use for criminal law, until a later period."[52]

While felonies may have been uncommon, minor violations of public order were a regular and tolerated part of western life. Early Kentuckians were extremely rowdy and competitive. At male gatherings such as log rollings and road building, "profanity, vulgarity & drinking were the most eminent characteristics." At militia musters, "Before dispersing at night, the training was quite eclipsed by a heterogeneous drama of foot racing, pony racing, wrestling, fighting, drunkenness and general uproar." At corn huskings, participants organized into teams and raced to finish first. At weddings, following the exchange of vows, the whiskey bottle made the rounds and the men commenced "shooting at a mark, some to throwing the rail or shoulder-stone, others to footraces." Likewise, while the women sewed at quilting bees, the men went off by themselves to joke, drink, and engage in various sorts of games. Nearly every sort of social gathering contained a competitive aspect, and those persons who were not directly involved often participated vicariously by placing bets on the outcome.[53]

Gruesome contests between animals were part of this insatiable need to compete. The boredom of station life seems to have encouraged an unusually imaginative variety of such events. According to William Clinkenbeard of Strode's Station, "The fort yard was a great place for wolf baiting." On one occasion a panther had been brought in alive and was being kept in an empty corn crib until a wolf could be captured to fight with it. (The contest was never held, however, because the women of the station insisted that the cat be killed for fear that one of the children would get too close to it.) Another experiment involved a wolf and a turkey buzzard, but proved disappointing because neither animal would fight. All this did not preclude, of course, more conventional contests between cocks, dogs, and fast horses. The latter were especially popular in Kentucky. At least with horses some argument could be made that racing contributed to the development of a better breed and Kentucky's rapidly spreading reputation for producing fine horseflesh.[54]

The most extreme form of this incessant rivalry involved a peculiar form of personal combat in which kicking, biting, gouging, and any other use of the body was permissible, but no weapons. "The drawing of a knife, for example, they all regarded as a great outrage." The prohibition against weapons reveals the ritualized nature of these otherwise passionate struggles. The fights were nonetheless often gory affairs. Tales abound of ears chewed off and eyes gouged out, and court records occasionally bear out such injuries. In June 1799, James Anderson Jr. appeared before the Bourbon County Court "and proved to the satisfaction of the Court, that he had lost a piece of his right Ear in a contest which happened between him and a certain Joseph Williams."[55] As reflected in the court's description of the encounter as a contest, the purpose was not really to resolve differences but rather to determine status.

Aggressive personal contests had long figured in American culture, particularly in the South, but in newly settled areas where an individual's social standing was often not fully evident, they assumed an added importance.[56] Westerners avoided such challenges to their detriment. As explained by the son of a western minister, "No man was permitted to insult another without resentment; and if an insult was permitted to pass unrevenged, the insulted party lost standing in society." Even men who did not approve of fighting realized its social significance. For instance, Samuel Rogers, a Presbyterian Church elder, "never quarreled with any one, but was ever ready to resent an insult with blows."[57] Most Kentucky men probably felt similarly.

Court day was especially prone to public disruption, and the presence of magistrates prevented neither the violence nor the unbridled betting that accompanied it. With Kentuckians "the passion for gaming and spirituous liquors is carried to excess, which frequently terminates in quarrels degrading to human nature," observed visitor François-André Michaux in 1802. "The public-houses are always crowded, especially during the sittings of the courts of justices." Likewise, in the town of Paris, Samuel Rogers, a boy at the time, later recalled, "Fellows would come in from the outskirts of the county, determined on having rows. . . . They would go up and down streets, seeking a fight, and not be satisfied to leave town without first having one."[58] Whatever the motivation, the result was public mayhem. Court days in early Mason County were marked by a "new trade in horses, another horse race, a cock fight, or a dog fight, a wrestling match, or a 'pitched' battle between two bullies, who in fierce recontre, would lie on the ground scratching, pulling hair, choking, gouging out each others eyes, and biting off each others noses, in the manner of bull dogs." Meanwhile, "a Roman circle of interested lookers on would encourage the respective gladiators with shouts which a passing demon might have mistaken for those of hell." Travelers marveled at the intense spirit of these public contests, and in their journals and letters they billed westerners as barbaric lunatics. Harry Toulmin, Kentucky secretary of state under Governor Garrard, tried to counter this impression, writing, "The land speculators of Philadelphia and others . . . tell you that half the people, through the practice of gouging, have no eyes."[59] Nonetheless, public occasions in eighteenth-century Kentucky frequently devolved into raucous competitions, and the presence of magistrates did little to temper this unruly atmosphere.

Justices not only overlooked such behavior; their own public behavior often lacked dignity and decorum as well. Justice William Routt of Bourbon County was involved in a case of assault and battery that reached the Kentucky Court of Oyer and Terminer. Thomas Kennedy, justice of the peace and member of the state legislature, was tried for murder—after he escaped from jail. Henry Lee, with a similar record of public trust, "whipped" a fellow Kentucky representative, Timothy Peyton. Such behavior hardly ever resulted in removal from office.[60]

One of the most notorious displays of unbecoming conduct by government officials occurred in 1792 between James Smith and John Waller, two Bourbon County justices also serving as state representatives. A citizen of modest means named Arthur McNickle who felt he had been horsewhipped unjustly by Justice Waller appealed to both the House of Representatives and Governor Shelby, who had appointed Waller to the Court of Quarter Sessions. One day during the ensuing investigation by the House of Representatives, a Bourbon County man named John Sanderson approached Colonel Smith before the House convened and inquired as to the whereabouts of Mr. Waller. Smith replied that "he was some where about, or he might have gone home." Sanderson, startled by this answer, asked whether Waller did not sit in the House. Smith responded that Waller could go into the House just like any citizen, but that he would not be permitted to take his seat until the charges against him were resolved. When Smith published a summary of this incident in the newspaper, Waller likewise took his case to the newspaper, charging Smith with bias and falsehood and challenging him to a duel. Smith responded by pointing out that, although the House investigation had cleared Waller of judicial malpractice, he could not "be said to be honorably acquitted, when other grievous crimes has been proven against him which did not come under the cognizance of the legislature." Smith concluded by challenging Waller to substantiate his claims of innocence. Waller responded in the next issue with an attack on Smith's character. Not only had Smith propagated known falsehoods, claimed Waller, but he had been "publicly pissed on in the town of Paris for lying." Waller also depicted Smith as a criminal who had fled Pennsylvania to escape the gallows.[61] Smith responded with a suit for libel, while Waller claimed his words were not libel but truth. Regardless of who was right, the protracted and public feud detracted from the dignity of both men and suggests one reason why authorities did not make more of an effort to control public disorderliness.

Gradually some citizens began demonstrating an increased sensitivity to public disorder and government apathy. Shortly after achieving statehood, in 1793, the Kentucky Assembly received a petition expressing public concern that the current criminal code was too sanguine and needed revision.[62] Such sentiments were not without foundation. The first decade of Kentucky statehood witnessed a noticeable rise in serious crime, and while falling well short of a crisis, the rise was nonetheless a troubling development. The most common serious offense was horse theft, the true extent of which only became evident in the later 1790s as Indian raids diminished.[63] But larceny, burglary, and murder also seemed on the increase. Bourbon County, for example, experienced several serious crimes in the decade preceding the Great Revival. A slave named Basil was executed for stealing seventy-five dollars in 1792. A weaver named David Boyd was convicted of murder and sentenced to hang, as was a local horse thief named John Smith, both in 1795. And, just prior to statehood, Bourbon County residents had been shocked when two men brutally raped and beat a local woman. Comparison with other neighborhoods reveals that Bourbon County's encounters with serious crime were fairly typical.[64]

The growing concern with public morality involved more than simply a desire to maintain public order and protect property. People believed that a virtuous society was essential for the survival of republican government. In late 1794, the House of Representatives received a petition from Bourbon County calling attention to the "alarming progress of vice" which "in a future day may sap the very foundation of government." The petition requested that laws be passed to "suppress vice and establish decency and good order in the community."[65] Shortly thereafter, a second petition requested that "a grand jury may be annually appointed in each county, to enforce the penal laws of this state, and to prevent vice and immorality."[66] Whether the problem lay with lax county magistrates or an overzealous segment of the county is impossible to establish, though the main concern may have been with conditions in town. Public disruption in Paris had been a long-standing problem, especially on court days, partly due to an inadequate number of resident justices. The town had been described two years earlier as a place "where riots is frequent."[67] Although the request for an annual grand jury was rejected, the House did pass "An Act for the Better Regulation of the Town of Paris." This seems to have had little effect, however, for a year later complaints about the chronic disorder in Paris were again brought to the assembly's attention.[68]

In accordance with the growing concern for crime and disorder, Bourbon County began making better provisions for local law enforcement. In 1795, the county allocated ten acres of ground for a prison. The following year the county finally erected a set of stocks and a whipping post. Also that year, new legislation increased the number of justices throughout the state. For Bourbon County this meant twenty-nine new justices over the next two years. In 1798, the County revamped the procedure for appointing constables and organized eleven districts.[69] These were supplemented with a corps of patrollers in 1801. By the turn of the century, the community's sense of security required that the prison have a ten-foot stone wall. Other Kentucky counties moved in a similar direction. Concern had grown in many parts of the state, and in Governor Garrard's address to the state senate in 1801, he called attention to "the alarming increase of capital crime."[70] By the time of the Great Revival, therefore, a growing number of Kentuckians perceived a moral decline.

Local Politics

In contrast to the unity and cohesiveness of station life, the new communities that formed as people settled out were plagued with discord and conflict. To some extent this may have been inevitable. At a time when most inhabitants had not forged many ties within the community, they faced numerous decisions about routing the roads, locating courthouses, and the like. By contrast, established communities did not face decisions like these very often. Furthermore, the prospect of future county divisions nourished existing animosities: why work for compromise when a new county boundary presented a chance for complete victory? Separation from Virginia and independent statehood in 1792 did not solve these problems. If anything, launching a new state raised the level of confusion.

Conditions would improve with time, but local government in Kentucky was often factious during the decade preceding the Great Revival.

Part of the difficulty stemmed from changes in county boundaries as Virginia and later Kentucky strove to keep pace with the flood of western immigrants. Everyone expected that the large frontier counties would be gradually subdivided as the area of settlement expanded. This had been the pattern for nearly two centuries in America. The standard county dimensions enabled most inhabitants to go to court and return home in a single day. Another common measure of appropriate county size was population, or more specifically, the burden placed on the county court docket. The number of men available for militia duty was also an important factor during the early years. Later, the number of tithables posed a major consideration. Whatever the criteria, the point at which a county merited division was seldom universally recognized. On the contrary, county divisions provoked vehement opposition by inhabitants who feared consequences such as higher taxes. County divisions were sometimes also opposed because of the impact on the composition of the legislature. New frontier counties threatened the hegemony of more established regions. The resulting delays meanwhile meant added burdens for the local courts.[71]

Under Virginia, the territory of Kentucky had proceeded through several divisions, but only nine counties existed by the time of statehood in 1792. The new state legislature immediately faced petitions for additional counties, creating seven new counties during its first year. Pressure for further divisions nonetheless continued as new settlers poured westward and the state's population increased from 73,677 in 1790 to 220,095 by 1800. That year the number of Kentucky counties reached forty-two. The number of unsuccessful requests for new counties was much larger, of course, with the result that few communities of the period escaped this source of local conflict.

Most proposals for county divisions followed a standard basic procedure. Petitions were circulated in the affected area and then submitted to the state legislature, usually the House of Representatives. The petition would then be referred to a committee (although sometimes it might be briefly tabled). The committee could suggest a different line of division, although most often the committee simply submitted or withheld their recommendation. Without recommendation, a proposed division was usually doomed. Recommended divisions were worked into a bill, read before the House three times, and then voted on. If passed, the bill proceeded to the Senate and, if it succeeded there, became law.

The experience of Bourbon County was fairly typical of central Kentucky. Bourbon had been established from Fayette County in 1785. In 1790, its area was divided along the Licking River, with the eastern section becoming Mason County. At that time Bourbon County had a population of nearly seven thousand white inhabitants, plus one thousand slaves. By 1800, this area had been further divided into the whole or parts of ten counties with a total population of more than thirty-five thousand. The creation of Nicholas County that same year reduced Bourbon County to roughly its modern size. Until that time county division had been practically an annual issue. Unfortunately, little is known concerning these efforts, although the state legislative journals outline numerous proposals for further county subdivision. Several suggest strong alignments among local inhabitants. One petition proposed dividing the county down the main street of Paris. Another proposed division would have resulted in a triangle measuring fifty miles long and only sixteen miles wide. The motivation behind these bizarre proposals is unknown, but others were clearly fueled by speculatory interests. Shortly after Kentucky became a state in 1792, for example, Matthew Walton of Nelson County apparently nominated John Caldwell as a county justice as part of a plan to divide the county and put the new courthouse on Walton's land. The proposed county, gerrymandered to avoid anticipated opponents, was supported with legislative petitions signed "privately & Quick." Few such efforts, however, met the Kentucky legislature's practical standards of convenience to local government. Meanwhile, the fluidity of county boundaries fostered a fractious and uncompromising spirit to an extent not usually experienced in older parts of the country.[72]

A second common source of political conflict involved official appointments. Kentucky's early governors exercised extensive appointive powers. When Kentucky's first governor, Isaac Shelby, assumed office in 1792, he immediately faced hundreds of appointments, often in unfamiliar parts of the state. Because the new state government could not get under way until these positions were filled, some prominent politicians submitted recommendations. Virginia appointees, incumbents who had valuable experience, were favored, but a complete rollover was not possible. Some men were inevitably selected over others, with predictable conflict. In one instance, John Edwards, the former Bourbon County clerk but in 1792 one of Kentucky's first U.S. senators, had offered Governor Shelby some recommendations that did not include fellow county justice John Waller, recently elected to the state House of Representatives. Waller accosted Edwards in front of a local crowd and accused him of making "improper" recommendations. Although Edwards had privately admitted his action to Waller, when confronted publicly before a crowd on court day, he denied it. Exasperated, Waller loudly declared that should the governor also deny what had occurred, he would think the governor "a Damned Rascall." Although tame by modern standards, the incident constituted a serious breach of gentlemanly conduct. Decrying Edwards's recommendation as aristocratic collusion, Waller incited the crowd to assault the senator.[73]

Eventually, Waller resigned his appointment to the Court of Quarter Sessions, informing Governor Shelby, "As long as I hold any office in the County of Bourbon, so long will I be the object of envy and persecution." He was moving to another county, away "from the Machinations of Bourbon politicians [*sic*]." Waller cast himself as unjustly persecuted, which was hardly accurate, but the factions and alignments in local affairs were very real.[74]

Local government was also plagued by new and changing procedures and policies. Nowhere is this more evident than in the collection of taxes. Large sums of money collected in small amounts proved tremendously difficult to handle. During the late 1790s, the Commonwealth of Kentucky filed lawsuits against Clark, Hardin, and Mason Counties for the taxes of 1795. Bourbon County had not submitted the monies for 1793. Nelson County owed for 1794, as did Mercer County. Harrison County owed for 1796. And Green County owed for 1790. Logan County may have been the worst case; the clerk of the court of quarter sessions was sued for taxes allegedly collected between December 1792 and November 1796. The total amount owed the state could not be determined, however, since the commissioners' accounts were missing for the years 1793 and 1794.[75] Much revenue was tied up for years, if not lost altogether. How the state budget coped is a mystery.

Public office, once an honor conferring much prestige, now posed great financial risk. In Bourbon County, for example, Sheriff Alvin Mountjoy took Deputy Thomas Hughes to court in 1794. Mountjoy's successor, John Gregg, was sued in the Supreme Court for the District of Kentucky for the 4,821 pounds of tobacco that Hughes was supposed to have collected but could not account for. Gregg futilely appealed to the state legislature for an extension. Gregg also appealed to the court for a judgment against Samuel Gibbons for £15 supposedly collected but unaccounted for. Gregg's successor, John McKinney, had to take three of his deputies to court for the same problem. McKinney in turn found himself sued for the taxes.[76]

Corruption may have been a factor, but the predicament of Bourbon County deputy Hezekiah Conn suggests that much of the blame lay with the newness of state government. Collection of the 1797 taxes had already begun by the time Conn received word that the legislature had reduced the tax rate at the last minute (mid-February 1798). Conn thereupon suspended his collections and awaited a copy of the new regulations, which took several months even though the state printer's office in Lexington was only one county away. He then had to begin a new set of accounts, and he hired his brother to help transfer the records. In the process, several errors were unfortunately committed. But, Conn insisted, these errors were not fraudulent. His political adversaries were merely using the confusion for their own benefit.[77] Such difficulties must have discouraged trustworthy men from undertaking public service.

A more competitive, interest-based style of politics was also apparent in the electoral process. One settler reported on the first elections after Kentucky became a state in 1792: "Our different Candidates for different posts are as numerous as Stud Horses at a Court House of an Election day." The Shelby County clerk described a local assembly campaign in 1794 as "a disgrace to human nature." Caleb Wallace, one of the new state's more prominent citizens, remarked, "Office hunting and factions have run high; and as great diversity of sentiments have prevailed as might have been expected in a Country, the inhabitants of which have come from almost every part of the World." John E. King resigned as a justice in 1796, and his foremost reason was that "a party spirit prevails Immoderately in the County." Planter Enoch Smith lamented to Governor Shelby in 1794, "It has been the unhappiness of Clark County ever since it had an existence to be in parties to the injury of the public good." The cause was everywhere to be seen. "Personal interest appears to be the standard of the actions of mankind in this corrupt age & the slightest hope of private emolument out weighs every consideration of publick advantage." The political scene resembled a "swarm of Hungry persons gaping for bread." And, in a sense even more frightening, some individuals refused public appointments from a selfish fear that the duties would detract from their personal business.[78]

Previously, governmental office had been the exclusive domain of the elite gentry class, who were expected to rule with disinterest for the greater good of society, with a sense of honor and duty. Electioneering was traditionally regarded as undignified, and political factions or parties hardly existed. Now, however, competition permeated public life, and concern for the public interest appeared to be in short supply. Contemporary observers perceived these trends as symptomatic of moral decay, but deep change can often appear sinister. Kentuckians were not alone in this experience; similar developments were occurring in many other parts of the country. But even had western citizens been more aware of this broader pattern of change, they would probably have felt little if any comfort.

The Great Kentucky Revival thus appeared in an unusually troubled social context. The prospect of obtaining excellent land, realistic or not, had drawn settlers from an extensive territorial range, bringing into close proximity several American subcultures. Furthermore, only a small portion of the population present in 1800 had been in the state for as long as a decade, and fewer still had remained in the same location for that period. Until the nineteenth century, hardly a voter in the state was a Kentucky native. Further hindering social development was the rootlessness of the western population, partially due to the lingering Indian danger. Developing community bonds under these circumstances would require some time. Many important decisions could not wait, however, making for a fractious political climate. Although local government institutions were effective in developing facilities necessary for economic development, numerous other matters threatened the fragile beginnings of a common public sensibility. Thus, for all of Kentucky's material progress in the years immediately preceding the Great Revival, social stability was even weaker than it had been during station times.

5

A New Political Culture

A nglo-American settlement of Kentucky coincided with the war for independence from Great Britain and the profound political transformation that followed in its wake. As on other Revolutionary frontiers along the colonial interior, establishing effective government institutions in Kentucky proved extremely difficult. The challenge involved far more than simply providing adequate civil administration in a wartime setting. The belief in individual rights to life, liberty, and the pursuit of happiness set forth in the Declaration of Independence heralded a fundamental reordering of American politics, a reordering still unfolding long after the last drums beat at Yorktown. This reordering dominated public affairs in every former colony. Along the Revolutionary frontier, where traditional political modes had not had much time to take root, it was especially powerful. Camp meeting revivalism thus appeared in an unusually troubled political setting, during a time when fundamental principles were undergoing critical reexamination.

Leadership on a Violent Frontier

Colonial politics had rested upon a fundamental belief that society was regimented but interdependent, the different segments forming an organic whole. Each segment had a role in this system, with public affairs reserved as the special domain of the gentry. Their greater wealth theoretically endowed them with superior opportunities to acquire education and experience. It raised them above corruptive influences. And it provided the leisure necessary for time-consuming public service, most of which carried little if any remuneration. The electoral process bound government officials to the interests of their community, but they were not simply advocates for a provincial constituency. Once in office, representatives deliberated independently, entrusted to exercise their best judgment for the common good. The citizens in turn deferred to the gentry's superior wisdom.[1]

This tradition survived the American Revolution, but not unscathed. No longer united by a common foe, anxious to recover from their material losses, Americans soon found themselves embroiled in bitter political conflict. A conception of society as being contentious and pluralistic began replacing the older conception of an organic and harmonious whole. To a growing number of citizens, the notion of a "natural" leadership class capable of representing a common interest seemed naïve if not actually dangerous. A noticeable number of officials soon began coming from the common ranks of society. Representation became more direct in other ways as well, such as the use of instructions advising representatives how to vote on particular issues. Members of the old guard viewed these developments as symptomatic of social decline, a threat to the very existence of the new republic. Their resistance, though, seemed only to confirm in the popular mind the need for direct representation and more democracy in general.[2]

The American Revolution rendered gentry leadership especially weak in Kentucky, not only because settlers there imbibed the same ideas of equality and democracy, but also because of the prolonged border warfare. While members of the gentry from Virginia and elsewhere might venture west to locate land claims, few stayed permanently until conditions became safer. Colonel John Strode, for example, was in Kentucky as early as 1776 with other men from Berkeley County to claim land. He returned with another party in late 1779, when Strode's Station was founded on his claim. Strode then returned to the safety of Berkeley County knowing that his land was secure from rival claimants. He did not move to his station until 1784. Strode, like other members of the Virginia gentry, enjoyed resources that allowed him to obtain rich Kentucky land with minimal personal risk. Any popular resistance to gentry leadership in western government thus had little provocation until security improved and men like Strode reappeared.

Yet habits of deference died hard. Those members of the gentry who did make a home in Kentucky during the early years quickly found themselves in public office, especially the appointive office of county justice. Nearly every aspect of local government came under the eye of the county justices, either singly or as the county court. Though often time-consuming, the position of justice carried no salary. It did, however, confer considerable prestige. And it was hard to achieve. County justices were appointed by the governor rather than elected. When a vacancy on the bench occurred, the remaining justices nominated suitable individuals to the governor for appointment. Although the governor was not bound by law to accept the court's nominees, he rarely failed to do so. Thus, the court was largely a self-perpetuating body. It likewise controlled most other important local offices. Each of Virginia's successive frontiers, including Kentucky, inherited this essentially closed system of local government.

Consider the original justice appointments for Bourbon County, established in 1785 from Fayette County. Bourbon County's most prestigious
settler was James Garrard, who had led a group of fellow Baptists from
Stafford County in tidewater Virginia westward to Kentucky in 1783.[3]
Garrard had previous experience in the Virginia Assembly and, with so
few of the gentry present in Kentucky at this early date, his political credentials were all the more impressive. In 1785, he returned to Virginia to
represent his new neighbors in Kentucky as one of the representatives to
the Virginia Assembly from Fayette County. Garrard's main achievement
was a subdivision of Fayette County, which resulted in the new county of
Bourbon. He also seems to have played an instrumental role in the selection of justices for the new county. One of the appointments was for
Garrard himself, whose social status and political experience made him
an obvious choice. More interesting is that no less than five of the remaining eight original justice appointments went to fellow Baptists from Stafford
County who had settled near Garrard in Kentucky. And, of nine individuals soon nominated by the new court for appointment as additional justices, at least three had formerly resided in Stafford County. Most of these
nominees came from elite families, in several instances with fathers or
other close relatives having served as Stafford County justices. Several of
them were also connected personally. Edward and John Waller, for example, were brothers. John Waller's father-in-law was Justice William
Routt. Justice Alvin Mountjoy was James Garrard's brother-in-law.
Mountjoy's brother Edmund married a daughter of Justice John Gregg in
1787. In 1786, Charles Smith Jr. married Elizabeth Mosby, whose guardian
was Justice John Grant.

It was a tight little group, whose power was concentrated even more
by recommendations to other county offices. Six of the eight individuals
nominated by the county court in May 1786 for appointment as militia
captains, for example, were either current justices or individuals whose
appointments were pending with the governor. Similarly, Garrard served
as county surveyor (an especially strategic office in newly settled areas),
and three of the four men he recommended as his deputies had also been
recommended by the court as additional justices. Through Garrard and his
counterparts elsewhere in Kentucky, the old patronage system survived.[4]

It did not, however, survive completely. In a setting where travel was
dangerous and settlements were widely separated, Garrard and his allies
simply could not govern by themselves. Early Bourbon County included
an extensive territory, and effective government necessitated that some
court appointments be allocated to outlying places.[5] Strode's Station, for
example, merited a resident justice because it was the largest settlement in
the southern part of Bourbon County and separated from Garrard's neighborhood by nearly ten miles. Garrard apparently recognized this because

the original panel of justices included Thomas Swearingen, who came from Berkeley County and had no discernible connection to Garrard. No one else then resident at Strode's Station could match Swearingen's social and political credentials. He had been a leading citizen of Berkeley County, where he owned a large mill, and had served as Berkeley County justice since 1770. He had represented that county in the Virginia Assembly in 1781. Unfortunately, Swearingen died soon after his appointment.

The obvious need for a justice for the settlements growing around Strode's Station, and the absence of Strode and other men with traditional credentials, forced the Bourbon County Court to consider more indigenous leaders. Swearingen's successor as the justice for Strode's Station, Andrew Hood, came from a much more modest background. One contemporary claimed that Hood "Didn't know the first letter in a book."[6] This was an exaggeration, but Hood's reputation clearly stemmed more from his military talent than from his learning or refinement. By almost any measure, Hood shared little with men like Garrard. He did, however, possess one essential quality for an officer of the law in a distant location: popular respect. According to a contemporary, "Old Major Hood and John Constant were good as wolves to track Indians." Hood was described as a "Low Dutchman" from the area of Staunton, Virginia, and "a brave enterprising man of fine mind, about six feet three inches high, verry stout, of excellent character & a first rate woods man."[7] When men with more traditional credentials were not available, men such as Hood offered the best alternative.

Geographical location continued to be an important factor in justice appointments for years to come, particularly in outlying settlements. An inhabitant of the Meyer's Station area of Lincoln County wrote Kentucky's first governor, Isaac Shelby, that "it is the wish of the people to have a justice appointed in this neighborhood, as there is none nearer than six or seven miles." Similarly, a citizen of Clark County informed the governor that local justices were unevenly distributed, with five justices in the "lower end of the County who are not more than five or six Miles distant from one another," two of whom lived within two miles of each other. Shelby was requested to eliminate them both and add two others in more dispersed settlements. In another case, a justice selflessly resigned his commission because his neighborhood already had three justices while another settlement cluster twelve miles away had none. Shelby's successor, James Garrard, received several petitions from a remote part of Mason County, one of which explained that "we have sum un Ruly people in this part of the Cuntry and it appears that their is a Rail Needsesity for Three Magistrates in this part of the Cuntry as we air so far from the sait of Goverment." Two local men were recommended for appointment, their main qualifications being simply that they were "Rail honest" and of "sound judgment."[8]

The pressure to bring the rule of law to remote settlements opened the way for nontraditional leaders to gain public offices otherwise reserved by the gentry. This did not, however, necessarily reflect a more democratic set of values. The tendency was rather to view such appointments as an expedient solution to avoid a far greater evil, anarchy. Western gentry, predictably, were often quite uncomfortable with the compromise. Planter Enoch Smith of Clark County, for example, wrote Kentucky's governor in 1794 urging him to postpone additional justice appointments until more members of the gentry had joined the settlement. Meanwhile, it was "better to suffer some inconveniency in neighbourhoods than justice should be trampled underfoot and men be fixed to execute Laws that never gives themselves the trouble to study either Law or justice."⁹ That Smith made this remark in 1794 attests to the persisting nature of the problem. Men with traditional gentry credentials remained in chronically short supply. Yet it was not just a self-interested gentry who still subscribed to ideas of political deference. Other segments of western society did, too. In 1797, for example, Ebenezer Alexander acknowledged to Governor Garrard receipt of a commission to the Court of Quarter Sessions for Logan County. "I can Inform you that I am unexperienced in that place, yet I think it my Duty to serve . . . untill a better can be recommended & it is the unhappy Case of our County that men fitly Qualifyed for that can scarcely be found."¹⁰ Although old political ideals survived, practical necessity widened the door to public office.

Just as important was the popular esteem accorded military skill. The twin themes of privation and danger reached epic proportions in the paradisiacal setting of Kentucky. Members of the gentry usually served as the militia officers, and a few, such as Isaac Shelby, Kentucky's first governor, demonstrated good military ability. More often, however, the heroes came from lower strata of society. The intrepid militia rangers who scouted the border area to intercept Indians headed toward the settlements were hailed as the "choicest men of the country. . . . Men of the greatest integrity, courage, and activity, and who were well skilled in all modes of savage warfare." Such men were regarded almost with reverence. "I was raised on the frontiers of Kentucky, in the midst of the Indian war," related one pioneer, "where men were only respected in proportion to their valor and skill in fighting Indians, and killing wild beasts; and I verily thought to be a brave skilful warrior: and a good hunter was the greatest honor to which any man could attain."¹¹ Many of these heroes were crude and impetuous, but a reputation for bravery overshadowed other valued qualities during this dangerous period. Because they possessed the one essential ingredient for governing remote settlements, the confidence of the people, some of these indigenous leaders attained public offices previously reserved for men of gentry rank.

One awesome demonstration of personal valor that almost instantly gained the status of legend and led to civic leadership involved "Wildcat" John McKinney, a talented young man of modest means from the Virginia backcountry.[12] McKinney eventually settled a few miles north of Strode's Station, but in the early 1780s he was teaching school in a small cabin immediately outside the stockade at Lexington. Teaching enabled McKinney to earn a living, for at the Battle of Pleasant Point in 1774, he had been "shot in the side, tomahawked in the back so as to loosen his ribs, and had his hand shot away so as to make a sort of club," recalled a pioneer who knew him. "He wore a glove always. Held a fork in it." One day a wildcat wandered into the schoolhouse when McKinney happened to be alone. Instead of fleeing when it saw him, the cat attacked. McKinney suffered severe wounds before finally strangling the cat with his good hand against the edge of his desk. This exploit understandably gained McKinney an instant reputation for valor—which was no hindrance when he ran for the Virginia Assembly in 1790 or five years later when he was elected Bourbon County sheriff. Although McKinney happened to be literate and public spirited, he was only a small landowner of Scots-Irish descent. His reputation for bravery may have been what most qualified him for public office in the minds of voters.

Such seems to have been true in the election of other early government officers as well. When James McMillan, one of the few heroes of General Josiah Harmar's disastrous 1791 military campaign in Ohio, stood for election to the Virginia House of Delegates for Fayette County, a fellow citizen remarked that "he didn't know what were his qualifications for the place, but he knew he handled a gun very well." Some of the Virginia gentry in Kentucky believed that McMillan was in for a big surprise when he reached Richmond. He "would never know he was a fool," some said, "till he saw how many smarter men there were there than himself."[13]

Michael Cassidy, a resident of Strode's Station and later the head of his own station, presents an extreme example of the status accorded to military ability. All accounts of Cassidy agree that he was short, fat, and brave.[14] Cassidy came from Ireland as a youth and began life in America as an indentured servant in Berkeley County, Virginia. In Kentucky the "little chunk of an Irishman" became well known as a hard drinker and a hard fighter. Benjamin Allen, who knew him at Strode's Station, asserted that Cassidy "had no earthly claims to office; was a man of no talents. But was elected to the [Kentucky] Legislature several times, alone because he was not killed that night when Bennet & Spohr [sic] were killed."[15] This incident, which quickly gained legendary stature, occurred in late 1785 during a surveying expedition with two friends from Strode's Station. The attack came late in the night, catching the three men asleep. Spahr and

Bennet died instantly. Cassidy struggled, taking blows to the head that fractured his jaw in two places. As he fell back, his hand came upon his tomahawk, and swinging wildly, Cassidy "cut his way" past the attackers and into the crisp autumn darkness. When Cassidy finally made it home to Hood's Station the next evening, barefoot and shivering, he "was not at first recognized, nearly naked & besmeared with blood." The injuries took several months to heal, and Cassidy carried a long scar on his face for the rest of his life.[16] Cassidy's reputation for bravery rested on more than just this single incident, but had Kentucky not undergone a prolonged period of danger, such adventures might not have led to elective office.

The result, unfortunately, did not work to universal satisfaction. Men who were unaccustomed to the power of public office could do much harm to a government still struggling to get on its feet. Some officials do seem to have had trouble exercising their recently acquired power properly. "We are under so different a kind of government from any I ever was acquainted with," complained Isaac Hite in 1783. The Jefferson County court officers were motivated by "some unknown Spirit." Specifically, "nothing cane [sic] be done but what their own Interest or inclination leads them to, and then every thing must bend to their superior power & dignity." On a similar note, William Breckinridge asked his brother in Virginia to send a copy of the recent acts of the Assembly because, "Our Delegates either Do [not] Know they ought to bring them or they think themselves above doing it and by such like doings as these the Country is in a manner left without laws."[17]

Both of the above observers identified with the gentry and were therefore more likely to resent new men in government, yet abuses of power did occur. The most notorious example of the problem involved Bourbon County magistrate John Waller. As previously mentioned, Waller came under investigation in 1792 for an incident involving a recent immigrant from Ireland named Arthur McNickle. Because McNickle refused to sign a confession of vagrancy, Justice Waller had, "wantonly and maliciously, and without even the colour of a plausible Cause," sentenced him to the humiliation of being horsewhipped. Fellow justice James Smith, writing in the newspaper under the pseudonym "Truth," claimed that Waller had "without even a fact either proved or alledged, inflicted disgraceful punishment upon a person, whose reputation for sobriety and honesty; stand as fair as any in the county; His seeming motive, was, only to shew his authority."[18]

Thus, government operated differently in Kentucky than elsewhere in the Old Dominion. The structures were the same, and many inhabitants were familiar with their workings, but western conditions had pried apart the gentry's tight hold on public affairs. The small core of individuals with traditional gentry attributes in newly settled areas had to be augmented with some additional local men chosen largely on the basis of their military accomplishments. Most lacked the traditional attributes of the ruling classes, but the popular respect they enjoyed lent crucial strength to western government. Though a necessary concession to frontier logistics, recruiting from beyond the gentry ranks also tacitly acknowledged the status hierarchy defined by military achievement and lent this alternative measure added legitimacy. As security improved and members of the gentry ranks finally proceeded westward, they would find their attempts to resume their customary position at the head of public affairs strongly contested. Government office was no longer their exclusive domain. Men like Andrew Hood, John McKinney, Michael Cassidy, and of course Daniel Boone had stepped in and helped fill the leadership vacuum. The rival leadership structures would break into open contention as Kentucky prepared for admission as a state.

The Pursuit of Statehood

The campaign for Kentucky's admission as a new state began as a means to attain better security. Virginia prohibited her trans-Appalachian citizens from taking offensive action against the native villages north of the Ohio River for fear of inciting an expensive war. Defensive measures alone, however, could not ensure security, and Kentuckians chafed under Virginia's policy. A special meeting of county militia leaders in 1784 decided that separation from Virginia merited further consideration, but as that lay beyond the meeting's authorized scope, Kentuckians were called upon to elect county delegates for a subsequent meeting specifically for that purpose. Several additional conventions would ensue before statehood was finally accomplished, but the real problem lay at the national level. Although Virginia willingly released the District of Kentucky, the Confederation of United States had no procedure in place for the admission of new states and, struggling to reach consensus on other crucial issues, was reluctant to upset the sectional balance. The pursuit of statehood thus proved a prolonged and frustrating experience. Only after a new national constitution was the way finally cleared for Kentucky's admission as the fifteenth state on June 1, 1792.[19]

Western support for statehood was mixed. Among the elite, a core group oriented around the courts pressed hardest for independence. Prominent figures included Harry Innes, John Brown, Caleb Wallace, Benjamin Sebastian, George Muter, Samuel McDowell, and James Wilkinson. Although most of these men originated from Virginia, they eagerly awaited a chance to direct western development without restrictions from Richmond. Centrally located in the Bluegrass region, eloquent and shrewd, the "court party" played an instrumental role in sustaining Kentucky's quest for statehood despite numerous obstacles and delays. A smaller contingent of western gentry, with Federalist sympathies, cautioned against premature separation from the parent state. By 1790 or so, however, western development had reached a point where conservatives had become more amenable to Kentucky statehood, if done through proper legal means.[20]

Popular attitudes are more difficult to gauge. Certainly many citizens paid little attention to politics. A Lexington resident observed in early 1791, "Our Indian Affairs seem to engage the attention of the Common people & a Separation [from Virginia] that of the Leading Men." Some people probably believed that statehood would open the way for a more aggressive Indian policy. Yet this and other possible benefits of statehood could not quell suspicions that separation from Virginia might be, or might become, a gentry grab for power. In one of the more explicit statements about the popular position, General Butler recorded in his journal in late 1785 that according to a party of travelers returning from Kentucky, statehood "is not so much the wish or voice of the people generally, as the uneasiness of the great landholders, who wish for power and offices in the government." Many people apparently also feared that statehood would mean higher taxes.[21] Several democratic-minded delegates to the statehood conventions, mainly men of modest property, attempted to address these concerns. Though not categorically opposed to statehood, they were suspicious of the "court party" pressure for a separation from Virginia. As for the public at large, whether because of deference to the "great landholders," simple apathy, or other reasons, the idea of statehood did not meet with much in the way of resistance.[22]

Only in 1791, after statehood had been approved, did an opposition movement really surface. The election of county delegates to the state constitutional convention was set for December, but popular agitation opened the campaign early. In August 1791, Judge Harry Innes observed with disdain and alarm that "the People of Kentucky are mere Fanatics in Politicks—Constitutions are forming in every neighborhood." Their unifying characteristic was a "great prejudice" against "men of Fortune, learned men, the Judiciary & Barr."[23] To forward popular opinion, several local organizations emerged calling themselves county committees, consciously modeled after the community groups organized during the American Revolution. These committees were probably connected to the democratic defenders of the general welfare who had resisted separation from Virginia, although too few members of either group can be identified to prove continuity.[24]

The most radical of the county committees, proposing specific mea-

sures for keeping political power in the hands of the citizenry, was that of
Bourbon County. Little about the various statehood conventions suggests
the immanent appearance there of a democratic movement. Its delegates
to earlier meetings to discuss statehood had been predominantly drawn
from James Garrard's group of gentry, although at least one democratic-
minded champion, James Smith, had also been chosen. The only hint that
Bourbon County would emerge as a bastion of democracy, and a vague
one at that, was the unusually large cohee population in the county's southern section, where Smith had quickly emerged as an influential voice.[25]
The first mention of a democratic committee in Bourbon County dates
from mid-September 1791, some four months preceding the election for
delegates to the new state's constitutional convention. Its chairman was a
man named William Henry, of whom little is known except that he was a
man of modest means and a local Presbyterian elder. In October the *Kentucky Gazette* printed an essay by Henry explaining the purpose of county
committees. Henry's serialized essays on behalf of the Bourbon County
Committee became the foremost expression of popular resistance to gentry leadership in the upcoming election of convention delegates.[26]

The immediate concern was to ensure the election of delegates to the
constitutional convention who would defend the interests of the general
citizenry. Elections, the primary means for popular participation in government, had unfortunately become "much corrupted by flattery, grog,
&c." The Bourbon County plan called for each militia company to choose
a committee, and each of these committees to send two delegates to meet
at the county seat with those sent by other militia companies. This general
committee would nominate a ticket of candidates, then send the ticket
back to the company committees for their assent. Through this procedure, "the minds of the people may in great measure be made up without
prejudice before the day of election," enabling voters to resist being
"wheedled out of our just rights, by flattery, grog, or the wag of a
ruffled hand." The corruption of elections was unquestionably a foremost concern, and as this statement implies, the gentry were considered prime culprits.[27]

The second function of the county committees, Henry explained, was
for the instruction of convention delegates. Instructions for elected representatives were not novel but were used with increasing frequency during
the postrevolutionary era as a means to bind representatives more firmly
to the popular will. The Bourbon County Committee proposed six recommendations for the new constitution, here again revealing the
Committee's democratic orientation. These recommendations called for a
unicameral legislature, for the exclusion of immoral men from public office, for local militia and county officers to be chosen through civic elections, and for the election process itself to be reformed by replacing viva

voce voting with ballots. It also recommended that instead of simply borrowing wholesale from antiquated and complicated legal codes, Kentucky should frame an original, simple, and comprehensible code and thereby reduce the expense of government and the need for attorneys. The last recommendation was for a more egalitarian tax structure.[28]

The third function of the county committees was to help ensure that the will of the people would be followed by an opportunity to ratify the proposed constitution. The constitution should be published and submitted to the committees so that "the sense of the people at large, may be easily and fully collected." Without such organizations to channel public sentiment, Henry warned his readers, "we must either be in a great measure dumb upon this occasion or nothing can be heard but a confused uproar."

As the Bourbon County program reveals, the committees of 1791 were thoroughly anti-elitist. Their avowed purpose was to ensure that "The farmer, the mechanic, and even the common labouring man have a voice . . . equal to the lawyer, the colonel or the general."[29] The Bourbon Committee claimed that the separation from Virginia had proceeded despite popular opposition, revealing that the "great men" placed their own pursuit of power and interest over the will of the people. They had failed to exercise public virtue, which the popular mind tended to confuse with personal virtue or morality.[30] This may have been especially true for the Bourbon Committee leaders. Both William Henry and John Boyd (who served as clerk) were Presbyterian elders, as was their neighbor Justice James Smith, who as a state representative would later seek to keep immoral characters out of public office. The concern with personal morality surfaced in other ways as well. The corruptive effect of luxury upon the gentry was implied in such phrases as "the wag of a ruffled hand." Slavery likewise raised questions about gentry virtue. Fearful no doubt of alienating the electorate, the Bourbon County democrats avoided taking an explicit position on this delicate issue, but their interest in extracting Kentucky from what they judged an immoral practice was nonetheless apparent to contemporaries. The conclusion was clear: the western gentry was immoral and therefore unworthy of public trust.

Critics of the county committees, mainly members of the gentry, countered with conservative warnings against the election of delegates who were honest but ignorant. They emphasized the importance and complexity of constitution writing and the need to elect delegates possessing judgment and wisdom. These critics defended the traditional system of political leadership, where the gentry dominated on the basis of their economic independence, education, and personal honor and ruled with the common good of society in mind, even if that sometimes meant taking an unpopular position. The common citizenry should defer to their superior judgment. No one disputed that political sovereignty lay with the people, but excessive democracy could be dangerous, and popular participation in government should be limited to the casting of an election vote.[31] County committees were deemed antithetical to this deferential tradition. Therefore, instead of debating the specific programs proposed by the Bourbon County Committee, criticism centered on the legitimacy of committees to exist. Opponents claimed that the county committees were not sanctioned by law, they fostered factionalism, and they negated the true meaning of representation.[32]

The committeemen defended themselves by emphasizing precedent organizations. Bourbon County Committee president William Henry pointed out, "At the time of the American revolution, when it was in the interest of our great men candidly to take the sense of every individual, the committees was proposed, and warmly urged."[33] Another defender of county committees wrote that the formation of such groups was a right that had been won in the Revolution, and now, he asked, how could anyone "look upon themselves as true friends to their country, that would endeavor to discourage and prohibit the exercise of that most valuable privilege[?]" This writer further declared, "Writing against committees duly elected by the people is . . . striking at the most sacred and essential rights of mankind."[34]

William Henry and his Committee struck a chord with the *Kentucky Gazette*'s readership, judging from the numerous sympathetic essays published that fall. A man who signed himself "Will Wisp" warned readers that the "great men" were almost all "designing men," who cared little for the good of the country. They posed a threat to liberty because "the great men will always out talk us and dispute us." Fortunately, "the little men are much the more numerous," and in the upcoming election, "we are determined to do ourselves justice."[35] A few weeks later appeared a letter written in a very similar vein signed "The Medlar," supposedly a woman.[36] "As far as I am capable to judge," she wrote, "I find the most solid wisdom among those who live above poverty and yet below affluence." The Medlar contrasted the raucous amusements and vices of the gentry with the virtue of the honest farmer "who can afford himself books and candles at night, and follows his farm in the day." Many of the great men were notorious for being "covetous, extortioners, profane swearers, sabbath breakers, drunkards, gamblers and even boasting of their scenes of brutality [over slaves]," claimed the Medlar. "Now how can you think a pure stream of government can flow from so corrupt a fountain?"

Another noteworthy contribution came from a certain "Philip Philips," posing as a barely literate Irishman transplanted to Mercer County. This essayist, whoever he was, sent the *Kentucky Gazette* a folksy summary of a local campaign debate between Samuel Taylor, a leading democrat, and

Colonel George Nicholas, a large planter and one of Kentucky's most respected attorneys. The main theme was the trustworthiness of the gentry. Philips wrote in his naïve style, "I never was a friend to larned men for I see it is those sort of fokes who always no how to butter their own bred and care not for others. I always thought it was not rite they shude go to convention or to the legislater." With rare exceptions, Philips believed that "larned men" could be trusted only to disarm the people of their political rights, to protect property interests, and to make cunning legislation that placed a disproportionate share of taxes on the common people. He reminded readers that the separation from Virginia had been pursued despite a lack of popular initiative or interest; the "larned men" forwarded their own interests—not those of common Kentuckians.[37]

Later in the campaign, two more voices spoke out in support of the county committees.[38] A contributor signing as "Salamander," and identifying himself as a "well wisher" of the Bourbon County Committee, openly expressed belief that if gentlemen gained election they would "make use of the best means in their power to suppress them [the people] in the beginning, before they had time to gather strength: for should the people in general begin to think for themselves and find that all mankind are made of one sort of clay, and that riches neither make a man wise or honest—ten to one but they fall into the measures of the Committee of Bourbon." On the same page of the newspaper, "Rob the Thrasher" responded to criticism of the Bourbon County Committee from "A.B.C.," who had ridiculed the appearance of "chimney corner constitutions" still stinking of smoke.[39] Rob sarcastically retorted, "But pray Mr. A.B.C., where do you live, is there no chimney in your house; sure you must have a stove then; or a very large lamp?" Rob's resentment toward the gentry was obvious as he observed, "You advised or dictated to us to send sensible men to the next convention, and men that understood the business well, you were perfectly right, but you thought we were fools."

A.B.C.'s ridicule of "chimney corner constitutions" also provoked two lengthy essays from a writer signing himself "H.S.B.M.," probably someone (or a group) close to the Bourbon Committee.[40] In answer to A.B.C.'s criticism of the Bourbon County Committee proposals for election reform, H.S.B.M. wrote that his opponent seemed to assume "that wise men, or good men, cannot miss being chosen at our Elections tho 'tis evident that those who are most liberal with their grog generally carries the election." The cutting response continued, "But perhaps he may look upon wise men, good men, and rich men, as Synonimous terms . . . for the Rich is always able to produce the greatest quantity of Spiritous Liquors in order to bribe the electors and by this means be elected." The H.S.B.M. essay then concluded, "[I]n general the rich have too much influence, and often make ill use of it." The key to liberty was the electoral process, but since the Revolution it had become "generally only a sham." H.S.B.M. lamented "to see it so corrupted; and I think it dangerous at this time, to risque our liberty and that of our posterity upon this rotten pillar only." Without safeguards such as those urged by the county committees, the current mode of elections was "calculated to cast us into an Aristocratic government or of establishing a government in the hands of a few wealthy men."

By the end of 1791, the Bourbon County Committee had counterparts in Mercer, Madison, Fayette, Mason, and Woodford Counties. Hardly anything is known about these groups, but their mere existence nevertheless attests to a broadly felt concern. Although the committees operated independently, at least one attempt was made to coordinate efforts as the election day approached. Representatives from three of the committees met at Harrodsburg, where they "compared their proceedings, which almost agreed in every particular."[41] Nonetheless, the county committees remained too unorganized to constitute a political party.

However disdainful of the county committees, the Kentucky gentry recognized their potential influence. Federal Court judge Harry Innes complained to his friend Thomas Jefferson early in the campaign for convention delegates, "The people of Kentucky are all turned Politicians." Innes continued, "The Peasantry are perfectly mad; extraordinary prejudices without foundation have arisen against the present officers of Government—the Lawyers and the Men of Fortune—they say that *plain honest Farmers* are the only men who ought to be elected to form our Constitution. What will be the end of these prejudices it is difficult to say, they have given a very serious alarm to every thinking man, who are determined to watch and court the temper of the people."[42] Unknown men with the most meager of credentials were publishing plans for the state government. Innes and his court party cohorts wondered audibly how long it might be before "Reason will resume her seat & get the better of Folly & Ignorance."[43]

The western gentry urged voters to disregard the pre-statehood alignments, meaning the divided support for separation from Virginia, and to consider candidates solely according to their personal qualifications. Voters were warned that the plain and honest farmer might be good, but ignorant, and the unintentional result a ruinous constitution.[44] Kentucky's gentry worked hard to justify themselves with voters. "Philip Philips" reported a campaign debate between democrat Samuel Taylor and George Nicholas, an earnest defender of gentry leadership in government. Nicholas argued, "[I]f unlarned men go to the legislater to make laws, they could not understand them when they had made them, and it would take all the larned men and all the squires in court to make it out."[45] For a candidate of Nicholas's standing to elicit voter support in this manner would have been considered demeaning in earlier times. A few candidates apparently responded to the heated campaign by trying to join the county committees, causing one member to denounce the "rich designing men" who "procure themselves to be elected into the county committees." Most adhered to traditional campaign practice, however, refusing to accept that it had become necessary to court voter support.[46]

When the election results became known, Kentucky's gentry were distraught at what they regarded as the mediocre quality of the delegates. Federalist Humphrey Marshall claimed that instead of choosing the "best talents from each county," the electorate had cast their votes for "those who had taken the most pains to please, or who happened at the time, to be, the greatest favorites with the people."[47] Marshall, however, exaggerated. Only about a half dozen of the forty-five delegates owned no land or had no previous experience in public office. Relatively few of the delegates could claim gentry credentials, but most had solid social standing in their communities. In many cases, that standing had been earned as a result of abilities demonstrated during the dangerous process of settlement. Even in Bourbon County, the choice of delegates reveals relatively little radicalism. All delegates had experience representing their fellow citizens, and all but one were county justices. Whether democrat or gentry, no other available county inhabitant possessed credentials for public responsibility superior to those of the five men who were chosen.[48]

Other counties too were represented by a mix of gentry and indigenous leaders, with enough of the latter to cause dread among the former. "Our Convention which is to meet on Monday next, will I am afraid committt many blunders," explained one conservative. "County Committees, composed of very many ignorant & some bad men have borne the sway in our Election's." According to this observer, "The exclusion of Lawyers not from the Legislature only, but from the barr [sic], the abolition of Slavery, and low Salaries to the officers of Government, and that to be paid in produce, The committees it is expected, will insist much upon." Other controversial proposals included taxes on land belonging to nonresident speculators and a unicameral legislature.[49] Transforming such ideas into constitutional provisions, however, required more than simply electing sympathetic representatives.

When the convention assembled on April 2, the democrats and their allies revealed themselves as remarkably unprepared to formulate a constitution. The delegates quickly fell under the spell of George Nicholas from Mercer County. Although a newcomer to Kentucky, Nicholas was an experienced legislator, a shrewd politician, and an extremely talented attorney. Nicholas distrusted popular politics, but not having been present during the statehood conventions, this was not yet fully apparent to Kentucky populists. And as the only delegate to arrive at the convention with a coherent set of resolutions, Nicholas quickly became the convention's most influential member.[50]

Nicholas's plan of government contained little novelty but was rather a collection of conservative elements from other American constitutions. It was designed to counterbalance Kentucky's broad suffrage tradition, which he dared not touch, and check popular government.[51] Nicholas favored a bicameral legislature, with direct election of the lower house and property qualifications and electors for the upper house or Senate. Voters would choose the executive directly to ensure selection according to merit and ability. All judiciary appointments were to be made by the executive, with the legislature having power to impeach. The objective was to make the higher courts strong and independent from popular pressure, with judges appointed during good behavior and with ample salaries so as to discourage corruption. Meriting particular note, land title disputes were not subject to the usual appeal process but reserved for the state supreme court, which would presumably be controlled by men of property. Nicholas's scheme of government appeared prudent and sound. Emphasizing in his speeches the sovereignty of the people and other main principles of republican government, he overwhelmed all resistance. Whether on the floor or behind the scenes, George Nicholas dominated the convention.

The democrats tried to resist. Because the convention quickly dissolved into a committee of the whole, enabling delegates to debate freely off the record, the details of their efforts are lost.[52] Early in the proceedings the convention received "Sundry petitions from the County of Bourbon praying for certain principles to be engrafted into the Constitution." Presumably these petitions reiterated the ideas forwarded by William Henry and his County Committee. A few of these ideas were also supported by Nicholas, such as free manhood suffrage and voting by ballot. The selection of county sheriffs, coroners, and minor militia officers through election rather than executive appointment was also accepted by the convention. Whether the convention ever seriously considered the remaining proposals is questionable. Much of the final Kentucky constitution nonetheless incorporated elements from that of Pennsylvania, one of the more democratic state constitutions.[53]

Democratic resistance is much more evident with another issue, slavery. Emancipation had surfaced peripherally during the campaign for delegates, but it developed into the convention's main controversy.[54] One of the democratic leaders introduced a resolution that the constitution allow gradual emancipation, enabling owners to absorb their losses. Presbyterian minister David Rice, one of Kentucky's most prominent churchmen, immediately delivered a lengthy address in support. Rice argued, as the published title of his speech announced, that slavery was inconsistent with justice and good policy.[55] Slavery violated natural law, Rice asserted. "As creatures of God we are, with respect to liberty, all equal." Slavery operated contrary to a moral society, thereby jeopardizing republican government. Rice urged that no additional slaves be brought into Kentucky and that the new state government eliminate slavery entirely. How to accomplish this he declined to say, believing it best left to the legislature.

Nicholas responded with more than a mere rebuttal. Many Kentuckians, like Americans elsewhere during this period, disliked slavery or were indifferent to it, and he worried that in a few years' time antislavery forces might grow strong enough to gain a majority in the statehouse. To counter such a possibility, Nicholas submitted a carefully drafted resolution that would prohibit the state legislature from emancipating slaves save with the consent of their owners or full compensation, prerequisites which rendered an end to slavery in Kentucky virtually impossible. In addition, individual owners who wished to emancipate slaves had to ensure that the freed slaves would not become a public charge. Nicholas's resolution also required that the Kentucky legislature could not prohibit prospective settlers from bringing slaves into the state, although it might regulate the slave trade. In short, Nicholas's resolution offered Kentucky masters fuller protection than they had had under the state of Virginia.

In a lengthy speech to the convention defending his proposal, Nicholas avoided engaging with Rice over the moral aspects of slavery and concentrated instead on property rights. He also shrewdly played on the racial prejudice of his audience and the widely held notion that black economic and political advancement could only occur at the expense of white citizens. Nicholas further pointed out that the majority of Kentucky settlers were from southern states, and a prohibition of slavery would deter the future migration of southerners with property. Meanwhile, if antislavery men were sincere in their condemnations, they could begin by emancipating their own blacks. In response to concerns that his proposed article placed unreasonable strictures on future legislative action, Nicholas argued that legislative prerogative should be subordinate to the sacred right of property.[56]

The antislavery delegates had not come prepared to push for a constitutional abolition of slavery. Most of them realized that such action was premature and recognized the need to win wider public support before pressing the legislature for legal action. Nicholas's clever resolution obstructed this strategy and threatened to put abolition permanently beyond reach. Thus, when the convention voted to accept Nicholas's resolution as the Ninth Article, Rice resigned his seat in protest. The issue surfaced again, however, a few days later when the convention considered the proposed constitution drafted by Nicholas's committee. Samuel Taylor of Mercer County and James Smith of Bourbon County—both prominent democrats and known opponents of slavery—moved and seconded that the slavery article be expunged. It was a pivotal moment, especially in the wake of Rice's dramatic resignation, and produced the convention's single roll call vote. Probably because of the western shortage of agrarian labor, the slavery contingent prevailed. The Ninth Article was retained by a vote of 16 to 26, making Kentucky the only American state to constitutionally protect slavery.[57]

Shortly after the convention had adjourned, George Nicholas assessed the new constitution in a letter to his old friend James Madison. He defended the principle of free manhood suffrage as necessary for the preservation of personal liberty. "Exclude any particular class of citizens and sooner or later they will certainly be oppressed." Property rights remained secure through the process of choosing state senators indirectly, through electors. Nicholas smugly predicted, "Notwithstanding *all* have a right to vote and to be elected, the wealthy will nineteen times out of twenty be chosen." Thus most of the House and the entire Senate would be propertied individuals. "I will give up my opinion as soon as I see a man in rags chosen to that body." Yet Nicholas left little to chance. He designed a proportionately large and insulated Senate to counterbalance the House and county courts with their many indigenous leaders. The judicial system was centralized and independent. Kentucky's executive branch was one of the most powerful in the country, with the governor appointing nearly all state officials. And, despite calls from the Bourbon County Committee, Kentucky's new constitution was not submitted to voters for ratification.[58]

The strong challenge to gentry control that emerged in response to statehood, just a few years before the Great Revival, would appear consistent with the long-standing beliefs about frontier settlement associated with historian Frederick Jackson Turner. The association seems all the more pertinent because Bourbon County was not only a center for democratic government but also the location of Cane Ridge Presbyterian meetinghouse, where the Great Revival reached its greatest height. Representative James Smith, moreover, was an elder at Cane Ridge and a supporter of the new and controversial form of worship that distinguished the Revival, the camp meeting.[59] But even if the role of men like Smith could be better documented, the result would probably reveal little more than coincidence. Not only were similar political controversies occurring throughout the country, but camp meeting revivalism quickly spread to a variety of settings. Bourbon County was conspicuous but hardly unique.

The campaign for constitutional convention delegates is probably more significant for revealing a profound difference of opinion concerning proper moral standards, as well as an extraordinary degree of political contention. The character of public leaders was hotly disputed, raising major questions about representative government. At issue was no single government issue or policy, but the very nature of government itself. Similar debates were occurring throughout America at this time, but the situation in Kentucky was particularly unstable. This was a new state, with no common colonial heritage upon which to draw. Furthermore, the separation from Virginia left the western gentry, most of whom were relative newcomers to Kentucky and lacking in military credentials, to now survive on their own. Those who believed they could do so on traditional terms encountered a rude surprise. The electoral success of the Bourbon County Committee and its democratic allies, though squandered in the convention proceedings, indicates widespread resistance to gentry rule. George Nicholas's nimble success at the convention did not change this.

Politics in the New State

As the course of politics during the rest of the decade would reveal, Nicholas had overplayed his hand. Kentucky's democratic delegation had been momentarily overwhelmed, but not persuaded. The early years of statehood were consequently no more peaceful than earlier. Proposals similar to those which had been advocated by the committees and their fellow democrats soon appeared in the state House of Representatives. And as the new government proved itself partial to the propertied classes, public debate over the role of the gentry resumed. Without a common political culture—a broad understanding of how government should operate and toward what ends—a written constitution could only go so far. Few problems could be satisfactorily resolved in the absence of a shared set of values. Before the decade was out, therefore, Kentucky would require a second constitution. The Great Revival was thus preceded by an unusually prolonged period of deep political distress.

When Kentucky became the fifteenth state on June 1, 1792, all seemed quiet enough. After the flurry of state elections, a gentry observer reported with relief that the "factious spirit which . . . prevailed in this country last summer and fall seems to be fast subsiding."[60] Messages from the county committees no longer appeared in the newspaper. Yet they continued to exert effect. The first sign came with the election. Among those elected in Bourbon County, for example, were James Smith and John "Wildcat" McKinney. The county's democratic contingent was also probably responsible for the election of George Michael Bedinger, a backcountry Virginian of German descent who had served with the militia at Boonesborough during the Revolution. Two of the electors chosen to determine the county's state senator, Thomas Jones and Andrew Hood, also probably owed their victory to the movement for democratic government. In other counties as well, elected officials included a sizable proportion who lacked traditional gentry credentials. Their local standing rested on other qualities. They tended to be early settlers, usually landowners, with a reputation for fairness and honesty. Most had been previously entrusted with public business, often as county justices.

The Bourbon County Committee and its allies, though thwarted at the constitutional convention, promptly presented several legislative proposals to the new House of Representatives. One of the first matters taken up involved the payment of government officers. The Bourbon County Committee had insisted that, due to the general shortage of specie, officials should accept payment in farm produce. Opponents had laughed at the image of a chief justice at the end of a term "riding upon a bag of corn," or the governor "trudging home with a basket of Eggs upon his arm." The new legislature was not prepared to act contrary to its own interests; the Bourbon County petition prompted an opposing bill entitled "That the expenditures of government ought to be levied and collected in specie only." The measure passed, although the issue resurfaced one last time, again unsuccessfully, before the close of the year.[61]

The House received two other petitions from Bourbon County during its next session, in the fall of 1792. One was from "sundry inhabitants of the County of Bourbon, stating their fears that the Legislature will allow two [sic] high Salaries to the officers of Government and praying that the same may be moderate." The other petition was one "praying that the practice of attorneys be regulated by law." Again, both appeals correspond to ideas originally advocated by the Bourbon County Committee. This second attempt to introduce the Committee's principles into government, however, proved equally futile. After brief consideration by the House Committee on Grievances and Procedure, the petitions were rejected.[62]

A fourth petition from Bourbon County, which addressed the statewide problem of uncertain land titles, met a better fate. The involvement of the Bourbon County Committee is less clear, but this petition embodied the same concern for common citizens that had been at the heart of the Committee's other reforms. The problem as stated in the petition was that "many persons have settled and improved lands at great trouble and expense under the belief that they were the real owners thereof, [but] who have afterwards lost the same by [other persons with] prior claim." Prosperous settlers might defend their claim and hope for a settlement, but few small farmers could endure the expense and anxiety of prolonged litigation. The petition sought a law that would compel the person with superior claim to compensate the occupant for his improvements and disallow retroactive rent charges. Due to the statewide nature of the problem and the popular sense of injustice surrounding it, the House readily responded with bills in 1794 and again in 1795. Both bills were obstructed by the Senate, functioning as Nicholas had intended, in the interests of property. Only after a new election of senators in 1796, the result of popular ire, would a third House bill finally succeed in becoming law.[63]

Meanwhile, frustrated no doubt by the failure of the petitions, a democratic organization resurfaced in Bourbon County, this time calling itself a democratic-republican society. Groups under this label were appearing throughout the United States in 1793, modeled after the political committees which had operated during the American Revolution, in opposition to Federalist policies.[64] One had surfaced in Lexington by August, with John Breckinridge, Kentucky's attorney general, as its president, and some of the state's leading government officials, lawyers, and merchants as members. The Bourbon County group was likewise Anti-Federalist, but that is where similarities ended. The Bourbon Democratic Society directed its main criticism against the "aristocrats" in state government, many of whom belonged to the Lexington organization. This naturally evoked reaction from that quarter.[65] As one essayist argued, democratic societies were useful "when they are conducted by men of understanding and prudence," as was the case in Lexington, but where "ignorance is allowed to prevail, democratic societies are a nuisance, and are only calculated to promote dissension, and prejudice the minds of the people against the government and those in office; especially when a few under the name of a democratic society will dare to speak in the name of the county, as the society of Bourbon have done."[66]

Nonetheless, what little is known concerning the Bourbon Democratic Society does not suggest a group of disreputable, bitter outcasts or dangerous insurrectionists. The eight known leaders all enjoyed solid local reputations. William Henry was president and John Boyd was clerk, the same positions these two men had held in the old Bourbon County Committee. Both men were Presbyterian elders, and Boyd had recently been elected a state representative. Colonel James Smith, also a Presbyterian elder, had represented Bourbon County at the state constitutional convention and also served as a justice of the peace. Reelected to the House through most of the 1790s, he was already well known as a champion of democratic government. Thomas Jones, an elector in 1792, had succeeded James Garrard as county surveyor. He was one of the wealthiest men in the town of Paris and played a key role in its development. State Senator John Allen, an attorney, came closest to traditional gentry credentials, but the other known leaders (James Kenny, Richard Henderson, and Isaac Ruddle) were early pioneers and familiar figures to local inhabitants. These men came from a variety of backgrounds and lived in different sections of the county, suggesting a fairly broad base of support.[67] Furthermore, the perceived radicalism of the Bourbon Society was probably as much a product of who did not participate as of who did. Conspicuously missing among the Bourbon Democratic Society leaders were members of the county government. Out of some eighteen county officers (1792–94), James Smith is the only justice known to have participated in the Democratic Society, probably because they were appointed officials and little motivated to court popular favor. That the Democratic Society vehemently criticized the court system and the distribution of government authority must not have helped.

Under the leadership of William Henry and John Boyd, the Bourbon Democratic Society revived the old Bourbon County Committee's call for democratic government. Its position was set forth in three essays printed in the *Kentucky Gazette*, two preceding the May 1794 state election and the third appearing the following autumn during the legislative session. The first of these, published in two parts, was signed "A Farmer," who distinguished himself from the Lexington Society by telling readers that he had submitted his piece "at the particular request of a *pure* Democratic Society."[68] This essayist, whoever he was, began his argument by reviewing the "machinations and ambitious plans of our newly modelled patricians." The separation from Virginia had been the scheme of "The rich, the great, the designing amongst us." These men had overwhelmed the general citizenry with "many pompous and plausible arguments." Now, two years later, the small farmers were worse off than ever previously. Unfortunately, though, too few of them even realized it. People were too apathetic and naïve, allowing a corrupt, self-interested aristocracy to control the government for their own purposes. Instead of promoting civic welfare, the legislature's work revealed that "the securing and dividing of the loaves and fishes were their principal and highest concern."

This misfortune had occurred, argued "A Farmer," because the Kentucky constitution allowed justices of the peace also to be eligible for the legislature, violating the principle of separation of power. They were both makers and judges of the law. Furthermore, their concentration of power was compounded by the governor's reliance on these same individuals for advice in making local government appointments. With fifteen counties, each with an average of fifteen justices, "A Farmer" warned that the likely result would soon be "two hundred and twenty-five petty tyrants in a petty state." Bourbon County justice John Waller's high-handed treatment of Arthur McNickle, the Irish immigrant Waller had horsewhipped for insubordination, was a prime example of the danger. Although the House investigation had revealed Waller's misconduct as even more flagrant than originally depicted, "A Farmer" reminded readers that neither the governor nor the legislature had removed him from office. As long as the law permitted justices to hold concurrent office in the legislature, no effective recourse existed to prevent corruption. The concentration of government power was dangerous and would inevitably enable the gentry to exert unwarranted power over "the poorer and more numerous part of the community."

"A Farmer" appealed to his fellow plebeians, "Let us be vigilant in season and out of season against the wiles and machinations of the ambitious aristocrats, who are ever ready to take every advantage of our remissness or inattention." Kentuckians were advised to vote in the upcoming election for state legislators who would "reform the aristocratic parts of our constitution." This was a reference to the Senate, which had repeatedly rejected popular bills from the House. Toward this end, voters were urged not to elect county justices. People should protect themselves from these petty tyrants by forming themselves into *"pure"* democratic societies similar to that of Bourbon County. These democratic societies were to function as local nominating committees, following a procedure strikingly similar to that previously proposed by the Bourbon County Committee. From these societies citizens should "chuse or delegate committees to meet at some convenient place to nominate farmers and mechanics in each county, respectively, to whom we ought to give our vote." Readers were warned that a successful campaign against the "ambitious Squires" required unity as well as vigilance and effort. The squires were highly motivated, well connected, and shrewd. The real power, however, lay with the people.[69]

A short time later, as new legislative elections approached, the Bourbon County Democratic Society held a public meeting in the town of Paris. The address, published in the *Kentucky Gazette* and signed by president William Henry, built upon the critique from "A Farmer," but shifted emphasis to the "undue, aristocratical influence" of the Kentucky Senate and urged voters to demand a new constitution.[70] At the last election for state legislators, in May 1793, the Democratic Society claimed that the people of Bourbon County had "almost unanimously manifested a desire to alter our Constitution." Now, in the May 1794 elections, voters across the state were urged to choose representatives "who will do their utmost to obtain a new Convention." Henry directed voters to write the word *convention* on their ballots, so "it may be clearly evinced to both branches of the Legislature that it is the wish of a great majority of the citizens." This action would be supported with legislative petitions "declaring our *determination* to obtain a new Convention."

The third statement from the Bourbon County Democratic Society did not appear in the *Kentucky Gazette* until the fall. A man who signed himself "Moses" had recently complained that such groups as the Bourbon Society were a nuisance to public order, stirring up discontent and undermining government authority. Another critic advised the Society's members to "quit politics and attend to your farms, your flocks and herds with diligence."[71] William Henry, in his capacity as the Society's president, responded to these "acrimonious invectives" and "chattering of the Magpie" with a full list of grievances and their history, calling once again for constitutional revision.[72] Foremost among these grievances, several of which echoed the recent complaints of "A Farmer," was the election of magistrates to the legislature. Henry asked, "Can a set of men be pointed out, whose judiciary powers is more extensive than that of Justices of the Peace, and Quarter Sessions Judges? and yet they are often our Legislators." A second grievance focused on the role of the governor, claiming that legislative recommendations and veto power gave the executive too much lawmaking authority. While conceding that Governor Shelby exercised his authority with discretion, the constitution offered inadequate protection against abuses of power. The Senate received a much more extensive critique. Henry spoke first against the indirect procedure of selecting senators through electors. He also recommended reducing the senatorial term of office from four years to only one. The Senate's power to fill its vacancies occurring during the four years between elections was also challenged, with Henry noting that six (nearly half) of the current state senators had not been elected. Only a new constitution could remedy such serious problems.

These complaints had an effect. The proportion of local representatives serving concurrently in the judiciary decreased sharply in the 1794 election, and in 1795 a new law made the Court of Quarter Sessions judges ineligible for elective office. But the reform was incomplete. Election results for later years indicates that voter sensitivity diminished quickly. Similarly, the law did not affect justices of the peace. Neither did it prove difficult to circumvent. Statewide, the proportion of legislators tied to the local courts changed very little.[73] Only a new state constitution would really separate the branches of government and reduce the centralized structure of power.

The 1792 constitution stipulated that a constitutional referendum should be conducted in 1797, with a convention to follow majorities in two consecutive referendums. This had been George Nicholas's idea, in the expectation that the new state would soon attract more members of the gentry and who would be better able to grapple with constitutional issues. He came to regret this provision, however, because it quickly became a rallying point for democrats, emancipationists, and other malcontents. Indeed, the state of Kentucky had been barely a year old before the Bourbon County Democratic Society began calling for a new constitution. Public discontent was sufficiently widespread that by 1794 the House responded to a Bourbon County petition "to take the sense of the people regarding a convention to amend the constitution." A similar bill was passed the following year. Both bills, however, were blocked by the Senate. Thus, declared the Bourbon County democrats and their allies, had the aristocratic few "trampled upon . . . the sovereign *will of the people.*" The Kentucky constitution, however, called for a referendum to be conducted as part of the state elections in May 1797. Unfortunately, the poll was inadequately publicized, and the confusion on election day resulted in embarrassingly irregular returns.[74]

The meaning of these "silent votes" became the focus of a critical showdown between House and Senate. Had the voters not participated in the referendum because they were content, or because they had not been told of it? The House insisted that the irregular returns still demonstrated that a majority of voters favored a convention. It therefore implemented the procedure stipulated in the state constitution and authorized a second poll for the May 1798 elections. The Senate, on the other hand, felt justifiably threatened by the prospect of a new constitution. In the few years since statehood, it had repeatedly blocked popular legislation. The indirect election of senators, through electors, and the Senate's authority to fill vacancies in its body through appointment came under increasing fire. Anxious to prevent the reduction of power a new constitution would certainly bring about, Kentucky's state senators tried various measures to avoid a second referendum. The result was a prolonged impasse with the House.

Public interest ran so high during all this turmoil that the newspapers published the legislative debates in full. No sign can be found showing organized democratic activity as had occurred earlier, even in Bourbon County. None may have been necessary. Letters from various convention proponents echoed the old democratic arguments, contending that the fundamental issue was the people's right to decide how to constitute their government and that an aristocratic minority represented by the Senate sought to undermine this right. The people held the right to reconstitute their government at any time they saw fit, proponents insisted, and the 1792 constitution merely specified that the people be consulted in 1797. Most Kentuckians apparently agreed that the Senate was wrong in insisting that the 1797 referendum was optional. As a result, when election day 1798 arrived with the Senate still stubbornly rejecting the House's enabling bill, a second poll occurred anyway. The extra-legal ballot confirmed that a majority of voters favored a second convention.[75] Public support was also evident in the legislative elections. Incumbents who had resisted a new constitution found reelection difficult. Voter opinion having made itself known, the next step lay with the legislature when it convened in the autumn.

At this crucial moment, popular outcry against the Alien and Sedition Acts enabled John Breckinridge, George Nicholas's protégé and the leading opponent of constitutional reform, to regain public favor.[76] The summer of 1798 was punctuated by a series of rallies in nearly half of the counties in Kentucky. The resolutions adopted at these meetings varied slightly in form, but followed a pattern set by Breckinridge. First, they denounced any alliance with the "corrupt and sinking monarchy of Britain" and charged hostile relations with France as being "impolitic, unnecessary and unjust." The old colonial apprehension that standing armies were a first step toward despotism resurfaced. Resolutions called for reducing the president's authority as commander-in-chief. The Alien and Sedition laws were denounced as "infractions of our constitution, injurious to the American character, and repugnant to the spirit of our government."[77] The unanimity of public feeling in Kentucky was unprecedented. By the time Breckinridge presented the Kentucky Resolutions to the legislature in November, his political popularity and that of his gentry allies seemed wholly restored if not actually enhanced.

Nothing, however, could halt the call for a new state constitution. When the Kentucky legislature reconvened that autumn, everyone resumed their old positions. The problem of the irregular 1797 poll remained unresolved, and the 1798 referendum had been unauthorized. Nonetheless, large proportion of voters desired a convention, and it seemed politically sensible to comply. After much bitter wrangling, a bill finally passed. Voters would choose convention delegates at the next state election, in May 1799, with a convention to be held the following July.

Coerced into a convention, Breckinridge, Nicholas, and other defenders of property turned their attention to the campaign for delegates. Properly organized, they believed that the problems encountered during the 1791 campaign for convention delegates could be avoided. They commenced early. In the months preceding the election, the pair corresponded closely with their allies in the various counties, orchestrating committee meetings and coordinating essays for the newspapers. They also deftly guided the nomination of local candidates through religious and militia organizations, a strategy ironically reminiscent of the county committees they had once so vehemently attacked. The Kentucky gentry still regarded themselves as the most qualified to lead, and many still regarded electioneering as undignified, but they had learned to do what was necessary to win election. George Nicholas wrote to former governor Isaac Shelby regarding the selection of candidates, "they should not only be good men, but such of that class as are most popular." Shelby was a perfect example of this model, being one of Kentucky's richest planters but one whose public reputation had originated from military leadership in the border warfare accompanying the War for Independence.[78]

The conservative platform, as unveiled by Nicholas at a large public rally held on January 26 at Bryan's Station Baptist meetinghouse in Fayette County, included legislative representation by population rather than by county, a measure which protected the hegemony of central Kentucky over the frontier interests of outlying regions. Other conservative planks called for a judiciary independent of legislative influence, protection of the compact with Virginia at the time of statehood ensuring the inviolability of land titles, and retention of the Ninth Article prohibiting legislative emancipation without the consent of slave owners or full compensation. The conservatives also insisted on a bicameral legislature, although possibly with the upper house directly elected and with shorter tenure. This latter point represented a major concession. The democrats had been demanding reform of the Senate since 1793. Poor relations between the House and the Senate had since convinced others. Nicholas and Breckinridge realized that levels of frustration had reached a point where some sort of reform was inescapable.

Having already capitulated on the need for Senate reform, emancipation remained as the last major issue. Public opinion was divided about emancipation. On one hand, the need for field labor had encouraged western slavery. Since Kentucky's admission as a state, the number of individuals owning slaves had increased significantly. A quarter of all taxpayers, more than thirty-two thousand in the state, owned slaves. These voters, and doubtless others yet too poor to purchase a slave, viewed the institution with an expansionist cast of mind. On the other hand, some citizens, particularly religious evangelicals, viewed slavery as immoral and a detriment to a republican society. Reverend David Rice believed that many poorer Kentuckians were sympathetic to gradual emancipation.[79] Just how many was nonetheless unclear.

While the main impetus for a new constitution centered around the "aristocratical Senate," Kentucky's small number of emancipationists welcomed an opportunity to purge the hated Ninth Article protecting slavery.[80] Essays in the newspapers discussed emancipation carefully, anxious to avoid accusations that they wished to unconditionally eradicate slavery. Slavery was wrong, they insisted, but abolition did not have to endanger property rights if implemented gradually. The legislatures of other states had successfully formulated such schemes, and so could that of Kentucky if the 1792 constitution's Ninth Article requiring full compensation prior to emancipation was eliminated. Drop the constitutional obstacles to creative legislation, they argued, and a just solution became possible.[81] Their position was summarized in a resolution adopted at a public meeting in Scott County for the nomination of emancipationist candidates: "That Slavery, as it now exists in this state, is a great national evil, and incompatible with a free government, and ought to be abolished as soon as equity and the safety of the state will admit. Therefore, no article shall be inserted in our constitution, which, either expressly, or by implication may warrant the enacting of laws continuing so impolitic a nuisance."[82]

To minds that viewed a convention with apprehension, reform of the

Senate and emancipation shared a similar thrust against property rights. Breckinridge had written Governor Shelby in 1798, "If they can by one experiment emancipate our slaves; the same principle pursued, will enable them at a second experiment to extinguish our land titles: both are held by rights equally sound."[83] An astute politician, Breckinridge realized that it was much easier to defend property rights than to defend the unpopularity of Senate actions. His public arguments against a second constitution had therefore dwelt more on the dangers of emancipation than any other issue, and as election day approached, Breckinridge resumed his critique. Besides posing a threat to the general social and economic order, he argued, emancipation was no different than any other sort of threat to property rights. Prolific and shrewd, Breckinridge managed to deflect criticism of elite dominance in government by turning emancipation into the campaign's central issue.

These efforts paid off well. By conceding in the Bryan's Station platform the need to reform the senate and judiciary, Breckinridge stole much of the momentum from reform advocates. The democratic partisans had already vented their main complaints during the long struggle for a new constitution. They had little more to say that was new. Most objections to the Bryan's Station resolutions were consequently reduced to minor issues. One critic, for instance, insisted that universal free manhood suffrage, already an established tradition in Kentucky, deserved a specific constitutional guarantee.[84] Breckinridge and Nicholas had left the old democratic champions with little room to maneuver. No county committee or similar group appeared, even in Bourbon County, although some emancipationists organized opposing slates of candidates. With the campaign reduced to practically a single issue, one in which about a quarter of all voters already had a vested interest, the Bryan's Station candidates met with general success. "In truth the emancipation fume has long evaporated," observed one man after the convention, "and not a word is now said about it." Only four emancipationists had been elected "upon any plan however modified."[85]

The contrast between the convention proceedings of 1792 and those of 1799 is striking from any point of view. Despite the success of the Bryan's Station resolutions, gentry interests did not dominate the deliberations of the convention. George Nicholas died just as the delegates convened, and even had he been present, it is doubtful whether he could have reprised his earlier role. Compared with the delegates in 1792, this second group included more established community leaders, justices of the peace, officers in the militia, and other men of property and standing. Many had gained substantial legislative experience since 1792. They were certainly less impressionable, holding their own opinions about the merits and shortcomings of the original constitution. Furthermore, differences of social rank among the delegates spanned a much narrower range by 1799. Not only had safer conditions diminished the premium placed on military ability; many of the men originally selected for public office on the basis of military skill had since seen significant improvement in their economic condition as well as their social standing. Meanwhile, the old gentry had been changing as well, learning to put themselves in front of popular issues including, but as will be shown, not only, protest against the Alien and Sedition Acts. Consequently, while the second constitutional convention had more roll call votes, none came from deep ideological alignments. Delegates formed and dissolved coalitions throughout the convention.[86] A new, more stable politics was finally emerging.

The convention itself produced few surprises. The two most controversial issues, Senate reform and emancipation, had been essentially predetermined by the voters in their insistence on a convention and their support of the Bryan's Station platform. Nicholas's Ninth Article was accordingly retained. The indirect selection of senators, through electors, was abandoned. In addition, the Senate was expanded to twenty-four members, each to be elected from a separate district. As Kentucky's population grew, a new seat in the Senate would be added for every three new seats in the House. Most of the other alterations decentralized the government's power structure, reversing what Nicholas had so carefully devised in 1792. Though important, these changes largely confirmed a trend which had commenced almost from the first day of statehood. The legislature, which included a significant number of county justices, had over the years redistributed powers originally reserved for the higher courts, particularly after a notorious decision in 1795 that had wreaked havoc on Kentucky land titles. Now the executive branch came under review. The governor's broad appointive powers were left virtually intact except for the state treasurer and public printer. More serious was that the governor's veto could now be overridden by a simple majority, rather than a two-thirds majority as before. The governor's strength was also reduced by making the incumbent ineligible for reelection. The other significant area of reform involved the reapportionment of the House. The creation of outlying counties as settlement expanded, often with small populations, threatened the hegemony of Kentucky's Bluegrass core. The convention eventually adopted a compromise that closely approximated existing levels of representation. The 1799 constitution also reversed a few measures that had originated with the county committees, such as the use of ballots, but these reversals were prompted more by practical considerations than by ideology.[87]

The second constitutional convention was thus as anticlimactic as the first, but for very different reasons. In 1792, Nicholas had overwhelmed and outmaneuvered the populist contingent. But the following years, particularly the insistent call for a new constitution, proved that he could not stem the movement it represented. Statehood had therefore brought little peace as legislative proceedings struggled to hammer out a more appropriate arrangement. The last major elements in this process were dealt with during the 1799 election for convention delegates. Thus, instead of overturning what Nicholas had accomplished in 1792, as the Bourbon County democrats had no doubt hoped when they initiated their call for a new constitution in 1793, Kentucky's second constitution represented the formal expression of an emerging consensus. At the time, unfortunately, it still looked to many Kentuckians less like the birth of a new political order than just a terrible and unending crisis.

The period preceding the Great Revival was thus one of exceptional political turmoil. Kentucky, like the rest of postrevolutionary America, was engaged in a painful transition between two political cultures, from one based on a hierarchical but organic conception of society to one more egalitarian and partisan. The adherents of each perspective were convinced that their opponents posed a moral threat. On one hand, the gentry feared that the ignorance of the masses would not only deprive them of their property but lead to anarchy. On the other hand, the democrats feared that the gentry's insatiable appetite for power and wealth, as well as their lack of personal virtue, made them unfit to lead a republic. This conflict was especially acute in Kentucky where the steadying influence of established practice and familiar leadership was largely missing. Statehood offered no cure. Quite the opposite, statehood brought the tension to the center of government, where it haunted public debate through the rest of the 1790s.

The political climate was much calmer by the time of the Great Revival, but with the 1799 constitution barely a year old, this had yet to be felt. For many of the people who camped together around Kentucky meetinghouses in 1800 and 1801, the political realm still appeared disturbingly contentious and corrupt. That religion might offer special appeal under such circumstances would seem wholly understandable. It was probably no accident that camp meeting participants were amazed by the loving atmosphere of the early camp meetings. For some ten thousand people to suddenly become capable of peaceful coexistence for several days running presented the sharpest possible contrast to secular reality. All the more remarkable, no government authority enforced the peace. Camp meeting revivalism offered respite as well as inspiration to a politically weary and anxious population.

6

WESTERN SETTLEMENT
AND NATIONAL POLICY

An important role awaited the U.S. government in supervising the settlement of its citizens in the North American interior, but this role remained largely unfulfilled during the eighteenth century. Western expansion was overshadowed by the more immediate problems of establishing independence and then creating a viable national government. Even the 1787 Northwest Ordinance, arguably the Confederation's most significant achievement, fell victim to other concerns on the national agenda. Ten years later, settlement of the Northwest Territory was barely under way.

Most Kentuckians believed their interests had met a similar fate. The rest of the country seemed little concerned that for trans-Appalachian settlers the conflict with Britain's native allies had not ended, only diminished. Neither did Americans elsewhere share western concerns that the peace with the European powers had not secured American navigation rights to the Mississippi. And the sectional jealousies that westerners thought lay behind this neglect seemed likely to worsen rather than improve, raising the possibility of discriminatory legislation. As one Kentuckian recalled a few years later, "It was a generally received opinion that the Eastern States were unfriendly to the population of the Western country," and unsympathetic to its special needs as a newly settled region. From a Kentucky perspective, therefore, the stronger national government established by the Constitution boded ill.[1]

This feeling solidified as President Washington's administration took shape. In particular, the inadequate resources given to Indian relations, the reluctance to press the Spanish for American trading privileges through New Orleans, and the federal excise on distilled spirits all seemed aimed at keeping the western settlements in a colony-like dependence. Federal policy seemed so uniformly injurious that some Kentuckians wondered whether a conspiracy might not be afoot. A few even entertained thoughts of secession. Although loyalty to the United States was too strong to allow such a radical step, a number of westerners displayed an alarming readiness to resist its authority, if necessary, with violence. For Kentucky's gentry elite, however, the federal crisis proved an excellent political opportunity. By positioning themselves as defenders against an external tyrant, they found they could restore their popularity with western voters who otherwise distrusted the gentry. Overall, instead of being a source of stability, the national government was a source of ferment, adding further to the disorganized condition of western society. The participants of the Great Revival thus lived in a world of acute political upheaval, not only at the local level but also higher.

Western Military Policy

General Cornwallis's surrender at Yorktown brought peace to most sections of the new United States, but not on the Native American frontier. Britain formally ceded the territory north of the Ohio River and east of the Mississippi in the Treaty of Paris, but U.S. sovereignty also had to be acknowledged by Britain's former Indian allies before the land could be opened to American settlement. The region in question was homeland for a number of native groups. The Iroquois Six Nations, headed by the shrewd Joseph Brant, claimed territory in western Pennsylvania and eastern Ohio. The Delaware and Wyandot occupied eastern and central Ohio. The Shawnee dominated western Ohio. The Mingo as well as branches of the Ottawa and Chippewa were also in the area. Along the Wabash River further to the west were the Miami, Wea, and Piankashaw. To the north were the Pottowatomi. Some of these groups, the Shawnee in particular, had been at war with American settlers since before the Revolution, and they remained a formidable enemy. Although the British had lost the war, their Indian allies remained undefeated. Furthermore, the prewar alliance remained intact, a source of arms and supplies from Canada.[2]

The new American government approached negotiations with the assumption that the Great Lakes Indians had lost their territorial rights through their unfortunate alliance with the British. The United States therefore demanded acknowledgment of American sovereignty north of the Ohio River and cessions of native territory in southern and eastern Ohio. In late 1784, at Fort Stanwick, the Iroquois Six Nations ceded land in western Pennsylvania. The following January at Fort McIntosh, the Delaware, Wyandot, Chippewa, and Ottawa agreed to retreat to the northwestern corner of Ohio. A year later at Fort Finney, located at the mouth of the Great Miami River, the Shawnee agreed to stay on the western side. The American emissaries congratulated themselves for their superb handling of their heathen guests, but these treaties actually achieved little. Not only was an important opportunity to establish goodwill squandered but the Indian participants proved unable to obtain their peoples' assent. American surveyors and settlers meanwhile began to infiltrate the Ohio territory, provoking renewed resistance. The Confederation government tried to rectify matters with two treaties in early 1789, offering nine thousand dollars worth of trade goods in exchange for a confirmation of the earlier treaties, but the Shawnees refused to participate, and their example was followed by other native groups.

As tensions increased between the United States and the Ohio tribes, daily life resumed its terror in Kentucky, particularly for stations facing the Ohio River. In 1786, Benjamin Logan reported to the governor of Virginia, "The Enemy are repeating there Barbarities almost every day in some part of the Country. . . . Several settlements are Avacuated in this country with the loss of defferent People." A year later, as the winter snows melted and the war season approached, Colonel Levi Todd reported similar difficulties in Fayette County: "We have every reason to expect, as soon as the season permits, to experience the united efforts of all the neighboring Indian Tribes. Apprehensive of this, our frontier settlements give way, and 'tis with difficulty that Settlers can be prevailed on to stay at such frontier places as we conceive of the greatest Importance." Shortly thereafter Todd reported that eastern Jefferson County and lower Mercer County had been wholly evacuated. The spring of 1788 saw little improvement. Rather, even well-populated districts experienced danger. One of the most shocking demonstrations of this occurred one night when a cabin in Bourbon County was surrounded and set ablaze, the family killed as they fled from the flames. The incident set off a local panic. "The Inhabitants . . . are alarmed and moving," reported two militia officers, "and when this once begins, 'tis Hard to say where the evil will terminate, or what part may be a frontier." The area of settlement in Mercer County had contracted by thirty miles just the previous year.[3]

Kentucky seemed as endangered as at any time during the Revolutionary struggle, but the intervening years had wrought a dramatic transformation. Whereas the settlements had once been too isolated and weak for much more than a defensive response, postwar growth encouraged a more aggressive strategy. Western inhabitants believed that preemptive strikes in Ohio were the surest way to prevent Indian raids in Kentucky, and they were eager for revenge. The governments of Virginia and the Confederation, however, were apprehensive of provoking a general Indian war for which they were ill prepared. Kentuckians could pursue attackers to the Ohio River, but were prohibited from crossing over after them. The policy caused much resentment. Levi Todd wrote to Virginia's governor in 1787, "We complain much that the Legislative Body have tied the Hands of the Kentucky people in such a manner as to prevent our lifting Arms against those who daily invade us." National policy elicited similar complaints. Recent political reports, wrote Judge Harry Innes, "serve but to convince us that Congress doth not mean to give us that protection, which as part of the Federal Union we are entitled to."[4] As the raids continued, western frustration became a growing factor in the campaign for independence from Virginia and admission as a state. A few radical souls were "decidedly of opinion that this western Country will, in a few years, Revolt from the Union and endeavor to erect an Independent Government."[5]

The new United States, racked by debts and sectional rivalries, could do little to aid western citizens. Neither could it prevent them from mounting occasional retaliatory raids across the Ohio. In 1788, for example, a party of sixty Kentuckians reached Vincennes intent on revenge and attacked friendly Piankashaws—while the handful of federal troops at Fort Knox stood by, too weak to intervene. As tensions mounted, such incidents occurred with increasing frequency. Yet Kentucky could not achieve permanent peace without national assistance. Unfortunately, Americans elsewhere opposed the expense of waging a fresh war when the country was yet recovering from its recent struggle with Britain. Some also worried about the moral aspect; as a nation so recently founded on principle, to now let power dominate seemed dangerously contradictory. Congress therefore authorized only the smallest possible force. Even so, recruitment was difficult. Quotas remained unfilled, and quality left much to be desired. According to one officer, the recruits were generally "the offscourings of large Towns and Cities;—enervated by Idleness, Debaucheries and every species of Vice." The hardship and low pay of military service made it nearly impossible to recruit anyone but criminals and boys eager for adventure. Forging this motley collection into professional soldiers posed innumerable difficulties.[6]

The lack of an effective professional army meant a heavy reliance on supplementary forces drawn from state militias. The main advantage of using militia to augment the army was cost; militia required pay and provisions only for their period of active service, usually only two to three months. Because military campaigning coincided with the agricultural seasons, however, filling militia quotas was sometimes nearly as difficult as for regular troops. And, once recruited, militia units demanded special treatment. Militia soldiers were extremely conscious of their status as free citizens and looked with disdain on regular soldiers, who fought for pay rather than patriotism. In addition, the western militia viewed themselves as experienced Indian fighters. As a result, discipline was usually lax. Especially problematic was that when a term of service had expired, sometimes at a crucial point in the campaign, few men could be prevailed on to remain longer. As one professional officer sent to Ohio observed, "Militia show great impatience; their officers appear to have little influence. One-third turn out with a determination to go back, a few are prevailed on to stay."[7] The need to avoid an expensive professional army, however, made militia participation necessary.

The first major attempt to pacify the Ohio frontier occurred soon after Washington took office. Secretary of War Henry Knox directed General Josiah Harmar, headquartered at Fort Washington (the future site of Cincinnati), to "extirpate utterly, if possible," the Indians who were raiding the settlements. The summer campaigning season was nearly over, but Harmar left Fort Washington in late September of 1790, proceeding slowly northward with a force of 1,453 men. Only 320 of these soldiers were regular troops; the rest were drawn from the Kentucky and Pennsylvania militias. Harmar's careful advance allowed the Indians ample time to evacuate their towns. These were torched, but the failure to engage the enemy was embarrassing. Harmar then detached three hundred men to find the Indians, who he believed had not gone very far off. When the troops returned without success, Colonel John Hardin of Kentucky boasted that he and his militia could do better. Eager to upstage the regular army troops, Hardin moved forward boldly but stepped into an ambush. The self-acclaimed superior talent of Kentuckians in Indian warfare was not much in evidence as most of the men fled in panic, abandoning a few brave souls to their deaths. Rather than retaliate, Harmar began the return to Fort Washington. But first he dispatched a force of three hundred militia and sixty regular troops to return to the burned village site in hopes of surprising the Indians as they returned. Although the plan worked, once again, the lack of discipline in the militia proved disastrous, and Harmar returned to Fort Washington in disgrace. Of 320 regular troops, 75 had been killed. The militia dead numbered 108, blamed by western citizens on the timid and inept federal commander. Worst of all, instead of being subdued, the Indians were furious at the destruction of their towns and emboldened by their victory.[8]

Anxious to minimize the political damage, Congress readily authorized an additional regiment of troops, but organizing a fresh expedition before the upcoming summer campaign season was difficult. Neither additional soldiers nor supplies were very forthcoming, which put any expedition seriously behind schedule. Generals Charles Scott and James Wilkinson of Kentucky led militia expeditions in early summer, trying to create enough havoc in Ohio to prevent the Indians from resuming their attacks on settlers. Though few Indians were killed, the campaigns helped placate western opinion, which had little confidence in the ability of regular troops for border warfare. Meanwhile, the army's preparations proceeded slowly. Not until September 17 did the refurbished army begin working its way northward into Indian territory.

The commander of this army was Arthur St. Clair, governor of the

Northwest Territory. His instructions were to establish a secure military post at the Maumee-Wabash portage, a strategically important location, which would be connected to Fort Washington by a chain of smaller posts. The first of these was Fort Hamilton, twenty-five miles north of Fort Washington, the construction of which consumed two valuable weeks. Constructing forts also eroded morale. The militia balked at having to work like common laborers when they had been recruited to fight Indians. The regular troops were not any happier. Getting the work done under these conditions took extra time and patience.

After stopping forty-five miles north of Fort Hamilton to construct Fort Jefferson, St. Clair moved northward again on October 24. It was now dangerously late in the season, and progress was slowed by miserable weather. Hacking their way through the wilderness, the cumbersome military train advanced only a few miles each day. St. Clair, laid low with an attack of gout and unable to ride, was carried in a litter. Discipline deteriorated to new lows. Despite strong evidence of Indians, standard precautions were allowed to lapse. Not surprisingly, when Indians sprang a dawn attack on November 4, the entire camp fled in a general panic. American casualties numbered nearly six hundred. St. Clair's defeat was a major disaster, but especially so in Kentucky where most of the militia had been recruited.[9]

The defeats of Harmar and St. Clair convinced Secretary of War Knox that the militia was "utterly unsuitable" except for use in "sudden enterprises, of short duration." Convincing Congress to strengthen the army was still not easy. Every possibility for peaceful resolution had to be exhausted before justifying military force. After lengthy debate, Congress passed legislation in March 1792 to repair and augment the western forces. A new recruiting drive increased the size of the army to approximately 5,128 men. These troops were to serve three years, or until the United States achieved peace with the Indians. Militia would not be involved except as cavalry, enabling the army to avoid the expense of a permanent unit. As commander of this new force, President Washington chose Revolutionary veteran Anthony Wayne.[10]

The soundness of Washington's choice was not immediately apparent. Wayne was determined to create an effective fighting force, one that would follow orders under any conditions—even an Indian ambush. This required strict discipline. Wayne worked through the winter training his men, and in early May he descended the Ohio to Fort Washington, where he impatiently awaited further orders pending a final peace initiative. But when word finally came to proceed, it was already mid-September and too late in the season for a full campaign. As 1793 drew to a close, little had been achieved other than the erection of a new stockade six miles north of Fort Jefferson, which Wayne named Fort Greenville.

Wayne's slow progress struck western critics as a repeat of the St.

Clair fiasco. Pressure again mounted to allow the Kentuckians, with their experience in Indian warfare, a free hand. Wayne's force included two brigades of mounted Kentucky militia under the command of General Charles Scott, and in large measure to appease his western critics, Wayne agreed to let them undertake an independent action. Scott's mounted Kentuckians were believed inadequate for an attack against the main body of Indians, so on November 3 they were detached to eliminate an Indian hunting camp serving as a base of support for raids into Kentucky. Despite Scott's popularity, about half of his men deserted, deciding that such an insignificant objective was not worth the short rations and cold rain. The remainder captured the camp, but the five Indians they found all escaped. It was an embarrassing finale. The Kentuckians headed home, and Wayne's army went into winter camp at Fort Recovery, built on the site of St. Clair's disastrous defeat two years earlier. Although symbolically important, it was apparent to all that Fort Recovery contributed little to the larger military objective.

Thus, yet another military season passed with little accomplished. One Kentucky gentleman reported that winter, "The people here have generally forfieted all patience with the Secretary of the Treasury & the Secretary of War—and it appears that not a man in the whole State could be found a friend to either of them & enmity with the Eastern States daily encreases." That winter several more Kentucky civilians died in small Indian raids, not to mention the loss of horses and other property, making Kentuckians angrier about the national government's military shortcomings. Most blamed the militia's poor showing on the federal commanders and remained confident that the Kentucky militia could do a much more effective job against the Ohio tribes—if only it were unfettered from federal constraints. Governor Isaac Shelby certainly thought so, and he urged Secretary Knox to grant the Kentucky militia a chance to prove it, but Knox was not about to place the fate of Ohio in the hands of a group whom he had come to view as full of bravado and utterly unreliable. Meanwhile, western sentiment was such that retaliatory raids into Ohio were seldom prosecuted by state authorities."

Kentuckians finally achieved security the following summer as a result of General Wayne's victory at Fallen Timbers. In spring 1794, the old Indian confederation of Shawnee, Delaware, Wyandot, Iroquois, Chippewa, Miami, and related groups reassembled. Amply supplied by the British, they presented a formidable force. On August 20, only about ten miles from the British garrison at Fort Miami, the Americans encountered a large contingent of Indians defensively positioned among a tangle of trees uprooted several years earlier by a tornado. Wayne, mistakenly believing that the entire Indian confederation stood before him, ordered a full bayonet charge. The thin line of Indians fell back in complete disarray, everything happening so suddenly that they had no chance to regroup and mount a counteroffensive. When the Indians retreated in desperation to Fort Miami a short distance away, the British commander had the stockade gates shut before them. Thus ended the old alliance. The battle of Fallen Timbers lasted barely an hour and involved combined casualties of fewer than a hundred men, but it shattered Indian power throughout the Great Lakes. In August the following year, the defeated tribes assembled for treaty negotiations at Fort Greenville, where they ceded most of Ohio.[12]

Those national leaders who believed that Fallen Timbers would quell western critics were much mistaken. Wayne's success brought little gratitude. Writing in late 1795, George Nicholas reported, Wayne's victory "is no more spoken of, than if it had never taken place at all."[13] The feeling prevailed in Kentucky that westerners could have eliminated the Indian danger faster and just as effectively had national authorities only permitted them to do so. Instead, hundreds of Kentucky militiamen lay in shallow, unmarked graves. Despite the official findings that attributed Harmar's and St. Clair's defeats to poor discipline in the militia, Kentuckians placed the blame squarely on government ineptitude if not downright disregard for western interests. Wayne's dramatic success at Fallen Timbers was therefore not enough to restore western faith in the national government. Though divided on internal political matters, Kentuckians were united in this perception. Just as significant were their other grievances with the national government.

The Mississippi Navigation

Long before Kentucky gained total security in 1794, western Americans realized that their future prosperity depended on access to the Mississippi River. The bountiful yields of Kentucky soil, increasing rapidly as settlement expanded, made planter and yeoman alike yearn for external markets. Already by 1787, reported one settler, Kentuckians were producing twice the produce they needed for subsistence.[14] Although the flood of immigrants provided a market for foodstuffs, all ranks of Kentuckians realized that long-term prosperity hinged on the opportunity to send American produce through the Spanish port of New Orleans. "I long much to hear some thing respecting the trade of the Mississippi[.] the time draws on that great quanti[ti]es of Tobo., Flour, Beef, pork, Hemp, &c. will be for market," wrote one Kentuckian in a 1793 letter to a Virginia kinsman. "Improvements in this Country is almost beyond conception, both as to society and agriculture."[15] Western expectations increased with every passing year. Without the Mississippi, Kentucky's prospects remained limited.

Unfortunately, just as the national government's slowness to adequately defend the Kentuckians had led them to mount their own military campaigns, so did its slowness in acquiring navigational privileges on

the lower Mississippi lead to efforts to deal with Spain directly. Kentuckians asserted that American possession of the Ohio Valley entitled the
citizenry to full privileges to all water courses running through it. They
had been disappointed when the close of the Revolution left Spain in control of the Mississippi, but had expected that a diplomatic resolution would
soon follow. These hopes came close to ruin as a result of negotiations led
by the American secretary of foreign affairs, John Jay, who like most Federalists believed that westward expansion would siphon off the young
republic's energy and strength. Neither was Spain eager to lure masses of
American settlers across the Appalachians. Negotiations stalled, and in
late May 1786 Jay requested from Congress permission to officially put
the Mississippi navigation on hold for twenty-five or thirty years. Westerners were livid when they learned of Jay's recommendation, and the
issue dominated congressional debate for the rest of the summer. A number of national leaders understood that sacrificing something so vital to
western interests for the national welfare might lead to a secession. And,
as Thomas Jefferson pointed out, should western Americans "declare themselves a separate people, we are incapable of a single effort to retain them."
Congress eventually refused Jay's request, and negotiations collapsed. The
episode nonetheless left a deep imprint on western relations with the national government.[16]

One result was that almost immediately thereafter, James Wilkinson,
former Revolutionary general and recent emigrant to Kentucky, attempted
an independent diplomacy. His object was both personal and political. In
addition to obtaining trading privileges for himself, he suggested to the
Spanish governor at New Orleans that Kentucky's desire for access to the
Mississippi might support a Spanish alliance if properly approached. By
the time Wilkinson returned to Kentucky in May 1788, however, the political climate had changed. Although Harry Innes and a few other leaders
looked favorably on a union with Spain, the ratification of the Constitution now dominated all political conversation.[17] The moment for secession had passed, and plans for union with Spain were quietly set aside lest
the proponents thereof appear disloyal.

Unfortunately, hope that the new government would be more respon-
sive soon subsided. Opposition in the form of a democratic-republican
society appeared by early August 1793 in Lexington. Modeled after a similar Anti-Federalist organization in Philadelphia, its members included some
of Kentucky's foremost political characters, with Kentucky's attorney general, John Breckinridge, selected as president. Breckinridge and his friends
possessed outstanding capabilities which, combined with inflammatory
words, gained for the Lexington Society widespread—indeed, national—
notoriety. Although Breckinridge and his fellow officers retained full control, the Lexington Democratic Society enjoyed popular support and

attracted some two hundred members. Several meetings were held at the statehouse.[18] Two similar organizations, in Bourbon and Scott Counties, appeared at about the same time. These two chapters displayed their own distinctive character and operated independently but shared the Lexington organization's Anti-Federal orientation.

According to Federalist Humphrey Marshall, a scathing critic, the democratic-republican societies "condemned and abused, . . . whatever had the name of federalist." For the most part, however, the Kentucky democratic societies reserved their criticism for those Federalist policies which most affected western settlement. As aptly summarized by Marshall, "The old subjects of Indian war, and the navigation of the Mississippi, were made to take up the front of complaint; while the excise [on whiskey] brought up the rear." According to John Bradford of the Lexington Society, "The leading object of the Society was to procure the navigation of the Mississippi river."[19] Although the democratic societies in Scott and Bourbon Counties shared this concern, the Lexington branch in Fayette County was its most ardent advocate, perhaps influenced by that society's more elite membership and Lexington's urban aspirations.

The Lexington Democratic Society picked up the cause of the Mississippi navigation only after more radical strategies had failed. In February 1793, before the appearance of democratic societies, an embittered George Rogers Clark had written to the French minister to the United States proposing a plan to lead a force of fifteen hundred Kentucky volunteers down the Mississippi against Spanish Louisiana. If successful, the expedition would not only open the Mississippi to American commerce but also strike a blow against Spain, which was then at war with France. The new French minister, Citizen Edmond Charles Genet, found Clark's letter awaiting him in Philadelphia upon his arrival in May. Genet's main objective as minister was to solicit American military support, drawing on American gratitude for the assistance that France had rendered during the Revolution. President Washington, however, was determined to maintain U.S. neutrality. Secretary of State Thomas Jefferson was more sympathetic, but when they met in July he warned Genet that encouraging Clark and his fellow Kentuckians was dangerous, "for they would surely be hung if they commensed hostilities against a nation at peace with the United States." Yet Jefferson's ambivalence is evident in his failure to alert the president that Genet intended to proceed with his plans. Nor did he alert the governor of Kentucky. Instead, Jefferson provided letters of introduction for Genet's chief agent, a French botanist named André Michaux.[20]

Michaux reached Kentucky by early September. Sending two subordinates to Louisville, probably to contact Clark, Michaux proceeded to consult with other political leaders at Lexington and Danville. On September 11 he contacted General Benjamin Logan, who with Clark was to lead the Kentucky expedition. Logan, however, withdrew from the venture, explaining that he "would be delighted to take part in the enterprise," but had recently received a cautionary letter from Kentucky senator John Brown. Brown's letter carried news of a new diplomatic initiative with Spain, which any hostile action against Louisiana would jeopardize. Shortly thereafter, Michaux conferred with Governor Isaac Shelby and probably divulged the nature of his mission. He then proceeded to Louisville to meet with Clark, who in the interim had concluded that France was uninterested. Moreover, a "fresh circumstance," possibly the same news that deterred Logan, now obstructed the plan. Although Clark's interest soon revived, Michaux judged Clark, who had developed a conspicuous drinking habit, "totally incapable of conducting such a business, and entirely without influence." As George Nicholas reported in a letter to James Madison, dated November 15, Michaux "sounded different characters in this country, but finding no disposition to engage in such an enterprise, he gave it up and has returned."[21]

Nonetheless, the Genet episode had a considerable effect. As Nicholas pointed out to Madison, "It has shewn us unquestionably that the French may be induced to join us in procuring what we are now satisfied our government wants inclination and spirit to obtain for us." A military solution suddenly seemed feasible. Nicholas was not alone in his belief that "the Western country united can bid defiance to the rest of America and to the Spaniards too." Just days before writing these words, Nicholas had met with Michaux and proposed an alternative to the Clark plan in which the French navy would capture the mouth of the Mississippi and invite the Americans to enjoy full navigational privileges. If the Spanish at New Orleans interfered with the American vessels, then the Americans could retaliate on grounds of self-defense.[22] Unfortunately, while this plan reduced American involvement, it required greater commitment of French resources, beyond what Michaux could personally authorize.

While Michaux awaited approval from his superiors, a very similar plan was being publicly advocated in Lexington. At a mass meeting on November 11, John Breckinridge led the Lexington Democratic Society in resolving, "That the free and undisturbed use and navigation of the river Mississippi is the NATURAL RIGHT of the inhabitants of the countries bordering on the waters communicating with that river, and is unalienable except with the SOIL." The Society also argued that the government's negotiations with Spain had been suspiciously feeble and that western interests were being sacrificed on behalf of the seaboard states. The Society resolved to petition both the president and Congress "in the bold decent and determined language proper to be used by injured freemen, when they address the servants of the people," demanding that "immediate and effectual steps" be taken to obtain navigation rights on the Mississippi.

These demands were accompanied by a threatening observation that "we are strong enough to obtain that right by force." Western readiness for action is also discernible in a resolution proposing to take an American boat "in a peaceable manner" down the Mississippi into the Gulf, so that "we may either procure an immediate acknowledgment of our right from the Spaniards; or if they obstruct us in the enjoyment of that right, that we may be able to lay before the Federal Government such unequivocal proofs of their having done so, that they will abandon or protect the inhabitants of the western country."[23] Copies of this brash document went to other western settlements accompanied by appeals for support. In addition, the Lexington Democratic Society pressed the Kentucky legislature and succeeded in obtaining a joint resolution that declared the navigation of the Mississippi as "the natural unalienable right of the citizens of this Commonwealth." The state's two senators were directed "to assert that right to the General Government."[24]

Meanwhile, knowledge of Genet's activities had reached Spanish authorities, who demanded that Washington take preventive action. Committed to American neutrality and angered by Genet's covert efforts to mobilize popular opinion against this policy, Washington responded decisively. In a letter dated August 29, Secretary of State Jefferson warned Governor Shelby of Genet's intentions and directed him to "take those legal measures which shall be necessary to prevent any such enterprise."[25] Shelby responded that he would be "particularly attentive to prevent any attempts" such as that described by Jefferson, but doubted that there was much to fear. Interestingly, he made no mention of his meeting with Michaux.[26] Shelby's response crossed in the mail with a second warning from Jefferson giving further details. In addition, Secretary of War Henry Knox authorized Shelby to "use effectual force to prevent the execution of the plan of the said Frenchmen, or any other persons who may support or abet their design."[27] General Anthony Wayne, commander of the western U.S. army, received orders to intercept any expedition out of Kentucky, and he placed a cavalry unit at Shelby's disposal. Although Shelby did not respond as firmly as did Governor St. Clair, who issued a proclamation requiring neutrality of all inhabitants under his jurisdiction in the Northwest Territory, Shelby appeared ready to uphold American policy. In late November one of the French agents wrote Shelby to verify rumors that Kentuckians who joined in the plans against New Orleans would be arrested. Shelby responded that any Americans preparing to invade Louisiana "should be warned against the consequences." Such action "will expose them to punishment, and . . . I should take those legal measures necessary to prevent any such enterprise."[28]

Despite these measures, plans for an American expedition against

New Orleans did not immediately die. The Lexington Democratic Society issued a handbill on December 31, 1793, announcing its readiness to send an American vessel through New Orleans, as had been proposed at the November 11 rally. The idea of a military expedition revived as well. Benjamin Logan, who had pulled out of the Clark expedition in September, now wrote Clark and offered his military services. In January, Clark publicly called for volunteers to assemble near Louisville, and he was reportedly gathering cannon and ammunition, although delays in the arrival of funds promised by the French hindered preparations. A resident of Cincinnati traveling through Kentucky in early April reported that some money had arrived and that "the boat builders, and other artificers for the expedition, had again recommenced, vigorously, their work at the rapids of the Ohio."[29]

The precise nature of the relationship between the activities of Clark and those of the Lexington Democratic Society, whose members included some of Kentucky's most prominent citizens, remains unclear. Secretary John Bradford testified many years later that the Lexington Democratic Society "positively refused to intermeddle with that enterprise." Other records, however, indicate that Bradford and several other leaders of the organization had pledged or furnished Clark with supplies and credit. Furthermore, the Society's leadership, after disassociating with Clark, continued to support his cause. In February, George Nicholas told James Madison, "The inhabitants of the western country have lost all confidence in the General government . . . what they demand is so clearly their right, and so indispensibly necessary to their welfare, that they must and will sacrifice every thing to obtain it."[30]

Efforts to resuscitate plans for an armed expedition were possible in part because of the ambivalence shown by Governor Shelby. In January 1794, Shelby responded to Jefferson's November letter and expressed doubts whether government intervention against private citizens who desired to leave the state was "necessary or proper," and he declared himself "averse to the exercise of any power which I do not consider myself as being clearly and explicitly invested with." Furthermore, Shelby felt "but little inclination to take an active part in punishing or restraining any of my fellow Citizens for a supposed intention only to gratify or remove the fears of a minister of a prince who openly withholds from us an invaluable right." Therefore, Shelby called upon President Washington to be "full and explicit as to the part he wishes and expects me to act." Shelby wanted no discretion, no responsibility. President Washington could not help but be disturbed by this, despite Shelby's promise that "whatever may be my private opinion . . . I shall at all times hold it as my duty to perform whatever may be constitutionally required of me as Governor of

Kentucky, by the President of the United States."[31] Governor Shelby would do his duty, but nothing more.

President Washington responded without hesitation. On March 24, he issued a proclamation declaring the plan against Louisiana illegal. Jefferson's successor as secretary of state, Edmund Randolph, dealt with Shelby, addressing the legal qualms raised in his January letter and reminding him of his duty. General Wayne received orders to re-garrison Fort Massac on the lower Ohio and intercept the Kentuckians should they proceed with their plans. Fortunately, matters never reached that point. By the time Wayne received his orders, western support was already receding. According to one observer, people felt that the Lexington Society had gone too far in the belligerent, threatening tone of its remonstrances. Perhaps more important, Breckinridge and his allies no longer supported a military expedition and had begun exploring less dangerous options. Clark, however, apparently did not abandon his plan completely until late April.[32]

In May Genet was recalled to France, but the final collapse of the French conspiracy against Louisiana by no means extinguished western discontent. Negotiations with Spain had not even begun when news of John Jay's appointment as minister to Great Britain inflamed westerners who remembered how less than a decade earlier as minister to Spain he had shown himself ready to "barter away" their "most valued right" to the Mississippi River. This traitor of western interests was now to confer with the other great enemy, Great Britain, whose flow of trade goods to the northern Indians enabled them to continue preying on American settlers. The Lexington Democratic Society promptly organized a large public meeting, held on May 24, where various speakers "address'd the people assembled upon the occasion in the most inflammatory & invective language."[33] The old claims to navigation rights on the Mississippi and the government's negligence in protecting these rights rang out once more. Again, the meeting produced a petition to the president and Congress, impatiently demanding redress. After stirring up the crowd, an effigy of Jay, "the Great Enemy of the Western Country," was in turn pilloried, guillotined, and burned. Having been filled beforehand with gunpowder, the phony Jay "produced such an explosion that after it there was scarcely to be found a particle of the *Dejecti membra Plenipo.*"[34]

After so many years of inaction and endless promises, assurances from Jefferson and others that the national government was now earnestly negotiating with Spain left many Kentuckians unimpressed. "We all agree the Spaniards are unjustly withholding our most invaluable rights," wrote a resident of Frankfort in 1794. "We fear the policy of the eastern States will prevent them from giving us any assistance. That their secret negotiations on the subject are . . . mere delusions."[35] In August, leading members of the Lexington Democratic Society attempted to verify the status of negotiations by interrogating John Edwards, Kentucky's Federalist senator, but his answers gave little if any reassurance.[36] Western discontent remained high, due in no small measure to the determined efforts of such figures as John Breckinridge, Harry Innes, Benjamin Sebastian, and George Nicholas. Even if most people were not ready to risk an illegal expedition against New Orleans, many agreed with the Democratic Society's president, John Breckinridge, when he declared, "Nature has done every thing for us; Government every thing against us." In his private correspondence and publicly as president of the Lexington society, Breckinridge continued to insist, "The Mississippi we *will* have. If government will not procure it for us, we must procure it for ourselves. Whether that will be done by the sword or by negotiations is yet to scan."[37] Coming from one of Kentucky's most talented and influential leaders, these were ominous words. Plans for sending an armed force against New Orleans, however, remained at rest.

The danger had nonetheless been serious enough for Washington and his advisers to take alarm. As Secretary of State Edmund Randolph confided to Jefferson, "What if the government of Kentucky should force us either to support them in their hostilities against Spain, or to disavow and renounce them? . . . The lopping off of Kentucky from the Union is dreadful to contemplate." Even President Washington, disgusted though he was by the impudence of his western critics, realized that further disturbances must be averted. In November he appointed Thomas Pinckney to open fresh negotiations with Spain for navigation privileges through New Orleans. In addition, Washington sent a special envoy to Kentucky to assure political leaders there that their concerns were receiving attention.[38] Little did he know that several of Kentucky's leading political lights had engaged in direct, covert, and treasonous negotiations with Spanish authorities at New Orleans. Though ultimately abandoned, these efforts nonetheless attest to western discontent at the highest levels.

Popular discontent also continued strong. In late 1795, public protests erupted again. This time the trouble was triggered by the news that Congressman Humphrey Marshall, one of the state's few Federalists, had defied western sentiment and voted in favor of the Jay Treaty with Great Britain. According to Francis Preston, writing to his brother in October, "I do believe if something decisive is not done by Congress to quiet the minds of the people much confusion will ensue, they have no confidence in the Government, distrust much their proceedings, and appear sore under their laws."[39] Fortunately, relief was already in sight. That same month, the Pinckney Treaty finally opened the Mississippi to American trade.

When news of it arrived in Kentucky, people in Lexington celebrated around public bonfires late into the night. Still, the government's standing with western citizens was not so easily repaired. Kentuckians had endured too many long years of frustration. Besides, another grievance remained unresolved.

The Excise on Domestic Distilled Spirits

Although resistance to the 1791 federal excise on domestically distilled spirits is most closely associated with western Pennsylvania, where President Washington used a militia force to quell resistance in late 1794, Kentucky posed no less a problem. There too the excise met with widespread, even violent, defiance. As in Pennsylvania, distilling was an important element in Kentucky's economy because it enabled farmers to render their surplus grain into a more marketable commodity. Most Kentucky whiskey was consumed locally, but it was already figuring as an item of exchange with settlements in other parts of the west such as Natchez, Illinois, and St. Louis. The federal excise thus affected a vital part of the western economy. Yet the opposition to it centered much more upon political than economic grounds. With remarkable uniformity, western distillers did not argue an inability to pay the excise; they argued the injustice of paying it. They saw the excise as a discriminatory tax because some citizens had to pay while others did not and because it burdened some regions much more than others. Many Kentuckians therefore agreed with Governor Shelby that the excise "seemed calculated to subvert the principles of the Revolution."[40]

The federal excise on domestic spirits also fit alarmingly well into the existing pattern of troubled relations with the national government, particularly the damning failure to secure American "natural rights" to the Mississippi River. Both issues seemed to demonstrate a lack of regard for the region's economic development. As one prominent Kentuckian reported to relatives in Virginia, "The Excise Law is much objected to in this country and is Doubtful whether some people will not Refuse paying it until the Mississippi is opened to . . . our produce." George Nicholas, one of Kentucky's best legal minds and himself a distiller, asked in a letter to James Madison, "Do you not think it is unjust to subject us to the excise until you give us the use of our rivers; is it not requiring us to make bricks without straw?" Other Kentucky distillers felt similarly. At a public meeting in Lexington on July 8, 1793, a group of distillers argued that because the Spanish at New Orleans prevented western access to markets, "the excise law is much more oppressive to the People of Kentucky than to those of other states." They declared, "The United States ought to see that we are equally protected in our trade before we are required to pay equal taxes under the law in specie only." The requirement that the excise be collected in specie drew particular protest because commercial relations with eastern merchants already siphoned off much of the circulating cash. In short, the government that unfairly suppressed Kentucky's development now seemed intent on bleeding it dry of what little prosperity it had yet cultivated.[41]

The excise proved difficult to enforce in Kentucky from the very outset. The chief revenue officer, Colonel Thomas Marshall, one of the very few Federalists in the western district, dutifully announced in the newspaper that the excise law would go into effect on July 1, 1791. Despite Marshall's diligence, problems began to surface almost immediately. The complicated method of calculating the excise required measuring the capacity of the stills, which, being custom made, followed no standard size. But because most stills were kept in steady use, excise agents found it practically impossible to measure their capacity. Frustrated, Marshall wrote in early 1792 to his superior in Virginia, "I presume you do not expect a strict compliance with those instructions, because that cannot be done." Marshall reported in the same letter that opposition to the excise was "visibly prevalent among the people." Two revenue agents had already been assaulted.[42]

Most distillers were passive in their resistance, either failing to register a still or failing to pay the tax on a registered still. Yet as Marshall's report indicates, violent resistance also occurred. Most such cases involved a lone distiller who lost his temper and forcibly drove the excise agents from the premises. A few incidents, however, suggest a degree of organization. In early 1793, for example, a quantity of whiskey that had been properly taxed and then purchased for the army was "rescued" from the collection agent. In 1797 the collector for Fayette County was pulled from his horse, tarred, and rolled in dry leaves. One of the better documented instances occurred in 1794 as collector William Hubble neared the end of his route through northeastern Kentucky and arrived at the house of Laban Shipp, a prosperous miller and distiller and a respected local figure in Bourbon County. Hubble stayed at Shipp's house for the night, intending to settle Shipp's account the next morning. During the night, however, the house was attacked by a group of men with blackened faces who absconded with Hubble's saddlebags containing more than one hundred dollars, the excise account book, and some personal items. Marshall strongly suspected Shipp "in some measure to be privy" to the crime, but even the unusual offer of one hundred dollars reward did not reveal the guilty parties.[43]

Violent resistance occurred rarely and caused little physical damage, but nonetheless opened the door to possible military intervention. President Washington responded with little hesitation in 1794 when whiskey rebels in western Pennsylvania torched the house of a local excise agent, personally leading a force nearly as large as his wartime army to quell the disturbance. When news of this reached Kentucky, many people worried that the government might resort to military force there, too. Judge Harry Innes of the Federal Court in Kentucky privately acknowledged, "The insurgents in the Western parts of Pennsylvania had done very little more than the people of Kentucky." Democratic societies in Kentucky and western Pennsylvania had engaged in a sympathetic correspondence with each other, and both had been extremely critical of Washington's western policies. One Kentuckian confessed that "many of us were almost ready to join our brethren insurgents," until dissuaded by Washington's firm handling of the Pennsylvania distillers.[44] Even as late as 1797, political leaders in Kentucky worried that sporadic resistance might prompt President Adams to follow his predecessor's example and resort to a military solution.[45]

Despite comparable degrees of unrest, a military response to the resistance in Kentucky involved much greater difficulty. In contrast to Pennsylvania, the discontented distillers were not concentrated in a remote corner of the state but rather dispersed over a wide area, making for a poor military target. Furthermore, their proximity to the state's political and cultural centers enabled distillers to elicit popular support for their position, thereby rendering the state militia unreliable. The troops garrisoned in Ohio under the command of General Wayne provided an alternative, but using a professional army against civilians seemed a dangerous violation of republican principles. Even had a military solution been more feasible, Secretary of State Edmund Randolph warned the president that, given the general level of discontent already existing in Kentucky, a military response might provoke outright rebellion.[46] Although the Kentucky distillers offered equal if not greater provocation than those in western Pennsylvania, the same sort of coercive response stood to backfire in Kentucky.

Instead, Treasury Secretary Alexander Hamilton tried inducements. As of mid-1793, Kentucky distillers could have their arrears forgiven for the first year of the tax, July 1791 through June 1792, if they agreed to pay from that date forward. The distillers, however, insisted that the grace period should be lengthened to two years. Not willing to concede another year's revenue but willing to make payment (and collection) easier, Hamilton devised a way in late 1794 for the tax to be paid in whiskey rather than exclusively in cash. Since the Treasury handled both tax collection and procurement for the army (which provided a daily ration of whiskey), the revenue agents received authorization to purchase whiskey for the troops. This was convenient, and it ensured that the army's whiskey had been properly taxed. Hamilton's provision received only a mild response from Kentucky distillers, though. Apparently the ones who paid in whiskey were mainly those who wished to sell to the army. Noncompliance continued to be embarrassingly widespread.[47]

Only after the near catastrophe of the Clark expedition in early 1794 did the national government truly grasp the depth of western discontent. In addition to assuring western leaders that the government was earnestly pursuing negotiations to secure American trading privileges through New Orleans, James Innes, President Washington's personal emissary to the west, also gathered information regarding opposition to the excise. Upon his return Innes advised Washington that unless the government extended the forgiveness of arrears to June 1794, Kentuckians were unlikely to cease their agitation.[48] In May 1795, having received no further word, a number of the principal distillers gathered in Lexington and again proposed an extension, this time presenting it to supervisor Marshall for him to relay to his superiors. Marshall did not forward the proposal, however, apparently believing that conciliation would be a mistake when an important principle was at issue. His supervisors, embarrassed by the widespread noncompliance and their inability to quell it through other means, were more flexible. In June 1796, Commissioner of the Revenue Tench Coxe wrote Marshall, "It appears to be expedient to renounce the claim for penalties and some part of the arrears, if by these means the laws can hereafter be put in regular execution."[49] With this concession, the Treasury Department assumed that an understanding had been achieved and that all duties owed since July 1, 1796, would be paid. Coxe did not know that Marshall, determined not to bow to the distillers, had withheld disclosure of the government's offer. Western distillers only learned of the new policy in May 1797, nearly a year later, when Marshall's political adversaries published Coxe's letter in the newspaper. These circumstances, of course, did little to lessen the political strain. Some western distillers even imagined a conspiracy afoot.[50] Compliance with the excise improved but remained reluctant and resentful.

A revealing picture of the general climate during this period is gleaned from an incident involving a figure no less prominent than the governor of Kentucky, Isaac Shelby, who for three years had avoided paying the excise. In February 1795, two excise agents visited Shelby's plantation in Lincoln County to measure his stills and calculate the amount of his excise duty. Shelby told collectors William Streshly and Edward Richardson that "it was a pity that young men of our appearance could find no business to follow for a livelihood but that of an excise officer—that it was one of the meanest offices we could fill, and advised us strongly to give it up." Streshly and Richardson replied that "it was a lawful calling, and that we were not ashamed of it (although he endeavoured to make us so)." Streshly then asked Shelby whether he intended to pay the tax, and Shelby sullenly replied "that he would see about it, that if others paid he supposed he should." After calculating the amount due from Shelby, Streshly told him that he was being recorded as liable for the tax and as having acknowledged the debt. Failure to pay would result in legal proceedings and the seizure of property. Irritated by Streshly's impudence in lecturing him on the law, the governor answered that anyone who took his property had better be ready to face the consequences. Shelby also complained that the excise "was an oppressive law, and a very bad one; that it was hard for him to pay . . . when his neighbour, that was worth as much as he was, paid nothing, because he had no distillery." This was a familiar complaint among distillers, and the collectors had an equally familiar answer. They pointed out that while the distillers remitted the tax, the amount was actually paid by the consumer in the form of a higher price. In that case, Shelby retorted, it would be nice to have ready consumers. Streshly was ready for this, too, and promptly offered to accept whiskey in payment at the current price per gallon, but Shelby's remark had not been intended literally. Though Governor Shelby did pay the excise on his stills, grudging compliance from men of his stature did little to foster western respect for the national government and its officials.[51]

Shelby and other members of the Kentucky elite played a pivotal role in local reactions to the excise. Several were, like Shelby, themselves distillers and directly affected by the excise, but their opposition was political as much as it was personal. They had come west to enhance their privileged rank and secure it for their offspring. They could be counted on to resist interference with these objectives, whether from the state of Virginia or the national government. Furthermore, organizing opposition to the excise presented an excellent opportunity to regain popularity with western voters and quash the democratic challenge in Kentucky's internal political alignments. In addition to allowing the Kentucky gentry to portray themselves as true and able defenders of western interests, the strategy deflected criticism aimed toward themselves and redirected it against a distant antagonist, the national government.

The support from Governor Shelby and others of the state's gentry, more than any other factor, distinguished the situation in Kentucky from that in Pennsylvania. As Thomas Marshall bitterly complained to his superior in 1792, opposition by "our influential men" posed the most serious obstacle to enforcing the excise law in Kentucky. The assistance provided by powerful state leaders made violent resistance unnecessary. Indeed, violent resistance became undesirable. George Nicholas was ready to represent any distiller "except where the defendants have been guilty of a clear breach of the Peace."[52] Even without the prospect that President Adams might use violent protest to justify a military invasion of Kentucky, nothing was more abhorrent to these survivors of the Revolution against British rule than the chaos and disorder of violence. Protest short of violence, however, received their protection. Not only were attorneys the caliber of Nicholas willing to defend accused excise violators, but they refused in any way to aid in their prosecution.

Nowhere was this more evident than the difficulty encountered in appointing a federal prosecuting attorney for Kentucky. The current holder of that office managed to avoid excise cases until his resignation in December 1792, and the search for a successor lasted for four years because no local attorney would accept appointment. As Kentucky senator John Brown remarked, "The Excise is so odious that No lawyer who has a reputation to loose [sic] will accept office." Members of the Kentucky bar so strongly and uniformly opposed the excise that Marshall could not even hire private counsel. Thoroughly frustrated, Marshall wrote to his superior in 1794, "The business is rendered so unpopular by some of our influential Characters that no lawyer unless it is made his particular duty will undertake it."[53]

The most important friend to western distillers was none other than district court judge Harry Innes. Although he kept a careful distance from overt political activity and insisted that his private political views did not conflict with his duties as an official of the United States, Innes was known as a strong Anti-Federalist, and his thoughts on the excise were no secret. A frustrated prosecutor quoted Innes as saying that "the defects were in the law, and until they were revised, the duties could never be collected to the extent that seemed proper, or that the distillers were liable."[54] Innes played a key role in the contest between the federal government and excise violators. Said one Kentuckian, "It was owing in a high degree to the temper and moderation of the Judge of the federal Court in Kentucky that prevented actual violence from bursting forth."[55] Innes did this in several ways. First, he did not insist that the federal marshal convene a grand jury for every court session. Second, until late 1798 he allowed distillers—even those with cases pending in the court—to serve on the grand jury. Third, Innes insisted on strict adherence to due process. Consequently, Kentucky distillers (unlike their brethren in Pennsylvania) had little to fear from the federal court. Completely frustrated with the situation by 1794, Marshall complained, "I really know not what to do . . . every attempt to execute the law gets defeated."[56]

Despite a couple of ill-fated efforts by Marshall, prosecution of excise violators languished until December 1796, when a Federalist from Maryland named William Clarke filled the position of federal attorney in Kentucky. A grand jury immediately brought presentments against two men for forcibly obstructing a revenue collector in the performance of his duty. During the next court session in March, presentments were brought against two more men, one for keeping two unregistered stills and the other for assault and battery against a revenue collector.[57] Attorney Clarke's boldest action was to file informations (criminal accusations by an agent of the government) against two prominent local distillers, John Brown and Thomas Jones. These charges were in rem, or against the still, rather than against the distiller. Although both men had complied with the excise, previous owners of the stills had not. Clarke's extreme action outraged area distillers, who called a meeting at a nearby tavern on court day. All that occurred, however, was Clarke's undramatic filing of charges against the two men; verdicts would not be reached for more than a year. As it turned out, the distillers had little to fear. Besides losing both cases, Clarke received a scathing public lecture from Judge Innes on proper legal procedure. By this point, July 1798, Clarke had revealed himself as a careless if not incompetent prosecutor.[58]

Clarke's other efforts to prosecute violators of the excise proved equally futile until November 1798, when Judge Innes announced a new court rule disqualifying distillers and their witnesses from serving as grand jurors. Finally, the grand jury began to issue presentments, charges based on personal knowledge of violations. Five persons were quickly charged with operating unlicensed stills. When the court reconvened in March 1799, thirteen distillers were presented, and the trend continued thereafter. Yet, convictions did not necessarily follow. Distillers remained eligible to serve on petit juries, and these bodies refused to convict defendants accused of excise violations. In the seven cases Clarke argued before petit juries, the defendant won every time.[59]

The November 1798 district court term was also significant because the prosecution finally switched strategies, from criminal procedure to civil suits for debt. Eliciting less hostility from Innes, prosecution for debt soon emerged as the primary method of enforcement. Dozens of suits were filed in rapid order at each subsequent court term, and the government finally began winning judgments on a regular basis. Excise violators remained difficult to convict, however, because Innes still disallowed testimony by revenue agents on the grounds that they had a pecuniary interest in the outcome of the case—not only a commission on all the excise money collected but also on penalties and forfeitures.[60] The other problem was Clarke's lazy disregard for proper legal form and Judge Innes's strict insistence on it. The final blow to Clarke's tattered reputation occurred in July 1799, when Marshall's successor as revenue supervisor charged Clarke with failing to pay the duties on his own still![61] By this time it was obvious that Clarke's effectiveness had grown negligible, and in late 1800 he was promoted to the new position of chief justice for the Indiana Territory. A replacement was not easy to find given the dearth of western Federalists, and Joseph Hamilton Daviess did not assume office until a year later. But when he did arrive, the difference was immediately perceptible. On his first day in court, Daviess obtained two indictments from the grand jury and docketed 121 civil suits for excise debts. Able, energetic, and professional, Daviess brought a new era to the excise law in Kentucky.

Nearly a decade after the original excise law, the federal government was finally obtaining judgments in its favor on a consistent basis, yet victory was still not absolute. Writs of fieri facias, an order to secure the amount of the judgment from the personal property of the unsuccessful litigant, remained difficult to execute. In 1800, the federal marshal and a deputy suffered bullet wounds attempting to serve a writ in Bourbon County.[62] Milder forms of defiance occurred regularly, as shown by numerous writs returned to the court with the notation, "Ex'd [executed] and . . . not Complyed with." In other cases the marshal reported, "No property found" or "Defendant has no property that I can find to make the within Debt & Costs." Even when property was found and the seized goods were offered at public auction, people often hesitated to bid— whether from a fear of revenge or a sense of solidarity is difficult to say. Numerous writs of execution were returned to the court with notations such as, "Ex'd [executed] on three Horses and not sold 35 miles," and "Ex'd on 3 hides leather + 1/2 side. Not sold for want of Biders [sic]."[63] By this time Jefferson had assumed the presidency, and general expectations were that the excise would soon be repealed. Resistance nonetheless continued to the bitter end.

The true extent of the resistance in Kentucky is impossible to determine beyond the 176 distillers who had appeared as defendants in the district court by 1800.[64] Noncompliance entailed considerable potential risk, and many western distillers chose instead to submit, especially after 1795. In February 1795, a Lincoln County citizen who saw the collection agent's account book noted that, in addition to Governor Shelby, "the accounts of many other distillers in the said county were also credited in full." When asked whether the distillers were complying, the collection agent replied that "all he had called upon had." Similarly, in March 1795 a prominent distiller named Jacob Spears delivered a wagonload of whiskey in payment of his excise debt and that of a neighboring distiller. Spears noted "a large number of casks," which the excise collector told him contained whiskey received in payment of excise. In addition, "a much larger amount" of the excise supposedly had been paid in cash. The previous year, revenue agent William Hubble had more than one hundred dollars in excise collections when his belongings were stolen at Shipp's house in Bourbon County. References such as these support claims from the distillers that after 1795 they had been "generally disposed to conform to the direction of the law, and large payments are said to have been made by them early in that year."[65]

None of these payments, however, ever reached the U.S. Treasury. In

1797, Commissioner of the Revenue Tench Coxe reported in a letter to Kentucky senator John Brown that "it does not appear *that any thing* has been received beyond what has been absorbed in spirit purchases [for the troops], and in charges and expenses." Marshall blamed the distillers and the "influential men" who protected them. Kentucky distillers, on the other hand, insisted that compliance had been good since 1795 and claimed that the U.S. Treasury had received no money because dishonest excise agents were siphoning excise payments into private speculatory schemes. Whatever the truth of these accusations, the quality of the excise agents did leave something to be desired; several were later sued for the monies they had collected but failed to submit to their superiors.[66] Unquestionably, whether through the evasive tactics of distillers, the collusion of leading Anti-Federalist politicians, or Marshall's inability to hire competent agents, the federal excise was a complete failure in Kentucky.

More serious, though, than the inability to generate needed revenue, the excise laws undermined a government authority that had yet to get completely on its feet. The excise agents faced constant abuse—occasionally to the point of violence. Thomas Marshall, one of Kentucky's most eminent citizens, suffered the humiliation of being burned in effigy. Especially serious is that some of these incidents, such as the midnight raid on Laban Shipp's house, involved apparent collusion by public officials and community leaders. Federal authorities could not help but worry that one of these events might spark a wider insurrection. Even the justice system worked to the detriment of government authority. Indeed, the situation in the district court approached comic proportions, with an incompetent attorney resorting to desperate measures, as when Clarke prosecuted the stills of Brown and Jones. The excise undermined what little respect federal authority enjoyed in Kentucky.

Instead of providing a moderating influence upon the ferment and confusion plaguing public affairs in Kentucky, national policy inflamed public sentiment. Western citizens openly and at times violently defied the government. Although catastrophe was averted, the absence of a respected higher authority created a noticeable void, particularly following Kentucky's separation from Virginia. As Kentucky took its first steps as a state, no kind parent stood by watching over. Instead, Kentuckians faced what they could only perceive as a hostile external power. From that viewpoint, and especially in the context of the recent struggle for independence from Great Britain, most Kentuckians felt fully justified in their fierce Anti-Federalism. Until Jefferson's election in 1800, the only stability rendered by the national government came from pursuing policies so odious to westerners that Kentucky's internal factions collapsed into a broad Anti-Federalist alliance based on sectional interests. The main beneficiaries were the western gentry, such as John Breckinridge, who positioned themselves as champions of western interests on the national political stage, thereby improving their shaky relations with Kentucky voters.

By the time of the Great Revival, national policy toward the west had greatly improved. Wayne's victory at Fallen Timbers had made westerners safe in their homes. The Pinckney Treaty secured the West's economic future. The excise on domestic distilled spirits had been effectively neutralized by the western courts, and repeal was pending. The resolution of these problems could not, however, immediately eradicate their effect. That would take time. Other parts of the nation had also suffered detrimental national policies, of course, but few as consistently as had the trans-Allegheny west. The Great Kentucky Revival thus appeared in a setting suffering instability at even the highest levels. The weakness of national authority helps explain not only the western location of the first camp meetings but also the timing of their first appearance.

7

SPIRITUAL CONDITIONS ON THE EVE OF REVIVAL

Religious revivalism almost by definition presumes a prior condition of ailing religious health. Such impressions may be especially strong for Kentucky's Great Revival because so many historians tend to associate that event with frontier conditions. Yet, as historians of other revivals have increasingly recognized, generating and sustaining any major religious revival requires considerable institutional resources, trained personnel, and organizational structure.[1] These "supply-side" factors were also important to Kentucky's Great Revival. They help explain why the western settlements did not host a revival earlier, during station times, when the effects of border warfare were causing serious property loss, human casualties, and psychological terror. But perhaps more important is how these factors provided an essential foundation for the Great Revival and set the stage for future growth. Although the early camp meetings often have been depicted as spontaneous affairs conducted by itinerant preachers in the backwoods, they were actually organized in advance, led by a professional corps of ministers, and hosted by established congregations.

Establishing Institutional Foundations

Despite the proud claims of local historians, religious institutions were actually a rarity during Kentucky's early frontier period. Those few which existed were usually fragile and isolated, meeting as circumstances allowed. Even some of the larger settlements lacked religious institutions during their early years. Strode's Station, for example, was a key settlement but did not support a religious congregation until 1791—more than a decade after its founding—and the station lacked a regular minister for several years more. Even then, the congregation never grew beyond eleven members at any time and remained so feeble that it eventually ceased to exist. Despite the concentration of Regular Baptists at Bryan's Station, one woman later claimed that she never heard a sermon during the entire time she lived there.[2] The Bryan's Station Baptist Church was not founded until 1786—after four years of settlement. Station inhabitants simply had little interest in establishing institutions when they expected to move soon to a permanent home, often located some distance away. Of course, believers could still read Scripture, hold family prayer, and sing hymns without an assembly of fellow worshipers and a minister. But sustaining personal faith in isolation was not easy, and many believers probably became lax when denied the discipline and support of a congregation for extended periods. When Reverend David Rice brought his family to Mercer County in 1784, he was thoroughly dismayed by the state of frontier religion. "After I had been here some weeks, and had preached at several places," he wrote, "I found scarcely one man and but few women who supported a credible profession of religion."[3]

One of the main obstacles to organized religious worship during the early years was the danger of travel. William Hickman, a Baptist preacher, recalled that people going to church service often traveled in groups, "sometimes twenty or thirty in a gang." The local men provided an armed escort for Hickman as they rode to the meetinghouse, so that "it looked more like going to war than to meeting to worship God."[4] Even as conditions improved, attending worship still entailed personal risk. For example, around 1789 a Bourbon County man and his wife were waylaid while riding double to a Presbyterian meetinghouse. The man was shot in the mouth, the bullet ripping through his jaw. The wife instantly moved to slip off behind so he could aim his rifle, but he told her not to, and whipping the horse, he managed to escape. This particular incident occurred in the heart of what was then considered a well-populated and safe neighborhood.[5] Churchgoers in outlying neighborhoods were even more at risk, and distances of five or more miles were common. The prolonged Indian danger not only deterred churchgoers but threatened the viability of smaller congregations through the actual loss of members. Five members of Cooper's Run Baptist Church were killed by Indians during its first year of existence, 1787, a misfortune which jeopardized the congregation's ability to survive.

The slow appearance of ministers was also a problem, for it was difficult to generate interest in organizing a congregation in the absence of religious leadership. A few ministers visited Kentucky during the Revolution, but none settled there permanently until later. Ministers were so scarce that even getting married was difficult. Living together out of wedlock carried especially serious consequences on a violent frontier: should the husband die intestate, his common-law wife and offspring could not inherit his property. In contrast to Sunday worship, wedlock was a single event for which the parties involved were probably prepared to travel some distance, yet Kentucky couples still found it hard to find a licensed minister. Some resorted to the practice followed in Pennsylvania and exchanged vows before a county magistrate—only to discover later that their union was possibly invalid under a law passed by the Virginia legislature in 1781 requiring that marriages be performed by a licensed minister.[6]

The number of western ministers improved slowly. By late 1786 western Presbyterians had six ministers for all of Kentucky plus a few adjacent settlements in Tennessee and Ohio. The Methodist system of preaching circuits served by itinerant ministers finally reached the western settlements in 1786. Baptist preachers were more numerous, but even they did not arrive in significant numbers until the mid-1780s. Court records indicate that ministers remained in short supply even in Kentucky's more densely populated central regions. As late as 1790 in Bourbon County, when the federal census recorded 7,837 inhabitants, only three ministers had registered with the court for leave to perform marriages. Madison County, where settlement had begun in 1775 with Boonesborough, had registered only four ministers by 1790. And, on the fringes of settlement, conditions were as bad as ever. A Baptist minister named Thomas Henderson at Morgan's Station in eastern Kentucky was the only preacher available for some twenty-eight miles in 1792.[7]

Even where a minister could be had, providing for his support was seldom easy. Since few congregations could afford a full-time pastor, it was common to join with a neighboring congregation and contract for a pastor together. When the sister congregations were of unequal strength, as was often the case, the minister served each in proportion to their contributing support. The arrangement, which typically included little cash, could be quite complicated, and despite various precautions, the promised support was not always forthcoming. Some ministers suffered genuine poverty as a result. Others augmented their income by teaching. Unfortunately, a complaining minister always looked more like a worldly money-grubber than a true man of God, no matter how justified. When chronic problems in collecting his support threatened the welfare of Reverend David Rice's family in 1797, he tried to force compliance by withholding his services. Although Rice ranked as Kentucky's leading Presbyterian, the dispute transformed him into a subject of public ridicule, with nasty rhymes submitted to the newspaper for publication.[8] Nothing was more embarrassing than a dispute between shepherd and flock over money.

A frontier pulpit offered so little money and so many challenges that ministerial quality often left something to be desired. According to one early authority, most of the frontier ministers were "not above mediocrity; nor was the dullness of the ax compensated by putting thereto more strength." Daniel Drake described the early Baptist preachers he knew as being "illiterate persons, but some were men of considerable natural talents." Still, "They all lacked dignity & solemnity, and some now & then uttered very droll expressions in the pulpit."[9] Presbyterian ministers had to have a college degree and one year of theological training under the guidance of a minister, but these requirements by no means guaranteed refinement of manner or sophistication of thought. David Rice had been educated at the College of New Jersey, yet a layman described him as a "tobacco preacher" because he "chewed tobacco & preached at the same time." Similarly, a pioneer critically recalled a Presbyterian meeting where "old parson Shannon, took out a long quid of green tobacco from his pants pocket, bit off a piece, put it back, and went on with his preaching." Standing nearby, his more sophisticated colleague, Reverend James Blythe of Woodford County, merely smiled with tolerant amusement. Although the frontier generation of ministers played an instrumental role in organizing congregations and instilling a degree of church order, Rice himself admitted that often they "did not appear to possess much spirit of the gospel."[10]

Despite various early hindrances to public worship, religious congregations began multiplying once people could leave the stations for permanent homes. The number of congregations in Transylvania Presbytery, which encompassed Kentucky and adjacent settlements in Tennessee and Ohio, increased from twenty-four in October 1790 to forty-six in April 1794. During roughly the same period, the number of member churches in the Elkhorn Association of Regular Baptists increased from fourteen to twenty-six. In Fayette County, dominated by the booming town of Lexington, an inhabitant estimated in 1792 that the county had two Presbyterian, three Methodist, and six Baptist ministers. Jefferson County, which included Louisville, had one licensed Presbyterian minister, plus "Itinerants . . . almost without number, and of every denomination." The number of ministers also increased in more rural counties. Nelson County had three Baptist ministers, plus about twelve who were mainly Presbyterian, as well as a Roman Catholic priest (the only one in Kentucky).[11]

The number of western ministers increased dramatically during the 1790s. The number of Presbyterians, for example, grew from five in 1785 to twenty-six by 1799. In Madison County, only four ministers had applied to the court for licenses to perform weddings before 1790; another twelve did so by the end of the decade. Bourbon County saw similar increases: three ministers before 1790 and fourteen by the end of the decade. The availability of ministers improved markedly even in more recently settled areas. In Mason County, where so many settlers made a temporary home, no less than twenty ministers applied for licenses between 1790 and 1800. Growing up in remote Logan County, Peter Cartwright's family had several churches nearby. A Baptist congregation existed a few miles west of the Cartwright farm, and a Presbyterian congregation was a few miles to the south. Cartwright's mother worshiped with the Methodists, about four miles to the south.[12] Although the denomination of choice might be some distance away, most neighborhoods, particularly in the Bluegrass region where settlement was most advanced, enjoyed reasonable access to public worship by the time of the Great Revival in 1800. Arguments that the fervor accompanying the Great Revival resulted from a dearth of opportunities for religious worship must therefore be set aside.

Somewhat less obvious but just as crucial to the growth of western religion was the organization of regional governing bodies. Local congregations would have found it extremely difficult to survive much less multiply without guidance and supervision. Religious leaders understood this perfectly. Even while the number of local congregations could be counted on one hand, western Baptists, Presbyterians, and Methodists began organizing themselves into associations, presbyteries, and conferences. These regional governing bodies assigned ministers, mediated disputes, maintained church discipline, and provided constant guidance. Bringing together strangers to form a religious congregation involved numerous difficulties, and few congregations escaped some sort of internal disruption during their early years. Without the stability provided by regional governing bodies, many local congregations would have surely disbanded. Instead, local congregations enjoyed an excellent rate of survival. Although local histories often overlook this intermediate level of the ecclesiastical hierarchy, the new religious communities sprouting on the edge of the wilderness found in it valuable support.

The Baptists constituted the leading religious denomination practically from the very beginning and promptly began organizing local congregations into regional associations. Despite earnest efforts, however, Kentucky Baptists could not overcome doctrinal differences between Regular Baptists, who were Calvinist and subscribed to the Philadelphia Confession of Faith, and the Separate Baptists, who rejected any outside authority or creed. This difference, along with the geographical concentration of Regular Baptists north of the Kentucky River and Separate Baptists south of it, resulted in the formation of two independent associations. The five congregations of Regular Baptists in central Kentucky, only one of which lay south of the Kentucky River, formed the Elkhorn Association in 1785. Another set of Regular Baptists, clustered near the future site of Louisville and cut off from the interior settlements by miles of uninhabited frontier, organized independently as Salem Association. The seven congregations of Separate Baptists located south of the Kentucky River organized as South Kentucky Association in 1787. Separate and Regular Baptists in Virginia had overcome their differences in 1787, but Kentucky Baptists would not unite until 1801. The organization of regional church bodies nonetheless proceeded around the division.

The spread of settlement led to the organization of three additional Baptist associations in the 1790s. Tate's Creek Association was organized in 1793 in reaction against the South Kentucky Separate Baptists, when the latter rejected the Regular Baptist proposal for unification. Calling itself "United Baptist," Tate's Creek Association originally comprised four churches. Unlike other Separate Baptists, the members of Tate's Creek accepted the Philadelphia Confession of Faith, although with some minor clarification. A fifth Baptist association resulted from the new settlements in Kentucky's northern and eastern counties. What had been the eastern territory of Elkhorn Association became Bracken Association in 1799. The five member churches soon increased to nine. The last association founded in Kentucky during the eighteenth century was that of Green River in the central region of southern Kentucky, established in 1799 with eight or nine member congregations of Regular Baptists.[13] The surge in church membership and the founding of new congregations during the Great Revival would lead to additional associations in the early nineteenth century.

The associations provided Kentucky Baptists with an ecclesiastical structure conducive to stability and growth. Delegates from each member congregation established the main points of church policy within the bounds of their association. Topics of concern varied widely, but most of the deliberations concerned either liturgical practice or church governance. Because church members coming to Kentucky often held divergent religious views and followed various practices, young congregations were plagued with frequent conflict. Most congregations worked hard to absorb these differences and reach some sort of consensus, but when an impasse occurred, they often turned to the association for help. For example, Elkhorn Association was asked to rule on the propriety of funerals; it decided against processions but in favor of a simple graveside sermon. In another instance, it was asked to formulate a procedure for marriage, and in a third, to compile a catechism. Salem Association, asked to rule on whether Christians could marry unconverted persons, responded that such marriages were permissible if the person did not lead a profane or debauched life or hold heretical beliefs. Controversial practices, such as footwashing and the laying of hands on newly baptized members, also came before western associations. The association's verdict was not binding, because each member church remained autonomous, but the ruling usually elicited respect and compliance.[14]

Matters of church governance also required frequent attention. Some questions sought to clarify associational authority, such as whether the association had the right to schedule the quarterly meetings and whether the association could expel churches that rejected its resolutions. Elkhorn Association was asked whether ministers could properly hold civil or military office, and some time later, the question arose whether elders and ministers shared the same privileges and responsibilities. The associations also arbitrated disagreements within congregations, such as when one congregation with a grievance against its pastor asked Elkhorn Association if financial support of ministers was a "debt or a liberal contribution." The Association sternly advised that it was a duty to provide ministers with reasonable support.[15] The associations also routinely corresponded among themselves, with the negotiations for uniting Kentucky's Separate and Regular Baptists being a topic of foremost concern until unification was finally accomplished in 1801.

Presbyterian rules of church governance gave regional bodies an even greater degree of influence. In 1785 David Rice and four colleagues, plus elders from twelve fledgling congregations, organized Transylvania Presbytery. In addition to encompassing all of Kentucky, the new presbytery included the beginning settlements in the Cumberland River valley in Tennessee and the Miami River valley in Ohio. When the Presbyterian General Assembly created the system of synods in 1788, Transylvania came under the care of the Synod of Virginia. The rapid expansion of western settlement led to the subdivision of Transylvania in 1799, with the region north and east of the Licking River now designated as Washington Presbytery. The area between the Licking and the Kentucky River became West Lexington Presbytery. Transylvania Presbytery, which had been the main governing body in Kentucky for most of the eighteenth century, continued to administer the region south and west of the Kentucky River. At the time of the division, in March 1799, Transylvania had ten ministers, West Lexington had nine, and Washington had seven. The number of congregations was somewhat larger. The division into three presbyteries not only accommodated church growth but was also a major step toward independence from the Synod of Virginia. The Synod of Kentucky, with the required minimum of three presbyteries, was duly authorized in 1802.

The presbyteries served member congregations in much the same capacity as the Baptist associations, but with undisputed authority and a clear hierarchical relationship. Presbyterian congregations had much less autonomy than did Baptist congregations. Construction of a meetinghouse or the hiring of a new minister required the Presbytery's prior approval. Similarly, ordinations were conducted not by the congregation but by the presbytery. The presbytery also examined catechists and licensed probationers. Matters pertaining to individual church members were usually handled by the congregation's Session, but even these internal proceedings were subject to review by the Presbytery.[16]

American Methodism, the third largest denomination in Kentucky, was yet in its infancy when people began moving west after the Revolution. With adherents thinly scattered over a wide distance, western Methodism could probably not have survived but for the flexible and extensive Methodist style of itinerant preaching. The first Methodist preaching circuit west of the Appalachians was organized in 1786 with two itinerant preachers. In 1796, the Methodist Annual Conference was subdivided into six regional conferences charged with governing the preaching circuits within their bounds. The Conference was headed by a presiding elder and convened on a quarterly basis. By 1800, the Kentucky Conference had grown to six circuits within the state, plus several others covering adjacent settlements in Tennessee and the Northwest Territory. About one dozen itinerant preachers regularly served this huge area, supplemented by a handful of preachers who were prevented from traveling by marriage or poor health.[17] Between visits by a preacher, each congregation (or class, as they were called) held worship under the direction of leading laymen. Itinerancy enabled the early Methodist Church to deploy its preachers more extensively than other denominations, but without the Conference to coordinate and advise, western Methodism would certainly have floundered.

Frontier images of a camp meeting population starved for religious worship is thus highly misleading. By 1800, the number of congregations had multiplied dramatically. Some were already a decade old. The proportion served regularly by ordained ministers had risen considerably, supported by stable regional governing bodies. Indeed, without this institutional framework, the Great Revival would have hardly been possible.

Competition and Conflict

Establishing an institutional structure of local congregations and regional governing bodies was crucial, but the task of transplanting religion in the western settlements remained far from finished. The fledgling religious communities faced innumerable difficulties during their early years. In some cases, the bonds holding church members together were strained nearly to the breaking point and occasionally beyond. One settler wrote home enjoining an old friend to emigrate to Kentucky, "if you will be Determined neither to Quarrel about religion nor go to Law about Lands[,] Evils that attend our Land."[18] Hardly a congregation escaped the pain of internal disputes, interdenominational rivalry, or lapses in church discipline. One of the most painful difficulties, in Kentucky as elsewhere in the new republic, revolved around the issue of slavery. These problems and related ones created an atmosphere of incessant conflict, which believers and nonbelievers alike perceived as contrary to the basic tenets of Christianity. Until these differences could be resolved, the western churches remained vulnerable.

The first problem, naturally enough, was religious neglect. Most late-eighteenth-century American churchmen agreed that the secular, rationalistic thinking of the Enlightenment was a major factor in a general decline of religion. The trans-Appalachian West was no exception. Methodist itinerant James Smith, traveling near Lexington in late 1795, noted that "the Universalists, joining with the Deists, had given christianity a deadly stab hereabouts."[19] Baptist minister David Barrow, after visiting various parts of the state that same year, remarked, "Of all the denominations that I remember to h[ave] seen in that country, the Deists, Nothingarians, and anythingarians, are the most numerous." Barrow attributed the strength of deism in Kentucky in large part to the popularity of Thomas Paine, whose *Rights of Man* had been serialized by John Bradford in the *Kentucky Gazette*. According to Reverend Robert Stuart, who was sent in 1798 by the Presbyterian Synod of Virginia to work as a missionary among the western settlements, "The writings of Infidels, and particularly *Tom Paine's Age of Reason* was extensively circulated, and his principles imbibed by the youth particularly, with avidity; so that Infidelity, with all its concomitant evils, like a mighty tide, was desolating the land, with respect to religion and morals." One farmer who lived in the Bluegrass County of Woodford insisted that nine-tenths of his neighbors were the "avowed disciples of Thomas Paine."[20] Surely this was an exaggeration, yet the Appalachian Mountains do not seem to have insulated westerners from intellectual fashions of the day.

Religion probably suffered greater injury from the desire for material gain. Throughout the new nation, the restoration of economic markets after the Revolution "served as a powerful bait, to entrap professors [of religion] who were in any great degree, inclined to the pursuit of wealth."[21] People in the new settlements were particularly absorbed in the business of clearing fields, building houses, and reaching markets. General James Wilkinson once lamented that Kentuckians were not sufficiently involved in civic affairs because they preferred to develop their lands. Ministers had a similar complaint. Reverend James McGready, serving Presbyterians in southern Kentucky, claimed, "The world is in all their thoughts by day and night. All their conversation is of corn and tobacco, or land and stock. . . . But for them the name of Jesus has no charms; and it is rarely mentioned unless to be profaned."[22] Baptist leader John Taylor confessed that, although there were a number of church members living near him in Woodford County, "We all seemed cold as death. Everybody had so much to do, that religion was scarcely talked of, even on Sundays." Worship services had "but little of the spirit of devotion."[23] As Methodist Bishop Francis Asbury understood painfully well, "Good religion and such good land are not so easily matched together." Indeed, it seemed to Asbury, who traveled extensively among the new western settlements, "When I consider where they come from, where they are, and how they are, and . . . with so many objects to take their attention, with the health and good air they enjoy; and when I reflect that not one in a hundred came here to get religion, but rather to get plenty of good land, I think it will be well if some or many do not eventually lose their souls."[24]

The debilitating effect of worldliness infected even preachers. The Craigs of Scott County, who had played an instrumental role in transplanting Virginia Baptists to Kentucky, came under criticism for becoming "land-jobbers, and immersed in the world." Similarly, Reverend William Wood, a pioneer Baptist preacher in Mason County, was expelled in 1798 for becoming "entangled in land speculation." In another case, a minister "became wealthy and worldly-minded, departed from preaching, became intemperate, abused his family . . . and died a miserable sot."[25] As Reverend David Rice sadly admitted, "By adopting and acting upon the principles & maxims of this world[,] Christians & ministers contribute more to the spread of infidelity & impiety than all the infidel writers of Europe and America."[26]

Western religion was also hurt by interdenominational rivalry. Americans moving west often did not have the denomination of their choosing nearby, but anxious to join a church, sometimes joined whatever one was located closest to their new home. The Presbyterian Church, which required an educated ministry, was particularly hurt by a shortage of western ministers and therefore found it difficult to defend against such incursions. John Lyle, a young Presbyterian minister who came to Kentucky in 1797 from the Virginia backcountry, claimed, "The Methodists had cunningly proselyted some of the Presbyterian societies in their infancy, and carried away many disciples among them."[27] Ecumenicalism therefore received little support or encouragement. In late 1789, for example, Mt. Pisgah congregation suspended Elder William Scott "for inviting the Baptists frequently and permitting a Methodist to preach in his house."[28] Transylvania Presbytery overturned Scott's suspension after much debate, but interdenominational worship was perceived as threatening and was generally avoided. As a new settler, Harry Toulmin sadly reported, "The zeal of the sects is said to be deformed by bigotry."[29] Another minister confessed that, although the western denominations "acknowledged each other as sisters, descended from the same stock, yet such was the zeal of each for their distinguishing tenets, and forms of worship, that they stood entirely separate . . . wounding, captivating, and bickering with one another."[30]

Religious heresy likewise had a very divisive effect. Ministers complained that heresies sprouted like weeds among the ignorant population. Despite endless toil, even the most conscientious ministers were sometimes shocked and dismayed by some of the beliefs and practices they encountered. Neither were the ministers themselves entirely immune from such pitfalls. Perhaps the most embarrassing doctrinal division involved Universalism, popularly known as "Hell Redemption" because it transformed the belief that heaven was open to all into the belief that no soul was condemned to hell. The Separate Baptists, perhaps as an outcome of their independent congregational structure, were apparently the most seriously affected of the western denominations. When Universalism began appearing among Kentucky's Separate Baptists, church leaders found it difficult to defend against. The doctrine took an embarrassing toll. In 1793, two influential preachers in the South Kentucky Association of Separate Baptists were expelled for espousing Universalism. The ensuing disruption was a major factor in the Association's dissolution in 1801. Salem Association of Regular Baptists also expelled several ministers for espousing Universalism. It caused a crisis in Tate's Creek Association, too.[31]

The Regular Baptists belonging to the Elkhorn Association were rocked by a different challenge, a doctrinal controversy within the prominent congregation of Cooper's Run centered around the congregation's leaders, James Garrard and Augustin Eastin. Garrard, who had begun two terms as governor in 1796, had appointed an accomplished Unitarian minister from England named Harry Toulmin as Kentucky secretary of state.[32] Eastin, a "brilliant man of good social standing and irreproachable morals," was unfortunately also highly impressionable and showed a "propensity to ape men of distinction."[33] Both he and Garrard fell under the influence of Toulmin. The Elkhorn Association would finally take action against these two revered but errant members in early 1803, finding them both guilty of propagating Arianism. Elkhorn Association subsequently dropped the entire Cooper's Run congregation except for a few black members, and defiant portions of several smaller neighboring congregations.[34]

For Kentucky Presbyterians, perhaps the most serious episode of doctrinal conflict involved the much respected but dogmatic minister at Lexington, Adam Rankin, who insisted that only the Psalms and songs of David were legitimate for holy worship.[35] Although cautioned against this rigid stance by Transylvania Presbytery, in 1789 Rankin stubbornly took his argument all the way to the Presbyterian General Assembly in Philadelphia. Instead of accepting the Assembly's admonition to exercise greater Christian charity toward people who did not share his opinion, Rankin denounced his colleagues as blasphemers and refused to administer the sacrament to people who continued to use the very popular hymns of Isaac Watts. Transylvania Presbytery finally found it necessary to intervene, but before it could do so, Rankin conveniently departed for religious study in Great Britain. When he returned in late 1791, his position on psalmody had not budged. Within months, the Presbytery felt compelled to suspend Rankin from the ministry. Rankin and his loyal followers then seceded and attached themselves to the archly conservative Synod of Associate Reformed Churches. Rankin's other pastoral charge, New Providence congregation in Mercer County, split in two, dividing even families. "The neighborhood of Lexington is at this time much Divided with Rankin

People," reported a settler in a letter home. "It is a Disagreeable Circumstance to be near (Even) our friends & them oposers [*sic*] of our Religion." Although Rankin's people were in the minority, their unyielding stance caused problems in several other congregations as well. A local church elder reported three years later, "The divisions about Psalmody seems rather to increase, many have entirely quit coming to meeting."[36] Unfortunately, as a result of the affray, "Fundamental doctrines and fundamental piety came to be regarded as subordinate matters." At a time when western Presbyterianism was in yet a feeble condition, the conflict caused great pain and its effects were discernible for many years afterward.[37]

Church growth was also hurt, or at least not helped, by personal quarrels between ministers, who should have been exemplars of Christian piety but too often succumbed to human flaws. Among the early Methodists, for instance, Presiding Elder Francis Poythress and pioneer itinerant James Haw maintained a long-term disagreement. Poythress, a former Anglican, had a reputation for being domineering and arrogant. In contrast to most other Methodist itinerants, Poythress would only stay at the best of houses. One pioneer recalled vividly that Poythress "prayed with his eyes open, looking around to keep order." James Haw also possessed a distinctive personality. Although "an able and successful laborer in the Lord's vineyard," one Methodist itinerant later disclosed, "It was thought that he indulged a little too much in jealousy and envy, and had lost his influence and usefulness."[38] Although the specific nature of the disagreement between Poythress and Haw remains obscure, it appears that personal animosity rather than doctrinal differences separated the two men. A similar conflict in 1791 between Elijah Craig and Joseph Redding split Great Crossings Baptist Church into two rival congregations. Craig and Redding were both important spiritual leaders, and their feud caused a major commotion throughout the Elkhorn Association.[39] Such conflicts reflected badly upon religion, making professors look petty if not downright hypocritical.

Ministerial misconduct posed a similar problem. Early minutes of Transylvania Presbytery, for example, included complaints of drunkenness, breach of promise, physical abuse of a slave, and "improper intimacy" with a woman slave.[40] The number of ministers who failed in their role as exemplars of Christian piety was not of crisis proportions, but it did not take many to have an effect. Church members often found themselves forced to take sides, and nonmembers seldom failed to note the hypocrisy of immoral clergy. Each such instance posed a delicate problem, which church leaders did their best to investigate and resolve.

One of the most troubling incidents involved Robert W. Finley, the pastor of Presbyterian congregations at Cane Ridge and Concord in Bourbon County, where he also conducted an academy. Thomas Rogers was only a boy at the time, but he recalled in a personal memoir years later, "I can remember well my father came home one day from the blacksmith shop. It was on the road from town to Cane Ridge. He seemed very sad." When his mother asked what was wrong, Mr. Rogers replied, "I have heard sad news. . . . Our pastor was seen passing his house so drunk he could scarcely ride." According to Rogers, "This struck a damp on all the neighborhood."[41] At a meeting of Transylvania Presbytery in February 1795, three members of Cane Ridge (supported by ten witnesses) accused Finley of habitual drunkenness and demanded an investigation. According to the minutes, "Reports of this nature respecting Mr. Finley have circulated in this country for some years past & appear now to have become recently flagrant." Finley in turn charged his three accusers with slander and submitted his own request that the hearing be conducted by a special sessional committee collected from neighboring churches. The Presbytery rejected Finley's request because, according to church rules, the proper jurisdictional body for investigating the conduct of a minister was the Presbytery. Finley thereupon submitted a written protest insisting "that the proceedings of [the] preby. is without warrant from the word of God & without precedent from any form of government in the church of Christ." Therefore, "I . . . consider myself no longer a member of your body nor under your government." Neither would Finley appeal to the Synod of Virginia, citing "the immense distance" and his own "want of health." Alarmed at Finley's defiance, Transylvania Presbytery suspended him and declared vacant the sister congregations of Cane Ridge and Concord.[42]

The Presbytery maintained its firm stand at the disciplinary hearing at Cane Ridge the following April. A calmer Finley contended that his rejection of the Presbytery's authority stemmed from a mere misunderstanding. Before readmitting him, however, the Presbytery required that he sign a formal confession and promise future submission. After procrastinating several days, Finley finally signed the prepared statement and was restored as the pastor of Cane Ridge and Concord. Transylvania Presbytery then proceeded to arrange its hearing of the drunkenness charges and notified the ten witnesses. But Finley apparently had second thoughts. Instead of appearing at this hearing, he sent a message recanting his previous statement and "holding forth that he was no longer to be considered as a member of our body nor under our body nor under our government." Finley was again suspended, and the congregations of Cane Ridge and Concord were declared vacant. Yet the matter was still not closed. Despite his suspension, Finley continued to preach at Cane Ridge and Concord, compelling the Presbytery to depose him in October 1795 from "the whole exercise of the ministerial office." Although this was undoubt-edly a sad and painful decision, Finley's incorrigible defiance left little alternative. Finley moved his family to Ohio shortly afterward.[43]

"O that God would heal the breaches in Zion, and send forth his word with power," prayed a Kentucky Baptist in 1794.[44] Scandal, worldli-ness, and discord marred western Christianity in the eyes of both believ-ers and nonbelievers. Minor conflicts easily flared into bitter standoffs. The authority of local and regional religious institutions was repeatedly tested. Western religion had made tremendous strides within a very short time. Yet it offered little refuge from the stresses of political partisanship, economic uncertainty, and a society of strangers. Religion, rather, seemed as troubled as any other facet of existence.

The Divisive Issue of Slavery

Of all the problems facing western religion, none caused greater trouble than emancipation. The experiences of the American Revolution and its aftermath impelled many citizens to rethink the principles of black sla-very. If all men were born equal, then black inferiority could only be as-cribed to deficiencies of environment. Enslavement on that basis suddenly seemed an outrageous injustice. Moreover, history taught that republican forms of government were extremely fragile. Checks upon government power, no matter how clever, would not work without an underlying foun-dation of virtue. Thus, to many white citizens, slavery was a moral blot on American society, and the survival of the country required that it be removed.[45] In the northern states these beliefs led to legislation for imme-diate or gradual emancipation. In the southern states, they were espoused mainly by members of evangelical denominations. Evangelical leaders ar-gued that, in addition to violating natural rights, slavery violated religious principle. The use of slaves to attain wealth, profit, and prestige was a prime example of how worldliness destroyed godliness. Furthermore, the evangelical rejection of worldly obsession gave special significance to the people that the world rejected—and no group was more rejected in Ameri-can society than black slaves.[46] Not only were they physically oppressed, but they were also spiritually oppressed by masters who kept them igno-rant of religious salvation. Particularly objectionable was the hereditary basis of American slavery, which contrasted with the character of biblical slavery. Eliminating this aspect of slavery would ease the way toward the eventual elimination of slavery altogether.

The blending of republican ideology and religious principle is evident throughout the postrevolutionary antislavery literature. In Virginia, for example, Baptist leaders contended that slavery was a "violent depriva-tion of the rights of nature, and inconsistent with a Republican Government." In 1784, the Virginia Baptist General Committee had resolved "Heredit[ary] slavery to be contrary to the word of God."[47] The Episcopal-Methodist Church Discipline in 1780 condemned the enslavement of blacks as "contrary to the law of God, Man, nature, and hurtful to society."[48] One of Kentucky's leading emancipationists, Baptist preacher David Barrow, decided to emancipate his slaves "from a conviction of the inequity, and a discovery of the inconsistency of hereditary slavery, with a republican form of government." Every slaveholder, Barrow reasoned, was just as *absolute, uncontroulable,* and *arbitrary*" as any king.[49]

During the 1780s the three main denominations in Kentucky each saw higher church bodies issue public condemnations of slavery. American Methodists, under the influence of Bishop Asbury, took the firmest stand against slavery and struggled hardest with it. Methodist preachers were directed in 1780 to provide slaves with religious instruction and to press for emancipation at every possible opportunity. All itinerant preachers were directed to free whatever slaves they owned. After 1784, church members were to arrange for the gradual emancipation of their slaves, according to their ages and their ability to support themselves.[50] Similarly, in 1787, the Presbyterian Synod of New York and Philadelphia, the highest governing body in the American church, endorsed what they called "the general principles of universal liberty" as well as the recent legal measures eliminating slavery in several states. The Presbyterian resolution for emancipation carefully recommended that church members should adhere to "the most prudent measures, consistent with the interest and the state of civil society."[51] Virginia Baptists, including those west of the mountains, were encouraged by the General Committee in 1789 "to make use of every legal measure to extirpate this horrid evil from the land, and pray Almighty God that our honorable legislature may have it in their power to proclaim the Great Jubilee, consistent with the principles of good policy."[52]

Although the state government of Kentucky protected slavery, Baptists, Presbyterians, and Methodists had been told it was wrong. If slavery could not be eradicated through political means, many church members believed that a moral responsibility remained to eradicate it within the church. How this might be accomplished in a fair and effective manner, however, was far from clear. Hardly a single congregation, regardless of denomination, escaped some level of disruption from internal struggles with this issue. Several congregations were almost destroyed by alignments over slavery. Desperate to preserve harmony within the young and fragile congregations, western churches eventually retreated to more accommodating positions. Unable to eliminate slavery, some professors of religion concentrated instead on eliminating its harsher aspects. The more general response, however, was to reposition slavery as a civil rather than a moral issue and thereby justify noninterference.

The Elkhorn Association of Baptists, concentrated in the Bluegrass region where slavery was strongest, was especially affected by the antislavery movement. Although in Virginia the Baptists had been associated with the poor and downtrodden, they soon figured among the more affluent of Kentucky's inhabitants. Probably a majority of Baptist adults owned slaves by the close of the century.[53] In 1791, on the eve of the first state constitutional convention, the Elkhorn Association declared slavery inconsistent with the principles of Christianity. Some member churches reacted so negatively, however, that the Association quickly called a special meeting and retracted its statement.[54] Emancipation remained an extremely divisive issue, and although the Association sought to preserve unity by avoiding any further pronouncements on the subject, escape proved impossible. A few congregations disagreed so strongly with the association's policy on slavery, either that it was too conservative or too radical, that they withdrew in protest. Sometimes the conflict occurred within the congregation. For example, two families belonging to Cooper's Run Baptist Church in Bourbon County withdrew in 1798 because they objected to holding fellowship with slaveholders.[55] In other instances, the disagreement was not whether slavery should be ended but how it should be ended. Few people were ready to require unconditional manumission, at least not when civil law permitted slavery. Unable to accommodate the broad range of opinions, Baptist church policy in Kentucky and elsewhere gravitated toward noninterference.

The proportion of Kentucky Methodists who owned slaves was probably less than in the other denominations, but the firm antislavery stance adopted by the church under Bishop Francis Asbury's influence created difficulties for them, too. In a Methodist society in Bourbon County, Mt. Gilead, the members strongly opposed slavery, and class leader Daniel Leer "had to step down over it."[56] In other Methodist classes both in Kentucky and elsewhere, the church's opposition to slavery caused problems. The national Methodist leadership finally concluded that the sanctions against slave owners were probably counterproductive. Now, instead of expelling slave owners, the church decided that a slave owner would not be admitted into membership until the preacher had "spoken to him freely and faithfully on the subject of slavery," so that the church's strong disapproval was clear.[57] The sale of a slave remained sufficient grounds for expulsion, and Methodists who purchased slaves were to have their quarterly meeting determine the term of labor, after which the slave was to be manumitted. Yet even this milder policy proved unacceptable. As with the 1784 rule, entrenched resistance from quarterly and annual conferences eventually compelled the General Conference to suspend it. Church leaders continued to preach a strong emancipationist ethic, but without attempting to compel compliance. They defended this milder stance by emphasizing the duty to preach the gospel to every soul, something which offended slave owners had the power to obstruct.[58]

Western Presbyterians found it equally difficult to find a satisfactory policy on slavery. In 1784, the Presbyterian General Assembly had officially disapproved of slavery and urged the adoption of "measures consistent with the interests of civil society" for eventually abolishing it. A decade later the Transylvania Presbytery, embracing all of Kentucky, resolved that Presbyterian slave owners should teach "every slave not above the age of fifteen years to read as may prepare them for the enjoyment of freedom."[59] For more radical Presbyterians, however, this was not enough. In 1796, the sister congregations of Cane Ridge and Concord, supported by a letter from Colonel James Smith, a Kentucky state representative and an elder at Cane Ridge, petitioned Transylvania Presbytery to take a braver stand. Apparently these two congregations wished to exclude church members who owned slaves. Confronted the previous year with "certain queries" regarding slavery, possibly from these same churches, the Presbytery had preserved harmony by referring the matter to the upcoming meeting of the Presbyterian General Assembly. Now the Transylvania Presbytery reiterated the policy that had been issued at that time, declaring that "although [the] Presby[tery] are fully convinced of the great evil of Slavery yet they view the final remedy as alone belonging to the civil power." Western Presbyterians were told that the word of God did not give sufficient authority to make emancipation a term of acceptance into the church. Slavery must remain a matter of conscience. Echoing their previous statements, the Presbytery recommended that church members "emancipate such of their Slaves as they may think fit subjects of liberty; and that they take every possible measure by teaching their young slaves to read and giving them such other instruction as may seem in their power, to prepare them for the enjoyment of liberty."[60] A year later the Transylvania Presbytery faced the slavery problem yet again. In its response the Presbytery affirmed that while slavery was a moral evil, not all slave owners were guilty of moral evil. As to distinguishing those who were guilty from those who were not, the Presbytery declined to judge, only saying that the importance of the question required further consideration and should therefore be "put off to a future day."[61]

The church's equivocation irritated ardent emancipationists, who continued their agitation. When Transylvania Presbytery was divided in 1800 and the congregations of Cane Ridge and Concord found themselves in the new presbytery of West Lexington, they promptly brought the issue to the new organization. Their petition denounced slavery as a moral evil, something "very henious, & consequently sufficient to exclude such [church members] as will continue in the practice of it from the privileges of the Church." After some deliberation, West Lexington Presbytery resolved to refer the matter to their superior ecclesiastical body, the Synod of Virginia. The appeal explained that it was "a Subject likely to occasion much trouble & discussion in the churches in this country," where a "large majority" of church members apparently sympathized with the petitioners. The Synod stood by official church policy: slave owners in the church had an "indispensable duty" to prepare their slaves for freedom and to grant them freedom when they had shown themselves ready. But to exclude church members for having slaves was a "very unwarrantable procedure." Besides violating church policy, the Synod pointed out, exclusion from the church was unlikely to end slavery. Those emancipationists were wrong who insisted on judging slavery a known sin and therefore all slave owners to be sinners: only those slave-owning church members who understood the sinfulness of slavery deserved to be excluded. Lacking an adequate means to distinguish the unpersuaded conscience from the defiant conscience, the Synod recommended that "mutual forbearance & charity ought to be exercised towards those who differ in opinion from one another."[62] Presbyterian church discipline thus constrained western extremists.

Overall, whether Baptist, Methodist, or Presbyterian, Kentucky churches experienced a painful and embarrassing struggle to reconcile their religious beliefs with the demand for agricultural labor. By the end of the eighteenth century, the denominations had all found it necessary to retreat from their earlier militancy to more accommodating positions. Slavery had become a matter of conscience, not of church discipline. In 1805, this policy was officially adopted by the Elkhorn Association, which declared, "This Association Judges it improper for ministers[,] Churches, or Associations to meddle with emancipation from Slavery or any other political Subject." Bracken Association was slightly more explicit, declaring, "It is our Opinion that as an Ass'n we have nothing to do with Slavery, seeing that it involves political questions, but do advise every soul to be subject to the higher power."[63] A similar retreat is observable among western Presbyterians. Reverend David Rice, who had resigned his seat in the constitutional convention of 1792 to protest protection for slavery, came to admit that "a slave let loose upon society ignorant, idle, headstrong, is in a state to injure others and ruin himself."[64] Rice argued that Christianity was as capable of ending slavery in Kentucky as it had been in Rome, "not by producing laws for . . . abolition, but by its effects on the hearts of christians[,] disposing them to justice and mercy."[65] Given the realities of a burgeoning agricultural district, the most that could be hoped for was that church members with slaves would become conscience-stricken and see the need to emancipate their human chattel.

As western slavery received accommodation from church and state, some disillusioned emancipationists left for the Northwest Territory. The

American victory at Fallen Timbers in 1794 was quickly followed by a heavy influx of settlement, much of it from Kentucky. Many of these people headed north for the chance to buy cheap land, but the federal territory also beckoned to ardent emancipationists and others simply not comfortable amid slavery. Thomas Rogers of Cane Ridge, only a boy at the time, remembered when Colonel James Smith returned from the 1792 state constitutional convention and told Mr. Rogers about the Ninth Amendment protecting slavery. "I remember well my father's expression after hearing Smith through. 'Well, well, Kentucky will not hold me much longer.'" Mrs. Rogers, standing nearby listening to the conversation, asked her husband, "Well, William, where next?" He replied, "I will be among the first to go to the Northwestern Territory." By 1797, the Rogers family had relocated to the area of Chillecothe. They were not alone in this choice. As another former inhabitant of Bourbon County explained, "My father moved to this place [Fayette County, Ohio] on account of slavery." Without leaving such an explicit statement of motives, hundreds and perhaps thousands of Kentuckians seeking new land around the close of the century chose to go north rather than to western Kentucky, Tennessee, or Missouri.[66] In the interim, however, Kentucky congregations struggled to discover a peaceable compromise.

Religious Slumber

Despite impressive institutional development and a growing corps of ministers, the 1790s marked a stagnant period for all three denominations in terms of attracting new church adherents. The problem was hardly unique to the western settlements. Clergymen throughout America found the closing years of the eighteenth century a time of religious slumber, if not sheer ungodliness.[67] Notwithstanding a few pockets of religious interest, church membership declined or faltered in various parts of the new United States. Most ministers and professors of religion probably shared Episcopal minister Devereaux Jarratt's feeling that the "prospect is gloomy and truly suspicious and discouraging."[68]

Western preachers likewise watched the slow progress of religion with concern, at times nearly overwhelmed by the indifference and even hostility they encountered. Methodist itinerant Benjamin Lakin, serving eastern Kentucky's Hinkston Circuit in 1794, lamented in his journal for the "low state of Zion." Lakin prayed and wept "for the Lord to revive his work." At the town of Cynthiana in Harrison County, for example, Lakin tried preaching to "a thoughtless people, but they refused to open a dore to receive the Gospel." Lakin judged another large gathering in the area as "the most Disorderly peopel that I have seen." Lakin met with more positive receptions on other occasions, but his preaching during the closing years of the eighteenth century met with frequent indifference or rejection.[69] As his superior, Bishop Francis Asbury, remarked during a trip west in 1800, on the eve of the Great Revival, "It is plain there are not many mighty among the Methodists in Kentucky."[70]

Western Presbyterians likewise found "great cause to mourn for the deadness which is too apparent in our Congregations." In early 1792, Transylvania Presbytery called for a special day of fasting and prayer "to implore the blessing of God upon his church & that the primitive Spirit of the Christian religion be revived." By 1794, the sense of alarm among the Presbytery's member congregations resurfaced with a resolution calling for a special meeting to investigate "the general causes, & implore the divine aid in this important case." A year later the "languishing State of religion among our churches" prompted yet another fast day. Similarly, shortly after its creation from the eastern section of Transylvania Presbytery in 1799, West Lexington Presbytery urged member congregations to join on the first Tuesday of each month in a "concert of prayer for a revival of religion." Again in 1800, Transylvania Presbytery deplored the "prevalence of vice & infidelity, the great apparent declension of true vital religion in too many places." These years also witnessed repeated calls for a return to family prayer.[71] Apparently even in the homes of church members, religious attention was weak or lacking altogether.

Identical complaints troubled the Baptist churches. Elkhorn Association in 1793 recorded that its twenty-five member churches "are in general peace but appear to be in a languishing state[,] few additions haveing [sic] been made this year." At the annual meeting in August 1795, Elkhorn Association recommended that member churches set aside the second Saturday in September as "a day of fasting and prayer to implore the divine blessing upon our state and upon the Churches that the Lord would bless his own institution of a preached Gospel[, and] that he would check the rapid [spread] of impiety & infidelity." A related problem was religious complacency. Shortly after arriving in Kentucky in 1795, Baptist minister David Barrow commented that religion in his new state was marked by a "good deal of fashionable, or Pharisaical conformity." Reverend John Taylor, living in the rich Bluegrass region immediately northwest of Lexington and one of the most active of the pioneer Baptist preachers, saw the 1790s as a time of severe religious drought. Despite the large number of Baptists throughout Kentucky, religion exhibited "but little of the spirit of devotion."[72] At the annual meeting of the Elkhorn Association in 1799, "complaints of deadness and supineness in religion" were heard all around. According to one Baptist leader, "It appeared as if every harp was untuned and hung upon the willows. Though peace and tranquility were prevalent, and the Churches appeared sound in the Faith, their general state seemed to strike all the friends of vital piety." According to this same observer, "It was likewise observed to be the case with every other denomination of Christian in this country."[73] Presbyterian David Rice discovered similar conditions when he settled in Green County in 1800: "I found that there were but few reputable characters as Christians. There were a few Presbyterians, a few Baptists, and a few Methodists, but a few upon the whole."[74]

Data on church membership for the years prior to the Great Revival bear out the truthfulness of these anxious laments. The arrival of a new minister might herald a brief flurry of "religious excitement," but after former members returned and perhaps a few new members arrived, interest would abate. Hardly any information exists concerning Presbyterian church membership during the eighteenth century, but records are good for Baptists and Methodists. Among the congregations in the Elkhorn Association, by far the largest of the western Baptist associations and encompassing most of the Bluegrass region, the 1790s marked a period of little growth, broken only by a brief evangelical excitement among new settlers in Mason County in 1797. After the initial period of settlement and reorganization, however, Baptist membership in general increased slowly.

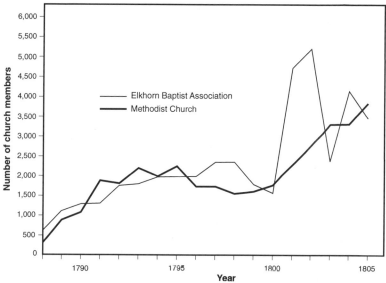

Fig. 2. Patterns of church membership for Kentucky Baptists and Methodists. Data was drawn from the "Minutes of Elkhorn Baptist Association," in William Warren Sweet, *Religion on the American Frontier: The Baptists, 1783–1830: A Collection of Source Materials* (New York: Henry Holt, 1931); *Minutes of the Annual Conferences of the Methodist Episcopal Church, 1773–1851,* 4 vols. (New York: T. Mason and G. Lane, 1840).

Indeed, toward the end of the decade, membership actually declined. Western Methodism presents a similar picture. The 1790s began with steady growth, followed by a more erratic pattern by mid-decade, and then faltering in the closing years of the century. The poor growth of western Methodism is especially striking because with each passing year the western preaching circuits were gaining additional itinerants. The closing years of the eighteenth century were truly a time of "religious slumber" in the West, regardless of denomination.[75]

The decline in church membership was all the more cause for concern because it occurred in the midst of phenomenal population growth. Between 1790 and 1800, the population of Kentucky more than tripled, from 73,677 to 220,955. Moreover, roughly 55 percent of this population was age sixteen or under—the highest proportion of children anywhere in the United States except Tennessee. Most of these young people were apparently approaching adulthood without much familiarity with a vigorous religious establishment. One Kentuckian coming of age in the decade before the Great Revival simply assumed that "young people had nothing to do with the sacrament, that it was intended for old people only."[76] As contemporary historian Robert Davidson explained, "It was the general impression that none but elderly persons, who from their years had acquired steady habits and were out of the way of temptation, should partake of the ordinances." The growing number of western young people felt alienated and therefore "gave themselves no concern about religion." The inevitable consequence was that "the Church, gaining no accessions, was in a fair way to becoming extinct through natural decrease."[77] An entire generation was coming of age almost ignorant of Christian principles, a backlog of potential converts for the Great Revival.

In short, Kentucky was not nearly the spiritual desert it has often been described as being before the Great Revival. Despite an initial slowness in transplanting organized religion caused by the chronic border warfare, the pioneer generation of preachers had built a sound institutional base. The 1790s witnessed a rapid proliferation of congregations, and by 1800 most Kentuckians enjoyed reasonable access to a local church. This was particularly true of the Bluegrass region, where the Great Revival exerted its greatest power. It is indeed doubtful whether the Great Revival could have occurred, or retained many of the new adherents, had it not been preceded by two decades of dedicated religious work.

Yet western religion remained quite fragile. The division and conflict afflicting public life also plagued the religious community. Rarely did a congregation escape some sort of serious difficulty during its early years. Some church leaders might even have pursued emancipation more vigorously had they not been constantly fending off disunity. Arguably more problematic was the inability to attract new adherents, something especially disturbing for evangelical denominations such as the Presbyterians, Baptists, and Methodists. But even more troubling was the mysterious inability to attract young people. The institutional foundation built by frontier churchmen seemed a hollow achievement when the rising generation showed so little interest in religion. This general, persistent sense of malaise during the closing years of the eighteenth century is significant because it made religious leaders more receptive to experimentation with new forms of worship.

Part III.
THE GREAT REVIVAL

The association of camp meeting revivalism with a Turnerian frontier environment has almost totally obscured important traits. Rather than being a wholly novel creation, the camp meeting format adapted and rearranged several existing religious elements. In a related vein, what distinguished the camp meeting revival from other existing forms of worship lay more with the ritual structure than the theology. Especially misunderstood is that the camp meeting was not a more individualistic form of worship but quite the contrary. It brought together a diverse and divided society and created a temporary ideal model of Christian society.

8

SPIRITUAL AWAKENING

In 1800, after a quarter-century of settlement, Kentucky was in several ways primed for a religious revival. Most inhabitants were nominal Christians but not connected to any particular congregation. Moreover, many were young adults and at a traditional point in the life cycle for a spiritual transformation. Religious institutions in Kentucky were not only present but had had time to take root. Some congregations were already a decade old by the time of the Great Revival, and nearly all belonged to regional governing bodies that provided valuable stability and support. Furthermore, and in contrast to Kentucky's parent state of Virginia, each of the three main Kentucky denominations had a strong evangelical character. By 1800, Kentucky also had an energetic ministry, one grown anxious about stagnant membership levels. The combined effect made a revival of religion a real possibility as the century came to a close.[1]

But the Great Revival was more than simply a fresh infusion of believers. Unlike most revivals, it produced a new form of evangelical worship, the camp meeting. For much of the twentieth century, historians of American religion looked at the western origins and believed that this newness was a product of a frontier setting. More recent studies have instead emphasized evangelical traditions and precedent. Camp meeting revivalism is more accurately considered as a combination of old and new elements. Traditional belief and practice provided the core to which were added seemingly simple and modest alterations. The result, largely unintentional and certainly unforeseen, was a very different sort of evangelical experience, one which resonated deeply with a generation disoriented by a war for independence, geographic relocation, a more competitive economy, and a disturbingly partisan political culture.

A New Light Tradition

In some respects the Great Revival in Kentucky was merely another episode in a strong tradition of Presbyterian revivalism that stretched all the way back to the Scottish Reformation. The Scots-Irish migration to North America in the early eighteenth century had not abandoned this heritage but rather transplanted it to a new setting in the backcountry of Pennsylvania, Virginia, and North Carolina.[2] A wave of local revivals in this region following the Revolution set the stage for the Great Revival west of the mountains at the turn of the century. Some of the participants were undoubtedly in Kentucky by the end of the century, and perhaps their experiences made them more receptive to revivalism when it later surfaced there. Unfortunately, with rare exceptions, this connection is nearly impossible to trace.

For the Presbyterian clergy active in Kentucky's Great Revival, however, the relevance of previous revival experiences seems fairly clear. A significant proportion of the Presbyterian ministers working in Kentucky by 1800 had participated in or were themselves products of this late-eighteenth-century wave of revivalism. At a formative moment in their professional lives, these men had personally witnessed the importance of evangelical preaching, and it altered the way they thought about their ministerial roles. Whereas the first western ministers had devoted their lives to organizing congregations and instilling church discipline and order, this younger generation of ministers believed that such work was secondary to saving souls. "Vital religion," as they called it, preceded all else.

Of the various postrevolutionary revivals in the Presbyterian Church, the one of greatest relevance for Kentucky occurred in Virginia, centered at Hampden-Sydney College in Virginia, and soon spread to her sister institution west of the Blue Ridge, Liberty Hall Academy. Many of the Southern Presbyterian ministers active in the late eighteenth century had been trained at one of these two institutions.[3] The Hampden-Sydney revival started in 1787 when a student named Cary Allen, later to work as a minister in Kentucky, heard the preaching of a Methodist preacher named Hope Hull and subsequently experienced a new spiritual birth.[4] Upon Allen's return to Hampden-Sydney, the dramatic change in his demeanor impressed several other students and moved them to seek a similar religious transformation. This small group began secretly meeting to sing and pray together. Concerned by the Methodist influence behind Allen's transformation, Hampden-Sydney's president, John Blair Smith, invited the students to hold their next meeting in the parlor of his home. By then the religious fervor had embraced almost the entire school, and on the appointed evening Smith's parlor could hardly accommodate the number of students who arrived.[5] The revival of religious interest soon spilled beyond Hampden-Sydney. One Presbyterian leader claimed that he "had seen nothing equal to it for extensive spread, power, and spiritual glory, since the years '40 and '41." Smith, who had played a prominent role in the Virginia debates concerning church and state relations, was deeply disillusioned with politics, and he poured himself into the revival. That summer he spent "riding to sacraments, and preaching everywhere."[6]

Smith belonged to the evangelical tradition of the Great Awakening and welcomed the revival of religious interest, but as a Calvinist he regarded the emotional forms of worship condoned by Methodism as unbecoming in the eyes of God. Smith therefore sought to control the Methodist influence behind Cary Allen's spiritual transformation, but without stifling the religious interest it had generated. Smith firmly steered his young charges away from Methodist styles of spontaneity and emotion and toward a more restrained demeanor. Whenever the people listening to his sermons verged on any sort of outburst, Smith would admonish them and wait for composure. A contemporary described Smith's preaching style as "plain, practical and very fervid; but perfectly free from ranting. The Calvinist doctrines were conspicuous in his sermons."[7] Thus, despite the glimmer of Methodist influence, the Hampden-Sydney revival remained well within the traditions of New Light Presbyterianism, which had been planted in America during the Great Awakening earlier in the eighteenth century.

Though conservative and brief, the Hampden-Sydney revival infused the Presbyterian ministry working in the South with a renewed dedication to evangelical preaching during a most discouraging time. No individual career better exemplifies this fresh infusion of evangelical fervor than that of James McGready, destined to play a critical role in Kentucky's Great Revival.[8] McGready had been born in 1758 in western Pennsylvania and had lived there until his family moved south to Guilford County, a stronghold of Presbyterianism in the backcountry of North Carolina. After the Revolution, McGready returned to Pennsylvania to study for the ministry under James McMillan, an heir of the Great Awakening and a graduate of the College of New Jersey. As a New Light Presbyterian, McMillan stressed regeneration in his ministry, but McGready apparently did not experience a personal conversion until 1786, following his recovery from smallpox. After being licensed to preach in 1788 by Redstone Presbytery of western Pennsylvania, McGready returned to North Carolina. Along the way he happened upon the revival under way at Hampden-Sydney College. Although McGready's precise level of involvement in the Hampden-Sydney revival remains a mystery, he interrupted his travel because of it and his autobiographical writings suggest that it was an influential event.

Soon after reaching North Carolina, McGready became the pastor for two congregations in the Guilford County area. His recent revival experience seems to have made a serious impression, for McGready soon revived religious interest among his new charges in North Carolina. By early 1790 he was at the head of a "great religious excitement." McGready's preaching especially affected the young men at Guilford Academy, a highly regarded school under the direction of Reverend David Caldwell, a fellow

Presbyterian New Light. Hearing McGready preach, a student and future colleague named Barton W. Stone wrote of him, "His person was not prepossessing, nor his appearance interesting. . . . His coarse tremulous voice excited in me the idea of something unearthly." Yet, "Such earnestness—such zeal—such powerful persuasion, enforced by the joys of heaven and miseries of hell, I had never witnessed before. My mind was chained by him."[9] McGready's passionate appeals to sinners, however, also provoked opposition. Death threats compelled him to move his family in 1795, settling eventually in southern Kentucky. There, by the end of the decade, McGready would again be at the center of a religious revival—this time evoking even greater controversy.

Notwithstanding the evangelical qualities of the Hampden-Sydney revival in Virginia and McGready's revival in North Carolina, the Calvinist tenets of Presbyterianism remained intact. The emphasis on regeneration in the theology of McGready, Smith, and their followers was not inconsistent with orthodox Calvinist doctrines of special election, total depravity, and irresistible grace. Presbyterian New Lights reconciled these beliefs with evangelicalism by viewing God's elect as not necessarily an exclusive minority. Ministers therefore had an obligation to grant priority in their preaching to spiritual rebirth, using, as McGready declared, "every possible means to alarm and awaken Christless sinners from their security, and bring them to a sense of their danger and guilt." Otherwise, "we will be the worst murderers; the blood of sinners will be required at our hands—their damnation will lie at our door."[10] McGready and his generation of Presbyterian ministers regarded themselves as direct descendants of the Great Awakening, legitimate sons. Although they laid greater emphasis on regeneration, they remained orthodox Calvinists.

Similarly, the ritual structure of Presbyterian revivalism also remained traditional, centered around the sacramental occasion. Scheduled annually for each congregation, or semi-annually in some areas, the sacramental occasion constituted a major event on the religious calendar. Preparatory observances, mainly prayer and fasting, might begin a week in advance. By Thursday evening small groups of neighboring church members met for prayer and hymns, led by an elder or perhaps by the pastor himself. The pastor usually held a special prayer session on Friday evening, either at the meetinghouse or in the home of a nearby elder. On Saturday, "public" events began at the meetinghouse. Preaching, prayer, and hymns took up most of the day, often followed by a special sermon in the evening. Sunday's activities oriented around the Lord's Supper. For Calvinists such as the Presbyterians, this was an exclusive event, restricted to those people who had experienced a conversion, that is, to God's elect. Before administering the sacrament, the pastor of the congregation would deliver what was called the "action sermon." Another minister would "fence the tables," reviewing in detail "all the sins forbidden in each of the ten commandments." Church members who qualified for the sacrament had previously received small lead or pewter tokens, which they surrendered as they approached the communion table where the pastor presided. When attendance was large, the successive seatings might take several hours. More prayer and hymns usually followed, continuing after nightfall by torchlight. The last participants separated for home on Monday morning after a brief closing prayer. The sacramental occasion could be an extremely emotional experience, particularly at certain points in the services, but ecstatic or enthusiastic behavior was not a prominent feature of late-eighteenth-century sacraments.[11]

Camping too was virtually unknown. As a special event on the church calendar, sacramental occasions usually drew a larger turnout than did regular Sunday worship. Services were therefore often held outdoors. In fact, the regional presbyteries scheduled sacramental occasions during summer for just this reason. For Presbyterians, summer was the "sacramental season." The sacramental occasion, it should be noted, was intended primarily for members of the local congregation. Those whose homes were inconveniently distant stayed overnight with various church members living near the meetinghouse. "The families residing in the vicinity of the place were usually thronged with lodgers." Proceedings were adjourned late at night and taken up again the following morning.[12]

In contrast to the sermons of regular Sunday worship, which usually explicated Scripture or addressed doctrinal matters, ministers found the sacramental occasion a natural forum for special evangelical preaching. Not only did the communion table dramatically distinguish the saved from the unsaved, but families often attended in whole, meaning that children of church members and other unredeemed persons were present in greater number than usual. But by no means did Presbyterians expect sudden conversions. The idea was completely inconsistent with Calvinism, which held that humankind was thoroughly depraved and regeneration was possible only as a gift of God's grace. This gift would be granted not as a result of any human merit but only through God's mercy and love. Therefore, grace would arrive in "God's own sovereign time, and for that time the sinner must wait." Convicted individuals might go through days, weeks, or months of spiritual agony before receiving that gift of grace. In North Carolina, during McGready's revival around 1790, young Barton Stone waited a full year from the time when he felt convicted of his sinfulness to when he received saving grace—and regarded this as normal. "According to the preaching, and the experience of the pious in those days," Stone later explained, "I anticipated a long and painful struggle . . . in the language then used, before I should get religion."[13] For Calvinists, "getting religion" was a distinctly two-step process of conviction and conversion.

Though triggered perhaps during a sacramental occasion, personal transformations from godlessness to conviction and especially from conviction
to conversion typically occurred in private, during "secret prayer." The
authenticity of this experience would have to be reviewed by the pastor
and elders before baptism. Thus, at the sacramental occasion, the Lord's
Supper dominated all else and the process of joining God's elect usually
transpired elsewhere.

Although the postrevolutionary revivalism was conservative, adher-
ing to Calvinist theology and the ritual of the sacramental occasion, it
reinvigorated New Light Presbyterianism tremendously. An estimated thirty
to forty graduates of Hampden-Sydney College and Virginia's other Presbyterian academy, Liberty Hall, entered the ministry in the years directly
following the revivals at those institutions. This rising generation of Southern Presbyterian ministers could be found a few years later preaching
throughout the reaches of American Presbyterianism and particularly in
the southern backcountry where the denomination was most concentrated.
These ministers had personally witnessed, at a formative point in their
professional lives, the power of evangelical preaching. Their subsequent
ministerial careers emphasized regeneration, faith, and repentance.

The effect for newly settled areas such as Kentucky, where Presbyterian ministers were in short supply, was enormous. Over the next few
years the Synod of Virginia, now with a small surplus of energetic young
ministers, dispatched several missionaries to Kentucky. One of the first
was Cary Allen, the young man who had initiated the revival at Hampden-
Sydney. Also from Hampden-Sydney came James Blythe and William
Calhoun. From Liberty Hall came Robert Marshall, Robert Stuart, and
John Lyle. From McGready's Revival in North Carolina came John Rankin,
William Hodge, and Barton W. Stone. Thus, in the closing years of the
eighteenth century, western Presbyterianism was infused with a younger
generation of ministers dedicated to evangelical outreach. By 1800, individuals with personal experience of revivalism and its techniques constituted one-third of the Presbyterian ministers active in Kentucky.[14]

The Creation of a New Evangelical Format

The breach with the New Light tradition and the beginnings of camp
meeting revivalism occurred under James McGready in 1800, and it is richly
documented in firsthand accounts left by clergy and laity. Religious conditions in Kentucky had not changed very much between David Rice's
arrival in 1783 and that of James McGready in 1797. Although McGready
did not struggle in the same sort of isolation as Rice had, he faced the
same problems of nurturing feeble congregations and catechizing persons
who had long neglected religion. Over the years the number of church

members and congregations in Kentucky had steadily increased, but this progress was practically obliterated by the much faster rate of population growth. Despite the achievements of Rice and his generation of colleagues, religion was yet a minor aspect of western life.

After a brief time in Tennessee, McGready joined a few friends from North Carolina who had settled in Logan County, a comparatively remote and still rustic area in southern Kentucky. There he assumed the care of three small congregations: Gaspar River, Muddy River, and Red River. McGready had a difficult task before him. Logan County was known as a rough neighborhood, even by western standards. The famous Methodist preacher Peter Cartwright said that the area in Logan County where he grew up went by the label "Rogue's Harbor." Reverend John Rankin had visited Logan County early the previous year, but "could not discover a single individual, who seemed to have any light or knowledge of living religion, or any desire for it."[15] In this setting, McGready resumed his gospel ministry of regeneration. Within months, "the ears of all . . . seemed to be open to receive the word preached." About ten new members joined McGready's congregation at Gaspar River, a noteworthy success given the circumstances. Following the summer sacramental season, however, the religious interest generally subsided and by the end of the year conditions had returned to a state of "general deadness."[16]

McGready and his small band of believers continued to pray and fast for the conversion of sinners. In 1798, with the onset of better weather in spring, the religious energy of the previous year resumed. At the sacramental occasion in late July, "a very general awakening took place." The ministers who assisted McGready likewise found "renewed zeal and fervor of spirit."[17] At his next sacramental occasion, in September at Muddy River, "The people seemed to hear as for eternity." As a result of McGready's personal dedication, religion became a foremost topic of daily conversation throughout the Logan County area. Apparently, however, McGready's zeal led him beyond normal standards of Presbyterian decorum. One of his more conservative colleagues, Reverend James Balch, ridiculed the emotional proceedings and disputed the propriety of evangelical preaching as practiced by McGready. Under Balch's harsh criticism, religious recovery subsided. Yet McGready did not surrender. Through another winter, he and his followers nursed along their hopes that God would send His saving grace.

The sacramental occasion at Red River, in July 1799, seemed to herald a return of religious interest. By the close of the service on Monday, "the power of God seemed to fill the congregation, the boldest, daring sinners in the country covered their faces and wept bitterly." When the service ended, people lingered, reluctant to leave. Their religious awareness had been greatly aroused, but they seemed not to know how to respond.

McGready and the ministers assisting him were themselves confused, but called the people back for more prayer. Suddenly, "The mighty power of God came amongst us like a shower from the everlasting hills . . . and some precious souls were brought to feel the pardoning love of Jesus." The specific manner in which this heavenly shower was experienced by the assembly McGready does not explain, but the problems he encountered with closing the sacramental occasion in the usual manner indicates that the old ritual was no longer sufficient. McGready was being driven to improvise.

Similar crises occurred at McGready's other sacramental occasions that summer. At the Gaspar River sacramental occasion held a month later, the people again remained after the close of proceedings, solemn, expectant, and tense. "Presently, several persons under deep conviction broke forth into a loud outcry—many fell to the ground, lay powerless, groaning, praying and crying for mercy." McGready and the assisting ministers earnestly sought to comfort and restore the stricken, but they also felt thoroughly awed by the scene. This meeting was followed by an equally moving sacramental occasion a few weeks later at Muddy River. The evangelical urgings from McGready and his colleagues were bringing people to an emotional precipice, but leaving affected individuals helpless in their seats, without means for relief. There matters remained as the sacramental season ended for 1799 and the religious excitement became dormant for winter.[18]

The sacramental occasions conducted under McGready's direction in 1800 reveal a distinct shift, with greater emphasis on regeneration. Indeed, the central focus soon become dual. The change occurred in late June when McGready's three congregations, Muddy River, Gaspar River, and Red River, met at the latter location for a sacramental occasion. Attendance was calculated at four or five hundred people, unprecedented in Kentucky. Assisting McGready were Presbyterian ministers William Hodge, John Rankin, and William McGee—all previously acquainted through the revival in North Carolina. Also present was a Methodist minister, John McGee, the brother of William. In a gesture of ecumenical unity unusual for the times, McGready invited him to address the gathering. McGee's presence would prove critical in breaking the impasse that had been encountered in closing sacramental occasions the previous year.

Throughout the weekend, people listened "with reverence and awe," and as the close of events approached on Monday, the religious tension had grown palpable. Hodge concluded the sacramental occasion with a powerful sermon, and then the assembly was dismissed. McGready, Rankin, and Hodge prepared to leave. Most of the listeners remained quietly in their seats, however, reluctant to depart. The McGee brothers also remained in their places. Once again, McGready's proceedings had generated an acute level of religious feeling. According to one account, a "solemn weeping" affected many of those present. At this critical moment, when the Presbyterian ministers seemed helpless, John McGee, the Methodist, "came forward and without hesitation, entered on the most heart-stirring exhortation, encouraging the wounded of the day never to cease striving . . . until they had obtained peace in their souls."[19] McGee later related that he "exhorted them to let the Lord God Omnipotent reign in their hearts, and to submit to Him, and their souls should live." McGee then proceeded to lead in singing a hymn while some of the people loudly began to praise God. He sang out an old Watts hymn,

> Come, Holy Spirit, Heavenly Dove,
> With all thy Quickening powers
> Kindle a flame of sacred love,
> In these cold hearts of ours.

According to a lay member, McGee "had not sung more than the verse quoted, when an aged lady, Mrs. Pacely, sitting quite across the congregation to the left, and Mrs. Clark, also advanced in years, seated to the right, began in rather suppressed but distinct tones, to hold a sort of dialogue with each other, and to reciprocate sentiments of praise and thanksgiving." Still singing, McGee slowly descended from the pulpit and moved toward these two ladies and other individuals who seemed particularly stricken. Alarmed, his brother warned, "You know, these people are much for order. They will not bear this confusion." Yet, amazingly enough, they did. No one was ready to take on the role Smith had at Hampden-Sydney and enforce Presbyterian restraint. As McGee slowly moved through the crowded meetinghouse, he reached out and clasped the hands of those persons nearest him. "Suddenly persons began to fall as he passed through the crowd—some as dead." Overpowered by religious feeling, some people physically collapsed into an unconscious state deeper, observers claimed, than simple fainting. McGee recalled years later, "I went through the house shouting, and exhorting with all possible ecstacy and energy, and the floor was soon covered with the slain."[20]

Although falling to the ground was a very old symbol of Christian submission, it was unfamiliar to the late-eighteenth-century Presbyterians, and for the moment, "All was alarm and confusion." Reverend Rankin later remembered that Hodge turned to him in a panic asking, "What shall we do? What shall we do?" Somewhat rattled himself, Rankin answered, "We can do nothing at present. We are strangers to such an operation." The Presbyterians had lost control of their meeting, but observing McGee's composure, they "acquiesced and stood in astonishment, admiring the wonderful work of God." Methodist clergy would be invited to

future sacramental occasions for help in the same situation, although Presbyterians could never readily admit their need for guidance and instead
claimed a new ecumenical spirit.[21]

As news of the extraordinary occurrences at Red River spread, people
prepared to attend McGready's next sacrament and witness matters for
themselves. At Gaspar River on the last weekend of July, "A surprising
multitude of people collected; many from a very great distance." Most
significantly, some arrived prepared to camp at the meetinghouse. According to McGready, "There were 13 waggons brought to the meetinghouse, in order to transport people and their provisions." And in August
at Muddy River, "an immense multitude assembled from far and near.
There were twenty-two waggons loaded with people and their provisions;
with many others provided for encamping at the meeting house." Referring to the customary hospitality, McGready pointed out, "The congregation could not have accommodated the one-half of the strangers if they
had not come so provided." Although the term would not come into use
for several more years, here began the idea of the camp meeting.
McGready's own descriptions reveal quite clearly that the initiative was
exercised by the laity rather than by the clergy. People were not coming to
escape spiritual isolation, for services had been available at the meetinghouse for several years, but to witness the marvel they had heard told of,
to see a spectacle. Just what they thought of it, of course, varied according
to belief, but camping at the site helped ensure that they would not miss
the emotional displays that tended to occur toward the end of the long
day's activities.[22] The clergy acquiesced because they correctly sensed that
removing people from daily life increased the likelihood of personal transformation.[23]

In the wake of Red River, the sacramental occasion at Gaspar River
carried a high level of general expectation. Tensions mounted throughout
Friday and Saturday. By the end of the Saturday night sermon, penitents
were "lying in every part of the house, praying and crying for mercy."[24]
Many others, however, found no relief, and tension continued to build
throughout the Sunday services. A general feeling of urgency permeated
the sultry summer air. As the conclusion of the sacrament neared, so did
the final opportunity for rebirth. That night William McGee exhorted the
assembly with all his powers, the pulpit illuminated by flaming torches.
His text was that of the apostle Peter sinking into the water due to his lack
of faith. By the time McGee finished, the assembly was thoroughly agitated. The cries of distressed sinners nearly drowned out the sound of his
voice. "No person seemed to wish to go home—hunger and sleep seemed
to affect nobody—eternal things were the vast concern," wrote McGready
later. "Here awakening and converting work was to be found in every
part of the multitude."[25] According to Reverend John Rankin, who had

also been present at Red River, the floor of the meetinghouse once again was "literally covered with the prostrate bodies of penitents." Few Presbyterians present had ever seen anything like it.

Thus, under McGready the primary function of the Presbyterian sacramental occasion began a subtle but unmistakable shift, from administering the sacrament to saving souls. An evangelical concern had always characterized the event, but was now elevated to greater prominence. Ritually, the event remained a sacramental occasion, but it was now accompanied by a rite of personal transformation—the product, apparently, of Methodist influences and acquiesced to by Calvinist Presbyterians in the interest of gaining converts. The strange manner in which affected individuals fell to the ground led to two additional changes. One was a universal call to participate regardless of denomination, and the other was the creation of a total environment through camping at the meeting site. These changes involved ritual more than belief, and nothing about them was inherently inconsistent with Calvinism. They nonetheless made a tremendous difference in the evangelical experience, for both those who responded to appeals and those who participated less completely.

A Spiritual Refreshing among Western Baptists

The new style of sacramental occasion attracted unprecedented levels of response every place it was introduced, but the altered format alone cannot be credited for producing Kentucky's Great Revival. Perhaps the clearest evidence for this was a parallel revival among Baptist congregations in the Bluegrass. The Baptist revival coincided closely with that begun by McGready miles away to the south, first appearing in the late summer of 1800, but it was clearly an independent phenomenon. By the next spring when news arrived of McGready's activities, nearly every Baptist church in the area was already in the midst of a powerful revival of religious interest.[26] Histories of the Great Kentucky Revival have almost completely overlooked the Baptist aspect, largely because it operated with less sensation. Its appearance is nonetheless important as a strong indication that the widespread popular appeal of McGready's new form of sacramental occasion involved more than mere spectacle. A more general set of preconditions, particularly in the Bluegrass region, made Kentucky ripe for evangelical appeal.

In 1800 western Baptists still possessed a living, if dormant, evangelical heritage. Most church members were converts from other denominations, and many of the ministers who had led them to the West were still active, including John Taylor, Richard Cave, Ambrose Dudley, Joseph Redding, John Gano, George S. Smith, Augustine Eastin, William Hickman, Elijah Craig, and his brother Lewis Craig. Neither the Presbyterians nor the Methodists could claim a similar continuity of leadership. Nonetheless, Baptist church growth generally stagnated during the 1790s and became an increasing point of concern. The religious zeal of the older generation, who had experienced persecution for their beliefs in Virginia, seemed a dim memory by the end of the eighteenth century.

This pattern changed abruptly in 1800. The Elkhorn Association's annual meeting in early August marked a sudden resurgence of religious interest, attracting more than two thousand people.[27] Shortly afterwards, the first signs of a religious revival were noted among several of the member congregations. And, in contrast to the seasonal pattern prevailing among the Presbyterians, the Baptist revival persisted through the difficult winter months. At Bryan's Station Baptist Church near Lexington, for example, at least 120 new members were baptized between February 8 and March 8. In the Elkhorn Association, which included most of the Bluegrass churches, new baptisms doubled the membership in no fewer than eighteen of the twenty-six member churches. Bryan's Station and three other congregations were especially affected, each gaining more than three hundred new brethren that year. One church member likened the religious interest to "a fire that has been long confined—bursting all its barriers, and spreading with a rapidity that is indescribable."[35] The Association's annual meeting in early August 1801 at South Elkhorn Baptist Church near Lexington drew between eight and ten thousand people.[29] Attendance on this scale was unprecedented among Kentucky Baptists and is all the more remarkable because it coincided with the massive sacramental occasion at the Cane Ridge Presbyterian Meetinghouse only a few dozen miles away. Contemporary accounts of the Baptist revival make no mention of camping. The induction of new members through the winter of 1800–1801, in contrast to the Presbyterian sacramental occasions in summer, suggest a different sort of evangelical format. It is certainly possible, however, that the crowds at South Elkhorn Meetinghouse may have adopted camping, or begun to, for the same practical reasons as at McGready's sacramental occasions.

The Baptist revival shared an amazing coincidence not only of timing but also of place. By the summer of 1801, the main revival activity among Presbyterians was no longer in Logan County but in the central part of Kentucky. This area had also seen the greatest increase in the number of new Baptists. "Last winter was a considerable addition to the Baptist Church," reported an anonymous observer, especially "in the interior parts of this state." Several congregations in the Elkhorn and Bracken Associations of churches experienced membership increases exceeding 70 percent over the previous year.[30] These Baptist activities were organizationally independent of the revival triggered by McGready's new style of sacramental occasion and by 1801 now appearing among other western Presbyterian

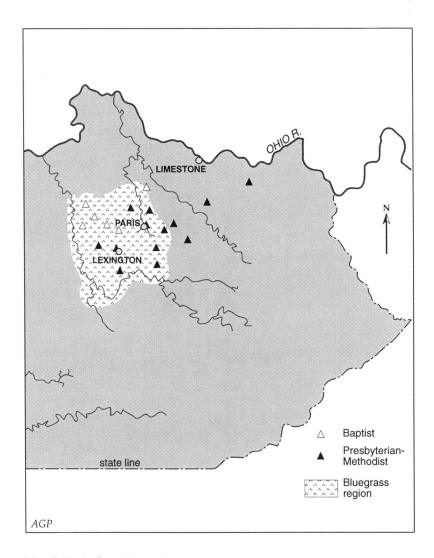

Map 7. Revival activity in the Kentucky Bluegrass region, 1801. Baptist centers of revival are represented by congregations where membership grew by 70 percent or more during the previous year. Presbyterian and Methodist revivalism followed the circuit of sacramental occasions scheduled by Transylvania and West Lexington Presbyteries. Sources: "Diary of Rev. John Lyle"; M'Nemar, *The Kentucky Revival*; Sweet, "Minutes of Elkhorn Association," in *The Baptists*.

churches. Both waves of revivalism swept the same territory, however, operating most intensely in the Bluegrass counties. This region had the religious institutions and ministry necessary for mounting a revival. It also had the densest population and, therefore, the largest body of potential converts. The people had struggled with political problems ranging from statehood to excise agents. And, in little more than a decade, the Bluegrass settlements had recovered from an Indian war and blossomed into a thriving agricultural region. In few other parts of the country, whether established or recently settled, did discord and strain converge to the degree they did in Kentucky's Bluegrass settlements during the 1790s.

The surge of religious interest among Kentucky Baptists owed little if anything to the new rites of personal transformation incorporated by McGready. "Bodily agitations" were not unknown to Baptists, even among the Calvinist Regular Baptists, but the emotional tumult breaking out at Presbyterian sacramental occasions struck many as bizarre and even dangerous. Baptist chroniclers of Kentucky religion described the sensational events occurring at Presbyterian meetinghouses in fascinated detail. In contrast, these writers said virtually nothing about the liturgical format within their own denomination, implying with their silence that little had changed. One of the very few Baptists who did was disturbed by what he observed at the joint Presbyterian-Methodist meetings, writing that he could only "hope the great power of God is in this work." He reported that no more than two churches in the Elkhorn Baptist Association had united with the Presbyterian and Methodist revivalists. These two "noisy" congregations were known to exhort, pray, and sing the whole night through. At times, some participants appeared enraptured, "as if they were ready to take their flight to Glory." As with McGready's followers, distressed persons would be "lying on the floor, crying out for mercy." The other twenty-four churches in the Elkhorn Association conducted their religious activities with "great solemnity and seriousness."[31] Except for the two "noisy" congregations, Baptist revival traditions apparently remained intact and unaltered in 1801. According to Richard Collins, one of Kentucky's early historians, "The work among the Baptists was deep, solemn and powerful, but comporting with that decency and order so emphatically enjoined in the Scriptures."[32]

Part of the Baptist revival's distinctiveness was attributable to its leaders, who generally steered clear of the new style of sacramental occasion. Presbyterian minister John Lyle, for instance, often recorded participating colleagues in his personal diary but seldom mentioned Baptists. Baptist ministers may have become a little less reluctant to join interdenominational proceedings as the Great Revival progressed. In September 1801, after a full summer of revival activities, Lyle noted an event attended by six Presbyterian ministers and three Baptists. At a sacramental occasion held at Paris nearly a year later, Lyle named ten Presbyterian ministers and then remarked, "No Methodist ministers on Sunday and but one Baptist, old Mr. Todd." The general underrepresentation by Baptist ministers sometimes caused the early camp meetings to be described as "Presbyterian and Methodist meetings." Being numerically superior to other denominations in Kentucky, their general absence was noticed.[33]

Although historically overshadowed by the sensational occurrences reported among the Presbyterians and Methodists, the independent appearance of a revival among the Baptist congregations is an important aspect of Kentucky's Great Revival. First, the church growth it produced probably matched, and may have exceeded, the increases that occurred among Presbyterians and Methodists. Second, the occurrence of a parallel revival, close in time and place but clearly independent, strongly implies that the revival of religious interest in Kentucky was a product of broadly existing circumstances. Whatever compelled several thousand people to join the Baptist Church in 1800, it was not the charismatic personality of McGready. Nor was it the awesome scene of sinners struck to the ground. Nor was it a release from Calvinistic gloom. Yet, regardless of denomination, large numbers of Kentuckians were suddenly more receptive to evangelical preaching.

Rehearsing the New Format

Logan County was a relatively remote and recently settled part of Kentucky. Had the camp meeting remained there and in similar regions, arguments that it stemmed from frontier conditions might be easier to defend. Instead, the center of religious excitement quickly shifted to the trans-Appalachian West's most advanced settlement region, the Bluegrass. Within a few years, of course, the camp meeting format would spread to areas long removed from their frontier beginnings, including towns and cities.

Descriptions of McGready's revival probably first reached Kentucky's Bluegrass settlements through Barton Warren Stone, the pastor of the sister congregations of Cane Ridge and Concord since late 1798. Like McGready and many of the younger Presbyterian clergy, Stone came to Kentucky with personal evangelical experiences. He was born in Maryland in 1772, and his family moved to Pittsylvania County, Virginia, during the Revolution. In 1790, Stone left to study at Reverend David Caldwell's Presbyterian academy in Guilford, North Carolina, where "McGready's Revival" was soon in full force. McGready's preaching deeply affected Stone and probably influenced his decision to enter the ministry. After brief employment teaching languages at a new Methodist academy near his brother's home in Georgia, Stone resigned and in early 1796 applied to the regional presbytery for a license to preach. He then progressed slowly through Virginia, North Carolina, and Tennessee. By the end of the year he was in Kentucky, where he received an invitation to serve from the vacant congregations of Cane Ridge and Concord. That winter, according to Stone, he refined his preaching techniques. Approximately fifty new church members were added to Concord and thirty to Cane Ridge. Stone soon became "much attached to these congregations, and . . . I at length yielded to their solicitations to become their settled and permanent pastor." The ordination was held on October 4, 1798.[34]

Word of McGready's success in Logan County reached Stone while he was returning from a brief visit to North Carolina, probably to close personal business, with a colleague named Hall who was headed for missionary work at Natchez. They encountered some Tennesseans carrying letters for Hall, including one describing McGready's revival in Logan County. This news was personally as well as professionally significant for Stone, since both McGready and fellow revivalist William Hodge had been instrumental to his spiritual development. Shortly thereafter, in October 1800, West Lexington Presbytery dispatched Stone to work the Natchez mission with Hall. Presumably it was during his return from Natchez, in the spring of 1801, that Stone visited McGready in Logan County and witnessed the remarkable religious outpouring there.[35] Through his experiences during McGready's revival in North Carolina and his time spent teaching among the Methodists, Stone was no stranger to emotional religion. Nonetheless, the events in Logan County impressed him. "The scene to me was new, and passing strange. It baffled description. Many, very many fell down, as men slain in battle, and continued together in an apparently breathless and motionless state. . . . After lying thus for hours, they obtained deliverance." The falling to the ground astounded Stone, as it did other Presbyterians. He carefully observed the activities and became thoroughly convinced that "it was a good work—the work of God."[36]

Stone returned to Bourbon County "with ardent spirits." Arriving at Cane Ridge on the Sabbath, he was greeted by an unusually large gathering of people eager to hear of the spiritual outpouring in Logan County. According to his later account, Stone climbed the pulpit and reported what he had witnessed, then opened his Bible and began preaching from the Scripture, "Go ye into the world and preach the gospel to every living creature. He that believeth and is baptized shall be saved, and he that believeth not shall be damned." As he later wrote of this moment, "On the universality of the gospel and faith as the condition of salvation, I principally dwelt, and urged the sinners to believe now, and be saved." Stone's heartfelt, urgent appeal moved his hearers deeply. "The congregation was affected with awful solemnity and many returned home weeping."[37]

After promising to return to Cane Ridge for a weeknight prayer meeting, Stone hurried to evening services at his other congregation, Concord. As he preached that night, two girls fell to the floor in a manner strikingly similar to Stone's description of events in Logan County. That the first individuals to succumb were children is probably not accidental. The girls were more likely victims of suggestibility, but eighteenth-century notions of child psychology pointed instead toward divine inspiration, and their exhortations made a deep impression on all those present.

A spiritual outpouring quickly surfaced at Cane Ridge as well. On Monday Stone returned to Cane Ridge for a group prayer meeting at the house of Elder William Maxwell. Several prominent members of the congregation greeted Stone with news that the previous day's sermon had left a number of people "solemnly engaged in seeking salvation, and some had found the Lord, and were rejoicing in him." One of these people was Nathaniel Rogers, a prominent member of the congregation and well known as "a man of first respectability and influence in the neighborhood." Rogers and his wife rushed out to greet Stone, ecstatically shouting praises to God. According to Stone, "We hurried into each others' embrace, he still praising the Lord aloud." All those present were greatly moved, and within twenty minutes the religious tension found release as "scores" fell to the ground. Stone's memory of this event, a private prayer meeting, probably exaggerates the number of participants, but people were clearly struck by what they saw. As Elder David Purviance, a political leader in the community, approached the site, "We found the people in the yard, mostly standing on their feet, but . . . found many persons under both physical and mental excitement." The gathering in Maxwell's yard did not break up until well after dark.[38]

Word of these developments spread to neighboring congregations, and sacramental occasions in central Kentucky began following the new model of McGready's, probably based on descriptions provided by Stone.[39] In early May, the sacramental occasions scheduled by Transylvania Presbytery for Flemingsburg and Reverend John P. Campbell's congregation in Mason County both evidenced a more evangelical tone. A sacramental occasion held at Cabin Creek Meetinghouse in late May also seemed more spiritually awakened. The congregation's pastor, Richard McNemar, wrote, "The scene was awful beyond description; the falling, crying out, praying, exhorting, singing, shouting, &c. . . . few, if any, could escape without being affected." The high point occurred on the third night, when an especially large number of people fell down. To prevent the fallen from being stepped on, McNemar had the prostrate bodies "collected together, and laid out in order, on two squares of the meetinghouse; which, like so many dead corpses, covered a considerable part of the floor." The first-hand accounts by McNemar and others focus on the dramatic falling and do not discuss the other two alterations introduced under McGready: the camping and ecumenicalism. These may have taken longer to implement, but the documentation is very meager and could easily have missed them at this early point. The gathering was larger than previous sacramental occasions at Cabin Creek. McNemar recognized people from Cane Ridge, Concord, Eagle Creek, and other neighboring Presbyterian congregations. While no surviving first-hand accounts mention Stone, he was very probably present as well.[40]

The sacramental occasion at Concord in Nicholas County followed the very next weekend. According to Colonel Robert Patterson of Lexington, a leading Presbyterian layman, "This was the first occasion that shewed the necessity of encamping on the ground; the neighbourhood not being able to furnish strangers with accommodation; nor had they [the participants] a wish to separate."[41] Patterson, who had not attended the proceedings at Flemingsburg and Cabin Creek, which were rather more distant from his home, was mistaken, but his remark nonetheless indicates that camping was occurring early on and that the impetus behind it came mainly from the laity. And, as was becoming common, the meeting at Concord Meetinghouse lasted longer than the normal sacramental occasion, from Saturday to Wednesday, "day and night, without intermission." Of the four thousand or so people who attended, Patterson estimated 250 communicants and 150 struck to the ground. The ministers included no less than seven Presbyterian ministers and at least one Methodist. Patterson described the night he was there as still and calm, illuminated with candles provided by the people of Concord. William Rogers of Cane Ridge commented, "It was no uncommon occurrence, for persons while listening to preaching, exhortation, prayer or singing, to fall from their seat or feet to the ground, and some appeared almost in lifeless condition." This phenomenon "took the name of the falling exercise, from its manner of operation."[42] Falling, the only variety of "bodily exercise" clearly identified in any descriptions written before 1802, continued all night. According to Patterson, the scene was utterly chaotic, with "exhortations, praying, singing; the cries of the distressed, on account of sin; the rejoicing of those that were delivered from their sin's bondage, and brought to enjoy the liberty that is in Christ Jesus; all going on at the same time."[43] McNemar, the pastor at Cabin Creek, was also present, and his account emphasized the broad composition of the crowd: "No sex or color, class or description, were exempted from the pervading influence of the Spirit." And Stone marveled at the ecumenical atmosphere. "All seemed heartily to unite in the work, and in Christian love," he wrote. "Party spirit, abashed, shrunk away."[44]

The summer schedule of sacramental occasions continued, the next one held in mid-June for the congregation of Salem in Clark County. Closer to the center of western population, the ministers present included at least five Presbyterians and two Methodists, with the meeting continuing from Friday to the following Wednesday. William Burke, a prominent Methodist minister, claimed that the Presbyterian ministers stood by helplessly as the emotional tumult intensified, relying on Burke and his fellow Methodists for guidance. According to Burke, "There was a great trembling among the dry bones. Great numbers fell to the ground and cried for mercy, old and young."[45] Young John Lyle, the pastor at Salem, estimated three hundred persons fell to the ground with religious conviction.[46]

The next sacramental occasion was held on the last Sabbath in June at Point Pleasant Meetinghouse in southern Bourbon County, where participants "engaged in singing and hearing and praying night and day from Friday morning to Tuesday evening." One of the Presbyterian ministers estimated the crowd at five or six thousand, while Lyle estimated three or four thousand people, with three hundred falling.[47] Colonel Patterson estimated eight thousand present, with 350 at the sacrament and 250 struck to the ground.[48]

In the same letter, Patterson provided some valuable information on early perceptions of such events. First, many Presbyterians "stood astonished, not knowing, and wondering what these things meant; not willing to reprobate it, and many at last closed in with it." Second, the "nominal professors" of religion, who Patterson declared to be the most inveterate, "call it enthusiasm, hypocrisy, witchcraft, . . . in fine, every thing but what it really is." Finally, the deists dismissed it as the product of mere "sympathy, agitation, delusion, &c."[49] Western observers clearly saw the new form of revivalism as distinctive despite its close association with the traditional Presbyterian sacramental occasion.

Two large sacramental occasions held at the end of June drew participants from overlapping areas. At Indian Creek in southern Harrison County, the proceedings lasted a full week, from Thursday to Thursday, and reportedly drew participants from as far as Woodford County some forty miles away. The greatest number, however, probably came from adjacent parts of the eastern Bluegrass region. Colonel Patterson reported that the Indian Creek meeting numbered approximately ten thousand people, with five hundred communicants and eight hundred "struck." The sacramental occasion at Lexington lasted from Friday to Tuesday. An estimated six thousand people attended, with an estimated three hundred communicants and seventy people affected by the falling exercise.[50]

In early July, the Presbyterian congregation located in the town of Paris, county seat of Bourbon County, hosted a sacramental occasion. Indian Creek, a few miles north of Paris, had a second sacrament a week later. Although no estimates of attendance are available, one of the Presbyterian ministers, Reverend John E. Findley, reported, "Hundreds fell to the ground at once." The meeting lasted about five days, according to Reverend McNemar, marked by "prayer, exhortation, singing, shouting and leaping for joy."[51]

Thus the revival sparked by McGready the previous year spread among the Bluegrass settlements, following Transylvania Presbytery's sacramental calendar through the summer of 1801. All of these gatherings shared a fundamental similarity. Though still recognizably a Presbyterian sacramental occasion, the events now encompassed a second purpose, the salvation of souls. To the rituals of spiritual renewal leading to the sacramental table were added rituals of spiritual awakening—the falling, camping, and ecumenicalism. In 1801, this alteration was accompanied by a level of disorganization and emotional intensity alien to Presbyterian liturgy and disturbing to more conservative church adherents. While the latter attributed these developments to satanic influences, historians have tended to credit a primitive frontier environment, but they are actually very characteristic of early stages in the process of ritual change. The sacramental occasions held during the summer of 1801 in Transylvania Presbytery marked a unique moment, differing from the traditional sacramental occasion format yet not fitting mature forms of camp meeting revivalism either.

The Meeting at Cane Ridge

The formative phase of camp meeting revivalism, the period when the events remained a Presbyterian sacramental occasion with the elements introduced under McGready superimposed, culminated at Cane Ridge Presbyterian Meetinghouse in early August. Building upon the previous events, surpassing them in size, Cane Ridge soon overshadowed them in reputation. Indeed, Cane Ridge has often been mistaken as the first camp meeting. Though untrue, its heavy attendance made it the most fully described of the early camp meetings. These descriptions of Cane Ridge capture camp meeting revivalism at a fleeting stage of development, before it became institutionalized and evolved into the forms by which it was more widely known.

Cane Ridge was located in rural Bourbon County, within the rich Bluegrass region which supported Kentucky's inner core of settlement. Presbyterian records first mention a congregation at Cane Ridge in October 1791, about which time the meetinghouse was built. As described by an early member, "For a log building, it is large. . . . The roof is of clapboards, a puncheon floor [originally a dirt floor], the cracks between the logs were open." The north and south walls had small alcoves built in the center, for a total area of fifty by thirty feet. The pulpit was in the north alcove, "boxed up, with entrance at the side reached by several steps, and its elevation so considerable that the speaker literally looked down upon his audience." Along the south wall was an upper gallery, reached by a ladder on the outside. The pews were "rough-hewn puncheons"—split logs with no backs.[52] In 1795, Cane Ridge and its smaller sister congregation of Concord included approximately three hundred families. Their first pastor had been Reverend Robert W. Finley, who served from 1793 to late 1795, when he was deposed by Transylvania Presbytery. After two years of being served on a rotating basis, the congregations gained their second pastor, Barton Warren Stone. Cane Ridge had developed a political reputation for taking strong moral stands, particularly against slavery, but the neighborhood generally resembled the rest of central Kentucky. Populated and prosperous, its frontier beginnings were rapidly fading into history.

In July 1801, Reverend Barton Stone married in Muhlenberg, Kentucky, and brought his bride back to Bourbon County to prepare for the sacramental occasion scheduled for Cane Ridge on the second Sabbath in August. Although John Bradford, a man of deist leanings who believed the revival exploited public credulity, refused to allow announcements for it to appear in his newspaper, *The Kentucky Gazette,* word of the upcoming event at Cane Ridge spread widely. With the benefit of ample advance notice, and coming toward the end of a summer of revivalism, the Cane Ridge meeting was guaranteed an especially large assembly.[53] Expectations rose as the event drew near. A neighboring Baptist, in a letter written on Saturday, August 7, explained, "I am on my way to one of the greatest meetings of the kind perhaps ever known; it is on a sacramental occasion. Religion has got to such a height here, that people attend from great distances; on this occasion I doubt not but there will be 10,000 people, and perhaps 500 waggons." He followed by relating the revival's most distinctive trait: "The people encamp on the ground, and continue praising God, day and night, for one whole week before they break up."[54]

As was customary, church members began spiritual preparations on the previous Sunday with fasting and prayer. By Thursday and Friday, the roads to the log meetinghouse at Cane Ridge "were literally crowded with wagons, carriages, horsemen, and footmen, moving to the solemn camp." According to a visitor from Ohio, "Whole settlements appeared to be vacated, and only here and there could be found a house having an inhabitant." As at previous events, the number of wagons helped establish the size of the crowd and was variously figured at between 125 and 148, considerably more than at previous revival meetings.[55] Most estimates of attendance ranged between ten and twenty-five thousand people. Some exaggeration must be assumed, but Bourbon County alone contained nearly thirteen thousand black and white inhabitants, and several adjacent counties were equally well populated. The main point, of course, is that the assembly at Cane Ridge was huge, exceeding even the summer's previous events. "For more than a half mile," wrote Elder David Purviance of Cane Ridge, "I could see people on their knees before God in humble prayer."[56]

Cane Ridge's greater scale is supported by the number of attending ministers. It had always been customary for one or two neighboring Presbyterian ministers to assist at sacramental occasions, and the revival meetings continued this practice. The Presbyterian ministers presiding at sacramental occasions during the Great Revival usually numbered between four and six, reflecting the larger scale of the revival, plus one or two Methodists and an occasional Baptist preacher. At Cane Ridge, however, the Presbyterian ministers numbered no less than eighteen, sixteen of whom can be identified from records of the event. The Methodists included William Burke, Benjamin Lakin, Benjamin Northcott, and Samuel Hitt. Accounts of the Cane Ridge meeting refer to Baptist participants, but the only Baptist minister present was Governor James Garrard of Cooper's Run Meetinghouse, located a few miles north. Garrard was hardly a representative member of the Baptist ministry, however, since he was already under suspicion for Arian leanings.[57] The absence of other Baptist ministers at Cane Ridge may have been because of the annual meeting of Elkhorn Baptist Association at South Elkhorn, where an estimated eight to ten thousand people also gathered that weekend.

Cane Ridge drew participants from great distances, but nowhere near as far as claimed by some defenders of the revival, who sought to offset accusations of excessive enthusiasm by demonstrating its effectiveness in attracting the godless. But in a statement years later, Presbyterian lay leader Robert McAfee stated that at Cane Ridge there were "nearly ten thousand people, from all the adjoining Countys."[58] Probably the best indication of where the participants came from can be derived from the ministers, because church members often followed their pastor to where he was preaching, there being no sermon from their own pulpit that week. Most of the ministers at Cane Ridge came from Bourbon or adjoining counties: James Welch and James Crawford from Fayette; John Lyle and Joseph P. Howe from Clark; and William Robinson from Harrison. Others came from more distant neighborhoods, involving between thirty and fifty miles of travel: Robert Marshall from Woodford County; John Evans Findley from Mason County, Richard McNemar from modern Lewis County, and Matthew Houston from modern Garrard County. John Rankin, who had worked with McGready in Logan County, had traveled nearly three hundred miles, but it seems unlikely that he ventured so far specifically for the event at Cane Ridge. Claims that some of the individuals at Cane Ridge came from "Ohio and other distant parts" thus held some substance in fact, but most people came from within a day's traveling distance.[59]

The spectacular nature of the Great Revival generated a number of firsthand descriptions, particularly by ministers. Of these, the diary kept by Reverend John Lyle is without question the definitive account. Lyle had been sent to Kentucky in 1797 as a missionary from the Synod of

Virginia. Since 1800 he had been the pastor of Salem congregation in Clark County. A contemporary described Lyle as a man of "moderate talents," but possessing "sound judgement and studious habits."[60] Lyle kept a regular journal of his ministerial activities, including a detailed account of the Cane Ridge meeting. In addition, Lyle's viewpoint was ambivalent. He believed that the revival was fueled by divine power, yet he was still suspicious of emotional excesses, sympathetic yet cautious. In contrast to other participant accounts, Lyle's was not intended for an audience. The result is an unusually balanced account of the event. Especially valuable is that Lyle wrote his account of the Cane Ridge meeting during the event or immediately thereafter, rather than months, years, or even decades later. Unique in this respect, the journal entries capture the improvised nature of daily proceedings. Supplemented by other firsthand descriptions, Lyle's journal establishes what actually transpired that week in August 1801 and helps distinguish reality from legend.

On Friday evening Lyle did not go to Cane Ridge Meetinghouse, where prayer services supposedly continued all through the night, but to the home of Elder Andrew Irvine. Most of the people at Irvine's were probably members of the Cane Ridge congregation. Lyle noted a certain tension, but there were no emotional outbursts. Presbyterian minister Joseph P. Howe was preaching in the meetinghouse the next morning when Lyle arrived at the camp meeting. The afternoon's preaching was by Reverend Richard McNemar (a former inhabitant of Cane Ridge). Lyle listened to McNemar with apprehension, and his description of the address mark the first signal of a departure from orthodox Presbyterianism. Lyle seemed to shudder as he watched McNemar carry on "much like a methodist."

On Saturday evening, people squeezed into the meetinghouse to hear preaching by Stone and other ministers. The sweltering heat and growing emotionalism as people began falling to the floor soon drove Lyle outside. "If Mr. Stone would not command order and silence," wrote Lyle, ". . . I would not go there no more." Lyle and McNemar joined with Reverend Matthew Houston at the central tent, or canopied platform, and each delivered a religious discourse to the crowd gathered below. The discourse this time was more orthodox. Lyle emphasized the Calvinist notion of human depravity and unworthiness, and McNemar followed with an orthodox exhortation. Lyle wickedly noted that McNemar "had nearly forgot his new gospel."

On Sunday morning, Lyle "traversed the camp." In the log meetinghouse he found Houston already exhorting, and he followed Houston with a discourse on the "Christian character as exemplified by our Savior in his life." The day was marked by pouring rain, but preparations for the afternoon's sacrament went ahead. At the central stand where the tables stood protected under a canopy, Reverend Robert Marshall gave the action sermon, a moving invitation to "Arise my fair one and come away, &c." Lyle left this scene for the meetinghouse, but finding it teeming with religious agitation, he proceeded to where William Burke, a noted Methodist leader, was addressing a large crowd. Because Stone and his Presbyterian colleagues kept postponing Burke's turn at the preaching stand, Burke, by his own account, took the initiative and began preaching late in the morning "on the body of a fallen tree, about fifteen feet from the ground." There, Burke "fixed my stand in the open sun, with an umbrella affixed to a long pole and held over my head by brother Hugh Barnes." A large crowd quickly gathered. Speaking on the text "For we must all stand before the judgement-seat of Christ, . . . Hundreds fell prostrate to the ground, groaning in distress and shouting in triumph." Lyle concluded from their noisy demeanor that Burke's listeners included many Methodists.[61]

At the sacrament on Sunday afternoon, Lyle assisted Reverend Blythe in serving the tables. Reverend Samuel Finley preached one of the favorite revival texts, "How shall we escape if we neglect so great salvation?" Lyle himself experienced "some reviving clearer views on divine things" and "felt uncommonly tender" as he in turn addressed the crowd. The full supply of more than eight hundred communion tokens had been distributed earlier. One of the elders thought that the number of communicants reached close to eleven hundred people. The long lines converging at the canopied stand took several hours to serve.

After communion, Lyle and Blythe confided in each other their fears "about disorder, the danger of enthusiasm, etc." As they talked, Reverend Marshall came to tell them that a prominent man named Preston Brown had fallen to the ground in religious conviction, and the three ministers went to comfort and pray—and perhaps quietly gloat. Heavenly power over earthly trifles seldom seemed more evident than when members of the gentry were spiritually humbled.[62]

By Sunday evening the rain had ended, and the revival proceeded in full force throughout the "Camp of Israel." One Presbyterian minister reported, "On Sabbath night, I saw above one hundred candles burning at once—and I suppose one hundred persons at once on the ground crying for mercy of all ages from 8 to 60 years."[63] According to Lyle, "Many were falling and rising and rejoicing &c. &c. . . . I turned into praying and exhorting among them, as did other ministers and continued I suppose near to one or two o'clock." Lyle recognized several of the people in the throes of spiritual turmoil. Late that night he "went around and through the meeting house[,] found many asleep in their seats and some [fallen] down but not much stir in the house—some out of doors were praying &c. and some [were fallen] down." Lyle noticed a black man preaching in one part of the grounds, and after following with an exhortation, Lyle then retired to bed.[64]

After breakfast on Monday morning, Lyle went to the meetinghouse, where Reverend Isaac Tull of Bourbon Academy was preaching. Lyle "exhorted after he prayed and then he exhorted and I prayed and he exhorted again and set the people to sing Come ye sinners, &c." Singing together seemed to have an added effect. "One and another fell down and the work went on briskly." As the meetinghouse grew "crowded and sultry," Lyle helped carry out the limp bodies of the fallen. Word then arrived that Robert Finley, probably the same Robert Finley who had formerly served as pastor of Cane Ridge, was speaking nearby. Lyle caught only Finley's closing words and followed with an exhortation. He then returned to the meetinghouse to help "carry out [the fallen] and pray and exhort till the middle of the day or about one o'clock."[65]

More frequently than during previous days, the crowds were addressed by stricken participants who delivered personal religious testimony. Singing together seemed to have an added effect. As noted by Lyle, "Their orations consist of the plain and esential [sic] truths of the gospel that they themselves have been powerfully convinced of, but they speak them with all the feeling and pathos that human nature affected with the most important objects is capable of." As Lyle further remarked, "They speak much of the fullness of Christ, his willingness to save &c."

On Monday afternoon Lyle encountered Governor James Garrard, an inhabitant of the county, who appeared overwhelmed by the religious fervor and told Lyle "that he was gone distracted, that his head was weak before, &c." Later that afternoon Lyle listened to Reverend John Rankin of Logan County preach "a plain sermon about conviction and conversion &c." Benjamin Northcott, a Methodist preacher settled at Flemingsburg, followed with an exhortation. Lyle then "gave a description of the heavenly city from Revelations." After dinner Lyle and other church leaders circulated among the fallen, talking to them about what they were feeling and praying with them.

Lyle's chronicle of activities on Monday evening emphasizes prayer and comfort for the fallen, describing several individuals affected by the proceedings. Like other revival narratives, Lyle made specific references to individuals who tried to resist religion, particularly deists, detractors of the revival, and people of bad reputation.

On Tuesday morning, Lyle "viewed the camp [and] saw a number down." Outside the meetinghouse he encountered some boys and girls, "singing and shaking hands, a sort of wagging that appeared like dancing at a distance." Lyle found them "verry loving and joyful[,] almost dizzy with joy." He attempted to gently instill better decorum, advising them to "sing the same hymn and not sing different ones so near together." When Reverend Rankin arrived, Lyle helped call people to assemble for worship, "which they did immediately and he spoke first and I next[.] the people were verry attentive and a good deal moved." Shortly afterwards, word spread that Reverend Burke, the Methodist, would preach at the tent. Lyle departed at noontime on Tuesday, anxious to return home, since his wife was expecting a child. Others lingered at Cane Ridge as late as Thursday. Thus ended the Great Revival's largest single event.

Contemporary observers of Cane Ridge and other early camp meetings tended to stress that which was novel, understandably overlooking the more familiar elements. Nonetheless, much about the early camp meetings harkened backward in time and eastward toward the rest of America. Perhaps most obvious is the debt to Presbyterianism's strong evangelical heritage, which had been recently reinvigorated by the Hampden-Sydney revival and the dedicated young ministers seeking pastorates among the western settlements. Also significantly, camp meeting revivalism used for its structural foundations a customary forum for evangelical outreach, the Presbyterian sacramental occasion. The importance of church structures is also evident in that these events were hosted by established congregations and scheduled in advance by the presbytery. Neither at this early point did camp meetings noticeably break with orthodox Calvinism. The strongest evidence of theological change involves Stone and McNemar, but whatever Lyle observed at Cane Ridge, they remained Presbyterians in good standing for another two years.

Nonetheless, the Kentucky Revival did not merely reprise established evangelical forms. McGready, Stone, and the other western clergymen were so anxious to build on the religious foundations established by the pioneer generation of ministers that they were unusually open to new methods. The first departure from tradition was McGready's invitation to the Methodist John McGee. McGready had been working earnestly for a revival for some time, but it did not really commence until the moment when John McGee stood up at Red River and the laity began to fall. From this innovation followed two other new practices that were less controversial but no less important: a universal call to participants regardless of religious affiliation, and the adoption of camping at the meeting site. The evangelical events remained recognizably sacramental occasions during this early period, but with these few simple changes superimposed, something new was being experienced as well. Soon this difference would be captured by the term *camp meeting*. For the moment, however, such distinctions mattered little. What did matter was that the new format had extraordinary popular appeal.

9

THE SOCIAL SIGNIFICANCE OF
CAMP MEETING REVIVALISM

Camp meeting revivalism's extraordinary popular appeal has long been attributed to frontier influences that supposedly fostered a religion more in keeping with the needs of people who were spiritually starved, more individualistic, and primitivized by the wilderness environment. This explanation, however, not only rests on erroneous characterizations of the frontier but also fails to appreciate the rapid pace of western development during the 1790s. Especially in the Bluegrass counties, where the Great Revival reached its greatest strength, many settlements had already existed for a quarter of a century and had not faced substantial Indian danger for more than a decade. The economy teetered on the brink of staple agriculture. Government institutions were accessible and active. By 1800 the western settlements bore a closer resemblance to the rest of rural America than to their violent beginnings.

Many of the ambiguities of recent settlement nonetheless persisted and contributed to a social disorder arguably more severe than in many other parts of the new nation. A diverse and mobile population kept the settlements churning. Hardly a voter in the state was a native Kentuckian. Although this self-selected population shared a keen interest in commercial development, the economic striving introduced a new and troubling level of competition. Despite the high quality of Kentucky soil, prospects for landownership remained moderate at best. Especially disturbing was the uncertainty of title. Neither could the establishment of government institutions, even as a separate state, provide much order. National policies exacerbated these problems rather than relieved them. Even recreational pastimes involved competition and conflict. Religious institutions which might have smoothed some of these problems were multiplying but beset by rivalries and internal disputes. From virtually any perspective, the western settlements were disturbingly divided and diverse.[1]

The camp meeting beginnings in this context have usually been attributed to popular desires for a more liberal form of religious worship, but the opposite is more probable. The people of post-frontier Kentucky, as well as many other parts of America during this period, had not yet abandoned traditional social ideals of cooperation and cohesion. They yearned for a restoration of community at the very same time that they were behaving in ways that seemed to move in a different direction. The camp meeting, in contrast to other forms of religious worship, provided an integrative mechanism. For a few days, people from every possible sort of background joined together to form a temporary community ruled by principles of harmony, virtue, and unity. The integrative aspects are especially apparent during the camp meeting's formative phase of development, through the meeting at Cane Ridge in August 1801.

Camp Meeting Orthodoxy

Kentucky's Great Revival belongs to a much broader era of religious energy, the Second Great Awakening. Like the Great Awakening of the previous century, the Second Great Awakening was no simple event but took various forms and surfaced at various times according to local circumstances. Practically the only characteristic that may link the events of the Second Great Awakening is the introduction of a more individualistic religion, one in closer alignment with emerging ideas of equality and freedom surfacing throughout the young republic.[2] Within decades, the dominant Protestant theology in America changed from Calvinism to Arminianism—from perceiving human nature as abominable and therefore salvation as possible only through God's unmerited gift of grace, to perceiving salvation as God's gift to all who seek it. In Calvinism, humans were passive and inconsequential, but in Arminianism, humans were agents of their own eternal destiny.

Because camp meeting revivalism later became so closely associated with Arminian theology, its Calvinist beginnings are often overlooked. During the formative phase, before the camp meeting format broke away from the Presbyterian sacramental occasion, New Light Calvinism dominated the event. McGready and his colleagues perceived nothing unorthodox about their new practices.[3] Nonetheless, the intensity and massive scale of the early camp meeting soon led some religious leaders to seriously reconsider central Calvinist beliefs, especially the doctrine of election, the idea that an almighty God had foreordained that only some sinners would ever be saved. Contrary to what is commonly thought, however, the theological shift followed the new form of worship rather than inspired it.

The key figure in the theological debates generated by camp meeting revivalism was the pastor at Cane Ridge, Barton Warren Stone, who with several Presbyterian colleagues declared independence from the Presbyterian Church in 1803. Stone later joined Alexander Campbell in establishing a new denomination, the Church of Christ, an effort to pare away the institutional and theological overgrowth and return to biblical essentials. In his autobiography, perhaps with the clarity of hindsight, Stone dated his heterodoxy to the time of his ordination at Cane Ridge in 1798. Supposedly as he prepared for his examination, Stone began to discover doubts regarding the trinity, election, reprobation, and predestination as these concepts were stated in the Presbyterian Confession of Faith. He had experienced similar doubts in 1793, while studying theology under William Hodge in North Carolina.[4] Fortunately for Stone, the late-eighteenth-century New Light Presbyterians had already found ways to make Calvinism less harsh. From Hodge, Stone learned "the way of divesting those doctrines of their hard, repulsive features, and admitted them as true, yet unfathomable mysteries. Viewing them as such, I let them alone in my public discourses, and confined myself to the practical part of religion, and to subjects within my depth." But as Stone reexamined the doctrines in preparation for his ordination, "I found the covering put over them could not hide them from a discerning eye with close inspection."

When Transylvania Presbytery assembled at Cane Ridge on October 14, 1798, for the ordination, Stone confided his troubled state of mind to the two ministers conducting the ceremony, James Blythe and Robert Marshall, and asked for a postponement. "They labored, but in vain, to remove my difficulties and objections," Stone recalled later. Finally, "They asked me how far I was willing to receive the confession? I told them, as far as I saw it consistent with the word of God. They concluded that was sufficient."[5] Blythe and Marshall may have interpreted Stone's misgivings as nothing more than the perfectionism of a very pious young man, but as products of the earlier revivals at Hampden-Sydney and Liberty Hall, they may also have been prepared to sidestep the fine points of orthodox belief. New Light Presbyterianism was long accustomed to navigating the narrow straits of Calvinism.

Stone's self-doubt was not deemed serious enough to prevent his ordination or bear mention in Presbyterian records, but years later in his autobiography Stone maintained that his reservations about Calvinism persisted. Sometime afterward he apparently experienced a spiritual crisis, his mind "continually tossed on the waves of speculative divinity." He believed in the total depravity of humankind, and saw it as inseparable with unconditional election and reprobation, as taught in the Westminster Confession, but objections agitated his mind. "I honestly, earnestly, and prayerfully sought for the truth, determined to buy it at the sacrifice of everything else." Stone pushed away all religious scholarship and began immersing himself in the Bible until he became "convinced that God did love the whole world, and that the [only] reason why he did not save all, was because of their disbelief." Their unbelief stemmed not from God's failure to exert his power in them, but from their refusal to accept the truth of Holy Scripture. The faith necessary to believe in Jesus Christ was freely available to everyone in the gospel. Nothing more was required. Salvation was offered to all who believed.[6] Stone's account, written much later in his career, does not specify when he reached this conclusion. Given the righteousness that the people of Cane Ridge and Concord are known to have displayed on other church matters, however, Stone probably treaded his way carefully.

Just how far Stone had progressed in his exit from Calvinism by the time of the Cane Ridge camp meeting in 1801 is difficult to discern. No sermons survive that can be dated to this period, but even if they did, the answer might prove elusive simply because the preaching at sacramental occasions traditionally emphasized evangelical rather than doctrinal themes. Both orthodox Calvinists and dissenters heralded God's love of humankind and his desire to save them. According to Calvinist tenets, God already knew which individuals would be among the saved. At some point in their lives, He would present each with an opportunity to accept Christ as their savior. The operating principle of revivalism was to bring this opportunity to as many individuals as possible. Both McGready, who remained Calvinist, and Stone, who did not, spoke in expansive, almost universalist terms. McGready referred to "the pardon of millions of rebellious sinners," while Stone proclaimed "free and full salvation to every creature."[7] The main thrust of revival preaching was to break down the barriers of personal indifference; meticulous doctrinal consistency was subordinated to this more urgent task.

Contemporary observations are few in number and far from clear. Reverend John Evans Findley, a sympathetic Presbyterian who remained orthodox, was one of the few witnesses to comment on the content of preaching. Favorite Gospel texts included "Ask and ye shall receive" and "All things are possible to him that believeth." In a letter written shortly before the meeting at Cane Ridge he reported, "The doctrines chiefly insisted on, are, an immediate closure with Christ by faith; at the same time shewing the imminent danger a sinner is in, while out of Christ." Some Presbyterians objected to this emphasis for "seeming to lay too much stress on the natural ability of the creature." Findley dealt with this problem as did many other moderate Calvinists, judging the new approach by its fruits. "It is apparent that the Lord is at work, and that many are changed from the ferocity of the lion, to a lamb-like temper."[8]

The diary of Reverend John Lyle (who was particularly sensitive to such matters) offers a more specific critique, yet one that also reveals a highly confused situation. Lyle described Reverend McNemar's preaching at Cane Ridge as "unintelligible," spouting "the substance of what Mr.

Stone and he call the true new gospel which they say none preach but [them]selves." Lyle accurately predicted, "The conduct of these hot-headed men and the effect of their doctrine will separate the church of Christ." Yet just how far Stone and McNemar had progressed with their "new gospel" remains questionable. As the sacramental season opened in 1803, nearly two years after the meeting at Cane Ridge, Stone sounded perfectly orthodox. At a sacramental occasion at Point Pleasant, Lyle noted that Stone preached "a good sermon on the perseverance of the saints. . . . The strong Calvinists seemed highly pleased, but the arminians were greatly hurt, some I understood agonized on account of it." On the other hand, just weeks later at Walnut Hill near Lexington on the first Sabbath in June, "Mr. Stone made an address on his antinomian scheme of faith. In which he intimates that people may come without feeling their need of Christ any further than we do by nature, . . . or that if we believe we shall be saved whether convicted or not." Still, at this point Stone possibly considered his preaching as merely a simplification rather than a rejection of Calvinism, for Lyle went on to complain that Stone "studiously avoids saying anything of the work of the spirit in conviction and calls such description legality."[9] While Stone's autobiography gives the impression that his break with Calvinism occurred early and decisively, Lyle's contemporary record depicts a much more complicated and gradual change.

The experience of David Purviance, an elder at Cane Ridge in 1801, presents a similar picture. Although troubled by "difficulty and distress on the doctrine of election and effectual calling," Purviance remained Calvinist in his beliefs. As such, he wrote, "I looked on my friends and associates with ardent desire for their salvation; I saw many of them living without hope and without God in the world." Privately he said of them, "Poor creatures, they cannot help it if they are not of the elect, . . . they must perish and that without remedy—it is hard." Purviance's exit from Calvinism did not occur until well after the Cane Ridge revival. Deeply moved by his experiences during the Great Revival, Purviance resolved to abandon his political career for the ministry. At the West Lexington Presbytery in October 1801, only two months after the Cane Ridge camp meeting, Purviance announced his intention to become a candidate for the Presbyterian ministry. Apparently at that time, on the way home with Reverend Stone, Purviance asked his pastor's advice on how to prepare for the examination on theology. Stone responded, "Read the Bible." In the Bible, probably under Stone's guidance, Purviance "learned that the invitations of the gospel extended to every sinner. . . . Here I commenced my exit from Calvinism." But at the time of Cane Ridge, Purviance insisted, "We yet retained the Calvinistic idea of the perseverance of the saints."[10]

The institutional break would not occur until 1803, two years after the massive event at Cane Ridge, when Purviance, Stone, McNemar, and three other Presbyterian ministers announced their leave of the Presbyterian Church. They rejected all "party spirit," sectarian biases, and "manmade creeds," and called themselves simply Christians, after the original disciples of Jesus. The Christians proclaimed "free and full salvation to every creature."[11] Not only does the break with Calvinism appear to have occurred later than Stone suggested in his autobiography, the majority of Presbyterian clergy who participated in the Great Kentucky Revival adhered to Calvinism. The orthodox revivalists included James McGready, William Hodge, John P. Campbell, Joseph P. Howe, and John Lyle.[12]

Meanwhile, in practical terms of the preaching heard at Cane Ridge and other early revival events, the impending doctrinal schism was largely unapparent. Participants who were not of churched families were probably not sufficiently conversant in theology to discern the difference between Calvinist and Arminian appeals. Even for those who were, the difference between Stone's beliefs and those of his critics was not all that perceptible.[13] Neither did Transylvania Presbytery, whose ministers included Lyle as well as other religious conservatives, see fit to take action until much later. Thus, while Calvinist doctrine was probably not emphasized, neither can the Great Revival be readily attributed to the appearance of Arminian theology and a more individualistic style of religion.

A Rite of Passage

One of the most important changes under McGready had been to create more room in the sacramental occasion for spiritual rebirth, a direct call for sinners to undergo a rite of passage to a new condition among the regenerate.[14] At the time this did not appear to be a major departure from established practice. The preaching at sacramental occasions traditionally called for a revitalization of Christian faith in preparation for the communion table as well as to provoke a spiritual crisis in the unregenerate who might be present, mainly the children of church members. While the first stage of the process, acknowledgment of one's sinful human nature, a state known among Calvinists as conviction, might commence at a sacramental occasion, it remained a sidelight to the primary focus on the communion table. It was even rarer for conviction to lead directly to rebirth. That event, if it occurred at all, was the gift of God rather than the outcome of a minister's urgent pleas. It tended to occur privately, after much Bible study, prayer, and moral reform.

Placing greater emphasis on spiritual rebirth during the sacramental occasion inevitably heightened its emotional level. Conviction of one's sinful nature raised feelings of remorse, shame, fright, and, most of all, helplessness. Convicted persons cried, moaned, and sank weakly to their knees. And now, under McGready, increasing numbers of them were doing so in each other's presence, contributing further pressure. Moreover, the transformation was suddenly signaled by "bodily exercises," physical expressions of spiritual agony seemingly beyond conscious control. Although bodily exercises might take a variety of forms, the most common during this period was falling suddenly to the ground, "as if shot." Persons convinced of their sinfulness, or "convicted" by a sense of their sinfulness and need for God's mercy, would fall limply to the ground. The afflicted often lay for hours, at varying levels of stupor. Some of those who succumbed could pray, some could only moan in spiritual agony, and some appeared to be unconscious.[15] According to one observer, persons who fell often retained the ability to speak, while in other cases, the stricken appeared quite lifeless. The "pulse grows weak, and they draw a hard breath about once in a minute. And in some instances their extremities become cold, and pulse, and breath, and all the symptoms of life, forsake them for nearly an hour." Lyle wrote in June, "Some lay as if about to expire in a few moments. Some gron'd and breathed and wrought hard, as in the agonies of death. Some shrieked, as if pierced to the breast with a sword on account of their hardness of heart." A few weeks later he further noted, "Sometimes the pulse is so weak and the nerves so tremulous that you cannot feel a pulse at all without great care." Most persons who fell claimed an inability to feel any physical pain, "and when recovered, they could relate every thing that had been said or done near them."[16] People were symbolically falling "dead to sin," submitting themselves to God in hope that he would send his saving grace and revive them to begin a new spiritual existence. Afterward, they claimed a profound spiritual transformation, often giving testimony to all who would listen. Numerous observers insisted that it was "neither common fainting, nor a nervous affection."[17]

The seemingly involuntary physical expressions or "bodily exercises" were new to western Presbyterians. "To all but Methodists the work was entirely strange," said one participant. "The Presbyterian clergy, as a body, are not to be held answerable for the extravagant irregularities and enthusiastic fantasies which deformed the Great Revival," disclaimed one early chronicler. "As a body, they neither originated nor countenanced them. . . . It is to the Methodists these measures are to be traced."[18] Similar phenomena had occasionally been noted during previous Presbyterian revivals, both in America and in Great Britain, but these earlier episodes had faded almost beyond memory by the time of the Great Revival in 1800.[19] "The falling down of multitudes, and their crying out . . . was to us so new a scene, that we thought it prudent not to be over hasty in forming an opinion of it," explained Reverend John E. Findley of Mason County.

"However, a little conversation with the affected persons, induced us to believe . . . it was the work of the Lord." For McGready, too, these were "things strange and wonderfully new to me." One Presbyterian leader remarked with dismay that the falling "was a new thing among Presbyterians. It excited universal astonishment, and created a curiosity which could not be restrained," even when it occurred in the more solemn points in the worship service. According to Elder Robert Patterson, most Kentucky Presbyterians "stood astonished, not knowing, and wondering what these things meant; not willing to reprobate it, and many at last closed in with it."[20] As remarked a local Baptist who may have been writing about scenes he witnessed at Cane Ridge, "It is different from anything I have seen, though I have seen great bodily agitations before this."[21] Even had these observers realized that the "falling exercise" was not unique, neither was it something previously in their realm of experience. Whether hoax or miracle—and this was hotly debated—few westerners had ever witnessed anything like it before.

Some of the more extraordinary reports come from defenders of the revival, offered as evidence of divine power. For example, at the Lexington revival meeting, Reverend Lyle had attempted to revive a man who had fallen, and inadvertently some of the ammonia "ran in his nostrils but he did not seem to feel it though he could talk of sin, &c. So much were his thoughts taken up with other subjects." Similarly, while some people felt an approaching sense that they might succumb, others were caught unexpectedly. Suddenly the body went limp and "fell to the ground as if shot." And, in numerous accounts, the subject resisted until overwhelmed. According to one Presbyterian elder, "Many [people] when they felt deep and serious impressions, would attempt to leave the crowd and get to themselves, but scarcely ever went far before they fell their whole length on the ground, and in their groans and cries would call a small crowd to them." Some people "would try to make their escape and flee away, like those who are pursued by an enemy in battle," wrote Reverend Richard McNemar, "and be over taken by the invisible power."[22]

Revival lore abounds with tales of deists and doubters humbled by religious forces. One story described a man who came to a meeting bringing a pole equipped with a nail at the end, "intending therewith to probe such as should fall down in the crowd, which (he was certain) would soon rouse them out of their lethargy." Instead, he himself was soon lying on the ground, praising God. Such individuals were compared to Saul of Tarsus, profane people "taken in the very act of persecuting the work." Proponents of the revival also expressed satisfaction when people of high social standing succumbed. At the Indian Creek meeting in 1801, a Presbyterian minister wrote, "Hundreds fell to the ground at once, among them a Doctor C——, a professed Deist. The news was spread, and 10 or 12 of his companions ran to see; but in half an hour, they were all lying on the ground near the Doctor; and I humbly hope, that most of them have experienced saving change."[23] Such accounts, sprinkled liberally throughout numerous descriptions of the revival, were intended to enhance the credibility of this behavior as the work of God.

Surely some accounts were exaggerated, but the rare perspective of a nonbeliever likewise depicts the new style of worship as exerting an extraordinary power. James B. Finley was a young man whose father had been the pastor at Cane Ridge and who later became a prominent Methodist preacher, but in 1801 he was leading a "thoughtless and wicked" life. Interested in possibly reforming and curious about the religious revival sweeping through his old neighborhood, Finley attended the Cane Ridge meeting with several companions, "and as I prided myself upon my manhood and courage, I had no fear of being overcome by any nervous excitability, or being frightened into religion." Despite his stout resolve, as young Finley viewed the scene around the log meetinghouse, "My heart beat tumultuously, my knees trembled, my lip quivered, and I felt as though I must fall to the ground. A strange supernatural power seemed to pervade the entire mass of mind there collected." Embarrassed, he fled to nearby woods "to rally and man up my courage."[24] Finley succeeded in forestalling a spiritual crisis, but he was clearly surprised and impressed by the event's powerful effect.

The ability to melt the hearts of sinners enabled Calvinists to more easily accept the tumultuous quality of these events. Proponents of the revival defended the emotional behavior as the mighty power of God bursting through a dense atmosphere of deism, infidelity, and indifference. Reverend Lyle believed that "the Lord was doing terrible things in righteousness with a kind design that they might see it and *fear and flow together*. That perhaps the falling down in distress &c. &c., might answer instead of ancient miracles to arouse the attention of a sleeping world and convince deists and gainsayers." Reverend Barton Stone of Cane Ridge offered a similar explanation of the bodily exercises: "So low had religion sunk, and such carelessness universally had prevailed, that I thought that nothing common could have arrested the attention of the world; therefore these uncommon agitations were sent for this purpose." Stone readily admitted that "there were many eccentricities, and much fanaticism in this excitement." Yet "the good effects were seen and acknowledged in every neighborhood."[25] Reverend John E. Findley, one of the more conservative ministers present at Cane Ridge, offered a similar defense. "There are many irregularities among us, so it was in 1776 among the whigs in their enthusiasm for liberty, and so is human nature every where," Findley explained. "I see several things I doo disapprove; but can say, if only the tenth person convicted is truly converted, 'tis a great work." Reverend

David Thomas addressed the problem with a homey metaphor. "The greener or wetter the wood is while the fire is kindling, the greater cloud of smoke it emits." Yet, once dried, the green wood might still burn down nicely, "reduced to glowing coals."[26]

The tendency to emphasize the ability of camp meetings to reach sinners has overshadowed the fact that many of the fallen were already church adherents. Being familiar with the basic ideas and symbols of Christianity, believers (or nominal believers) were probably more susceptible to evangelical urging than other segments of the population. The prominence of believers among the stricken surfaces in many descriptions. In his account of events at Gaspar River in 1800, for instance, McGready reported that "Sober professors, who had been communicants for many years, [were] now lying prostrate on the ground," urging all who were present to listen to the gospel message. Noted another witness, "Some pious people have fallen under a sense of ingratitude and hardness of heart; and others under affecting manifestations of the love and goodness of God." Similarly, a Baptist leader who attended the sacramental occasion at Concord in June 1801 wrote that "30 or 40 persons would be lying on the ground at one time, crying for mercy, some saying, they had been professors of religion from early life, but were strangers to its life and power till now."[27] For these people, falling signified a revitalization of faith rather than conversion. Although they formed only a small segment of the total crowd, they no doubt exerted considerable influence upon fellow participants.

Falling by nonbelievers has usually been interpreted as signifying religious conversion, but initially this was not necessarily the case. While the reaction of Methodists at this time is unknown, few Presbyterian ministers (who usually dominated the proceedings) interpreted the falling as a conversion experience. They viewed it rather as part of the preliminary condition of conviction, whereby subjects are overtaken by a sense of their sinful nature and their need for God's mercy and saving grace. Whether all participants shared this distinction is questionable, but orthodox Presbyterians certainly did and they actively upheld it. At Cane Ridge, for instance, Lyle noted that on Monday John Rankin delivered "a plain sermon about conviction and conversion." The distinction is also evident in more casual statements, such as when Reverend John E. Findley wrote that "if only the tenth person convicted is truly converted, 'tis a great work."[28] People unfamiliar with Calvinism were probably confused or did not care; all they knew was that they had had a profound religious experience. Most Presbyterians, however, adhered to traditional criteria.

One of the most explicit statements to this effect was left by George Baxter, the head of Liberty Hall Academy in Lexington, Virginia, and a man of considerable repute in the Presbyterian Church. A few weeks after the event at Cane Ridge, Baxter traveled to Kentucky and witnessed the revival firsthand. He set his observations down in a letter that was widely reprinted in the religious press. Baxter viewed the Kentucky Revival and the falling with some degree of sympathy and awe, but as a phenomenon well within the New Light tradition. A letter followed in the *Christian Observer* claiming, as Baxter put it in his rebuttal, "that I have brought forward the falling down as a certain test of true religion and that I have expressed no doubt respecting the real conversion of those who thus fell down." Rather, the reverse was the case. According to Baxter, "The clergy in Kentucky so far from considering the falling down as a test of religion, have perhaps been rather more careful during the late revival than on former occasions." Baxter actually wondered just how much religious feeling the falling reflected: the falling supposedly signified religious "discovery," but he knew of instances where it had preceded any such experience.[29] Baxter and most other Presbyterians knew better than to rely on such phenomena as signs of divine grace.

Often lost in the dramatic descriptions of seas of stricken sinners is the fact that only a portion of the participants fell. For instance, Colonel Robert Patterson, a prominent Presbyterian layman, estimated that of the approximately ten thousand people who attended the sacramental occasion held at Lexington in late June 1801, some eight hundred fell and five hundred communed. Later that summer at Point Pleasant in southern Bourbon County, eight thousand people were said to attend, with 250 falling and 350 communing. At Indian Creek, six thousand were present, seventy were struck down, and three hundred communed. Written soon after the reported events, these estimates add an important sense of proportion.[30] Patterson offered these figures as positive evidence of the revival's power, but that power was clearly not universal in scope. As many as 90 percent of the participants seem not to have undergone a religious transformation, a surprisingly high proportion unless one assumes that people came for a variety of reasons, only some of which were of a spiritual nature.

Perhaps nothing has been more obscured by later forms of camp meeting revivalism than the extent to which falling was a collective experience. Falling could strike individuals unpredictably, but at times it seemed to sweep up every person standing in its path, creating a strangely synchronized scene of prostrate sinners. Perhaps no other aspect of the early camp meetings offers stronger testimony to the importance of the group setting. At Cane Ridge young James Finley was awed by the scene of several thousand people "tossed to and fro, like the tumultuous waves of the sea in a storm, or swept down like the trees of the forest under the blast of the wild tornado." Finley claimed to see at one point "at least five hundred swept down in a moment, as if a battery of a thousand guns had been opened upon them, and then immediately followed shrieks and shouts that rent the very heavens." As Reverend Robert Stuart explained, "The process was briefly this: an individual to your right . . . is taken with the exercise [of falling], of which you were notified by a shriek; there is an immediate rush to the place; a circle collects around the individual, and commences singing, and then praying, and then exhorting." Then, "Another is seized to your left, another in front, which soon spreads over the whole extent of the congregation." At large camp meetings such as Cane Ridge, numerous small support circles around the fallen might be active simultaneously, making for a chaotic scene. Participants might fall at any point during the proceedings, but were especially apt to fall during group activities, such as the singing of hymns. Reverend John Evans Findley reported, "The falling down of multitudes . . . happened under the singing of Watt's Psalms and Hymns, more frequently than under the preaching of the word." Falling also tended to follow the emotional structure of the proceedings, sweeping the crowds toward the end of the day or toward the meeting's close, as religious feeling became more urgent. At such times, "a universal agitation pervaded the whole multitude; who were bowed before it as a field of grain waves before the wind." As Reverend McNemar remarked, "How striking, to see hundreds, who never saw each other in the face before, moving uniformly into action, without any preconcerted plan." To members of a society severely divided by culture, economic differences, and political ideology, the camp meeting seemed to exert a miraculous unifying power over the crowd of participants.[31]

The falling that occurred at the early camp meetings has been almost completely overshadowed in modern historical studies by more extreme "bodily exercises," such as dancing, barking, running, rolling, and—the most notorious of all—the jerks. A person captured by the jerks would shake, or jerk, rapidly. As the head snapped back and forth, sometimes so rapidly that the person's facial features appeared blurred, a quick cry or yelp might be uttered. Both saints and sinners might succumb. And though the movement seemed violently strong, subjects rarely experienced any pain or injury.[32] Initially, however, these more spectacular "bodily exercises" were unusual. A few firsthand accounts of the meeting at Cane Ridge mention individuals with convulsions, possibly an attempt to describe the jerks, but contemporary accounts usually associate instances of convulsive behavior more to a lack of food and sleep than anything else— and these may have been different from the infamous jerks.[33] Several accounts insist that the jerks did not appear until some time later. Indeed, some sources set 1802 as the first year in which jerking appeared, although itinerant preacher Lorenzo Dow traveled extensively in Kentucky and Tennessee that year without mentioning it. Not until 1804 did he write that he "had heard about a singularity called the *jerks* or *jerking exercise* which appeared near Knoxville, in August last, to the great alarm of the people."[34] For those Kentuckians who sought the power of religion during the summer of 1801, "to be struck down . . . was the real sign." At Cane Ridge, "The falling exercise was the most noted."[35]

Thus, adding a rite of passage to the Presbyterian sacramental occasion did not in itself create a more individualized form of worship, as is usually thought, but rather the opposite. Spiritual crisis became a group event. Particularly indicative of the camp meeting's integrative function, people did not experience renewal and conviction randomly, as wholly autonomous individuals. They did so rather in a patterned fashion, in accord with others, in many cases falling "as if shot by a volley." Later in the nineteenth century, as the camp meeting format matured and spread, the rite of passage would take on a different character. Bodily exercises appeared in a greater variety of forms, occurring in a more random fashion. And, once Arminianism replaced Calvinism as the ruling theology, the entire transformation from conviction to conversion was condensed into a single event. An individual could arrive a sinner and leave a saint. From the vantage point of Cane Ridge in 1801, however, this was not part of the foreseeable future.

A Ritual of Community

The new style of sacramental occasion exerted such extraordinary power over individuals in part because it offered them something painfully lacking in normal social life, a sense of connection and belonging. Many types of public assemblies serve to integrate participants, but camp meeting revivalism was particularly effective—and never more so than during its first full season of existence, through the event at Cane Ridge.

Many scholars of ritual follow anthropologist Victor Turner's use of the term *communitas* to connote the quality of intense, ritually generated, and usually brief human interconnection. Turner described communitas as "full, unmediated, communication, even communion." When the structures that ordinarily separate, categorize, and organize people succumb to rapid social change, all fall together into one undifferentiated mass. Feelings of isolation and alienation, which may have existed beforehand, are replaced by integration and a profound sense of the shared human condition. The experience is as intense as it is fleeting because efforts to stabilize or channel it appear almost immediately. While the resulting institutionalized forms of communitas are inevitably milder, they are usually more easily sustainable. Eventually, the institutionalized communitas undergoes challenge, either because more structures are added over time that further reduce the communitas or because people suddenly need more communitas due to forces undermining normal social bonds. Reform sometimes forestalls this process, but an ultimate return to full communitas is practically inevitable. Every set of rituals thus proceeds through cyclical phases of breakdown and development.[36]

Significantly, camp meeting revivalism evolved not from regular Sunday worship but from a special church occasion, when the religious community reassembled as completely as possible, reaffirming its bonds by worshipping together and especially by sharing the holy sacrament together. A special degree of communitas was therefore already present. McGready's alterations to the Presbyterian sacramental occasion nonetheless greatly enhanced it. First, the camp meeting proceedings were characterized by a fresh degree of indeterminacy, or absence of structure. The lack of organization, the sheer scale of the crowds, and the toleration of emotional display were particularly disturbing for Presbyterians, who perceived disorderly worship as offensive to God. Second, the new style of public worship was a much more inclusive event. Segments of the population normally neglected, particularly the youth, became full participants. Even non-Presbyterians were welcomed. And, whereas the sacramental occasion carefully screened participants from the sacramental table, such measures were now greatly relaxed. Third, the adoption of camping transformed the sacramental occasion into a total environment, where people lived, ate, and slept religion for several days without interruption. Fourth, the camping effectively leveled economic and social distinctions. Compared with normal daily life, the camp meeting temporarily created a distinctively egalitarian and harmonious society. Most important, while the communitas played an instrumental role in the event's explicit purpose, the salvation of souls, it was also experienced by virtually everyone present.

The almost total lack of organizational structure or form probably ranks as the most controversial aspect of camp meeting communitas. According to a lay participant at Cane Ridge, "These meetings exhibited nothing to the spectator unacquainted with them but a scene of confusion, such as scarcely could be put into human language."[37] Unlike later camp meetings, the only scheduled event at Cane Ridge was the sacrament on Sunday afternoon. Stone conducted the rest of the activities informally, if not spontaneously. The role of the Methodist preachers, for instance, was not agreed upon until after their arrival at Cane Ridge. Methodist William Burke relates that he became frustrated and finally assumed the initiative and began addressing the crowd independently. Lyle also participated as the opportunity arose, serving in various ministerial capacities as he roamed among the people. Other ministers followed a similar course. At any one moment, several different ministers could be seen addressing portions of the crowd, with others leading prayers and hymns or assisting those persons stricken to the ground. One participant at Cane Ridge counted "seven ministers, all preaching at one time, some on stumps, others in wagons, and one—the Rev. William Burke, now of Cincinnati—was standing on a tree which had, in falling, lodged against another."[38] According to one of the ministers present, some people were "crying for mercy; some shouting redeeming grace; and others collected in numberless small circles of twelve or twenty singing hymns; all serious; many walking to and fro, with anxiety pictured on their countenances."[39] The camp meeting presented an awesome scene, with "Sinners dropping down on every hand, shrieking, groaning, crying for mercy. . . . Some singing and shouting, clapping their hands, hugging and even kissing, laughing; others talking to the distressed, to one another, or to opposers of the work; and all this at once."[40] Contemplating Cane Ridge, one young man remarked, "The noise was like the roar of Niagara. . . . Some of the people were singing, others praying, some crying for mercy in the most piteous accents, while others were shouting vociferously."[41] Confusion reigned even among believers. Lyle commented, "Sometimes almost all the serious people were praying at once, each with his own voice. In the meeting house[,] sung six songs at once."[42] Conservative Presbyterians such as Lyle disapproved, yet such practices functioned to obliterate the traditional structure and form of the sacramental occasion and replaced it with a fluidity that brought participants—no matter their denominational background—into direct contact with one another.

Somewhat related to these patterns of lay participation was the frequency with which people assumed preaching roles. "During this time I heard a number of those that were delivered arise and speak for their friends and the people and numbers got convicted and fell down," Lyle noted. "Their orations consist of the plain and essential truths of the gospel that they themselves have been powerfully convinced of, but they speak with all the feeling and pathos that human nature . . . is capable of. They speak much of the fullness of Christ, his willingness to save &c." Lay exhortations challenged the usually hierarchical power relations of public worship, reducing the authoritative difference between laity and clergy. At the early camp meetings, the clergy and laity shared control of the proceedings. The result was a more balanced or egalitarian event.[43]

Communitas was also produced by the more inclusive composition of early camp meetings. Probably the most conspicuous indication is the ecumenical character. Sacramental occasions had nearly always involved additional ministers to assist the local pastor, but starting with McGready's sacrament at Red River, these ministers included some who were not Presbyterian. While Presbyterians retained the key roles in administering the sacrament, now ministers of other denominations, particularly Methodists, became actively involved as well. Genuine efforts were made to bypass doctrinal differences for the greater glory of God. For example, Reverend John Rankin defended John McGee's participation with

McGready by explaining, "All of our gifts and ministerial efforts were united and tended to the same end, the conviction, conversion and salvation of souls." Interdenominational cooperation was not unprecedented in American Protestantism, but it was rare. In Kentucky, where the ministers had previously competed for westerners with no church affiliation, it was unprecedented.[44]

Despite the apparent sincerity of Rankin and other western revivalists, doctrinal difference and years of rivalry could not be instantly forgotten. At the revival meeting hosted by Concord in June 1801, Methodist Benjamin Northcott had been welcomed and invited to preach but was informed by the Presbyterian ministers that "there was too much prejudice among their people against Methodist preachers for him to be known as such."[45] At the Cane Ridge camp meeting, Methodist and Presbyterian relations seemed little improved. Stone tried to get Methodist William Burke to publicly distinguish Methodist doctrine. Feeling the insult, Burke challenged Stone to do likewise, and Stone quickly backed down, explaining that it was not he but his elders who were concerned. Burke resented that the Presbyterian ministers desired Methodist help in guiding the emotional currents of the event, but were not ready to share the preaching stand or allow Methodists to administer the sacrament. Said Burke in his memoirs, "We were fully satisfied that they only wanted the Methodists to shake the bush, and they would catch the birds."[46] Baptists elicited similar reactions. In mid-August, during a meeting at Paint Creek Presbyterian Meetinghouse in Madison County, Moses and Isaac Renfro preached, both Baptists, and Lyle noted, "This disturbed some of the Old Presbytereans verry much." Stone glossed over such problems when writing about the revival years later, however, and proudly claimed, "The Methodist and Baptist preachers aided in the work, and all appeared cordially united in it."[47]

Nonetheless, western Christians were worshiping God with unprecedented if imperfect unity. According to Elder David Purviance, "The dogma's [sic] and speculations of the sects, were now but little requested, even among the clergy. Themes of a much more noble character inspired their hearts . . . the salvation of souls." Another Presbyterian minister present at Cane Ridge defensively explained: "Some, perhaps, will censure us for associating with the Baptists and Methodists; But, my dear Sir, we are all very friendly . . . and is this not better, than to be devouring one another?" Earlier in the year, an unidentified gentleman had taken a more radical stand, wishing all denominations to unite as Christians: "And that the profession in the belief in one Lord, one Faith, one Baptism, one God and Father, might take place: that there might be but one visible household of Faith, that all might be of one heart, and one mind, and join hands in building up the torn down walls of Zion, which party zeal has almost demolished." Other participants were likewise impressed by the camp meeting's ability to overcome interdenominational rivalry. Young Lewis Garrett, later a Methodist preacher, contended, "The barriers which had kept different sectaries apart, seemed to have given way; non-essential peculiarities were measurably forgotten. . . . The love of Christ and souls seemed to be the governing principle."[48] Much acclaim was raised that "Presbyterians, Methodists, Baptists . . . preached and prayed and praised together." The new emphasis on essential tenets of Christianity brought a society long troubled by religious division new hope for future harmony.[49]

The early camp meetings were also noticeably more inclusive for their presence of western youth. In contrast to regular church services, in which young people played a passive and marginal role, young people were conspicuous participants at camp meetings. McGready wrote, "It was truly affecting to see little boys and girls, of nine, ten, and twelve years of age, and some younger, lying prostrate on the ground, weeping, praying, and crying out for mercy, like condemned criminals at the place of execution, and that in the presence of multitudes." At Cane Ridge, Reverend Findley saw "one hundred persons at once on the ground crying for mercy of all ages from 8 to 60 years." According to another witness, "I have seen a great many down and lay[ing] a great while & as soon as they are able begin to sing and pray for the World, particularly Boys and Girls about 8 or 10 years old." Reverend Lyle's account of his activities at Cane Ridge frequently refer to affected individuals as someone's son or daughter, presumably because their parents were church members. In the religious revival among the Baptists, "a great many" of the converted were children of church members.[50] Having already had some religious indoctrination, such children were especially vulnerable to religious impressions. It is probably no accident that the first to fall after Stone's return from Logan County were two girls. While the actual proportion of children is impossible to calculate, the generally youthful age structure of the western population as well as the revival's broad popular appeal make it reasonable to assume that they comprised a major segment of the camp meeting crowd.

Indeed, the active involvement of western youth probably contributed significantly to the Great Revival's more sensational aspects. Descriptions of the early camp meetings frequently mention highly excited children, singing, crying out, and falling to the ground. Particularly noteworthy is the respect that adults accorded exhortations by children. At Gaspar River James McGready "stood by some dear young creatures, little boys and girls, and heard their groans and cries in the pangs of the new birth, like the shrieks and cries of condemned criminals at the place of execution. . . . I have likewise stood present, when the light of the knowledge of the glory of God in the face of Jesus broke into their souls; and to the astonishment of all around them, these little creatures have started to their feet, and told all present their sweet views of the lovely, precious Lord Jesus." Wrote McGready, "I say, to hear them speak upon these subjects, the good language, the good sense, the clear ideas, and the rational, scriptural light in which they spoke, truly amazed me. I felt mortified and mean before them."[51] The modern understanding of human psychology would attribute the particular responsiveness of these children to mere suggestibility, but eighteenth-century Americans believed that children were especially likely to be used by God as divine messengers. As one witness at Cane Ridge explained, "Children were often made the instruments through which the Lord wrought." Another noted that "children are the most active in the work. When they speak, it appears that the Lord sends his Spirit, to accompany it with power to the hearts of sinners."[52]

One of the more vivid instances was related by Reverend McNemar and probably occurred at the Indian Creek meeting, approximately ten miles north of Cane Ridge. In the afternoon, a boy about twelve years old mounted a log and began speaking extemporaneously to the nearby crowd. "With tears streaming from his eyes, he cried aloud to the wicked, warning them of their danger. . . . He was held up by two men, and spoke for about an hour." As the boy neared total exhaustion, "he raised his hand, and dropping his handkerchief wet with sweat from his little face, cried out: 'Thus, O sinner! shall you drop into hell, unless you forsake your sins and turn to the Lord.'" At that moment, a number of listeners fell to the ground, "like those who are shot in battle."[53] Although children had figured very little in religious worship before the Great Revival, adults now granted children such as this one status because they believed that their innocence and eloquence had divine origin.

Somewhat less apparent to participants was how the children contributed to the event's communitas. Normally subordinate to adults, a reversal of status transpired when children preached. Sometimes the reversal was quite explicit. For example, at a meeting held at Walnut Hill in early September, a month after Cane Ridge, Lyle noted, "In the meeting house John and Samuel Martin & Sallie Martin & Alex Eubanks & James McDonals daughter fell & the two boys got up and exhorted powerfully & the daughter of James McDonals advised her father and mother very tenderly." This incident reversed both the child/adult and the child/parent relationship. Symbolic inversion of status essentially put all participants on a more egalitarian footing.[54]

Participation by women, however, received much less attention. Women's emotional susceptibility was not novel nor did it attest to the divine power of the revival. Most contemporary accounts of camp revivals were written at least in part to persuade critics that such meetings provided a rare opportunity to reach those westerners usually resistant to religion.[55] Apparently the revival's effects on women seemed mundane compared with the sight of a "bold Kentuckian (undaunted by the horrors of war) turn pale and tremble . . . sink in deep remorse, roll and toss, and gnash his teeth, till black in the face; . . . and obtain deliverance." Reverend McNemar asked, "Who would not say the change was not supernatural and miraculous?" The camp meeting's ability to affect men held special significance, as when Lyle reported hearing after he left Cane Ridge that "they were nearly all men that fell on Tuesday." The effect on men was constantly noted in less pointed descriptions as well. "Some old men fell, some young ones of robust constitution, some children about 11 (as Betsy Rogers) about 7 or 8 (as Adams [sic] two children)," noted Lyle at the Pleasant Point meeting earlier that summer. "One Miller fell who was telling his daughters lying in distress that if they would come again to such meetings he would beat them well. He fell with these words in his mouth."[56]

Both male and female alike responded to the evangelical appeals, although the only church records that can bear this out are for Baptists. Two selected congregations, located in different parts of central Kentucky, admitted an almost equal proportion of male and female members during this period. Interestingly, this was true for both white and black members. Providence Baptist Church in Madison County, between May and October 1801, admitted for baptism forty-five white males, forty-eight white females, thirteen black males, and fourteen black females. At Bryan's Station Baptist Church in Fayette County, the revival proceeded strongly from September 1800 through August 1801. During this year, Bryan's Station admitted for baptism 119 white males, 103 white females, 77 black males, and 67 black females.[57]

It is nonetheless possible if not probable that, while the submission of men was more noteworthy, women predominated at camp meetings. Lyle and other observers make frequent references to women. One account, a letter from a layman named Henry Alderson, specifically mentions that the afflicted tended to be women.[58] Similarly, François-André Michaux, a Frenchman who visited Kentucky in 1802, and was probably more objective than the ministers and elders who created most other extant descriptions of the revival, stated that women were particularly susceptible to the religious excitement. When women succumbed, he reported, they were "carried out of the crowd, and out under a tree, where they lie a long time extended, heaving the most lamentable sighs."[59]

At first glance the participation of women seems to have demonstrated merely a greater emotional susceptibility, but several accounts included incidents that reveal departures from normal social status. Some women began exhorting, for example, publicly advising nearby listeners. One of the first individuals affected at the sacramental occasion held at Lexington in 1801 was a woman who delivered stirring religious testimony. Agitated, gesturing wildly, the woman spoke "of a glorious deliverance from distress, clouds and darkness. . . . [S]he said she was poor and wretched[,] she was nothing [,] but she had great hopes in Jesus of the happiness in the world to come." Other incidents also suggest that the early camp meetings reduced the normal status differential across gender. McGready related an incident intended, like so many others left by defenders of the camp meeting format, to demonstrate its powerful effect on men, but it also sheds light on women. On Monday morning after a sacramental occasion in Logan County, "a man who lived in the congregation, came to the meeting-house, bitterly exasperated against his wife, who had remained at the meeting-house all night." According to McGready, "He ordered her home, but she refused to go: he then gave her very abusive language, and went home very angry." There, predictably, the man was "struck with deep conviction, and lay powerless on his own floor." Reverend Lyle also recorded an interesting example of the revival's empowerment when a woman "in a kind of agony" told him to set his slaves free. Lyle, who clearly thought the woman had overstepped herself, especially with a minister, replied politely but firmly that "the setting of my slaves free depended on the will of another." And if free, "they could not support themselves."[60] Such incidents suggest that the camp meeting communitas temporarily narrowed gender differences.

The inclusiveness of the camp meeting also encompassed race. Although most blacks were slaves and probably there primarily to wait upon their masters, many also participated. For example, McGready had observed at Red River, "Some of the Negroes appeared to be powerfully seized with convictions." On Sunday night at Cane Ridge, Reverend Lyle "went where a negro was preaching and after he was done[,] exhorted." According to another witness at Cane Ridge, the blacks assembled approximately 150 yards south of the meetinghouse, listening to exhortations delivered mainly by their own people. At a sacramental occasion held at Walnut Hill Meetinghouse near Lexington a month after the one at Cane Ridge, Lyle noted, "The negroes had a preaching to themselves." At a sacramental occasion held there in 1802, the twelve black communicants were served separately, after all the whites were finished. Some intermingling apparently occurred as well. Lyle saw a "woman (near where two or three negro wenches were down) crying glory to god in a shrieking voice."[61] Unfortunately, little other mention is made of black participation during this early period.

The presence of blacks marked a significant departure from normal religious worship. In Virginia, where a majority of western blacks originated, a significant percentage of church members were black, especially among Baptists. But in Kentucky, black church membership was a rarity.[62] Baptist congregations there seldom included more than three or four slaves before the Great Revival, and the situation among western Presbyterians and Methodists was apparently similar if not worse.[63] The evangelical character of these denominations welcomed black participation, and racial distance between church members was smaller than in society at large. Blacks clearly held an inferior position, being served last at the sacramental occasion, but no one questioned their right to be served. Interracial fellowship, however, may not have been as important to blacks as to whites. A desire for separate black worship had surfaced repeatedly in the Baptist congregations for which records survive, but with little success.[64] The separate worship activities at camp meetings was therefore possibly not imposed by whites (although whites retained control). The relative autonomy instead may have represented positive community development among western blacks. No evidence suggests a status reversal, with blacks preaching to whites—a useful reminder that the social ideals celebrated at camp meetings were those of the hegemonic white population. The new style of sacramental occasion was nonetheless a new high point in transcending normal social barriers as numerous blacks joined what had previously been almost entirely a white activity. On another level, of course, their marginalized presence reflected and perhaps reinforced secular norms.

In addition to the greater degree of indeterminacy and inclusiveness, the new style of sacramental occasion created an experience of communitas by removing participants from their normal activities. It went further in this respect than any other type of outdoor evangelical meeting. Previously, most participants at sacramental occasions had belonged to the host congregation, and they did not travel enough distance to justify camping. Those who did stayed not at the meetinghouse grounds but with a neighboring member of the congregation. The spectacle of prostrate sinners, however, quickly drew believers and nonbelievers from further away. The crowds soon exceeded anything the host congregation could possibly have accommodated in the traditional manner. Whether members who lived close enough to sleep at home continued to do so is unclear, but in 1801 activities were continuing unabated through the night. McGready's account indicates that camping originated with the laity, with no resistance from the ministers, who were mainly just grateful to see the spiritual drought end.

Camping arrangements during this early period were improvised and haphazard, contributing further to the sense of communitas. Those people who came in wagons, a small segment of the participants, adapted them for sleeping quarters. Other participants slept on the ground around campfires. A few rested as best they could on the pews of the meetinghouse, but that was usually noisy and crowded.[65] With proceedings persisting throughout the night, some people probably went without much sleep, not always voluntarily. Firsthand descriptions from this period suggest very little functional differentiation of space; sleeping and preaching occurred in close proximity. And when weather was wet, such as at Cane Ridge, any picnic atmosphere soon dissolved. Tents would later become the standard type of accommodation at camp meetings, relegated to a separate part of the grounds, laid out like a small town. But during this early phase, as a lay observer from Logan County recalled, "There were no camps, no arbor, not a board on the ground except for a few on the preacher's stand." Similarly, the only tent at Cane Ridge, recalled Methodist William Burke, was the one covering the preaching stand. Initially, participants were left to make their own arrangements, leading to a haphazard situation.[66]

Feeding the masses also seems to have elicited little planning or coordination. "There was no regular intermission, for eating and sleeping," recalled one minister later. "We must, therefore, add these as going on together with religious service." Stone later related that at Cane Ridge, some seven miles from the nearest sizable town, "The members of the church and the neighbors brought their provisions to the encampment, for themselves and strangers. Long tables were spread with provisions, and all invited to eat." It seems unlikely, however, that the Cane Ridge hospitality could have lasted long in a crowd whose numbers probably exceeded ten thousand. All other sources are silent about how the masses were fed, presumably because no organized effort was undertaken. In keeping with the Christian principles that guided the event, people probably shared what they had, cooking and eating with strangers around the open fires and thereby contributing further to the sense of communitas.[67]

Camping also added to communitas by removing people from the distinctions of regular daily life. Contemporaries seem to have had some sense of this, as when John McGee wrote of an early camper in Logan County, "He had left his worldly cares behind him, and had nothing to do, but attend on divine service."[68] Occupational status, family roles, and other identifiers carried less meaning for the three or four days of the camp meeting. The other institutions and structures that organize society were also left behind. Wealthy people, for example, had built large and imposing dwellings to differentiate themselves from people of lower economic ranks. At the camp meeting, these distinctions faded away. Regardless of social or economic status, people coexisted at the camp meeting in close contact, with virtually everyone sleeping on the ground. Privacy was minimal. Eating, sleeping, and other ordinarily domestic acts became public, an implicit reminder of the basic sameness of the human condition. Moreover, participants probably spent a good proportion of their time informally gathering around the open fires, exchanging observations and discussing spiritual matters well into the night. In many instances no doubt the conversations took place between relative strangers, creating personal bonds where none previously existed. This less formal aspect of camp meeting revivalism is almost completely overlooked in the written descriptions left by contemporaries, which focused instead on aspects of the event bearing more directly on the saving of sinners. Nonetheless, it played a crucial role in the creation of communitas for many participants.

Communitas constituted the camp meeting revival's premier characteristic. As one witness declared, the new form of religious revival "has united all in the strongest bonds of love."[69] By defying denominational boundaries, broadening participation, and leveling many social distinctions, the camp meeting created a situation where participants underwent heightened perceptions of human interconnection. The experience was not perfect, but still represented a major improvement over normal reality. Nor should camp meeting revivalism be regarded as unique or the sole mechanism by which early national Americans sought to reaffirm social connectedness. The immediate, widespread enthusiasm that greeted the camp meeting format nonetheless strongly suggests that camp meeting communitas fulfilled an important need, one not being adequately met through other means as western Americans struggled to come to better terms with social instability, economic striving, and political partisanship.[70] Camp meeting revivalism was a product of this atmosphere of community dissolution. It was not, however, simply a direct reflection of a more diverse, commercial, and liberal society. Rather, the relationship, as is often the case in religious ritual, was inverted. The camp meeting symbolically reminded an alienated audience of their shared human condition, thereby serving as a mechanism for reintegration.

Reaction and Refinement

Descriptions of the camp meeting revival were quickly relayed across all of religious America and even beyond. Before George Baxter left Lexington, Virginia, in October 1801 to observe the Kentucky revival firsthand, he had "heard many accounts and seen many letters respecting it." The *Connecticut Evangelical Magazine* included Baxter's report in its March 1802 issue. The *Christian Observer* published Baxter's report in October 1802. The *Methodist Magazine* featured Baxter's report yet again in its February 1803 issue and added a detailed account by Presbyterian layman Robert Patterson. In March 1803 it published an account by Presbyterian minister John Evans Findley. The *Western Missionary Magazine* serialized McGready's account of how it all began. But private letters shared among the clergy and leading laymen circulated descriptions of the Kentucky camp meetings even more quickly. The president of Hampden-Sydney College in Virginia reported in January 1802 that a twenty-mile area of North Carolina was experiencing a revival "with similar appearances."

The assemblies were purported to be "nearly as large, and instances of falling down as common as in Kentucky."[71] Revivals in the "Kentucky style" were soon noted in numerous places, especially in the western and southwestern parts of the country.[72]

Among the very first churchmen to hear about the occurrences in Kentucky was Bishop Francis Asbury, the leader of American Methodists. Initial reports reached him by early September. A journal entry for mid-October reports that he had recently read an account written by James McGready of the revival in Logan County. Asbury grasped the potential of the camp meeting format almost immediately. "This is field fighting," Asbury exclaimed, "this is fishing with large nets," and he urged his clergymen to embrace the new format. "Campmeetings! Campmeetings!" Asbury exclaimed. "The battle ax and weapon of war, it will break down walls of wickedness, part of hell, superstition, [and] false doctrine."[73] Methodist quarterly meetings were, like the Presbyterian sacramental occasion, special religious celebrations of renewal and reintegration and often held outdoors in order to accommodate crowds. The rituals adapted by McGready were therefore just as easily superimposed on the Methodist quarterly meeting.[74] In the hands of the Methodists and other denominations, camp meeting revivalism would develop into one of the most important forms of public worship in nineteenth-century America.

Even before descriptions of the western revival reached Asbury, camp meetings were already evolving into a more stable institution. The first steps in this direction were taken within weeks of the Cane Ridge sacrament. At a sacramental occasion a few miles away, at Paris, the Presbyterian clergy discovered two participants in the act of adultery, the first mention of any such offense. Another growing problem was the vending of whiskey. Following a troubling incident at Walnut Hill Meetinghouse in September, the Presbyterian clergy convened at the pastor's home one evening to consider how these new problems might be controlled. Reverend David Rice "presented a plan for regulating the camps at night." Basically, the participants sleeping in the meetinghouse were to be separated by sex, with the ministers taking turns at watch. In a related vein, the clergy agreed that participants needed to get more sleep. Otherwise, events ran a risk of "religious insanity." Transylvania Presbytery helped by scheduling multiple sacramental occasions, thereby distributing attendance and making crowds on the scale of Cane Ridge much less likely in the future. Not only was a smaller crowd easier to supervise, but it reduced the need to have several ministers speaking concurrently and thereby helped minimize disorder. Efforts were also made to reduce the level of disorganization by scheduling activities and speakers beforehand. Likewise, religious proceedings were no longer allowed to spill halfway through the next workweek. Spatially, the camp meeting were becoming more organized, with the grounds divided and designated for particular activities. Eating and sleeping areas were removed from the religious activities. And, of course, as people became more familiar with the falling and other "bodily exercises," they created less disruption. Camp meeting revivalism thus became institutionalized, entering a new stage of development.[75]

Later in the nineteenth century, camp meetings would be conducted literally "by the book," according to published instruction manuals.[76] Men and women were assigned separate seating areas. The convicted sinners gathered by the "mourner's bench," a special section of roughly hewn benches for the religiously affected, centrally placed just below the preaching stand. In some cases, this area was separated by an enclosure and gate. Instead of participants providing their own shelter, standard tents were supplied for all. These usually formed the perimeter of the grounds, in a horseshoe shape, square, or circle and aligned to form streets, accompanied by hygienic facilities. Nightly patrols ensured that the close sleeping arrangements did not lead to immorality. The preaching schedule was prearranged, with the time of worship announced with trumpets or some similar type of general notice. In many cases, facilities became semi-permanent, with tents set over plank floors and roofed assembly arenas at locations specifically reserved for the annual revival. Thus camp meeting revivalism became "civilized." Although diminishing the intensity of communitas, institutionalization enabled camp meeting revivalism to grow.[77]

Delineating the shape of camp meeting revivalism is easier than delineating its effects. The most obvious and easily measured effect was a surge in church membership. Within a few years, Kentucky's three major denominations experienced dramatic growth spurts. The Kentucky District of Methodists roughly doubled, from 1,741 members in 1800 to 3,961 by 1805. During the same period, Elkhorn Baptist Association, the largest of six Baptist associations in Kentucky, increased from 1,642 members to 3,550. Church members in Green River Association, Kentucky's other main Baptist association, in McGready's part of the state, increased from 361 in 1800 to 1,014 a year later.[78] Kentucky Presbyterians are said to have increased less dramatically, but membership figures are unavailable. Largely due to the achievements of the frontier generation of preachers in transplanting institutional structures, incorporating the sudden swell of converts was straining but not a serious problem. Some backsliding certainly occurred, as in any such movement. A year after Cane Ridge, for example, Lyle reported various individual failures, such as "'Becca Bell who is with child to one Brown" and "Patty and John McGown—the one has been whoring[,] the other drinking and fighting." Yet many others seemed to "hold up well" and an overall, permanent increase in western church membership is undeniable.[79]

The dramatic increase in church adherents apparently had a noticeable effect on public morals. The revivalists had not set out to change society; their concern was the individual soul, and they wished to extend the message of salvation to as many souls as possible. They nonetheless believed the final result should be a Christianized social order, and they detected some progress in this respect.[80] Terah Templin, one of Kentucky's pioneer Presbyterian ministers, claimed, "There is a considerable difference in the face of families, neighborhoods, and these congregations, compared with what formerly appeared." Said McGready in 1802, "Innumerable instances we have of those, who four or five years ago were drunkards, dancers, Sabbath-breakers, Deists, &c. &c. who are now humble, praying, sober, temperate Christians." When Reverend George Baxter came to Kentucky from Virginia in the autumn of 1801, "I was told by settlers on the road, that the character of Kentucky travellers was entirely changed, and that they were now distinguished for sobriety as they had formerly been for dissoluteness." After some observations of his own, Baxter wrote, "Indeed, I found Kentucky the most moral place I had ever been in; a profane expression was hardly heard; a religious awe seemed to pervade the country." Though surely an exaggeration, some reform had seemingly occurred. "A Great change of manners, at least, has largely taken place in this part of the world," insisted another Kentuckian. "This is too evident for anyone to deny." Even deists supposedly admitted that "from whatever cause the revival might originate, it certainly made people better." While most of these improvements proved temporary, Christian standards of social conduct nonetheless gained significant ground. As a traveler remarked a year after Baxter's observations, "Religion has obtained the preeminent influence. That is[,] those that have it shows it, and those that have it not wish to be considered religious for the credit it gives in society."[81]

Various studies of the Second Great Awakening suggest that further investigation of the Great Kentucky Revival's aftermath would also reveal some less obvious, more diffuse effects. Several historians of the early nineteenth century studying revivals elsewhere have detected, for example, connections between evangelical Protestantism and the emerging democratic culture. Evangelical religious practice provided opportunities for common citizens to develop leadership skills that were transferable to the public sphere. Furthermore, a shift occurred in the meaning of political virtue, from the pursuit of the common good to personal morality, which indirectly weakened elite dominance of political leadership. Other historians have emphasized the ways in which evangelical Protestantism influenced definitions of gender. Although men continued to monopolize church offices, evangelical religion offered women fresh opportunities for activity beyond the home in Sunday schools, charitable causes, and vice crusades. Their increased moral authority ultimately played a major part in the shaping of nineteenth-century middle-class culture. Evangelicalism also affected relationships in a rapidly changing economic order. Some historians have argued that religion provided a rising industrial class with a tool of social control over an undisciplined proletariat. Others have stressed religion's ability to temper the socially negative aspects of liberal individualism by placing limits on the pursuit of self-interest. In other ways as well, the growth of evangelical Protestantism during the early nineteenth century transformed the face of American culture.[82]

How did religion come to exert such far-reaching power? The early national period was one of profound cultural crisis. The experience of the American Revolution and its supporting ideology had essentially demolished the main pillars of traditional culture. Principles of deference and order were being supplanted by ideals of equality and freedom.[83] In addition, the Revolution accelerated the transition toward capitalism, redefining relationships and values in ways that sometimes seemed ruthless and antisocial if not downright immoral. In Kentucky, these problems were compounded by the effects of geographic relocation during wartime. And in no part of the new nation had much sense of "imagined community," or shared national identity, yet developed.[84] For those people who therefore found life confusing and fraught with uncertainty, religion offered valuable comfort and guidance. As historian Donald Mathews suggested in his classic essay, the Second Great Awakening of which the Great Kentucky Revival was a part, "helped to give meaning and direction to people suffering in various degrees from the social strains of a nation on the move into new political, economic, and geographical areas." Religion "provided values or goals for which to work and codes which regulated behavior giving ideological as well as social order to life." At the same time, it organized American society structurally into a quilt of local communities, held together not only by shared faith but also by church governance.[85] This achievement was facilitated by a general theological shift toward Arminianism. The early nineteenth century witnessed a national wave of evangelical movements, cutting across denominational boundaries, which offered a more democratic religious culture. Focusing on the leaders of this development, including Barton Warren Stone, and their readiness to take their cause to the public via print, Nathan Hatch has shown in rich detail how Christianity became embedded in the foundation of the emerging national culture, making religiosity an enduring trait in American life.[86]

Camp meeting revivalism constituted a vital component in this process, as evidenced in its widespread and enduring popularity. As historian Stephen Watts has noted, postrevolutionary Americans "promoted competition, fragmentation, and individualism in practically all realms of life, while at the same time making them more palatable with new strategies for reassurance, security, and order."[87] The camp meeting revival was one of these strategies. The core experience of communitas, especially intense during the formative phase of development, appealed to participants disoriented by the changes taking place in American society during the early years of nationhood. This communitas, as much as any touching exhortation delivered by a clergyman, was crucial to camp meeting revivalism's superior ability to elicit spiritual transformation. Indeed, many participants experienced conversion or renewal in unison, falling together "as if shot by a volley of guns." The freedom attained through salvation was thus symbolically orchestrated with the earthly church. Whereas previously most sinners sought spiritual relief privately, they now did so in public, amidst an audience. The camp meeting demonstrated dramatically, far more than did established religious forms, that when Americans exercised their spiritual freedom they also joined a community. By afterwards joining a religious congregation, individuals could partially preserve the sense of connection and acceptance.

But what of the numerous other camp meeting participants, the majority, who did not succumb to evangelical appeals? For some participants, the camp meeting experience was probably little more than a catharsis. For others, however, the effects may have been more meaningful, even if impossible to actually measure. Various anthropologists have pointed out how certain types of rituals address underlying social arrangements. For example, anthropologist Victor Turner used the term *social drama* to describe rituals that play out contemporary values and ideals. Milton Singer introduced the similar concept of a cultural performance: "occasions in which as a culture or society we reflect upon and define ourselves, dramatize our collective myths and history, present ourselves with alternatives, and eventually change in some ways while remaining the same in others."[88] Such ideas suggest that camp meeting revivalism held meaning not only for those who were spiritually transformed, but also for many other participants. Some more recent scholars go even further, emphasizing the instructive quality of rituals as models of "ideal relations and structures of values." Though somewhat similar to Durkheim's notion of how rituals function as a mechanism of social control and integration, ritual here merely clarifies or defines social norms and presents them for internalization.[89] Periods of profound change and cultural strain such as what was being experienced in late-eighteenth-century Kentucky are especially conducive to the development of clarifying or confirming ritual forms.

The idea that the camp meeting format carried an important social message was not entirely alien to contemporaries, but the tendency was toward literal Bible interpretations. Barton Warren Stone and several of his colleagues believed that the camp meeting format was a call to restore

Christianity to its original purity, when the disciples of Jesus Christ gathered for worship without the mediation of an educated clergy, impressive church structures, or doctrinal intricacies. This vision formed the foundation for the religious denomination soon organized by Stone and his adherents, named most appropriately the Christian Church. The Stonites rejected all creeds save the New Testament.[90]

Neither Stone nor any of his fellow revivalists who left a personal account of their experiences seem to have noticed that the particular aspects of Christianity being expressed at camp meetings also resembled republican social ideals. This oversight is hardly surprising, since defenders of the new evangelical format attributed its power not to earthly concerns but to divine favor. Yet the character of early camp meeting revivalism reveals an emphasis on key qualities of morality, egalitarianism, and unity that were central to both worlds. The camp meeting, which on one level was the temporary creation of an ideal Christian society, was also the temporary creation of an ideal republican society. Moreover, camp meeting participants were not required to distinguish between the two ideals. Indeed, they were encouraged not to do so, but rather to infuse the young nation with renewed Christian virtue. And, if a Christian republic could be realized for a few days at a camp meeting, hope also existed for a more permanent achievement. Thus camp meeting ritual contained an instructive aspect, not only religiously but also socially.

Although the full effect of camp meeting revivalism remains impossible to gauge, the extraordinary popularity of camp meeting revivalism among Americans in the nineteenth century offers indirect yet indisputable testimony for its tremendous importance. This popularity has often been under-appreciated, but the camp meeting's success lay not with the clergy but with the laity. Had people not found the new religious format meaningful, they would have declined to participate. Camp meeting revivalism would have gone down in history as merely a freak episode of spiritual excess. The specific meaning was certainly far from uniform, yet at least one general observation can be offered, an observation which pertains just as much to those participants who experienced religious transformation as to those who did not. The communitas experienced at camp meetings brought together people from different backgrounds in ways thought appropriate for both Christians and republicans. For a few days, to a varying degree, these Americans became, in the words of a popular hymn by Isaac Watts, "Citizens of Zion."

NOTES

Introduction

1. Catherine C. Cleveland, *The Great Revival in the West, 1797–1805* (Chicago: Univ. of Chicago Press, 1916); Peter G. Mode, *The Frontier Spirit in American Christianity* (New York: Macmillan, 1923); Frederick Jackson Turner, *The Significance of the Frontier in American History,* ed. Harold P. Simonson (New York: Frederick Ungar, 1963).

2. Among the historians to follow the lead of Cleveland and Mode are the following: Charles A. Johnson, *The Frontier Camp Meeting: Religion's Harvest Time* (Dallas: Southern Methodist Univ. Press, 1955); William Speer, *The Great Revival of 1800* (Philadelphia: Presbyterian Board, 1872); William Warren Sweet, *Revivalism in America* (New York: Abingdon Press, n.d.); T. Scott Miyakawa, *Protestants and Pioneers, Individualism and Conformity on the American Frontier* (Chicago: Univ. of Chicago Press, 1964); Bernard A. Weisberger, *They Gathered at the River: The Story of the Great Revivalists and Their Impact upon Religion in America* (Chicago: Quadrangle Books, 1966). On the last point see Peter G. Mode, "Revivalism as a Phase of Frontier Life," *Journal of Religion* 1 (1921): 337–54; William Warren Sweet, "Churches as Moral Courts of the Frontier," *Church History* 2 (1933): 3–21. Such is also implied in Donald G. Mathews, "The Second Great Awakening as an Organizing Process, 1780–1830: An Hypothesis," *American Quarterly* 21 (1969): 23–43; Ralph E. Morrow, "The Great Revival, the West, and the Crisis of the Church," in *The Frontier Re-Examined,* ed. John Francis McDermott (Urbana: Univ. of Illinois Press, 1967), 65–78; Dickson D. Bruce Jr., *And They All Sang Hallelujah: Plain-Folk Camp-Meeting Religion, 1800–1845* (Knoxville: Univ. of Tennessee Press, 1974). More recently, Stephen Aron presents a less Turnerian portrait of early Kentucky but still treats the Great Revival as a response to frontier disappointment and "possibilities lost." See Aron, *How the West Was Lost: The Transformation of Kentucky from Daniel Boone to Henry Clay* (Baltimore: Johns Hopkins Univ. Press, 1996).

3. John B. Boles, *The Great Revival, 1787–1805: The Origins of the Southern Evangelical Mind* (Lexington: Univ. Press of Kentucky, 1972); Leigh Eric Schmidt, *Holy Fairs: Scottish Communions and American Revivals in the Early Modern Period* (New York: Cambridge Univ. Press, 1989); Paul K. Conkin, *Cane Ridge, America's Pentecost* (Madison: Univ. of Wisconsin Press, 1990), 63.

4. The literature is extensive, but good places to start include the following: Patricia Nelson Limerick, *The Legacy of Conquest: The Unbroken Past of the American West* (New York: W. W. Norton, 1987); Patricia Nelson Limerick, Clyde A. Milner II, and Charles E. Rankin, eds., *Trails toward a New Western History* (Lawrence: Univ. Press of Kansas, 1991); William Cronon, George Miles, and Jay Gitlin, eds., *Under an Open Sky: Rethinking America's*

Western Past (New York: W. W. Norton, 1992); Donald Worster, "New West, True West: Interpreting the Region's History," *Western Historical Quarterly* 18 (1987): 141–56.

5. Ellen T. Eslinger, "The Great Revival in Bourbon County, Kentucky" (Ph.D. diss., Univ. of Chicago, 1988). At the time this study commenced, early Kentucky history was in what might be fairly described as a moribund condition. The last few years, however, have seen a flurry of revisionist studies: Fredrika Johanna Teute, "Land, Liberty, and Labor in the Post-Revolutionary Era: Kentucky as the Promised Land" (Ph.D. diss., Johns Hopkins Univ., 1988); Stephen Aron, "How the West Was Lost: The Transformation of Kentucky from Daniel Boone to Henry Clay" (Ph.D. diss., Univ. of California, Berkeley, 1990); Elizabeth Ann Perkins, "Border Life: Experience and Perception in the Revolutionary Ohio Valley" (Ph.D. diss., Northwestern Univ., 1992); Gail S. Terry, "Family Empires: A Frontier Elite in Virginia and Kentucky, 1740–1815" (Ph.D. diss., College of William and Mary, 1992); Craig Thompson Friend, "Inheriting Eden: The Creation of Society and Community in Kentucky, 1792–1812" (Ph.D. diss, Univ. of Kentucky, 1995). Aron's work has recently reached publication: *How the West Was Lost.*

6. Gregory H. Nobles, "Breaking into the Backcountry: New Approaches to the Early American Frontier," *William and Mary Quarterly,* 3d ser., vol. 66 (1989): 641–70; Albert H. Tillson Jr., "The Southern Backcountry: A Survey of Current Research," *Virginia Magazine of History and Biography* 98 (1990): 387–422; Warren R. Hofstra, "The Virginia Backcountry in the Eighteenth Century: The Questions of Origins and the Issue of Outcome," *Virginia Magazine of History and Biography* 101 (1993): 485–508. Some of the major works include Richard R. Beeman, *The Evolution of the Southern Backcountry: A Case Study of Lunenburg County, Virginia, 1746–1832* (Philadelphia: Univ. of Pennsylvania Press, 1984); Ronald Hoffman, Thad W. Tate, and Peter J. Albert, eds., *An Uncivil War: The Southern Backcountry during the American Revolution* (Charlottesville: Univ. Press of Virginia, 1985); Albert H. Tillson Jr., *Gentry and Commonfolk: Political Culture on a Virginia Frontier, 1740–1789* (Lexington: Univ. Press of Kentucky, 1991); Robert D. Mitchell, *Commercialism and Frontier: Perspectives on the Early Shenandoah Valley* (Charlottesville: Univ. Press of Virginia, 1977); David Hackett Fischer, *Albion's Seed: Four British Folkways in America* (New York: Oxford Univ. Press, 1989); Peter C. Mancall, *Valley of Opportunity: Economic Culture along the Upper Susquehanna, 1700–1800* (Ithaca: Cornell Univ. Press, 1991); Alan Taylor, *Liberty Men and Great Proprietors: The Revolutionary Settlement on the Maine Frontier, 1760–1820* (Chapel Hill: Univ. of North Carolina Press for the Institute of Early American History and Culture, 1990); Rachel N. Klein, *Unification of a Slave State: The Lives of the Planters in the South Carolina Backcountry, 1760–1808* (Chapel Hill: Univ. of North Carolina Press for the Institute of Early American History and Culture, 1990).

7. Richard White, *The Middle Ground: Indians, Empires, and Republics in the Great Lakes Region, 1650–1815* (New York: Cambridge Univ. Press, 1991); Daniel Usner Jr., *Indians, Settlers, and Slaves in a Frontier Exchange Economy: The*

Lower Mississippi Valley before 1783 (Chapel Hill: Univ. of North Carolina Press for the Institute of Early American History and Culture, 1992); Aron, *How the West Was Lost.*

8. Key recent works include Allan Kulikoff, *The Agrarian Origins of American Capitalism* (Charlottesville: Univ. Press of Virginia, 1992); Christopher Clark, *The Roots of Rural Capitalism: Western Massachusetts, 1780–1860* (Ithaca: Cornell Univ. Press, 1990); Daniel Vickers, *Farmers and Fishermen: Two Centuries of Work in Essex County, Massachusetts, 1630–1850* (Chapel Hill: Univ. of North Carolina Press for the Institute of Early American History and Culture, 1994).

9. James T. Kloppenburg, "The Virtues of Liberalism: Christianity, Republicanism, and Ethics in Early American Political Discourse," *Journal of American History* 74 (1987): 9–33; Daniel T. Rodgers, "Republicanism: The Career of a Concept," *Journal of American History* 79 (1992): 11–38; Isaac Kramnick, "The 'Great National Discussion': The Discourse of Politics in 1787," *William and Mary Quarterly,* 3d ser., vol. 45 (1988): 3–32; Ruth Bloch, "The Gendered Meanings of Virtue in Revolutionary America," *Signs* 13 (1987): 37–58; Gordon S. Wood, *The Radicalism of the American Revolution* (New York: Alfred A. Knopf, 1992); Joyce Appleby, *Capitalism and a New Social Order: The Republican Vision of the 1790s* (New York: New York Univ. Press, 1984).

10. See, e.g., Randolph A. Roth, *The Democratic Dilemma: Religion, Reform, and the Social Order in the Connecticut River Valley of Vermont, 1790–1850* (New York: Cambridge Univ. Press, 1987); Steven Watts, *The Republic Reborn: War and the Making of Liberal America, 1790–1820* (Baltimore: Johns Hopkins Univ. Press, 1987); Clark, *Roots of Rural Capitalism;* Allan Kulikoff, *The Agrarian Origins of American Capitalism;* Vickers, *Farmers and Fishermen.*

11. The term is from Benedict Anderson, *Imagined Communities: Reflections on the Origin and Spread of Nationalism* (London: Verso, 1983).

12. Émile Durkheim, *The Elementary Forms of the Religious Life,* trans. Joseph Ward Swain (London: G. Allen and Unwin, 1915).

13. Catherine Bell, *Ritual Theory, Ritual Practice* (New York: Oxford Univ. Press, 1992), 20.

14. Arnold Van Gennep, *The Rites of Passage,* trans. M. B. Vizedom and G. L. Caffee (1909; rpt., Chicago: Univ. of Chicago Press, 1960). See also Bruce, *And They All Sang Hallelujah.*

15. Victor Turner, *The Ritual Process: Structure and Antistructure* (Chicago: Aldine, 1966), 96; Victor Turner, *Dramas, Fields, and Metaphors: Symbolic Action in Human Society* (Ithaca: Cornell Univ. Press, 1974), 45–52.

16. Anthony F. C. Wallace, *Religion: An Anthropological View* (New York: Random House, 1966), 36.

17. Turner, *Dramas, Fields, and Metaphors,* 37–41.

18. The classic study of the Second Great Awakening in New York is Whitney R. Cross, *The Burned-Over District: The Social and Intellectual History of Enthusiastic Religion in Western New York, 1800–1850* (Ithaca: Cornell Univ. Press, 1950). More recent investigations include Mary P. Ryan, *Cradle of the Middle Class: The Family in Oneida County, New York, 1790–1865* (New York: Cam-

bridge Univ. Press, 1982); Curtis D. Johnson, *Islands of Holiness: Rural Religion in Upstate New York, 1790–1860* (Ithaca: Cornell Univ. Press, 1989).

19. Max Weber, *The Theory of Economic Organization,* trans. A. M. Henderson and Talcott Parsons (London: Oxford Univ. Press, 1947; rpt., New York: Free Press, 1964).

20. Wallace, *Religion,* 36. See also Sally Falk Moore, "Epilogue: Uncertainties in Situations, Indeterminacies in Culture," in *Symbol and Politics in Communal Ideology,* ed. Sally Falk Moore and Barbara G. Myerhoff (Ithaca: Cornell Univ. Press, 1975), 210–39.

21. Bell, *Ritual Theory, Ritual Practice,* 41; Victor Turner, *Schism and Continuity* (Manchester: Manchester Univ. Press, 1957), 93; Clifford Geertz, *The Interpretation of Cultures* (New York: Basic Books, Inc., 1973).

22. Weber, *Theory of Economic Organization;* Victor Turner, "Liminality and the Performative Genres," in *Rite, Drama, Festival, Spectacle: Rehearsals toward a Theory of Cultural Performance,* ed. John J. MacAloon (Philadelphia: Institute for the Study of Human Issues, 1984), 25. In the same volume see also Bruce Kapferer, "The Ritual Process and the Problem of Reflexivity in Sinhalese Demon Exorcisms," 179–207; Turner, *Dramas, Fields, and Metaphors,* 56.

23. Sally Falk Moore and Barbara G. Myerhoff, eds., *Secular Ritual* (Assen: Van Gorcum, 1977), 5.

24. Bell, *Ritual Theory, Ritual Practice,* 221.

Chapter 1. The Revolutionary Frontier in Kentucky

1. Jack M. Sosin, *Whitehall and the Wilderness: The Middle West in British Colonial Policy, 1760–1775* (Lincoln: Univ. of Nebraska Press, 1961); Helen Hornback Tanner, ed., *Atlas of Great Lakes Indian History* (Norman: Univ. of Oklahoma Press, 1986); White, *The Middle Ground;* Michael N. McConnell, *A Country Between: The Upper Ohio Valley and Its Peoples, 1724–1774* (Lincoln: Univ. of Nebraska Press, 1992); Gregory Evans Dowd, *A Spirited Resistance: The North American Indian Struggle for Unity, 1745–1815* (Baltimore: Johns Hopkins Univ. Press, 1992). Native American opposition also came from the Cherokees and other southern groups, but the main threat to Kentucky settlement came from north of the Ohio River.

2. On the status of native claims in eighteenth-century Kentucky, see McConnell, *A Country Between;* White, *The Middle Ground;* Sosin, *Whitehall and the Wilderness.* For native occupation of Kentucky, see Lucien Beckner, "Eskippakithiki: The Last Indian Town in Kentucky," *Filson Club History Quarterly* 6 (1932): 355–82 (this publication is hereafter cited as *FCHQ*); and A. Gwynn Henderson, "Dispelling the Myth: Seventeenth- and Eighteenth-Century Indian Life in Kentucky," *Register of the Kentucky Historical Society* 90 (1992): 1–25 (this publication is hereafter cited as *RKHS*).

3. Thomas Perkins Abernethy, *Western Lands and the American Revolution* (New York: Russell and Russell, 1959).

4. William Waller Hening, ed., *The Statutes at Large, Being a Collection of All the Laws of Virginia from the First Session of the Legislature in 1619,* 13 vols. (Richmond: printed for the author by George Cochran, 1819–1823), 9: 257–61, 9:

349–68, and 10: 35–50. Those who qualified for the four hundred acres also had a right to preempt and purchase one thousand adjoining acres. Those settlers who arrived between January 1, 1778, and January 1, 1779, received no settlement grant but could preempt four hundred acres for a modest price. A special land commission was created to administer these provisions. Settlers could also obtain land through military warrants or direct purchase at the state land office. Kentucky's early land system is dealt with more extensively in chapter 3.

5. John Floyd to William Preston, 21 July 1776, in Otto A. Rothert, "John Floyd—Pioneer and Hero," *FCHQ* 2 (1927): 173. Eighteenth-century grammar and spelling differed in various ways from modern practice. I have made every effort to retain the original form of quoted material, with occasional modifications to punctuation and the addition of a few editorial insertions in square brackets for clarity of meaning.

6. Harrodsburg had eighty-one able-bodied defenders, Boonesborough had twenty-two, and St. Asaph's had fifteen. See John Cowan diary, McAfee Papers, Lyman C. Draper Collections, State Historical Society of Wisconsin (microfilm), 4CC30; Levi Todd narrative, George Rogers Clark Papers, Draper Coll., 48J10–11. The Draper Collection probably ranks as the premier collection for early trans-Allegheny settlement, with special mention needed for the numerous interviews that John D. Shane conducted with aging pioneers in the early nineteenth century. See Josephine Harper, *Guide to the Draper Manuscripts* (Madison: State Historical Society of Wisconsin, 1983); and Perkins, "Border Life."

7. Clark's Illinois campaigns have been the subject of numerous studies, but a good summary may be found in Abernethy, *Western Lands and the American Revolution,* 193–204.

8. George Rogers Clark quoted in Charles Kerr, *History of Kentucky,* 5 vols. (Chicago: American Historical Society, 1922), 1: 179.

9. Native participation was fluid throughout this period, largely a reflection of internal disruptions traceable to the North American presence of Europeans. See Tanner, *Atlas of Great Lakes Indian History*; White, *The Middle Ground*; McConnell, *A Country Between*; Aron, *How the West Was Lost.*

10. Milo M. Quaife, "When Detroit Invaded Kentucky," *FCHQ* 27 (1953): 53–67; Maud Ward Lafferty, "Destruction of Ruddle's and Martin's Forts in the Revolutionary War," *RKHS* 54 (1956): 297–338.

11. The most engaging account of this disaster is probably John Mack Faragher, *Daniel Boone: The Life and Times of an American Pioneer* (New York: Henry Holt, 1992), 216–23.

12. Josiah Collins interview, Draper Coll., 12CC67; John Floyd to Thomas Jefferson, 16 Apr. 1781, *Calendar of Virginia State Papers and Other Manuscripts,* 20 vols., ed. William P. Palmer et al. (Richmond, 1881; rpt., New York: Kraus, 1968), 2: 48–49; John Todd Jr. to Thomas Jefferson, 15 Apr. 1781, *Calendar of Virginia State Papers,* 2: 44–45; John Floyd to Thomas Nelson, 6 Oct. 1781, *Calendar of Virginia State Papers,* 2: 530–31.

13. George Slaughter to Thomas Nelson, 9 Aug. 1781, *Calendar of Virginia State Papers,* 2: 306–7. See also John Montgomery to the governor of Virginia, 10 Aug. 1781, *Calendar of Virginia State Papers,* 2: 313.

14. "Diary of Major Eskuries Beatty, Paymaster of the Western Army" (typescript), Reuben T. Durrett Collection, Department of Special Collections, Univ. of Chicago Library, 10.

15. Consider the situation during the Seven Years' War related in Joseph Doddridge, "Notes on the Settlement and Indian Wars of the Western Parts of Virginia and Pennsylvania," in *History of the Valley of Virginia*, ed. Samuel Kercheval (Winchester, Va.: Samuel H. Davis, 1833), 341–42; James Smith, *An Account of the Remarkable Occurrences in the Life and Travels of Colonel James Smith, during his captivity among the Indians from the Year 1753 until 1759. Written by Himself* (Lexington: John Bradford, 1799).

16. The most comprehensive analysis of the Kentucky station is probably Nancy O'Malley, *"Stockading Up": A Study of Pioneer Stations in the Inner Bluegrass Region of Kentucky*, Archaeological Report 127 (Frankfort: Kentucky Heritage Council, 1987).

17. H. V. McChesney, ed., "The Certificate Book of the Virginia Land Commission of 1779–1780," *RKHS* 21 (1923): 90; William Spahr statement, Draper Coll., 25S250.

18. Lucien Beckner, ed., "Reverend John D. Shane's Interview with Pioneer William Clinkenbeard," *FCHQ* 2 (1928): 112; Lucien Beckner, ed., "Rev. John D. Shane's Interview with Mrs. Sarah Graham of Bath County," *FCHQ* 9 (1935): 240; Lucien Beckner, ed., "John D. Shane's Interview with Benjamin Allen, Clark County," *FCHQ* 5 (1931): 70; Josiah Collins interview, Draper Coll., 12CC67.

19. Beckner, "Shane's Interview with Clinkenbeard," 98, 101–7; Isaac Clinkenbeard interview, Draper Coll., 11CC1; James Wade interview, Draper Coll., 12CC16; Leon Stockton interview, Draper Coll., 12CC231; Mr. Hardesty interview, Draper Coll., 11CC171; Mr. and Mrs. Darnaby interview, Draper Coll., 11CC166.

20. Lucien Beckner, ed., "A Sketch of the Early Adventures of William Sudduth in Kentucky," *FCHQ* 2 (1928): 47; John Clinkenbeard statement, Draper Coll., 24S250; William Spahr statement, Draper Coll., 25S256; James Wade interview, Draper Coll., 12CC38; Josiah Collins interview, Draper Coll., 12CC67.

21. Beckner, "Shane's Interview with Clinkenbeard," 103; Otto A. Rothert, ed., "John D. Shane's Interview with Pioneer John Hedge," *FCHQ* 14 (1940): 177 and 179. See also: Isaac Clinkenbeard interview, Draper Coll., 11CC1; Donald F. Carmody, ed., "Spencer Records' Memoir of the Ohio Valley Frontier, 1766–1795," *Indiana Magazine of History* 55 (1959): 340.

22. "Col. William Fleming's Journal in Kentucky from Nov. 10, 1779, to May 27th 1780," in *Travels in the American Colonies*, ed. Newton D. Mereness (New York: Macmillan, 1916), 627 and 630; O'Malley, *"Stockading Up,"* 30.

23. Beckner, "Shane's Interview with Clinkenbeard," 99–101; A. Goff Bedford, *Land of Our Fathers: History of Clark County, Kentucky*, 2 vols. (n.p., 1958), 1: 77.

24. Beckner, "Shane's Interview with Allen," 90; Beckner, "Shane's Interview with Clinkenbeard," 117 and 122.

25. J. F. D. Smyth, *A Tour in the United States of America Containing an Account of the Recent Situation of That Country; The Population, Agriculture, Commerce, Customs, and Manners of the Inhabitants*, 2 vols. (London: printed for G. Robinson, J. Robinson and J. Sewell, 1784) 1: 345–46; Beckner, "Shane's In-

terview with Mrs. Sarah Graham," 232. See also Beckner, "Early Adventures of Sudduth," 50; "Personal Narrative of William Lytle," *Quarterly Publication of the Historical and Philosophical Society of Ohio* 1 (1906): 13–15.

26. Beckner, "Shane's Interview with Clinkenbeard," 105-6.

27. This account of the attack on Strode's Station is drawn from the William Clinkenbeard interview, Draper Coll., 11CC56; Isaac Clinkenbeard interview, Draper Coll., 11CC1–4; William Spahr statement, Draper Coll., 25S251–53; Jesse Kennedy interview, Draper Coll., 11CC9–10; Thomas Jones interview, Draper Coll., 12CC232. According to William Clinkenbeard, eight men made up the escort, leaving thirteen or fourteen men at Strode's Station plus another three or four visiting from David McGee's Station.

28. Isaac Clinkenbeard interview, 11CC2.

29. Although women figured among the earliest inhabitants at Strode's Station, most of them remain anonymous or known only through male relations. Unfortunately, the experiences of women in other stations are just as mysterious, but see, e.g., Mrs. John Arnold interview, Draper Coll., 11CC241–45; Mrs. Sarah Graham interview, Draper Coll., 12CC45–53; and Mrs. John Morrison interview, Draper Coll., 11CC150–54.

30. Beckner, "Shane's Interview with Clinkenbeard," 101.

31. Ibid., 122. Sudduth also credits Hood with a more aggressive response in Beckner, "Early Adventures of Sudduth," 45.

32. Beckner, "Shane's Interview with Clinkenbeard," 104–5 (a similar incident is related on p. 106); John Brady statement, Draper Coll., 15S248. See also Simon Kenton Papers, Draper Coll., 8BB33–35. The social and political importance of bravery has surfaced only in recent years. See Eslinger, "The Great Revival in Bourbon County," 31–38; Perkins, "Border Life," 235–38; and Faragher, *Daniel Boone*, 214–25.

33. Beckner, "Shane's Interview with Clinkenbeard," 119. For similar episodes of practical joking see Danske Dandridge, *George Michael Bedinger: A Kentucky Pioneer* (Charlottesville: Michie, 1909), 48–49; W. P. Strickland, ed., *Autobiography of Rev. James B. Finley, or Pioneer Life in the West* (Cincinnati: Methodist Book Concern, 1854), 37–38; and Robert Jones interview, Draper Coll., 13CC180–81.

34. Strickland, *Finley*, 127.

35. See also: Beckner, "Early Adventures of Sudduth," 70; Charles Drake, ed., *Pioneer Life in Kentucky: A Series of Reminiscential Letters from Daniel Drake, M.D., of Cincinnati to His Children* (Cincinnati: Robert Clarke, 1870), 23.

36. Otto A. Rothert, ed., "John D. Shane's Interview with Mrs. John McKinney and Her Son Harvey, Bourbon County, Including Data on John McKinney's Fight with a Wildcat," *FCHQ* 13 (1939): 157.

37. Beckner, "Shane's Interview with Clinkenbeard," 107. See also: Francis Cassidy statement, Draper's Notes, Draper Coll., 21S176; *Tyler's Quarterly Historical and Genealogical Magazine* 33 (1952): 136; Beckner, "Shane's Interview with Allen," 65 and 86; William McIntire statement, Draper Coll., 20S227; George M. Bedinger Papers, Series A, Draper Coll.; Madison County Circuit Court Depositions (typescript), Kentucky Historical Society, Frankfort, 149–50.

38. William McClellend interview, Draper Coll., 11CC181; John M. Ruddell interview, Draper Coll., 22S41.

39. Mrs. Jane Stevenson interview, Draper Coll., 13CC135–43.

40. The core list of early inhabitants at Strode's Station was derived from material collected in the early nineteenth century by John Shane, particularly the interview he did with William Clinkenbeard, a founder and longtime resident of Strode's Station. A few of the people named by Clinkenbeard, such as "Granny West," appear nowhere else in the Strode's Station literature. Most names, though, do appear in other records. A revised list was compiled by adding these supporting sources to the Clinkenbeard description. It includes all white male adults identified by name with Strode's Station before the 1781 Indian attack. Kinship was determined using the Shane interviews and available family genealogies. See Ellen T. Eslinger, "Kinship and Migration on the Trans-Appalachian Frontier: Strode's Station, Kentucky," *FCHQ* 62 (1988): 52–66.

41. Beckner, "Shane's Interview with Clinkenbeard," 109; Rothert, "Shane's Interview with Hedge," 181.

42. Bourbon County Court, Order Book A (microfilm), Kentucky Historical Society, 353. The other witnesses were one Robert Ellison and the schoolmaster, a man named Ogden. Daniel Deron interview, Draper Coll., 12CC239.

43. Beckner, "Shane's Interview with Allen," 67–68.

44. Ibid., 87.

45. Based on an analysis of Bourbon County Court, Order Books A and B (1786–95), where most Strode's Station people transacted their affairs. Eslinger, "Kinship and Migration," 62–65.

46. Beckner, "Shane's Interview with Clinkenbeard," 109–10; Beckner, "Shane's Interview with Allen," 83–84.

47. Charles Brunk Heinemann and Gaius Marcus Brumbaugh, *"First Census" of Kentucky, 1790* (Washington, D.C.: G. M. Brumbaugh, 1938), 3.

48. Nancy O'Malley, in her archaeological study of inner Bluegrass stations, also argues for a sequential scheme, delineating four stages of development. This temporal model nonetheless seems inadequate for larger study regions. O'Malley, *"Stockading Up,"* 30–33.

49. Daniel Deron interview, Draper Coll., 12CC239; James Wade interview, Draper Coll., 12CC14.

50. James Wade interview, Draper Coll., 12CC14; Beckner, "Shane's Interview with Clinkenbeard," 109.

51. William Sudduth interview, Draper Coll., 12CC62.

52. Beckner, "Shane's Interview with Allen," 67; John I. Rogers, ed., *Autobiography of Elder Samuel Rogers,* 3d ed. (Cincinnati: Standard, 1881), 4. See also J. Rankin interview, Draper Coll., 11CC82; Daniel Deron interview, Draper Coll., 11CC239.

53. James Wade interview, Draper Coll., 12CC14.

54. Rothert, "Shane's Interview with Hedge," 179; Beckner, "Shane's Interview with Clinkenbeard," 112–14; Thomas Pasley interview, Draper Coll., 13CC66; Henry Parvin interview, Draper Coll., 11CC72–75; Walter Kelso interview, Draper Coll., 12CC55; James Wade interview, Draper Coll., 12CC14–28; Daniel Deron

interview, Draper Coll., 12CC239; Beckner, "Shane's Interview with Allen," 68.

55. Harry Toulmin, *The Western Country in 1793: Reports on Kentucky and Virginia,* ed. Marion Tinling and Godfrey Davis (San Marino, Calif.: Henry E. Huntington Library, 1948), 64; Walter Kelso interview, Draper Coll., 12CC55; George Trumbo interview, Draper Coll., 12CC113.

56. Toulmin, *Western Country in 1793,* 64; Beckner, "Shane's Interview with Allen," 68; James Wade interview, Draper Coll., 12CC14. See also Drake, *Pioneer Life,* 14.

57. Beckner, "Early Adventures of Sudduth," 56–57; William Sudduth interview, Draper Coll., 12CC63; James Wade interview, Draper Coll., 12CC24.

58. Benjamin Hardesty interview, Draper Coll., 11CC171; Robert Jones interview, Draper Coll., 13CC165; Beckner, "Shane's Interview with Clinkenbeard," 113; Henry Parvin interview, Draper Coll., 11CC75; James Wade interview, Draper Coll., 12CC19.

59. Rothert, "Shane's Interview with Hedge," 178. See also James Wade interview, Draper Coll., 12CC29.

60. William Clinkenbeard interview, Draper Coll., 11CC61. Clinkenbeard's narrative of the attack is accompanied by a map of Constant's Station. Henry Parvin interview, Draper Coll., 11CC75; Robert Jones interview, Draper Coll., 13CC165; Drake, *Pioneer Life,* 14.

61. Daniel Deron interview, Draper Coll., 12CC239; James Lane interview, Draper Coll., 12CC55; Beckner, "Shane's Interview with Clinkenbeard," 113.

Chapter 2. The Rural Economy of the Early National West

1. St. John de Crèvecoeur, "Sketch of the River Ohio," quoted in Patricia Watlington, *The Partisan Spirit: Kentucky Politics, 1779–1792* (Chapel Hill: Univ. of North Carolina Press for the Institute of Early American History and Culture, 1972), 95.

2. Walker Daniel to Benjamin Harrison, 21 May 1784, *Calendar of Virginia State Papers* 3: 587.

3. Strickland, *Finley,* 35. See also Carmody, "Spencer Records' Memoir," 361.

4. Drake, *Pioneer Life,* 20 (quotation); James Galloway narrative, Draper Coll., 8J292.

5. Joseph Wood, 11 Mar. 1792, Wood Family Papers, Special Collections and Archives Service Center, Univ. of Kentucky, Lexington.

6. Drake, *Pioneer Life,* 45.

7. Lexington, *Kentucky Gazette,* 16 Sept. 1797; Toulmin, *Western Country in 1793,* 81; Gilbert Imlay, *A Topographical Description of the Western Territory of North America, Containing a Succinct Account of its Climate, Natural History, Population, Agriculture, Manners and Customs, with an Ample Description of the Several Divisions Into Which That Country is Partitioned, And an Accurate Statement of the various Tribes of Indians that inhabit the Frontier Country. To Which is Annexed a Delineation of the Laws and Government of the State of Kentucky. Tending to Shew the Probable Rise and Grandeur of the American Empire. In a Series of Letters to a Friend in England* (London: printed for J. Debrett, 1792), 93. See also Harry Toulmin, *A Description of Kentucky in*

North America: To Which Are Prefixed Miscellaneous Observations respecting the United States, ed. Thomas D. Clark (Lexington: Univ. Press of Kentucky, 1945), 88; "Some Particulars Relative to Kentucky," in *Travels in the Old South, Selected from the Periodicals of the Times,* 2 vols., ed. Eugene L. Schwab (Lexington: Univ. Press of Kentucky, 1973), vol. 1: 56.

8. R. C. Thruston, ed., "Letter by Edward Harris, 1797," *FCHQ* 2 (1928): 166.

9. Toulmin, *Western Country in 1793,* 82; "François-André Michaux's Travels West of Allegheny Mountains, 1802," in *Early Western Travels, 1748–1846,* 32 vols., ed. Reuben Gold Thwaites (Cleveland: Arthur H. Clark, 1904), 3: 238.

10. Drake, *Pioneer Life,* 64; Toulmin, *A Description of Kentucky,* 88 and 136; Toulmin, *Western Country in 1793,* 74 and 81; Imlay, *A Topographical Description,* 93.

11. Toulmin, *A Description of Kentucky,* 99.

12. Lucien Beckner, ed., "John D. Shane's Notes on an Interview with Jeptha Kemper of Montgomery County," *FCHQ* 12 (1938): 156.

13. Bourbon County, Will Books A and B (microfilm), Kentucky Historical Society, Frankfort; Toulmin, *Western Country in 1793,* 96–97; "The Monitor, No. IV," *Kentucky Gazette,* 18 Nov. 1797. The will books were inventories for family households, omitting eight inventories for single males who died during these years.

14. Mitchell, *Commercialism and Frontier*; George Melvin Herndon, "The Story of Hemp in Colonial Virginia" (Ph.D. diss., Univ. of Virginia, 1959), 133–69.

15. Toulmin, *Western Country in 1793,* 82. See also Beckner, "John D. Shane's Interview with Jeptha Kemper," 156; Hubbard Taylor to James Madison, 3 Jan. 1793, *The Papers of James Madison* 16 vols., ed. R. A. Rutland et al. (Charlottesville: Univ. Press of Virginia, 1983), 14: 436.

16. *Kentucky Gazette,* 15 Mar. 1790. See also Toulmin, *Western Country in 1793,* 97; James F. Hopkins, *A History of the Hemp Industry in Kentucky* (Lexington: Univ. Press of Kentucky, 1951).

17. "Michaux's Travels," 245; "The Monitor, No. IV," *Kentucky Gazette,* 18 Nov. 1797; Drake, *Pioneer Life,* 73; Toulmin, *Western Country in 1793,* 97.

18. Among several excellent studies challenging the notion of eighteenth-century self-sufficiency, see Carole Shammas, "How Self-Sufficient Was Early America?" *Journal of Interdisciplinary History* 8 (1982): 247–72; Bettye Hobbes Pruitt, "Self-Sufficiency and the Agricultural Economy of Eighteenth-Century Massachusetts," *William and Mary Quarterly,* 3d ser., vol. 41 (1984): 333–64; Daniel Vickers, "Competency and Competition: Economic Culture in Early America," *William and Mary Quarterly,* 3d ser., vol. 47 (1990): 3–29; Clark, *Roots of Rural Capitalism.*

19. Howard C. Rice, *Barthelemi Tardiveau: A French Trader in the West* (Baltimore: Johns Hopkins Univ. Press, 1938), 32. See also Thomas Chapman, "Journal of a Journey through the United States, 1795–1796," in *Travels in the Old South,* 1: 31; "Some Particulars Relative to Kentucky," in *Travels in the Old South,* 1: 60; and "The Monitor, No. III," *Kentucky Gazette,* 11 Nov. 1797.

20. Elizabeth A. Perkins, "The Consumer Frontier: Household Consumption in Early Kentucky," *Journal of American History* 78 (1991): 500–502.

21. "Michaux's Travels," 241; Enoch Smith to Isaac Davis, 6 Dec. 1795, Isaac Davis Papers (#320), Special Collections Dept., Univ. of Virginia Library; James Davis to Zachariah Johnston, 4 May 1790, Zachariah Johnston Papers, Special Collections, Leyburn Library, Washington and Lee Univ., Lexington, Va. On the lower status accorded homespun see also "The Monitor, No. III," *Kentucky Gazette,* 11 Nov. 1797.

22. Benjamin Wood to Joseph Lawrence, 27 June 1792, Wood Family Papers.

23. *Kentucky Gazette,* 18 May 1793; Paris, Ky., *The Rights of Man, or The Kentucky Mercury,* 15 Nov. 1797; James Davis to Zachariah Johnston, 4 May 1790, Zachariah Johnston Papers. See also "Michaux's Travels," 203.

24. Perkins, "Consumer Frontier," 495–96; "Michaux's Travels," 241.

25. Johanna Miller Lewis makes similar observations in her discussion of women artisans, *Artisans in the North Carolina Backcountry* (Lexington: Univ. Press of Kentucky, 1995), chap. 6. Female labor also enjoyed a special importance in other newly settled areas. See Glenda Riley, *Frontierswomen: The Iowa Experience* (Ames: Iowa State Univ. Press, 1981); John Mack Faragher, *Sugar Creek: Life on the Illinois Prairie* (New Haven: Yale Univ. Press, 1986), 104–5.

26. Toulmin, *A Description of Kentucky,* 99; "Diary of Major Eskuries Beatty," 61.

27. James Rood Robertson, ed., *Petitions of the Early Inhabitants of Kentucky to the General Assembly of Virginia, 1769–1792,* Filson Club Publications, no. 27 (Louisville: John P. Morgan, 1914), 102 and 105.

28. Hening, *Statutes at Large,* 12: 258; Bourbon County Court, Order Book A, 108 and 471.

29. *Kentucky Gazette,* 11 Nov. 1797; Toulmin, *Western Country in 1793,* 86.

30. "Some Particulars Relative to Kentucky," in *Travels in the Old South,* 1: 60; Lucien Beckner, ed., "John D. Shane's Interview with Jesse Graddy of Woodford County," *FCHQ* 20 (1946): 13; Imlay, *A Topographical Description,* 94; William Dodd Brown, "A Visit to Boonesborough in 1779: The Recollections of Pioneer George M. Bedinger," *RKHS* 86 (1988): 322.

31. Imlay, *A Topographical Description,* 41–42; Toulmin, *Western Country in 1793,* 82. See also "Diary of Major Eskuries Beatty," 116.

32. Clement L. Martzolff, ed., "Reminiscences of a Pioneer [Thomas Rogers]," *Ohio Archaeological and Historical Publications* 19 (1910): 197.

33. Imlay, *A Topographical Description,* 135; Drake, *Pioneer Life,* 76–77; "Michaux's Travels," 246; "Some Particulars Relative to Kentucky," in *Travels in the Old South,* 1: 56.

34. Toulmin, *Western Country in 1793,* 65; Toulmin, *A Description of Kentucky,* 89; "Michaux's Travels," 201.

35. Toulmin, *Western Country in 1793,* 78–79.

36. Drake, *Pioneer Life,* 54. Household exchange was a widespread practice in early America, especially in newly settled areas where cash was not plentiful. See, e.g., Faragher, *Sugar Creek,* 133–36.

37. The classic works on Kentucky slavery are J. Winston Coleman Jr., *Slavery Times in Kentucky* (Chapel Hill: Univ. of North Carolina Press, 1940); and Ivan E. McDougle, *Slavery in Kentucky, 1792–1865* (Lancaster, Penn.: Press of the New Era, 1918). For more recent perspectives on slavery's early years in Ken-

tucky, see Ellen Eslinger, "The Shape of Slavery on the Kentucky Frontier, 1775–1800," *RKHS* 92 (winter 1994): 1–23. An expanded version of this work appears in *Diversity and Accommodation: Essays on the Cultural Composition of the Virginia Frontier,* ed. Michael J. Puglisi (Knoxville: Univ. of Tennessee Press, 1997), 172–93. See also Gail S. Terry, "Sustaining the Bonds of Kinship in a Trans-Appalachian Migration, 1790–1811: The Cabell-Breckinridge Slaves Move West," *Virginia Magazine of History and Biography* 102 (1994): 455–76.

38. John Cowan diary, McAfee Papers, Draper Coll., 4CC30. See also "Col. William Fleming's Journal," in *Travels in the American Colonies,* ed. Mereness, 654–55, for information on Whitley's, St. Asaph's (Logan's), Clark's, and Dougharty's Stations.

39. Heinemann and Brumbaugh, *"First Census" of Kentucky, 1790,* 3; G. Glenn Clift, *"Second Census" of Kentucky, 1800* (Baltimore: Genealogical, 1982), v–vi.

40. Madison County Tax Lists, 1787 (microfilm), Kentucky Historical Society; Joan Wells Coward, *Kentucky in the New Republic: The Process of Constitution Making* (Lexington: Univ. Press of Kentucky, 1979), 62–63.

41. Eslinger, "Shape of Slavery"; Toulmin, *Western Country in 1793,* 108; Drake, *Pioneer Life,* 90.

42. Eslinger, "Shape of Slavery." On eighteenth-century slave culture, see Allan Kulikoff, *Tobacco and Slaves: The Development of Southern Cultures in the Chesapeake, 1680–1800* (Chapel Hill: Univ. of North Carolina Press for the Institute of Early American History and Culture, 1986); Ira Berlin, "Time, Space and the Evolution of Afro-American Society in British Mainland North America," *American Historical Review* 85 (1989): 44–78; Philip D. Morgan, *Slave Counterpoint: Black Culture in the Eighteenth-Century Chesapeake and Lowcountry* (Chapel Hill: Univ. of North Carolina Press for the Omohundro Institute of Early American History and Culture, 1998).

43. Eslinger, "Shape of Slavery," 9.

44. John Breckinridge to Gen. Samuel Hopkins, 15 Sept. 1794, Breckinridge Family Papers, Manuscript Division, Library of Congress.

45. Beckner, "Shane's Interview with Mrs. Sarah Graham," 240; Jesse Kennedy interview, Draper Coll., 11CC37.

46. Ethnic German women were sometimes an exception. "Michaux's Travels," 201 and 248; 48.

47. Drake, *Pioneer Life,* 45–48, 52, 57–58, 70, 72, 78, 85, 92, 95–96. Daniel Drake's memoirs provide perhaps the most complete account of childhood in late-eighteenth-century Kentucky.

48. Strickland, *Finley,* 73; Robertson, *Petitions,* 144–45, 150. See also Drake, *Pioneer Life,* 58–60; "Michaux's Travels," 240; Friend, "Inheriting Eden," 114.

49. "Narrative of John Heckenwelder's Journey to the Wabash in 1792," *Pennsylvania Magazine of History and Biography* 12 (1888): 38.

50. Bourbon County Court, Order Book A; Toulmin, *Western Country in 1793,* 92–93.

51. Lucien Beckner, ed., "John D. Shane's Copy of Needham Parry Diary of Trip Westward in 1794," *FCHQ* 22 (1948): 232. William Miller's mill dated to 1788.

52. Robert B. McAfee, "The Life and Times of Robert B. McAfee and His Family

and Connections," *RKHS* 25 (1927): 218; Drake, *Pioneer Life*, 54 and 83; Willard Rouse Jillson, *Early Kentucky Distillers, 1783–1880* (Louisville: Standard Printing, 1940).

53. David Meade letter, June 1797, William Bolling Papers, Duke Univ. Library.

54. Toulmin, *Western Country in 1793*, 62.

55. *Kentucky Gazette*, 27 June 1799.

56. Henry G. Crowgey, *Kentucky Bourbon: The Early Years of Whiskeymaking* (Lexington: Univ. Press of Kentucky, 1971); Jillson, *Early Kentucky Distillers*; "Michaux's Travels," 242.

57. Toulmin, *Western Country in 1793*, 113.

58. James R. Bentley, ed., "Letters of Thomas Perkins to General Joseph Palmer, Lincoln County, Kentucky, 1785," *FCHQ* 49 (1975): 148.

59. Humphrey Marshall, *The History of Kentucky. Exhibiting an Account of the Modern Discovery; Settlement; Progressive Improvement; Civil and Military Transactions; and the Present State of the Country*, 2 vols. (Frankfort: George S. Robinson, printer, 1824), 1: 271. Tobacco prices may be found in Leland Smith, "A History of the Tobacco Industry in Kentucky, 1783–1860" (M.A. thesis, Univ. of Kentucky, 1950), 63; Colonel Slaughter to [his son] Ransdell Slaughter, 21 Nov. 1788, Filson Club Historical Society, Louisville.

60. Robertson, *Petitions*, 120. This incident is also summarized in Stephen Aron, *How the West Was Lost*, 117–20, but Aron mistakenly overlooks the significant local market for corn. For the original analysis of early Kentucky legislative petitions as a means of gauging economic ambitions see Eslinger, "The Great Revival in Bourbon County," 122–30.

61. Mountjoy's petition received unusually prolonged debate. The original application was submitted in September 1788. At the next court term in October, its probable impact on navigation was deemed insignificant. At the November term, however, Mountjoy was ordered not to obstruct the migration of fish or the navigation of boats. Apparently he persevered, and in March 1789 his dam received tentative court approval. When the writ was finally issued in May 1789, however, it specifically required that the dam not obstruct boats twenty feet wide by forty feet long. Bourbon County Court, Order Book A, 182, 190–91, 207, 234, 245.

62. Ibid., 258–59.

63. Robertson, *Petitions*, 146–47.

64. The navigability was challenged by Shipp in Robertson, *Petitions*, 148–49, and a subsequent supporting petition on pages 150–51. A personal reminiscence adding credence to their assessment may be found in "Address of General Garrard, before the Bourbon Agricultural Society, on the 9th of June, 1838," Frankfort, Ky., *Franklin Farmer*, 4 July 1838.

65. The petition for a second warehouse may be found in Robertson, *Petitions*, 152–53. Only twenty-six (5 percent) of the signatures on the opposing petitions overlap, an indication of strong opposing alignments.

66. Eslinger, "The Great Revival in Bourbon County," 124–27.

67. Aron, *How the West Was Lost*, 119–20.

68. Hubbard Taylor to James Madison, 3 Jan. 1793, *Papers of James Madison* 14: 436.

69. "Address of General Garrard," *Franklin Farmer*, 4 July 1838.

70. James Davis to Zachariah Johnston, 4 May 1790, Zachariah Johnston Papers.

71. "Narrative of John Heckewelder," 38 (quotation); "The Monitor No. 1," *Kentucky Gazette*, 4 Nov. 1797. The Maysville road figures prominently in Friend, "Inheriting Eden."

72. "Narrative of John Heckewelder," 38; "Michaux's Travels," 195 (quotation). For the military's dilemma, see Henry Lee to Edmund Randolph, 30 June 1788, *Calendar of Virginia State Papers* 4: 46; John Logan et al. to Edmund Randolph, 16 June 1788, *Calendar of Virginia State Papers* 4: 456. On immigrant responses, see "Address of General Garrard," *Franklin Farmer*, 4 July 1838; Toulmin, *Western Country in 1793*, 82; Gilbert Imlay to Harry Toulmin, 2 Feb. 1793, in Toulmin, *A Description of Kentucky*, 118.

73. Peyton Short to Sir Peyton Skipwith, 12 Feb. 1789, Skipwith Family Papers, Swem Library, College of William and Mary; McAfee, "Life and Times of Robert B. McAfee," 116. Immigrant-driven prosperity was a common phenomenon in new settlement areas. See John J. McCusker and Russell R. Menard, *The Economy of British America, 1607–1789* (Chapel Hill: Univ. of North Carolina Press for the Institute of Early American History and Culture, 1985), 96; and Merle Curti, *The Making of an American Community: A Case Study of Democracy in a Frontier County* (Stanford: Stanford Univ. Press, 1959).

74. William Sudduth interview, Draper Coll., 12CC62. Harry Innes to Col. Wilson C. Nicholas, 10 June 1807, Harry Innes Papers, Codex 208, Reuben T. Durrett Collection, Department of Special Collections, Univ. of Chicago, 14; Harry Innes to Col. Wilson C. Nicholas, 16 July 1807, Innes Papers, Codex 208, Durrett Coll., 20. See also John Breckinridge to Samuel Hopkins, 15 Sept. 1794, Breckinridge Family Papers.

75. *Kentucky Gazette*, 16 Sept. 1797 and 11 Nov. 1797; "Michaux's Travels," 198 (quotation); John Harper to Thomas Thompson, 26 Nov. 1795, Zachariah Johnston Papers.

76. Bourbon County Court, Order Books A and B; Harrison County Court, Order Book A (microfilm), Kentucky Historical Society.

77. Bourbon County Court, Order Book B, 293.

78. "Merlin," *Frankfort Palladium*, 18 Nov. 1797; *Kentucky Gazette*, 11 Nov. 1797, 18 Nov. 1797, and 3 Jan. 1798. See also "The Monitor No. 1," *Kentucky Gazette*, 4 Nov. 1797. The "American Farmer" essay was already a classic, having been reprinted throughout the United States for at least a decade. See Shammas, "How Self-Sufficient Was Early America?"

79. *Kentucky Gazette*, 18 Mar. 1800.

80. *Kentucky Gazette*, 12 July 1788. See also 24 July 1789 for a petition from leading politicians calling for a "practical frugality." The same concern surfaced in numerous other parts of the country. See Drew R. McCoy, *The Elusive Republic: Political Economy in Jeffersonian America* (Chapel Hill: Univ. of North Carolina Press for the Institute for Early American History and Culture, 1980).

81. "Merlin," *Frankfort Palladium*, 18 Nov. 1797; *Kentucky Gazette*, 3 Jan. 1798; "A Worn-Out Merchant," *Kentucky Gazette*, 17 Jan. 1798, and "A New and True

Friend," *Kentucky Gazette*, 24 Jan. 1798. Similar economic advice was offered by "Aristides," *Kentucky Gazette*, 11 Oct. 1803 and 25 Oct. 1803. Nonconsumption was held up to public ridicule by Humphrey Marshall, in *History of Kentucky*, 2: 325.

82. "Aristides," *Kentucky Gazette*, 13 Sept. 1803, 27 Sept. 1803, 4 Oct. 1803, 11 Oct. 1803, 25 Oct. 1803.

83. "Diary of Major Erkuries Beatty," Durrett Coll., 3, 40, 49, 51, 53.

84. City, "Second Census" of Kentucky, 1800, vi. The classic work on the region's urban beginnings is Richard C. Wade, *The Urban Frontier: Pioneer Life in Early Pittsburgh, Cincinnati, Lexington, Louisville, and St. Louis* (Cambridge: Harvard Univ. Press, 1959). See also Charles R. Staples, *The History of Pioneer Lexington, 1779–1806* (Lexington, Ky.: Transylvania Press, 1939).

85. "Michaux's Travels," 198–99; "Cuming's Tour to the Western Country, 1807–1809," *Early Western Travels, 1748–1846*, 32 vols., ed. Reuben Gold Thwaites (Cleveland: Arthur H. Clark, 1904), 4: 102.

86. Robert Poage to Archibald Woods, 1 July 1803, Archibald Woods Papers, Swem Library, College of William and Mary; Becker, "Shane's Copy of Needham Parry's Diary, 1794," 232–33; Levis Condict, "Journal of a Trip to Kentucky in 1795," *New Jersey Historical Society Proceedings*, n.s., 4 (1919): 120; Toulmin, *Western Country in 1793*, 96 and 102; *Kentucky Gazette*, 9 Apr. 1796.

87. "Michaux's Travels," 200–202; "To the West on Business in 1804: An Account, with Excerpts from the Journal of James Foord's Trip to Kentucky in 1804," *Pennsylvania Magazine of History and Biography* 64 (1940): 6. For a detailed description of Lexington in 1807 see "Cuming's Tour of the Western Country," 182–87.

88. Richard Terrell to Lucy Terrell, 31 May 1793, Papers of the Carr and Terrell Families (#4757), Special Collections Dept., Univ. of Virginia Library.

89. The literature on the transition to capitalism extensive; but for an excellent summary, see Kulikoff, *Agrarian Origins of American Capitalism*, 13–33.

90. Toulmin, *A Description of Kentucky*, 101; Drake, *Pioneer Life*, 74.

Chapter 3. A Best Poor Man's Country?

1. This has been amply demonstrated for regions settled under the federal land survey system. See esp. Paul W. Gates, *Frontier Landlords and Pioneer Tenants* (Ithaca: Cornell Univ. Press, 1945); Robert P. Swierenga, *Pioneers and Profits: Land Speculation on the Iowa Frontier* (Ames: Iowa State Univ. Press, 1968); Allan G. Bogue, *From Prairie to Cornbelt: Farming on the Illinois and Iowa Frontier in the Nineteenth Century* (Chicago: Univ. of Chicago Press, 1963). It has also been a subject of interest for historians of the colonial era. See, e.g., James T. Lemon, *The Best Poor Man's Country: A Geographical Study of Early Southeastern Pennsylvania* (New York: W. W. Norton, 1972); Beeman, *Evolution of the Southern Backcountry*; Taylor, *Liberty Men and Great Proprietors*.

2. Samuel R. Walker, ed., *Memoir of the Late the Hon. Felix Walker, of North Carolina* (New Orleans: A. Taylor, printer, 1877),10; "General Levi Todd's Narrative," in *Tales of the Dark and Bloody Ground*, ed. Willard Rouse Jillson (Louisville: C. T. Dearing, 1930), 73; John Joyce to the Rev. Robert Dickson, 24

Mar. 1785, *Virginia Magazine of History and Biography* 23 (1915): 413; Toulmin, *Western Country in 1793,* 132; George Rogers Clark to Jonathan Clark, 6 July 1775, in *George Rogers Clark Papers, 1771–1781,* ed. James Alton James (Springfield, Ill.: State Historical Library, 1912), Illinois Historical Society Collections, VIII, Va. Ser. III, 1: 9–10; John Brown Sr. to William Preston, 5 May 1775, Preston Papers, Draper Coll., 4QQ15.

3. Imlay, *A Topographical Description,* 149–56.

4. Beckner, "Shane's Interview with Clinkenbeard," 89; Drake, *Pioneer Life,* 10.

5. Toulmin, *Western Country in 1793,* 81; *Kentucky Gazette,* 16 Sept. 1797 and 11 Nov. 1797; Drake, *Pioneer Life,* 48; Harry Innes to John Brown, 7 Dec. 1787, in G. Glenn Clift, ed., "From the Archives, the District of Kentucky, 1783–1787, As Pictured by Harry Innes in a Letter to John Brown," *RKHS* 54 (1956): 368–72. For Pennsylvania, see Lemon, *The Best Poor Man's Country,* 152.

6. Toulmin, *Western Country in 1793,* 83, 64. For a comparison with prices in Philadelphia see Hazel Dicken Garcia, "'A Great Deal of Money': Notes on Kentucky Costs, 1786–1792," *RKHS* 77 (1979): 199–200; and "Michaux's Travels," 202–4.

7. Beckner, "Shane's Interview with Clinkenbeard," 98 and 107.

8. Imlay, *A Topographical Description,* 518.

9. Eslinger, "The Great Revival in Bourbon County," 108–11.

10. Asa Farrar interview, Draper Coll., 13CC2; Mrs. James Arnold interview, Draper Coll., 11CC250. See also Strickland, *Finley,* 70; Rogers, *Autobiography of Elder Samuel Rogers,* 4; Drake, *Pioneer Life,* 46; Toulmin, *Western Country in 1793,* 64.

11. Alexander Martin to Zachariah Johnston, 26 Apr. 1791, Zachariah Johnston Papers.

12. Drake, *Pioneer Life,* 21–22.

13. Ibid., 30. The prices are based on valuations of personal estates in Bourbon County Court, Will Book A.

14. Levi Todd to Harry Innes, Isaac Shelby, and Benjamin Logan, 14 June 1791, Harry Innes Papers, Library of Congress; James Barnett to Edmund Randolph, 28 June 1789, *Calendar of Virginia State Papers,* 4: 652; Beckner, "Shane's Interview with Clinkenbeard," 106.

15. Drake, *Pioneer Life,* 26, 34, and 64 (quotation).

16. Drake, *Pioneer Life,* 49, 77 (quotation), and 132–34; Toulmin, *Western Country in 1793,* 74; "Michaux's Travels," 228–37.

17. Toulmin, *Western Country in 1793,* 80; Strickland, *Finley,* 38; "Michaux's Travels," 245–46.

18. Journal of General Butler, 2 Jan. 1786, quoted in Malcolm J. Rohrbough, *The Trans-Appalachian Frontier: People, Societies, and Institutions, 1775–1850* (New York: Oxford Univ. Press, 1978), 54; "Michaux's Travels," 227; Alexander Martin to Zachariah Johnston, 26 Apr. 1791, Zachariah Johnston Papers; Thruston, "Letter by Edward Harris, 1797," 167. See also Enoch Smith to Isaac Davis, May 1791, Isaac Davis Papers.

19. Nearly every historian of early Kentucky has been obliged to describe t plicated land system. For detailed recent treatments see Neal O.

Early Kentucky Land Records, 1773–1780, Filson Club Publications, 2d ser., no. 5 (Louisville: Filson Club, 1992); and George Mason Chinn, *Kentucky Settlement and Statehood, 1750–1800* (Frankfort: Kentucky Historical Society, 1975), 209–22.

20. Bourbon County Court, Order Book B, 15 Mar. 1796, 250; Dandridge, *George Michael Bedinger,* 185.

21. Enoch Smith to Isaac Davis, 30 May 1791, Isaac Davis Papers; Marshall, *History of Kentucky,* 1: 150.

22. William Pollard to Charles Biddle, Biddle Family Papers, Library of Congress; Marshall, *History of Kentucky,* 1: 97.

23. Martzolff, "Reminiscences of a Pioneer," 199.

24. Michael Cogan to Zachariah Johnston Sr., 7 Apr. 1793, Zachariah Johnston Papers.

25. Strickland, *Finley,* 99 (quotation); "Meeting of Farmers and Planters of the County of Fayette," 28 Apr. 1798 (copy), Broadside Collection, Special Collections and Archives Service Center, Univ. of Kentucky. See also Robertson, *Petitions,* 76; Enoch Smith to Isaac Davis, 30 May 1790, Isaac Davis Papers.

26. Bourbon County Court, Order Book A, 186, 228–29, and 267.

27. Rothert, "John D. Shane's Interview with Hedge," 181.

28. William Littell and Jacob Swigert, *A Digest of the Statute Law of Kentucky, Being a Collection of All the Acts of the General Assembly of a Public and Permanent Nature, From the Commencement of the Government to May Session, 1822,* 2 vols. (Frankfort: Kendall and Russell, 1822), 1: 641–45; Marshall, *History of Kentucky,* 2: 208–10. The state senate's persistent failure to remedy this problem would figure among the reasons given for a new constitution, formulated in 1799.

29. Marshall, *History of Kentucky,* 2: 208.

30. Ibid., 1: 153. See also Hubbard Taylor to James Madison, 3 Feb. 1795, *Papers of James Madison* 15: 464.

31. "Cuming's Tour of the Western Country," 179; "Michaux's Travels," 228; Sylvia Pettit Welch, ed., "Six Letters by Pioneer John McKinney and Other Data Bearing on His Life," *FCHQ* 14 (1940): 113.

32. Drake, *Pioneer Life,* 33–34 and 113.

33. McCoy, *The Elusive Republic,* 67–70.

34. Bentley, "Letters of Thomas Perkins to General Joseph Palmer [1785]," 150; John Crawford interview, Draper Coll., 12CC156; Toulmin, *Western Country in 1793,* 65, 96, 101, and 104.

35. Toulmin, *Western Country in 1793,* 76–77 (quotation); Imlay, *A Topographical Description,* 148–49.

36. Teute, "Land, Liberty, and Labor," 185; Coward, *Kentucky in the New Republic,* 55. Of 12,554 households in 1792, 8,177 owned no land; of 32,503 households in 1800, 16,500 owned no land.

37. Turner, *The Significance of the Frontier in American History*; Lee Soltow, *Distribution of Wealth and Income in the United States in 1798* (Pittsburgh: Univ. of Pittsburgh Press, 1989).

Thomas Perkins Abernethy, *From Frontier to Plantation in Tennessee: A Study of Frontier Democracy* (Chapel Hill: Univ. of North Carolina Press, 1932); John

D. Barnhart, *Valley of Democracy: The Frontier versus the Plantation in the Ohio Valley, 1775–1818* (rpt. Lincoln: Univ. of Nebraska Press, 1970); Teute, "Land, Liberty, and Labor"; Aron, *How the West Was Lost.*

39. The data presented here come from Coward, *Kentucky in the New Republic,* 55 and 63. In 1800 the proportion of householders who owned land in Woodford County was 52.4 percent, in Franklin County, 48.5 percent, and in Boone County, 47.3 percent.

40. Teute, "Land, Liberty, and Labor," 263 and 269–70. Teute also includes data for 1797, but in several instances the data for that year defy the pattern evident for the rest of the decade, raising the possibility that a mid-decade event such as alteration in county boundaries temporarily affected cumulative rates of land-holding in some areas. A similar trend is detected for western Pennsylvania by R. Eugene Harper, *The Transformation of Western Pennsylvania, 1770–1800* (Pittsburgh: Univ. of Pittsburgh Press, 1991), 33.

41. In 1778 the Virginia Assembly had invalidated the Transylvania Company treaty at Sycamore Shoals: Hening, *Statutes at Large* 9: 571–72. The data are from Coward, *Kentucky in the New Republic,* 55.

42. Caleb Wallace to James Madison, 12 July 1785, *Papers of James Madison* 8: 321. See also Enoch Smith to Isaac Davis, 30 May 1797, Isaac Davis Papers.

43. David Meade to Judge Prentis, 30 Apr. 1798, Webb-Prentis Papers (#4136), Special Collections Dept., Univ. of Virginia Library; George Nicholas to Wilson Cary Nicholas, 13 Feb. 1795, Wilson Cary Nicholas Papers (#2343), Special Collections Dept., Univ. of Virginia Library.

44. Watlington, *Partisan Spirit,* 95.

45. Stephen Aron writes of the "stranglehold of landlords," particularly absentee owners, in *How the West Was Lost.*

46. John May to Samuel Beall, 9 Dec. 1782, Beall-Booth Family Papers, Filson Club Historical Society.

47. William Christian to Elizabeth Christian, 12 Dec. 1785, and Ann Christian to Ann Fleming, 26 Mar. 1786, Hugh Blair Grigsby Papers, Virginia Historical Society, Richmond; George Nicholas to Samuel Smith, 25 Oct. 1789, Carter-Smith Family Papers (#1729), Special Collections Dept., Univ. of Virginia Library.

48. John Breckinridge to Letticia Breckinridge, 7 May 1789, Breckinridge Family Papers; John Breckinridge to James Monroe, 20 July 1798, Breckinridge Family Papers. See also the David Meade letter dated 6 May 1798, William Bolling Papers.

49. C. Morgan to Patrick Joyes, 29 Aug. 1799, Read-Sutherland Papers, Filson Club Historical Society; John Breckinridge to Samuel Hopkins, 15 Sept. 1794, Breckinridge Family Papers.

50. Teute, "Land, Liberty, and Labor," 232–39.

51. John Breckinridge to Smythe Payne, 15 Sept. 1794, Breckinridge Family Papers.

52. Robert Smith to John Breckinridge, 1 Oct. 1795, Breckinridge Family Papers.

53. William Lytle to John Breckinridge, 11 Mar. 1797, Breckinridge Family Papers; Leven Powell to Burr Powell, 9 June 1797, Leven Powell Papers, Swem Library, College of William and Mary. See also Paul W. Gates, "Tenants of the Log Cabin," *Mississippi Valley Historical Review* 49 (1962): 19.

54. Coward, *Kentucky in the New Republic,* 52–53.

55. David Meade to Ann Meade Randolph, 1 Sept. 1796, *William and Mary Quarterly*, 2d ser., vol. 21 (1941): 341; John Breckinridge to James Breckinridge, 9 May 1797, Breckinridge Family Papers.

56. Wade Hall, ed., "Along the Wilderness Trail: A Young Lawyer's 1785 Letter from Danville, Kentucky, to Massachusetts," *FCHQ* 61 (1987): 290.

57. "A Memorandum of M. Austin's Journey from the Lead Mines in the County of Wythe in the State of Virginia to the Lead Mines in the Province of Louisiana West of the Mississippi," *American Historical Review* 5 (1899): 525–26.

58. Toulmin, *Western Country in 1793*, 68.

59. U.S. Bureau of the Census, *A Century of Population Growth from the First Census of the United States to the Twelfth, 1790–1900* (Washington, D.C.: Government Printing Office, 1909), 94. For the classic statement on age and the acquisition of land, see James A. Henretta, "Families and Farms: Mentalité in Pre-Industrial America," *William and Mary Quarterly*, 3d ser., vol. 35 (1978): 3–32.

60. Thruston, "Letter by Edward Harris, 1797," 167; Spencer Records interview, Draper Coll., 23CC27; Toulmin, *Western Country in 1793*, 80. Lee Soltow and Kenneth W. Keller argue that tenancy was viewed in a similar manner in western Pennsylvania during this period: "Tenancy and Asset Holding in Late-Eighteenth-Century Washington County, Pennsylvania," *Western Pennsylvania Historical Magazine* 65 (1982): 1–4.

61. Rothert, "John D. Shane's Interview with Hedge," 177; Thruston, "Letter by Edward Harris, 1797," 167. See also Teute, "Land, Liberty, and Labor," 314–16, 327–28. Favorable terms also prevailed in other border settlement areas: Mancall, *Valley of Opportunity*, 105–7; Harper, *Transformation of Western Pennsylvania*, 158.

62. Drake, *Pioneer Life*, 27–28.

63. John McDowell to James McDowell, 22 Mar. 1794, James McDowell Papers, Southern Historical Collection, Wilson Library, Univ. of North Carolina at Chapel Hill.

64. Toulmin, *Western Country in 1793*, 76. Lease agreements took various forms during this period. See, e.g., Robert Jones interview, Draper Coll., 13CC161; Benjamin Hardesty interview, Draper Coll., 11CC171; Thruston, "Letter by Edward Harris, 1797," 167.

65. William Russell to John Breckinridge, 13 Mar. 1791, Breckinridge Family Papers.

66. John McDowell to James McDowell, 29 Dec. 1795, James McDowell Papers. See also John McKinney to Joseph Brown, 20 Aug. 1808, in Welch, "Six Letters by Pioneer John McKinney," 115.

67. Turk McClesky, "Rich Land, Poor Prospects: Real Estate and the Formation of a Social Elite in Augusta County, Virginia, 1738–1770," *Virginia Magazine of History and Biography* 98 (1990): 449–86; Lemon, *The Best Poor Man's Country*, 12; Soltow and Keller, "Tenancy and Asset Holding," 1–15; Lee Soltow, "Inequality amidst Abundance: Land Ownership in Early Nineteenth Century Ohio," *Ohio History* 88 (1979): 133–51.

68. Gates, "Tenants of the Log Cabin." More recently, see Teute, "Land, Liberty, and Labor," and Aron, *How the West Was Lost*.

Chapter 4. Ordering a Heterogeneous Society

1. Mitchell, *Commercialism and Frontier*; Fischer, *Albion's Seed*; Maldwyn A. Jones, "The Scotch-Irish in British America," in *Strangers within the Realm: Cultural Margins of the British Empire*, ed. Bernard Bailyn and Philip D. Morgan (Chapel Hill: Univ. of North Carolina Press for the Institute of Early American History and Culture, 1991), 284–313; Kenneth W. Keller, "What Is Distinctive about the Scotch-Irish," in *Appalachian Frontiers: Settlement, Society, and Development in the Preindustrial Era*, ed. Robert D. Mitchell (Lexington: Univ. Press of Kentucky, 1991), 69–86.

2. Richard H. Thornton, *An American Glossary, Being an Attempt to Illustrate Certain Americanisms upon Historical Principles*, 2 vols. (Philadelphia: J. P. Lippincott, 1912), 2: 910. The distinction persisted in Virginia: Alexander S. Paxton, *Memory Days, in Which the Shenandoah Valley Is Seen in Retrospection, with Glimpses of School Days and the Life of Virginia People of Fifty Years Ago* (New York: Neale, 1908), 16–18.

3. Rothert, "Shane's Interview with Hedge," 177–78; Robert Johnson to Gov. Patrick Henry, 5 Dec. 1786, *Calendar of Virginia State Papers*, 4: 191. See also Perkins, "Border Life," 168–72, 180–81, and 189–90.

4. Thomas L. Purvis, "The Ethnic Descent of Kentucky's Early Population: A Statistical Investigation of European and American Sources of Emigration, 1790–1820," *RKHS* 80 (1982): 253–66. Another surname analysis, but of a much narrower sample, may be found in John B. Sanderlin, "Ethnic Origins of Early Kentucky Grantees," *RKHS* 85 (1987): 103–10.

5. Revolutionary pension records for numerous counties have been abstracted for genealogical purposes and are on file at the Kentucky Historical Society, Frankfort. The sample of counties analyzed here were Nelson, Mercer, and Madison. The proportion of cohees ranged from 27.5 percent in Mercer County to 43 percent in Madison. Origin was defined as the most recent place of residence prior to removal to Kentucky. Only those applicants present in Kentucky before 1792 were included. The original pension records are in the National Archives and available on microfilm.

6. Deposition of George Shortridge, *Calendar of Virginia State Papers*, 4: 187 (quotation). The episode is related at length in numerous letters and depositions in *Calendar of Virginia State Papers* 4: 186–201.

7. Robert Johnson to Patrick Henry, 5 Dec. 1786, *Calendar of Virginia State Papers* 4: 191.

8. Walker Daniel to Benjamin Harrison, 19 Jan. 1784, *Calendar of Virginia State Papers* 3: 555–56; Walker Daniel to Benjamin Harrison, 21 May 1784, *Calendar of Virginia State Papers,* 3: 584–85; Christopher Greenup to Leven Powell, 8 Aug. 1783, Leven Powell Papers; James Speed to Benjamin Harrison, 22 May 1784, *Calendar of Virginia State Papers* 3: 589.

9. Joseph Ficklin interview, Draper Coll., 16CC271.

10. The term *Dutch* connoted speakers of both German and Dutch, but Germans were much more numerous in early America. See A. G. Roeber, "'The Origin of Whatever Is Not English among Us': The Dutch-speaking and the German-speaking Peoples of Colonial British America," *Strangers within the Realm,* ed. Bailyn and Morgan, 220–83.

11. Bourbon County Court, Will Book A, 231; Letter of Charles Anderson to Lyman C. Draper, 11 Mar. 1891, published in *Kentucky Genealogist* 25 (1983): 7. Peter Smelzer migrated to Kentucky from Berks County, Pennsylvania, according to Alvie Lee Pollock, *Asters at Dusk: The Smelser Family in America* (Dayton, 1961). The German communities in Bourbon and Jefferson Counties began as stations, called by English-speaking neighbors the Dutch and Low Dutch Stations, respectively. See also Perkins, "Border Life," 172–75. For the personal memoir of a German pioneer, see Solomon Zumwalt, ed., "Biography of Adam Zumwalt" (typescript), Lane County Pioneer Historical Society, Eugene, Ore.

12. Roeber, "The Origin of Whatever Is Not English among Us," 220–83; Kenneth W. Keller, "The Outlook of Rhinelanders on the Virginia Frontier," in *Diversity and Accommodation*, 99–126; Turk McCleskey, "The Price of Conformity: Class, Ethnicity, and Local Authority on the Colonial Virginia Frontier," ibid., 213–26; Elizabeth A. Kessel, "Germans in the Making of Frederick County, Maryland," in *Appalachian Frontiers*, 87–104; Klaus Wust, *The Virginia Germans* (Charlottesville: Univ. Press of Virginia, 1969); John Walter Wayland, *The German Element of the Shenandoah Valley of Virginia* (1905; rpt., Bridgewater, Va.: C. J. Carrier, 1964); Purvis, "Ethnic Descent," 263.

13. Joseph Ficklin interview, Draper Coll., 16CC267; Josiah Collins interview, Draper Coll., 12CC102; Nathaniel Hart Jr. interview, Draper Coll., 17CC208.

14. James Davis, Lincoln County, to Zachariah Johnston, 10 August 1789, Zachariah Johnston Papers; Eslinger, "Shape of Slavery," 13–15. The literature on slavery in recently settled areas is modest, but see: Peter H. Wood, *Black Majority: Negroes in Colonial South Carolina from 1670 through the Stono Rebellion* (New York: W. W. Norton, 1974); Allan Kulikoff, "Uprooted Peoples: Black Migrants in the Age of the American Revolution, 1790–1820," in *Slavery and Freedom in the Age of the American Revolution*, ed. Ira Berlin and Ronald Hoffman (Urbana: Univ. of Illinois Press for the United States Capitol Historical Society, 1983), 143–71; Philip D. Morgan and Michael L. Nicholls, "Slaves in Piedmont Virginia, 1720–1790," *William and Mary Quarterly*, 3d ser., vol. 46 (1989): 211–51.

15. Rhys Isaac, *The Transformation of Virginia, 1740–1790* (Chapel Hill: Univ. of North Carolina Press for the Institute of Early American History and Culture, 1982); Robert B. Semple, *A History of the Rise and Progress of Baptists in Virginia, by Robert B. Semple, Minister of the Gospel in King and Queen County, Virginia* (Richmond: privately printed, 1810), 14; James D. Essig, *The Bonds of Wickedness: American Evangelicals against Slavery, 1770–1808* (Philadelphia: Temple Univ. Press, 1982); Donald G. Mathews, *Religion in the Old South* (Chicago: Univ. of Chicago Press, 1977).

16. Semple, *Rise and Progress of Baptists in Virginia*, 25.

17. Spottsylvania County Court Records, quoted in ibid., 30.

18. West of the Blue Ridge, where the number of Baptists was very small, harassment occurred rarely. Lewis Peyton Little, *Imprisoned Preachers and Religious Liberty in Virginia* (Lynchburg: J. P. Bell, 1938), 516–21.

19. Walter Brownlow Posey, *The Baptist Church in the Lower Mississippi Valley, 1776–1845* (Lexington: Univ. of Kentucky Press, 1957), 4; Chester Raymond Young,

ed., *Baptists on the American Frontier: A History of Ten Baptist Churches of Which the Author Has Been Alternately a Member, by John Taylor* (Macon: Mercer Univ. Press, 1995).

20. William Mosby interview, Draper Coll., 11CC184; Gen. James Taylor, "Anecdotes of Genl. Chs. Scott," Draper Coll., 8CC166–67. Baptist opposition is also related in "Diary of Major Eskuries Beatty," 110.

21. "Diary of Major Eskuries Beatty," 60. See also "New Haven March 2d 1786: Extract of a letter from a gentleman in the Western Country, to his friend in this city, dated Fort Finley, near the Miami, Dec. 22 1785," *Massachusetts Gazette,* 13 Mar. 1786, in George Rogers Clark Papers, Draper Coll., 32J108.

22. Caleb Wallace to James Madison, 12 July 1785, *Papers of James Madison* 8: 321; George Nicholas to James Madison, 5 Sept. 1792, *Papers of James Madison* 14: 359; Caleb Wallace to William Fleming, 11 Aug. 1792, Hugh Blair Grigsby Papers.

23. Based on data for District B, Mercer County, in Netti Schreiner-Yantis and Florene Speakman Love, comps., *The 1787 Census of Virginia,* 3 vols. (Springfield, Va.: Genealogical Books in Print, 1987), 1452–56.

24. Teute, "Land, Liberty, and Labor," 295.

25. John Todd Jr. to Thomas Jefferson, 15 Apr. 1781, *Calendar of Virginia State Papers* 2: 44; "Pursuant to Instructions from the Executive," Danville, Kentucky, 16 Apr. 1788, *Calendar of Virginia State Papers* 4: 428; Gov. Isaac Shelby Official Papers [1792], Office of the Public Records Division, Kentucky Division for Archives and Records, Frankfort; Winchester, Va., *Virginia Gazette, or The Winchester Advertiser,* 16 Jan. 1790. The Ohio River quickly superseded the Wilderness Road as the primary route west.

26. John Edwards to Edmund Randolph, 26 Aug. 1790, *Calendar of Virginia State Papers* 5: 202. See also Levi Todd to Patrick Henry, 22 June 1786, *Calendar of Virginia State Papers* 4: 151; and Levi Todd to Edmund Randolph, 14 Feb. 1787, *Calendar of Virginia State Papers* 4: 237.

27. Lee Soltow, "Kentucky Wealth at the End of the Eighteenth Century," *Journal of Economic History* 43 (1983): 621; U.S. Bureau of the Census, *A Century of Population Growth,* 207.

28. Richard H. Collins, *History of Kentucky by the Late Lewis Collins,* 2 vols., rev. (rpt., Berea, Ky.: Kentucky Imprints, 1976), vol. 1: 22 and 25; "Michaux's Travels," 226.

29. Bourbon County tax lists (microfilm), Kentucky Historical Society.

30. Albert Ogden Porter, *County Government in Virginia: A Legislative History, 1607–1904* (New York: Columbia Univ. Press, 1947), 109–10; Charles S. Sydnor, *Gentlemen Freeholders: Political Parties in Washington's Virginia* (Chapel Hill: Univ. of North Carolina Press for the Institute of Early American History and Culture, 1952), 84–85; Thomas Jefferson, *Notes on the State of Virginia* (Chapel Hill: Univ. of North Carolina Press for the Institute of Early American History and Culture, 1955), 131–32; William C. Richardson, *An Administrative History of Kentucky Courts to 1850* (Frankfort: Kentucky Department for Libraries and Archives, 1983), 2–6. See also Levi Purviance, *The Biography of Elder David Purviance, with His Memoirs. Containing His Views on Baptism, the Divinity of Christ, and the Atonement. Written by Himself:*

With an Appendix Giving Biographical Sketches of Elders John Hardy, Reuben Dooly, William Samuel Kyle, and Nathan Worley. Together with a Historical Sketch of the Great Kentucky Revival (Dayton: published for the author by B. F. and G. W. Ells, 1848), 19.

31. "To Governor Harrison of Virginia," 11 Sept. 1782, *Calendar of Virginia State Papers* 3: 301–2 (quotation). See also Levi Todd to Benjamin Harrison, 11 Sept. 1782, *Calendar of Virginia State Papers* 3: 300–301; Andrew Steele to the governor of Virginia, 12 Sept. 1782, *Calendar of Virginia State Papers* 3: 303–4.

32. John Todd to Thomas Jefferson, 15 Apr. 1781, *Calendar of Virginia State Papers* 2: 45 (quotation); John Todd and Robert Patterson to Thomas Nelson, 21 Oct. 1781, *Calendar of Virginia State Papers* 2: 564.

33. John Floyd to Thomas Jefferson, 16 Apr. 1781, *Calendar of Virginia State Papers* 2: 47–49.

34. Benjamin Logan to Benjamin Harrison, 29 Apr. 1782, *Calendar of Virginia State Papers* 3: 142; Benjamin Logan to Benjamin Harrison, 31 Aug. 1782, *Calendar of Virginia State Papers* 3: 281.

35. James Garrard to Edmund Randolph, 1 May 1788, *Calendar of Virginia State Papers* 4: 433; John Edwards to Edmund Randolph, 4 Nov. 1788, *Calendar of Virginia State Papers* 4: 506–7.

36. Levi Todd to Edmund Randolph, 29 Mar. 1788, *Calendar of Virginia State Papers*, 4:420; "Statement of the Rank in which the Justices of Jefferson County Stood, at the Time of the Seperation of Kentucky, from the State of Virginia," [1792], Gov. Isaac Shelby Correspondence, Office of Public Records, Kentucky Division for Libraries and Records.

37. Benjamin Logan to Edmund Randolph, 17 May 1787, *Calendar of Virginia State Papers* 4: 287.

38. Hening, *Statutes at Large* 9: 260.

39. Thomas Speed, *The Political Club*, Filson Club Publications, no. 9 (Louisville: John P. Morton and Co. for the Filson Club Historical Society, 1894), 125. See also George F. Taylor, "Suffrage in Early Kentucky," *RKHS* 61 (1963): 22–37.

40. John Frederick Dorman, comp., *Petitions from Kentucky to the Virginia Legislature, 1766–1791, A Supplement to "Petitions of the Early Inhabitants of Kentucky to the General Assembly of Virginia, 1766–1792"* (Easley, S.C.: Southern Historical Press, 1981), 254. The disregard for Virginia property qualifications is also noted in Marshall, *History of Kentucky* 2: 197–98.

41. Bourbon County Petitions to the General Assembly, 28 Oct. 1789, Library of Virginia, Richmond.

42. William Martin to Lyman C. Draper, 7 July 1842, Tennessee Papers, Draper Coll., 3XX43; Smyth, *A Tour in the United States* 1: 330.

43. Robertson, *Petitions*, 44–45; Beckner, "Shane's Interview with Clinkenbeard," 116. See also Col. John Floyd to John May, 8 Apr. 1782, *Calendar of Virginia State Papers*, 3: 121; Rohrbough, *Trans-Appalachian Frontier*, 20–21; Faragher, *Daniel Boone*, 214–19.

44. Col. John Floyd to John May, 8 Apr. 1782, *Calendar of Virginia State Papers* 3: 121.

45. Beckner, "Early Adventures of Sudduth," 49.

46. Bourbon County Court, Order Book A; Beeman, *Evolution of the Southern Backcountry,* 44; Mancall, *Valley of Opportunity,* 115–24.

47. Toulmin, *Western Country in 1793,* 92–94.

48. A skewed pattern of early court activity was likewise noticed by Beeman in his study of Lunenburg County, *Evolution of the Southern Backcountry,* 44–47. See also Mancall, *Valley of Opportunity,* 119.

49. Caleb Wallace to James Madison, 12 July 1785, *Papers of James Madison* 8: 321.

50. Toulmin, *Western Country in 1793,* 92–93.

51. These cases involved charges of horse theft, bestiality, and the rape and murder of a local woman. Bourbon County Court, Order Book A, 156, 286–87, and 423–24.

52. Marshall, *History of Kentucky* 1: 199.

53. Drake, *Pioneer Life,* 180–89; Strickland, *Finley,* 71. James Galloway (Xenia) to Benjamin Drake, 12 Jan. 1839, Draper Coll., 8J258.

54. Beckner, "Shane's Interview with Clinkenbeard," 105; Eslinger, "The Great Revival in Bourbon County," 40–41.

55. H. T. Duncan interview, Draper Coll., 16CC51 (quotation). See also Rogers, *Autobiography of Elder Samuel Rogers,* 4; "Diary of Major Eskuries Beatty," 100–102; Bourbon County Court, Order Book B, 723.

56. Elliot J. Gorn, "'Gouge and Bite, Pull Hair and Scratch': The Social Significance of Fighting in the Southern Back Country," *American Historical Review* 90 (1985): 18–32; Arthur K. Moore, *The Frontier Mind: A Cultural Analysis* (Lexington: Univ. Press of Kentucky, 1957), 77–122; Isaac, *Transformation of Virginia,* 95–98; Bertram Wyatt-Brown, *Southern Honor, Ethics and Behavior in the Old South* (New York: Oxford Univ. Press, 1982).

57. James B. Finley [the son of Rev. Robert B. Finley] quoted in Chinn, *Kentucky Settlement and Statehood,* 358; Rogers, *Autobiography of Elder Samuel Rogers,* 5–6.

58. "Michaux's Travels," 247; Rogers, *Autobiography of Elder Samuel Rogers,* 4.

59. Drake, *Pioneer Life,* 188–89; Toulmin, *Western Country in 1793,* 70.

60. Dr. Marshall interview, Draper Coll., 16CC44; Coward, *Kentucky in the New Republic,* 80.

61. *Kentucky Gazette,* 24 Nov. 1792, 1 Dec. 1792, and 8 Dec. 1792. Smith had a past as a vigilante patriot against the British and had also been involved in a territorial dispute between Pennsylvania and Virginia. In 1774, Governor Dunmore of Virginia had attempted to assert authority in the area around Fort Pitt. Smith and several other Pennsylvania justices were arrested.

62. *Journal of the House of Representatives at the First Session of the Second General Assembly for the Commonwealth of Kentucky* (Lexington: John Bradford, 1794; microfilm, Washington, D.C.: Library of Congress Photoduplication Service, 1942), 15 Nov. 1793.

63. Arthur Hopkins to John Breckinridge, 27 Jan. 1794, Breckinridge Family Papers; Beckner, "Shane's Interview with Jeptha Kemper," 161.

64. Bourbon County Court, Order Book A, 423–24, 555; Bourbon County Court, Order Book B, 101; Order Book of the Kentucky Court of Oyer and Terminer, Office of Public Records, Kentucky Division for Libraries and Records, 33, 39, 51, 54–55. Slaves accused of capital crimes were tried by the county court.

65. *Journal of the House of Representatives at the First Session of the Third General Assembly for the Commonwealth of Kentucky* (Lexington: John Bradford, 1794; Washington, D.C.: Library of Congress Photoduplication Service, 1942), 5 Nov. 1794.

66. Ibid., 12 Nov. 1794. The increasing concern about crime during this period is also noted in Friend, "Inheriting Eden," 96.

67. John Edwards to Isaac Shelby, 24 June 1792, Gov. Shelby Official Papers.

68. On the day after the petition requesting an annual grand jury, Representative John Boyd introduced a bill "for the better regulation of Paris." This bill was readily enacted into law. *Journal of the House,* 24 Nov. 1794; 26 Nov. 1794. For the persistence of the problem see *Journal of the House of Representatives at the Sixth Session of the General Assembly for the Commonwealth of Kentucky* (Lexington: John Bradford, 1796), 202.

69. Bourbon County Court, Order Book B, 178, 274, 379, and 663. A set of stocks had been ordered in 1790 as well: Bourbon County Court, Order Book A, 270.

70. *Journal of the Kentucky Senate,* 4 Nov. 1801 (Washington, D.C.: Library of Congress Photoduplication Service, 1942).

71. Coward, *Kentucky in the New Republic,* 56–62.

72. *Journal of the House of Representatives . . . Commonwealth of Kentucky,* 23 Nov. 1792, 27 Nov. 1793; Charles Ewing to Isaac Shelby, Shelby Family Papers, Manuscripts Division, Library of Congress. County subdivisions also affected expenditures for new courthouses and official appointments. The problems in Logan County are discussed in a letter by a citizen named Caldwell to John Breckinridge, 24 Oct. 1799, Breckinridge Family Papers. The trouble caused by a disputed sheriff's election in Woodford County is related by Edmund Searcy to John Breckinridge, 6 May 1793, Breckinridge Family Papers. For similar conflict in Clark County, see Enoch Smith to Isaac Shelby, 13 Dec. 1794, Gov. Shelby Official Papers. These conflicts often devolved into public disorder.

73. James Brown to Isaac Shelby, 15 Aug. 1792 and 25 Aug. 1792, Shelby Family Papers; John Edwards to Isaac Shelby, 7 July 1792, Shelby Family Papers; "Truth," *Kentucky Gazette,* 28 July 1792.

74. John Waller to Isaac Shelby, 22 Sept. 1793, Gov. Shelby Official Papers. For other local political conflicts, see Thomas Fletcher to Isaac Shelby, 22 Aug. 1792, Gov. Shelby Official Papers; John Allen to Isaac Shelby, 6 June 1793, Gov. Shelby Official Papers; Charles Smith Jr. to John Breckinridge, 29 Apr. 1798, Breckinridge Family Papers.

75. Order Book of the General Sessions of the District Courts, 1797–1799, and General Court, 1800, Division of Public Records, Kentucky Department for Libraries and Archives, 6–25.

76. Bourbon County Court, Order Book B, 60, 162, 335, 657, 681, and 686. A similar situation, caused by the economic disruptions of the Revolution, is depicted in a recent study of Charles County, Maryland. See Jean B. Lee, *The Price of Nationhood: The American Revolution in Charles County* (New York: W. W. Norton, 1994).

77. *Kentucky Herald,* 28 Feb. 1800.

78. Francis Ransdell Slaughter to John Randsell, 6 June 1792, Filson Club Historical Society; James Craig to Isaac Shelby, 17 May 1794, Shelby Family Papers;
Caleb Wallace to William Fleming, 11 Aug. 1792, Hugh Blair Grigsby Papers;
John E. King to Isaac Shelby, 13 May 1796, Shelby Family Papers; Enoch Smith
to Isaac Shelby, 23 Dec. 1794, Gov. Shelby Official Papers; George Rogers Clark
to Jonathan Clark, 20 Apr. 1788, Jonathan Clark Papers, Draper Coll., 2L26.
For an example of the increasingly common refusal to serve in public office,
see Daniel Standiford to Isaac Shelby, 20 Feb. 1793, Shelby Family Papers.

Chapter 5. A New Political Culture

1. The classic description is found in Sydnor, *Gentleman Freeholders.* Other ma-
jor works include: Bernard Bailyn, *The Ideological Origins of the American
Revolution* (Cambridge, Mass.: Harvard Univ. Press, 1967); Gordon S. Wood,
The Creation of the American Republic, 1776–1787 (Chapel Hill: Univ. of North
Carolina Press, 1969); and *The Radicalism of the American Revolution* (New
York: Alfred A. Knopf, 1992). Virginia has figured prominently in the litera-
ture: Jack P. Greene, "Society, Ideology, and Politics: An Analysis of the Politi-
cal Culture of Mid-Eighteenth-Century Virginia," in *Society, Freedom, and
Conscience: The American Revolution,* ed. Richard M. Jellison (New York:
W. W. Norton, 1976), 14–76; Isaac, *Transformation of Virginia;* Beeman, *Evolution of the Southern Backcountry;* Kulikoff, *Tobacco and Slaves;* Tillson, *Gentry and Common Folk.*

2. The literature is extensive, but see Alfred F. Young, *The Democratic Republicans of New York: The Origins, 1763–1797* (Chapel Hill: Univ. of North Carolina Press, 1967); Andrew R. L. Cayton, *The Frontier Republic: Ideologies and
Politics in the Ohio Country, 1780–1825* (Kent, Ohio: Kent State Univ. Press,
1986); Thomas P. Slaughter, *The Whiskey Rebellion: Frontier Epilogue to the
American Revolution* (New York: Oxford Univ. Press, 1986); Taylor, *Liberty
Men and Great Proprietors.*

3. Garrard was descended from one of Stafford County's leading families. See
Allen Johnson and Dumas Malone, eds., *Dictionary of American Biography,*
20 vols. (New York: Charles Scribner's Sons, 1931–36), vol. 7: 159–60; H. E.
Everman, *Governor James Garrard* (n.p.: Cooper's Run Press, 1981).

4. Two good descriptions of how the "county oligarchies" worked in colonial
Virginia may be found in Sydnor, *Gentlemen Freeholders,* 74–85; and Kulikoff,
Tobacco and Slaves, 267–77.

5. Nathaniel Turk McCleskey, "Across the First Divide: Frontiers of Settlement
and Culture in Augusta County, Virginia" (Ph.D. diss., College of William and
Mary, 1990).

6. Beckner, "Shane's Interview with Allen," 90.

7. Beckner, "Shane's Interview with Clinkenbeard," 122; William Sudduth to Lyman
C. Draper, 22 May 1843, Frontier Wars Papers, Draper Coll., 14U10.

8. Thomas Davis to Isaac Shelby, 21 Nov. 1792, Gov. Shelby Official Papers; Doughty
to Isaac Shelby, 1 Dec. 1792, Gov. Shelby Official Papers; John Paul to Isaac
Shelby, 26 June 1793, Gov. Shelby Official Papers; James Young to James Garrard,

29 Jan. 1796, Gov. James Garrard Official Papers, Office of the Public Records Division, Kentucky Department for Libraries and Archives. See also Coward, *Kentucky in the New Republic,* 61–62.

9. Enoch Smith to Isaac Shelby, 13 Dec. 1794, Gov. Shelby Official Papers.

10. Ebenezer Alexander to James Garrard, 24 Jan. 1797, Gov. Garrard Official Papers. For another example, see John McIntire to John Breckinridge, 10 Feb. 1799, Breckinridge Family Papers. Note the dates of these statements, nearly two decades after the American Revolution.

11. Strickland, *Finley,* 44; William Kinkade statement, in Purviance, *Biography of Elder David Purviance,* 272. A similar situation has been detected for other areas thrown upon their own resources during wartime: Tillson, *Gentry and Common Folk;* Michael A. McDonnell, "'Loaded Guns and Imprudent Expressions': Military Culture and Gentry-Smallholder Relations in Virginia during the Revolutionary Crisis, 1774–1783," paper presented at the Southern Historical Association annual meeting, 1994.

12. G. W. Stipp, comp., *John Bradford's Historical &c. Notes on Kentucky from the Western Miscellany* (San Francisco: Grabhorn Press, 1932), 166–70; Walter Kelso interview, Draper Coll., 12CC42; James Wade interview, Draper Coll., 12CC44; Mrs. Morrison interview, Draper Coll., 11CC152; Rothert, "John D. Shane's Interview with Mrs. John McKinney and Her Son Harvey," 157–66.

13. John D. Shane, "The Henderson Company Ledger," 21 *FCHQ* (1947): 41; Beckner, "John D. Shane's Notes on an Interview with Jeptha Kemper," 160.

14. Beckner, "Shane's Interview with Clinkenbeard," 108 and 120–25; Beckner, "Shane's Interview with Allen," 85; R. S. Cotterill, "John Fleming, Pioneer of Fleming County," *RKHS* 49 (1951): 198; Michael Strode statement, Draper's Notes, Draper Coll., 20S175–96; John Clinkenbeard statement, Draper's Notes, Draper Coll., 25S250; Francis Cassidy statement, Draper's Notes, Draper Coll., 21S175–83; William Cassidy statement, Draper's Notes, Draper Coll., 21S196–99; William Spahr statement, Draper's Notes, Draper Coll., 25S254.

15. Beckner, "Shane's Interview with Allen," 93.

16. William Cassidy statement, Draper's Notes, Draper Coll., 21S199; Francis Cassidy statement, Draper's Notes, Draper Coll., 21S181–82; Samuel M. Cassidy, *Michael Cassidy, Frontiersman* (Lexington: privately printed, 1979).

17. Isaac Hite to Abraham Hite, 26 Apr. 1783, Filson Club Historical Society; William Breckinridge to John Breckinridge, 5 Feb. 1785, Breckinridge Family Papers.

18. Arthur M'Nichol petition, Gov. Shelby Official Papers; "Truth," *Kentucky Gazette,* 28 July 1792.

19. Kentucky's pursuit of statehood is related in detail in three studies: Watlington, *Partisan Spirit;* Coward, *Kentucky in the New Republic;* Lowell H. Harrison, *Kentucky's Road to Statehood* (Lexington: Univ. Press of Kentucky, 1992).

20. Copy of a letter from Thomas Marshall to George Nicholas, 26 Apr. 1789, Harry Innes Papers, Manuscript Division, Library of Congress. (Marshall, Kentucky's most prominent Federalist, was father of Chief Justice John Marshall.) The court party also investigated the possibility of a separation from the Union. See Watlington, *Partisan Spirit,* 120–25, 140–47.

21. Nathaniel Richardson to John Breckinridge, 11 Feb. 1791, Breckinridge Family Papers; "Journal of General Butler," in Neville B. Craig, *The Olden Time,* 2 vols. (rpt., Cincinnati: Robert Clarke, 1878), entry for 9 Oct. 1785, vol. 2: 444. See also Samuel Terrell to Garrett Minor, 7 July 1790, Papers of the Carr and Terrell Families; "An Address to the freemen of the district of Kentucky," *Kentucky Gazette,* 15 Oct. 1791; and "H.S.B.M.," *Kentucky Gazette,* 25 Feb. 1792.

22. The proponents of a more democratic government are referred to as "Partisans" by the two main chroniclers of statehood, Patricia Watlington and Joan Wells Coward, who adopted it in an effort to connote a political party or proto-party. Yet sources suggest that they were united by little more than a broad opposition to gentry rule. The term itself was not used by contemporaries except in the generic sense to connote, from a gentry perspective, a dangerous faction. The main spokesmen for democratic government at this point were Samuel Taylor, Ebenezer Brooks, and James Smith. See Watlington, *Partisan Spirit,* and Coward, *Kentucky in the New Republic.*

23. Harry Innes to William Fleming, 10 Aug. 1791, William Fleming Papers, Special Collections, Leyburn Library, Washington and Lee Univ.

24. "Philip Philips," *Kentucky Gazette,* 26 Nov. 1791; "H.S.B.M.," *Kentucky Gazette,* 24 Dec. 1791. The relationship between democrats in the statehood conventions and the county committees is also explored in Coward, *Kentucky in the New Republic,* 15.

25. Smith stands as one of Kentucky's most fascinating characters. He had grown up on the dangerous Pennsylvania frontier. Captured and adopted by Hurons in 1755, Smith mastered their language and culture. He later wrote a treatise on modes of border warfare. Back in the settlements of western Pennsylvania, he led a local vigilante group called the "Black Boys," which agitated for a more aggressive Indian policy. In 1776, Smith represented Westmoreland County in the Pennsylvania Assembly and later saw active service with the Pennsylvania troops. He had explored Kentucky shortly after the Seven Years' War and moved there in 1788. He represented Bourbon County in several conventions discussing statehood, distinguishing himself as a voice for democratic government, and in 1790 he became a justice of the peace. He was also a leading Presbyterian layman, helping to found the congregation of Cane Ridge in 1791 and serving as one of its elders. Dumas and Malone, *Dictionary of American Biography* 17: 284–85. See also the memoirs of his youth, *An Account of the Remarkable Occurrences in the Life and Travels of Colonel James Smith.*

26. Henry belonged to the Sinking Spring congregation at Paris and Smith to the neighboring Cane Ridge congregation. Both men attended meetings of Transylvania Presbytery and were presumably well acquainted. "An Address to the freemen of the District of Kentucky," *Kentucky Gazette,* 15 Oct. 1791 and 22 Oct. 1791.

27. In February 1792, after the election of delegates but before the constitutional convention met, the Bourbon County Committee published a second scheme for conducting elections. This scheme was very similar to the original one, except for added detail and the substitution of election districts for militia companies. *Kentucky Gazette,* 25 Feb. 1792.

28. This departure from tradition was also occurring in many other parts of the

country, although most other states had resumed a more conservative governmental structure by this time. Wood, *Creation of the American Republic*. Pennsylvania's constitution, with which Smith and other Kentucky cohees were familiar, may have been influential. See John D. Barnhart, "Frontiersmen and Planters in the Formation of Kentucky," *Journal of Southern History* 7 (1941): 19–36.

29. "An Address to the free men of the District of Kentucky," *Kentucky Gazette*, 15 Oct. 1791.

30. Other historians, studying different settings during this same period, have likewise noted the popular tendency to conflate public virtue and personal morality. See, e.g., Kloppenberg, "The Virtues of Liberalism."

31. See "The Disinterested Citizen," *Kentucky Gazette*, 11 Dec. 1790, 5 Mar. 1791, 12 Mar. 1791, 2 July 1791, 22 Oct. 1791, 29 Oct. 1791, 31 Dec. 1791. For the broader context see Wood, *Creation of the American Republic*.

32. See "A.B.C.," *Kentucky Gazette*, 24 Sept. 1791, 8 Oct. 1791, 10 Dec. 1791. See also "A Citizen," *Kentucky Gazette*, 17 Dec. 1791; and "Philanthropos," *Kentucky Gazette*, 14 Jan. 1792.

33. "An Address to the free men," *Kentucky Gazette*, 15 Oct. 1791. See also *Kentucky Gazette*, 22 Oct. 1791.

34. "H.S.B.M.," *Kentucky Gazette*, 19 Nov. 1791, 26 Nov. 1791, 24 Dec. 1791.

35. "Will Wisp," *Kentucky Gazette*, 15 Oct. 1791.

36. "The Medlar," *Kentucky Gazette*, 19 Nov. 1791.

37. "Philip Philips," *Kentucky Gazette*, 26 Nov. 1791.

38. "Salamander" and "Rob the Thrasher," *Kentucky Gazette*, 24 Dec. 1791.

39. "A.B.C.," *Kentucky Gazette*, 3 Dec. 1791. See also "Philomy O'Brand," *Kentucky Gazette*, 7 Jan. 1792 and "Torismond," *Kentucky Gazette*, 28 Jan. 1792.

40. "H.S.B.M." was possibly an acronym for William Henry, James Smith, John Boyd, and John "Wildcat" McKinney. All prominent Presbyterians residing in southern Bourbon County, they consistently resisted political dominance by the gentry. McKinney and Smith won election to the constitutional convention and the first Kentucky House of Representatives, where their voting record follows the committee's recommendations closely. Boyd, an officer in a similar organization two years later, subsequently served in the Kentucky House and Senate, where he too advocated committee proposals. *Kentucky Gazette*, 19 Nov. 1791, 26 Nov. 1791, 24 Dec. 1791. "H.S.B.M." also wrote a rebuttal to "Felt Firebrand," *Kentucky Gazette*, 7 Jan. 1792.

41. "H.S.B.M.," *Kentucky Gazette*, 24 Dec. 1791. See also Watlington, *Partisan Spirit*, 217–18; Coward, *Kentucky in the New Republic*, 21–22.

42. Harry Innes to Thomas Jefferson, 27 Aug. 1791, Thomas Jefferson Papers, Manuscripts Division, Library of Congress.

43. Harry Innes to William Fleming, 10 Aug. 1791, William Fleming Papers. See also Alexander S. Bullitt to William Fleming, 8 Mar. 1792, Frontier Wars Papers, Draper Coll., 5U10.

44. "A.B.C.," *Kentucky Gazette*, 24 Sept. 1791, 1 Oct. 1791, 8 Oct. 1791, 10 Dec. 1791.

45. "Philip Philips," *Kentucky Gazette*, 26 Nov. 1791. Little is known of Taylor other than he was a man of modest means who as a convention delegate had opposed separation from Virginia. Watlington, *Partisan Spirit*, 109–10, 119–20, and 184–85.

46. "Torismond," *Kentucky Gazette,* 28 Jan. 1792. For a description of eighteenth-century political campaigning, see Sydnor, *Gentlemen Freeholders,* and more recently, John C. Kolp, "The Dynamics of Electoral Competition in Pre-Revolutionary Virginia," *William and Mary Quarterly,* 3d ser., vol. 49 (1992): 652–74.

47. Marshall, *History of Kentucky* 1: 394. See also "X.Y.Z.," *Kentucky Gazette,* 14 Jan. 1792. Such complaints, it should be noted, were by no means unique to Kentucky during this period.

48. Coward, *Kentucky in the New Republic,* 21; Watlington, *Partisan Spirit,* 221. It is not known whether any members of the Bourbon County Committee stood for election. The only known members were William Henry and John Boyd, and neither was elected. James Smith's membership in a very similar group two years later as well as subsequent legislative activities highly consistent with the County Committee platform, however, strongly suggest committee membership. John "Wildcat" McKinney's future voting record also suggests that he may have had committee support. That Smith and McKinney enjoyed sterling reputations for bravery may have helped in their election as well. See Eslinger, "The Great Revival in Bourbon County," 155–59.

49. J. Hughes to Charles Simms, 30 Mar. 1792, Charles Simms Papers, Peter Force Coll., Manuscript Division, Library of Congress (quotation); "An Address to the free men," *Kentucky Gazette,* 15 Oct. 1791 and 22 Oct. 1791; "H.S.B.M.," *Kentucky Gazette,* 19 Nov. 1791 and 25 Feb. 1792; "Salamander," *Kentucky Gazette,* 24 Dec. 1791. The lack of preparation is inconsistent with Watlington's argument that the democratic "Partisans" constituted a political party. Watlington, *Partisan Spirit,* 204–6.

50. *Dictionary of American Biography* 13: 482–83. Nicholas's influence is discussed in detail in Watlington, *Partisan Spirit,* 200–201, 218–22.

51. Watlington, *Partisan Spirit,* 211–12; Coward, *Kentucky in the New Republic,* 17–18. See also George Nicholas to James Madison, 2 May 1792, *Papers of James Madison* 14: 296–97.

52. *Journal of the First Constitutional Convention of Kentucky, Held in Danville, Kentucky, April 2 to 19, 1792* (Lexington: State Bar Association of Kentucky, 1942).

53. Barnhart, "Frontiersmen and Planters in the Formation of Kentucky."

54. No statement from the Bourbon County Committee criticized slavery, but two of its defenders did. See "The Medlar" and "H.S.B.M.," *Kentucky Gazette,* 19 Nov. 1791 and 25 Feb. 1792. Slavery may have figured more prominently in the campaign than the newspaper suggests: see the words of democrat Samuel Taylor in "Philip Philips," *Kentucky Gazette,* 26 Nov. 1791; and J. Hughes to Charles Simms, 30 Mar. 1792, Charles Simms Papers. See also Coward, *Kentucky in the New Republic,* 20.

55. David Rice, *Slavery Inconsistent with Justice and Good Policy, Proved by a Speech Delivered in the Convention, Held at Danville, Kentucky* (New York: Isaac Collins and Son, 1804). Rice had studied at the College of New Jersey under Samuel Davies and had been licensed to preach since 1763. He was one of Kentucky's first Presbyterian ministers, having settled there in 1783. Robert Davidson, *History of the Presbyterian Church in the State of Kentucky with a Preliminary Sketch of the Churches in the Valley of Virginia* (New York: Robert Carter, 1847), 66–70; *Dictionary of American Biography* 15: 537–38.

56. Coward, *Kentucky in the New Republic,* 40–43; George Nicholas Papers, Reuben T. Durrett Collection, Department of Special Collections, Univ. of Chicago.

57. *Journal of the First Constitutional Convention,* 10; "Philip Philips," *Kentucky Gazette,* 26 Nov. 1791; Thomas Rogers to Lyman C. Draper, 17 Dec. 1862, Simon Kenton Papers, Draper Coll., 4BB21.

58. George Nicholas to James Madison, 2 May 1792, *Papers of James Madison* 14: 296–97; Coward, *Kentucky in the New Republic,* 26–36.

59. Ellen Eslinger, "Some Notes on the History of Cane Ridge prior to the Great Revival," *RKHS* 91 (1993): 1–23.

60. Caleb Wallace to William Fleming, 29 Jan. 1793, William Fleming Papers.

61. Among the Bourbon County representatives, Charles Smith and John Waller voted for the resolution while Bedinger, McKinney, and James Smith opposed it. *Journal of the House of Representatives,* 5 June 1792; "H.S.B.M.," *Kentucky Gazette,* 7 Jan. 1792; "An Address to the free men," *Kentucky Gazette,* 22 Oct. 1791. See also "At a meeting of the Democratic Society of Kentucky, in Bourbon County," *Kentucky Gazette,* 12 Apr. 1794.

62. *Journal of the House of Representatives,* 9 Nov., 16 Nov., 29 Nov., and 30 Nov. 1792; "H.S.M.B.," *Kentucky Gazette,* 7 Jan. 1792.

63. *Kentucky Gazette,* 15 Nov. 1792 and 29 Nov. 1793; Coward, *Kentucky in the New Republic,* 89. In 1796, the Senate increased to fifteen members and experienced a significant turnover.

64. Grievances varied somewhat between societies, but centered upon the excise on domestic distilled spirits, the withholding of American support for revolutionary France, and Federalist John Jay's assignment as diplomat to Great Britain. At least forty-two democratic-republican societies are known to have existed in the United States during this period. See Eugene P. Link, *Democratic-Republican Societies, 1790–1800* (Morningside Heights, N.Y.: Columbia Univ. Press, 1942); Noble Cunningham, *The Jeffersonian Republicans: The Formation of Party Organization, 1789–1801* (Chapel Hill: Univ. of North Carolina Press, 1957).

65. *Kentucky Gazette,* 2 Nov. 1793.

66. "Moses," *Kentucky Gazette,* 24 Aug. 1794.

67. The eight men are identified from articles appearing in the *Kentucky Gazette,* 2 Nov. 1793, 12 Apr. 1794, 12 July 1794. Eslinger, "The Great Revival in Bourbon County," 165, 179–80.

68. Italics added. "A Farmer," *Kentucky Gazette,* 1 Mar. 1794 and 8 Mar. 1794. The identity of "A Farmer" remains a mystery, although it can be safely assumed from the writer's description of himself as not holding any government office that he was not James Smith. That the writer was William Henry is also unlikely because Henry signed his own name to other published essays. During the constitutional debates in 1791, this pseudonym had been used by Harry Innes, but support for the Bourbon County democrats would have conflicted with his political beliefs.

69. "A Farmer," *Kentucky Gazette,* 8 Mar. 1794.

70. "At a meeting of the Democratic Society of Kentucky, in Bourbon County, held at Paris, March 31st 1794," *Kentucky Gazette,* 12 Apr. 1794.

71. "Moses," *Kentucky Gazette,* 24 Aug. 1794; "Joseph," *Kentucky Gazette,* 4 Oct. 1794. See also "Fools Will Be Medling," *Kentucky Gazette,* 18 Oct. 1794.

72. "Wm. Henry, President," *Kentucky Gazette,* 4 Oct. 1794 and 11 Oct. 1794.

73. In Bourbon County the proportion of representatives serving concurrently as justices decreased from 100 percent to 40 percent and would have been even lower but for democrat James Smith (who soon resigned his justice commission). Eslinger, "The Great Revival in Bourbon County," 189; Coward, *Kentucky in the New Republic,* 77–82.

74. "A Farmer," *Kentucky Gazette,* 1 Mar. 1794; "At a Meeting of the Democratic Society of Kentucky, in Bourbon County, held at Paris, March 31st, 1792," *Kentucky Gazette,* 12 Apr. 1794; "Wm. Henry," *Kentucky Gazette,* 4 Oct. 1794 and 11 Oct. 1794; *Journal of the House of Representatives,* 29 Nov. 1794, 2 Dec. 1794, and 8 Dec. 1794. See also Coward, *Kentucky in the New Republic,* 103–4.

75. Coward, *Kentucky in the New Republic,* 109. This work is the definitive account of Kentucky's second constitutional convention and the preceding campaign for delegates.

76. James Morton Smith, "The Grass Roots of the Kentucky Resolutions," *William and Mary Quarterly,* 3d ser., vol. 27 (1970): 222. For the national context, see James Morton Smith, *Freedom's Fetters: The Alien and Sedition Laws and American Civil Liberties* (Ithaca: Cornell Univ. Press, 1956); and more recently, Stanley Elkins and Eric McKitrick, *The Age of Federalism: The Early American Republic, 1788–1800* (New York: Oxford Univ. Press, 1993).

77. *Kentucky Gazette,* 11 July 1798, 1 Aug. 1798, 15 Aug. 1798, 29 Aug. 1798, 5 Sept. 1798, 12 Sept. 1798; *Stewart's Kentucky Herald,* 3 July 1798, 4 Sept. 1798, 18 Sept. 1798; Marshall, *History of Kentucky* 2: 251–74.

78. George Nicholas to Isaac Shelby, 27 Dec. 1798, Shelby Family Papers (quotation); Coward, *Kentucky in the New Republic,* 116–17. The change was under way in many other parts of the country as well. See Alan Taylor, "From Fathers to Friends of the People: Political Personas in the Early Republic," *Journal of the Early Republic* 11 (1991): 465–92; Richard R. Beeman, "Deference, Republicanism, and the Emergence of Popular Politics in Eighteenth-Century America," *William and Mary Quarterly,* 3d ser., vol. 49 (1992): 401–30; Wood, *Radicalism of the American Revolution,* 296–97.

79. David Rice to Pennsylvania Abolition Society, 4 Nov. 1794, Pennsylvania Abolition Society Collection, Pennsylvania Historical Society, Philadelphia. On southern evangelicals and slavery in the Revolutionary era, see Essig, *The Bonds of Wickedness*; Donald G. Mathews, *Slavery and Methodism: A Chapter in American Morality, 1780–1845* (Princeton: Princeton Univ. Press, 1965); W. Harrison Daniel, "Virginia Baptists and the Negro in the Early Republic," *Virginia Magazine of History and Biography* 80 (1972): 60–69; Mechal Sobel, *Trablin' On: The Slave Journey to an Afro-Baptist Faith* (Westport, Conn.: Greenwood Press, 1979); David Brion Davis, *The Problem of Slavery in the Age of the Revolution* (Ithaca: Cornell Univ. Press, 1975).

80. Marshall, *History of Kentucky* 2: 247; Coward, *Kentucky in the New Republic,* 118–21. See also *Stewart's Kentucky Herald,* 10 Apr. 1798; "An Independent Elector," *Kentucky Gazette,* 2 May 1799; "A Voter," *Stewart's Kentucky Her-*

ald, 17 Apr. 1798; "Scaevola," *Kentucky Gazette,* 25 Apr. 1798; "Cassius," *Kentucky Gazette,* 2 May 1798. Aron considers the abolition of slavery to be a "possibility lost," as though emancipation stood a realistic chance of succeeding. The tide against slavery had already turned back in much of the rest of the country by this time, however, and in Kentucky election results indicate that the persistent debate owed more to a small core of dedicated agitators than it did to widespread support. See Aron, *How the West Was Lost.*

81. "Scaevola," *Kentucky Gazette,* 12 Feb. 1799; "A Slave Holder," *Kentucky Gazette,* 7 Mar. 1799; "The Bag," *Kentucky Gazette,* 18 Apr. 1799; "An Independent Elector," *Kentucky Gazette,* 2 May 1799; "A Voter who does not wish to be a Committee Man," *Stewart's Kentucky Herald,* 12 Mar. 1799.

82. *Kentucky Gazette,* 4 Apr. 1799.

83. John Breckinridge to Isaac Shelby, 16 Mar. 1798, Breckinridge Family Papers; "A Friend to Order," *Stewart's Kentucky Herald,* 1 May 1798.

84. "An Independent Elector," "The Bag," and "A Layman," *Kentucky Gazette,* 18 Apr. 1799.

85. Coward, *Kentucky in the New Republic,* 121–23. Letter from David Meade, 4 Sept. 1799, Webb-Prentice Family Papers. See also Purviance, *Biography of Elder David Purviance,* 39; and "The Woodford Voter, No. 2," 6 Apr. 1800, Breckinridge Family Papers. The public's rejection of emancipation but support for champions of the people is nowhere more evident than in the electoral results for emancipationists William Garrard and David Purviance, both of whom were rejected as delegates to the constitutional convention yet won election to the legislature later that spring.

86. Coward, *Kentucky in the New Republic,* 123–36.

87. Ibid., 140–60.

Chapter 6. Western Settlement and National Policy

1. John Bradford deposition, Harry Innes Papers, Codex 208, Durrett Coll., 45. Apprehension about a stronger national government prompted eleven of the fourteen Kentucky delegates to Virginia's ratifying convention to vote against the Constitution. Watlington, *Partisan Spirit,* 147–56.

2. Francis Paul Prucha, *The Sword of the Republic: The United States Army on the Frontier, 1783–1846* (Lincoln: Univ. of Nebraska Press, 1969), 1–6; Tanner, *Atlas of Great Lakes Indian History,* 71–73 and 84–86; Reginald Horsman, *The Frontier in the Formative Years* (New York: Holt, Rinehart, and Winston, 1970), 32–40; Dowd, *A Spirited Resistance.*

3. Benjamin Logan to Patrick Henry, 19 Apr. 1786, *Calendar of Virginia State Papers* 4: 120 (quotation); Levi Todd to Edmund Randolph, 14 Feb. 1787, *Calendar of Virginia State Papers* 4: 237 (quotation); Levi Todd to Edmund Randolph, 30 Apr. 1787, *Calendar of Virginia State Papers* 4: 277; Levi Todd and James Garrard to Edmund Randolph, 29 Mar. 1788, *Calendar of Virginia State Papers* 4: 419 (quotation); Levi Todd to Patrick Henry, 22 June 1786, *Calendar of Virginia State Papers* 4: 151. See also Thurman B. Rice, "The Shanks (Skaggs, Skeggs, Scraggs) Family Massacre," *RKHS* 49 (1951): 83–92.

4. Levi Todd to Edmund Randolph, 30 Apr. 1787, *Calendar of Virginia State*

Papers 4: 277; Harry Innes to John Brown, 7 Dec. 1787, Harry Innes Papers, Library of Congress. See also Harry Innes to John Brown, 20 Feb. 1788, Harry Innes Papers.

5. Harry Innes to Edmund Randolph, 21 July 1787, *Calendar of Virginia State Papers* 4: 322 (quotation); John Brown to John Breckinridge, 20 May 1786, Breckinridge Family Papers; *American State Papers: Legislative and Executive, of the Congress of the United States, from the First Session of the First to the Third Session of the Thirteenth Congress, Inclusive,* 2 vols. (Washington, D.C.: Gales and Seaton, 1832), vol. 1: 84–96. See also Harry Innes to John Brown, 7 Dec. 1787 and 4 Apr. 1788, Harry Innes Papers, Library of Congress. Two years later, Innes wrote Secretary of War Henry Knox a detailed history of the Indian wars, relating a "general disgust towards Government": Harry Innes to Henry Knox, 7 July 1790, Harry Innes Papers. See also Mann Butler, *A History of the Commonwealth of Kentucky* (Louisville: Wilcox, Dickerman, 1834), 144–45.

6. Prucha, *Sword of the Republic,* 25–27. See also Gerald Clarfield, "Protecting the Frontiers: Defense Policy and the Tariff Question in the First Washington Administration," *William and Mary Quarterly,* 3d ser., vol. 32 (1975): 443–64. Part of the ambivalence involved long-standing suspicion toward standing armies in peacetime. See Elkins and McKitrick, *The Age of Federalism,* 594.

7. William H. Denny, ed., "Military Journal of Major Ebenezer Denny, an Officer in the Revolutionary and Indian Wars. With an Introductory Memoir," entry dated 31 Oct. 1792, in *Memoirs of the Historical Society of Pennsylvania,* vol. 7 (Philadelphia: J. B. Lippincott for the Historical Society of Pennsylvania, 1860), 366.

8. Prucha, *Sword of the Republic,* 20–21.

9. Horsman, *The Frontier in the Formative Years,* 40; Prucha, *Sword of the Republic,* 22–27; Harry M. Ward, *Charles Scott and the Spirit of '76* (Charlottesville: Univ. Press of Virginia, 1988), 115–17.

10. Prucha, *Sword of the Republic,* 27–28; Paul David Nelson, *Anthony Wayne, Soldier of the Early Republic* (Bloomington: Indiana Univ. Press, 1985).

11. Ward, *Charles Scott,* 131–34; Hubbard Taylor to James Madison, 13 Jan. 1794, *Papers of James Madison* 15: 181; Isaac Shelby to Henry Knox, 10 Jan. 1794, Filson Club Historical Society. See also Harry Innes to Edmund Randolph, 21 July 1787, in *The Voice of the Frontier: John Bradford's Notes on Kentucky,* ed. Thomas D. Clark (Lexington: Univ. Press of Kentucky, 1993), 89–90.

12. Prucha, *Sword of the Republic,* 36–37; Ward, *Charles Scott,* 139–47; Reginald Horsman, "The British Indian Department and the Resistance to General Anthony Wayne, 1793–1795," *Mississippi Valley Historical Review,* 49 (1962): 269–90; Nelson, *Anthony Wayne,* 269–83; Richard C. Knopf, ed., *Anthony Wayne, a Name in Arms: Soldier, Diplomat, Defender of Expansion Westward of a Nation* (Pittsburgh: Univ. of Pittsburgh Press, 1960).

13. George Nicholas to James Madison, 6 Nov. 1795, *Papers of James Madison* 16: 118.

14. Harry Innes to John Brown, 7 Dec. 1787, Innes Papers.

15. Hubbard Taylor to James Madison, 23 May 1793, *Papers of James Madison* 15: 20–21. See also James Davis to Zachariah Johnston, 4 May 1790, Zachariah Johnston Papers.

16. Slaughter, *The Whiskey Rebellion*, 40–43.
17. Ibid., 54–55; Watlington, *Partisan Spirit*, 120–22 and 139–48.
18. *Kentucky Gazette*, 24 Aug. 1793; John Nicholas to John Breckinridge, 15 July 1794, Breckinridge Family Papers; "The Democratic-Republican Societies of 1793 and 1794 in Kentucky, Pennsylvania, and Virginia," *William and Mary Quarterly*, 2d ser., vol. 2 (1922): 251, 253; Lowell H. Harrison, *John Breckinridge, Jeffersonian Republican*, Filson Club Publications, 2d ser., no. 2 (Louisville: Standard Printing, 1969): 54–55. See also the depositions by Bradford and other members in the Harry Innes Papers, Codex 208, Durrett Collection.
19. Marshall, *History of Kentucky* 2: 95–96 and 91; John Bradford deposition, Harry Innes vs. Humphrey Marshall Papers, Codex 206, Reuben T. Durrett Collection, Department of Special Collections, Univ. of Chicago Library, 206.
20. "Jefferson's Minute of Conversation with Genet," *Selections from the Draper Collection in the Possession of the State Historical Society of Wisconsin, to Elucidate the Proposed French Expedition under George Rogers Clark against Louisiana, in the years 1793–94*. American Historical Society Publication (Washington, D.C.: Government Printing Office, 1897), 983–85; Genet to [French] minister, 25 July 1793, ibid., 987–88. Clark's proposal, dated 5 Feb. 1793, was written to Genet's predecessor. Clark felt unappreciated by the American government after the war. See also Richard Lowitt, "Activities of Citizen Genet in Kentucky, 1793–1794," *FCHQ* 22 (1948): 252–67.
21. "André Michaux's Travels into Kentucky, 1793–1794," in *Early Western Travels, 1748-1846*, 32 vols., ed. Reuben Gold Thwaites (Cleveland: Arthur H. Clark, 1904), vol. 3: 39–45; George Nicholas to James Madison, 15 Nov. 1793, *Papers of James Madison* 15: 137; *American Historical Association Report for 1896*, 1007–9; Stuart Seely Sprague, "Kentucky and the Navigation of the Mississippi: The Climatic Years, 1793–1795," *RKHS* 71 (1973): 369–70.
22. George Nicholas to James Madison, 15 Nov. 1793, *Papers of James Madison* 15: 137; "André Michaux's Travels into Kentucky, 1793–1794," 44.
23. *Kentucky Gazette*, 16 Nov. 1793. See also "André Michaux's Travels into Kentucky, 1793–1794," 44.
24. *Acts Passed at the First Session of the Second General Assembly* (Lexington: John Bradford, 1793), 54. See also Hubbard Taylor to James Madison, 13 Jan. 1794, *Papers of James Madison* 15: 180–81.
25. Thomas Jefferson to Isaac Shelby, 29 Aug. 1793, *American State Papers, Documents, Legislative and Executive of the Congress of the United States, from the First Session of the First to the Third Session of the Thirteenth Congress, Inclusive: Commencing March 3, 1789, and ending March 3, 1815*, vol. 1: 455 (hereafter cited as *American State Papers: Foreign Relations*).
26. Isaac Shelby to Thomas Jefferson, 5 Oct. 1793, Letters from State Governors, Department of State series, Record Group 59, National Archives (printed in the *Kentucky Gazette*, 19 July 1794).
27. Thomas Jefferson to Isaac Shelby, 6 Nov. 1793, *American State Papers: Foreign Relations* 1: 455; Henry Knox to Isaac Shelby, 9 Nov. 1793, *American State Papers: Foreign Relations* 1: 458. The governor of the Northwest Territory, Arthur St. Clair, also received an alert. See Henry Knox to Arthur St. Clair, 9 Nov. 1793, *American State Papers: Foreign Relations* 1: 458.

28. Anthony Wayne to Isaac Shelby, 6 Jan. 1794, quoted in James Hall, *Sketches of History, Life and Manners in the West,* 2 vols. (Philadelphia: Harrison Hall, 1835), vol. 2: 38; Isaac Shelby to Charles DePauw, 28 Nov. 1793, George Rogers Clark Papers, Draper Coll., 11J199.

29. Benjamin Logan to George Rogers Clark, 31 Dec. 1793, *Amer. Hist. Assoc. Report for 1896,* 1026; Cincinnati, *Centinel of the North-Western Territory,* 25 Jan. 1794; "Extract of a letter from Constant Freeman, Agent for the Department of War, in Georgia, to the Secretary of War," 18 Apr. 1794, *American State Papers: Foreign Relations* 1: 459–60. See also George Nicholas to James Madison, 9 Feb. 1794, *Papers of James Madison* 15: 255.

30. "Report of Committee Relative to Address by La Chaise, No. 2," Harry Innes Papers; letter from Baron de Cardonelet to Duke de la Alcudia, *Selections from the Draper Collection,* 1051–56.; George Rogers Clark Papers, Draper Coll., 55J21; John Bradford letter, George Rogers Clark Papers, Draper Coll., 11J209; John Bradford deposition, Innes vs. Marshall Papers, Codex 206, Durrett Coll., 103 and 206 (quotation). For Bradford's pledge to support an expedition see "Clark's Claims," in *Selections from the Draper Collection,* 1074. Certainly the national government in Philadelphia perceived a connection. See John Brown to Harry Innes, 31 Dec. 1793, Harry Innes Papers. The statement from Nicholas to James Madison is dated 9 Feb. 1794, *Papers of James Madison* 15: 255. See also Nicholas's earlier comments dated 15 Nov. 1793, *Papers of James Madison* 15: 135–37.

31. Isaac Shelby to Thomas Jefferson, 13 Jan. 1794, *American State Papers: Foreign Relations* 1: 455–56.

32. Edmund Randolph to Isaac Shelby, 29 Mar. 1794, *American State Papers: Foreign Relations* 1: 456–57; Knox to Wayne, 31 Mar. 1794, *American State Papers: Foreign Relations* 1: 458–59; J. W. Cooke, "Governor Shelby and Genet's Agents," *FCHQ* 37 (1963): 162–70; Harold C. Styrett, ed., *The Papers of Alexander Hamilton* (New York: Columbia Univ. Press, 1972), vol. 16: 136–37; Hubbard Taylor to James Madison, 10 Mar. 1794, *Papers of James Madison* 15: 277. See also Arthur Preston Whitaker, "Harry Innes and the Spanish Intrigue, 1794–1795," *Miss. Valley Hist. Rev.* 15 (1928): 236–48.

33. Anthony Wayne to Henry Knox, 11 June 1794, quoted in Styrett, *Papers of Alexander Hamilton* 16: 589.

34. *Kentucky Gazette,* 31 May 1794; Address protesting Jay's appointment as minister to Great Britain, dated 29 May 1794, Breckinridge Family Papers. Several weeks later the Bourbon County Democratic Society held a similar rally in Paris and unanimously endorsed the resolutions adopted in Lexington on May 24. *Kentucky Gazette,* 12 July 1794.

35. John Smith to John Preston, 27 June 1794, Preston Family Papers, Virginia Historical Society. See also George Nicholas to James Madison, 15 Nov. 1793, *Papers of James Madison* 15: 137, and Hubbard Taylor to James Madison, 13 Jan. 1794, *Papers of James Madison* 15: 181.

36. Sprague, "Kentucky and the Navigation of the Mississippi," 384–86.

37. John Breckinridge to Samuel Hopkins, 15 Sept. 1794, Breckinridge Family Papers; Harrison, *John Breckinridge, Jeffersonian Republican,* 57. See also E. Merton Coulter, "Efforts of the Democratic Societies of the West to Open the Navigation of the Mississippi," *Miss. Valley Hist. Rev.* 11 (1925): 387.

38. Edmund Randolph to Thomas Jefferson, 28 Aug. 1794, quoted in Sprague, "Kentucky and the Navigation of the Mississippi," 386. The envoy was James Innes, the brother of Harry Innes, a prominent anti-Federalist and a respected judge on the U.S. district court in Kentucky.

39. Francis Preston to William Preston, 20 Oct. 1795, Preston Family Papers, Davie Collection, Filson Club Historical Society. The responses to Marshall consumed several issues of the *Kentucky Gazette*. See the issues for 26 Sept. 1795, 3 Oct. 1795, 10 Oct. 1795, 17 Oct. 1795, 24 Oct. 1794, and 7 Nov. 1795. Western citizens distrusted Jay for his earlier willingness to sacrifice American rights to the Mississippi and Britain for its alliance with the Ohio Indians.

40. Isaac Shelby deposition, Innes vs. Marshall Papers, Codex 206, Durrett Coll., 130. See also *Kentucky Gazette*, 7 Feb. 1797.

41. Robert Johnson to Benjamin Johnson, 18 Jan. 1792, Barbour Family Papers, Manuscript Division, Univ. of Virginia; George Nicholas to James Madison, 20 June 1791, *Papers of James Madison* 14: 33–34. See also George Nicholas to James Madison, 16 Sept. 1791, *Papers of James Madison* 14: 75; "Address to the Public," *Kentucky Gazette*, 10 Aug. 1793. Several historians have also noted this connection: Jacob E. Cooke, "The Whiskey Insurrection: A Re-evaluation," *Pennsylvania History* 30 (1963): 316–46; James Roger Sharp, "The Whiskey Rebellion and the Question of Representation," in *The Whiskey Rebellion: Past and Present Perspectives,* ed. Stephen R. Boyd (Westport, Conn.: Greenwood Press, 1985), 131 n. 7.

42. Thomas Marshall to Edward Carrington, 8 Mar. 1792, Whiskey Rebellion Papers, Records of the Internal Revenue Service, Record Group 58, National Archives. See also Mary K. Bonsteel Tachau, "A New Look at the Whiskey Rebellion," in *The Whiskey Rebellion,* ed. Boyd, 101.

43. George Nicholas to Thomas Marshall, 25 Aug. 1793, Whiskey Rebellion Papers; William Clarke to Tench Coxe, 11 May 1797, Tench Coxe Papers, Historical Society of Pennsylvania, Philadelphia; Thomas Marshall to Edward Carrington, 20 Mar. 1794, Whiskey Rebellion Papers; *Kentucky Gazette,* 22 Feb. 1794. In 1796, Laban Shipp would be appointed as a justice of the peace for Bourbon County.

44. Harry Innes to Col. Wilson C. Nicholas, 10 June 1807, Innes Papers, Codex 208, Durrett Coll., 17. (See also p. 15 of this letter.) "A Reader," *Kentucky Gazette,* 26 Sept. 1795.

45. Innes vs. Marshall Papers, Codex 206, Durrett Coll., 106, 128, 143, 206–7; Marshall, *History of Kentucky* 2: 124; Harry Innes to Col. Wilson C. Nicholas, 10 June 1807, Innes Papers, Codex 208, Durrett Coll., 18; William Irvine deposition, Madison County, 15 Oct. 1801, Innes Papers, Codex 208, Durrett Coll., 36; Mary K. Bonsteel Tachau, *Federal Courts in the Early Republic: Kentucky, 1789–1816* (Princeton: Princeton Univ. Press, 1978), 45.

46. Tachau, "A New Look," 110. Edmund Randolph to George Washington, 11 Mar. 1794, in Styrett, *Papers of Alexander Hamilton* 16: 140.

47. Tachau, "A New Look," 102.

48. Tachau, *Federal Courts in the Early Republic,* 49–51.

49. The distillers also proposed a legal test of the excise, with the promise to

conform to the court's judgment. "A Citizen," *Stewart's Kentucky Herald,* 23 May 1797; Tench Coxe to Thomas Marshall, 30 June 1796, in *Stewart's Kentucky Herald,* 23 May 1797.

50. "A Citizen," *Stewart's Kentucky Herald,* 2 May 1797 and 23 May 1797.

51. *Stewart's Kentucky Herald,* 7 Feb. 1797.

52. Thomas Marshall to Edward Carrington, 8 Mar. 1792, Whiskey Rebellion Papers; George Nicholas to Thomas Marshall, 25 Aug. 1793, Whiskey Rebellion Papers. See also John Bradford deposition, Innes Papers, Codex 208, Durrett Coll., 45.

53. "Extract of a Letter from Kentucky Dated Lexington, Jan. 25, 1794," enclosed in E. Randolph to George Washington, 27 Feb. 1794, Misc. Letters, Department of State, M-179, reel 11, General Records of the Department of State, Record Group 59, National Archives; Thomas Marshall to Tench Coxe, 24 Mar. 1794, Whiskey Rebellion Papers.

54. James Morrison deposition, Innes vs. Marshall Papers, Codex 206, Durrett Coll., 139. Innes's use of legal procedures to protect distillers is described in Oliver Wolcott to Harry Innes, 25 Feb. 1800, Harry Innes Papers, Library of Congress.

55. William M. Bledsoe deposition, 30 Oct. 1808, Innes Papers, Codex 208, Durrett Coll., 47.

56. Thomas Marshall to Tench Coxe, 24 Mar. 1794, Whiskey Rebellion Papers.

57. U.S. Court for the District of Kentucky, Order Book A (microfilm), Special Collections, Univ. of Kentucky, entries dated 21 Dec. 1796 and 21 Mar. 1797, 146–47.

58. *Kentucky Gazette,* 7 Mar. 1798; Tachau, *Federal Courts in the Early Republic,* 108–11.

59. Tachau, "A New Look," 104–5; Tachau, *Federal Courts in the Early Republic,* 111–13.

60. Tachau, *Federal Courts in the Early Republic,* 114–15.

61. Morrison vs. Clarke, U.S. Court for the District of Kentucky, Order Book B (microfilm), Special Collections, Univ. of Kentucky, 113.

62. Tachau, *Federal Courts in the Early Republic,* 113.

63. Writ #331, 14 July 1800, Matthew Hemphill; Samuel Morgan; Writ #353, 14 July 1800, Alexander Robinson; Writ #350, 14 July 1800, James Mitchell; Writ #395, 19 July 1800, James Twineham, all in Miscellaneous Manuscripts: Kentucky, National Archives and Records Center–Great Lakes Region (Chicago).

64. Jillson, *Early Kentucky Distillers,* 44–49.

65. "To the Printer of the Kentucky Herald," *Stewart's Kentucky Herald,* 7 Feb. 1797; Thomas Marshall to Edward Carrington, 20 Mar. 1794, Record Group 58, National Archives; "A Citizen," *Stewart's Kentucky Herald,* 23 May 1797.

66. Tench Coxe to John Brown, 30 Mar. 1797, published in *Stewart's Kentucky Herald,* 23 May 1797; "A Citizen," *Stewart's Kentucky Herald,* 2 May 1797. See also Marshall, *History of Kentucky* 2: 124.

Chapter 7. Spiritual Conditions on the Eve of Revival

1. Curtis D. Johnson, "Supply-Side and Demand-Side Revivalism? Evaluating the Social Influences on New York State Evangelism in the 1830s," *Social Science History* 19 (1995): 1–30; Roger Finke and Rodney Stark, *The Churching of*

America, 1776–1990: Winners and Losers in Our Religious Economy (New Brunswick: Rutgers Univ. Press, 1992). See also Timothy Smith, *Revivalism and Social Reform: American Protestantism on the Eve of the Civil War* (New York: Harper and Row, 1965); Richard Carwardine, *Trans-Atlantic Revivalism: Popular Evangelicalism in Britain and America, 1790–1865* (Westport, Conn.: Greenwood Press, 1978); Terry Bilhartz, *Urban Religion and the Second Great Awakening: Church and Society in Early National Baltimore* (Rutherford, N.J.: Fairleigh Dickinson Univ. Press, 1986).

2. Beckner, "Shane's Interview with Allen," 91 and 97; Samuel Treble interview, Draper Coll., 12CC43; William Warren Sweet, *Religion on the American Frontier*, vol. 2: *The Presbyterians, 1763–1840: A Collection of Source Materials* (New York: Harper, 1936), 705 (hereafter cited as *The Presbyterians*); Bedford, *Land of Our Fathers* 1: 332–33; Rogers, *Autobiography of Elder Samuel Rogers*, 14; Mrs. John Arnold interview, Draper Coll., 11CC241.

3. Robert Hamilton Bishop, "The Memoirs of David Rice," in *An Outline of the History of the Church in the State of Kentucky during a Period of Forty Years; Containing the Memoirs of Rev. David Rice, and Sketches of the Origin and Present State of Particular Churches . . .* (Lexington: Thomas Skillman, 1824), 68.

4. William Hickman, "A Short Account of My Life and Travels for more than Fifty Years; a Professed Servant of Jesus Christ, To which is added a Narrative of the rise and progress of religion in the early settlement of Kentucky, giving an account of the difficulties we had to encounter" (typescript), Reuben T. Durrett Collection, Department of Special Collections, Univ. of Chicago Library, 59.

5. Daniel Stranham interview, Draper Coll., 12CC246. See also John Hinkston Jr. statement, Draper's Notes, Draper Coll., 2S338; Robert Jones interview, Draper Coll., 13CC152; Samuel Shepard, "Extracts from the Journal of Samuel Shepard, April 10, 1787–December 3, 1796" (Cambridge: Massachusetts Institute of Technology Microreproduction Laboratory, 1967), 21. Shepard had to ride six miles to attend worship in 1788.

6. "An Act declaring what shall be a lawful marriage," in Hening, *Statutes at Large* 10: 361–63; Dorman, *Petitions from Kentucky to the Virginia Legislature*, 257–58.

7. James Wade interview, Draper Coll., 12CC22; Eslinger, "The Great Revival in Bourbon County," 57–59.

8. John Opie, "The Melancholy Career of 'Father' David Rice," *Journal of Presbyterian History* 47 (1969): 295–319. See the pastoral arrangement between Little Mountain and Springfield congregations, Clark County, and Rev. Joseph P. Howe, dated 4 Oct. 1794, in Sweet, *The Presbyterians*, 703–4.

9. Davidson, *Presbyterian Church in the State of Kentucky*, 103; Drake, *Pioneer Life*, 193.

10. Ben Snelling interview, Draper Coll., 12CC110–11; James Stevenson interview, Draper Coll., 11CC250; Bishop, "Memoirs of David Rice," 69.

11. Presbyterian Church, "Transylvania Presbytery Minutes, 1786–1860," microfilm (Lexington: Univ. of Kentucky Photographic Service, 1952), entries dated 6 Oct. 1790 and 24 Apr. 1794, 46–47 and 113–15 (an extensive but edited version can

also be found in Sweet, "Minutes of the Transylvania Presbytery," *The Presbyterians*); William Warren Sweet, "Minutes of the Elkhorn Baptist Association," *Religion on the American Frontier,* vol. 1: *The Baptists, 1783–1830: A Collection of Source Materials* (New York: Henry Holt, 1931), 438, 463–64 (hereafter cited as *The Baptists*).

12. Toulmin, *Western Country in 1793,* 91–94; Peter Cartwright, *The Autobiography of Peter Cartwright* (New York: Abingdon Press, 1956), 33. County figures were compiled from court order books available on microfilm at the Kentucky Historical Society.

13. J. H. Spencer, *A History of Kentucky Baptists from 1769 to 1885, Including More than Eight Hundred Biographical Sketches,* 2 vols. (Cincinnati: J. R. Baumes, 1885), vol. 2: 7–9, 44–45, 80–81, 88–90, 96–97, and 105–6.

14. Ibid., 48; Sweet, "Minutes of the Elkhorn Association," *The Baptists,* 476 and 421, 426, 427, and 430

15. Spencer, *A History of Kentucky Baptists* 2: 48; Sweet, "Minutes of the Elkhorn Association," *The Baptists,* 419, 421, 430, 436, 439, and 454.

16. Sweet, "Minutes of the Transylvania Presbytery, 1786–1837," *The Presbyterians,* 134–81.

17. *Minutes of the Annual Conferences of the Methodist Episcopal Church, 1773–1851,* 4 vols. (New York: T. Mason and G. Lane, 1840), vol. 1: 89–95.

18. Elijah Poage to Archibald Woods, 23 June 1798, Archibald Woods Papers, Swem Library, College of William and Mary. See also James Poage to Archibald Woods, 28 July 1792, Archibald Woods Papers.

19. James Smith, "Tours into Kentucky and the Northwest Territory: Three Journals by the Rev. James Smith of Powhatan County, Virginia, 1783–1798–1799," *Ohio Archaeological and Historical Publications* 16 (1907): 374.

20. Rev. David Barrow journal, Draper Coll., 12CC180; Robert Stuart, "Reminiscences, Respecting the Establishment and Progress of the Presbyterian Church in Kentucky," *Journal of the Presbyterian Historical Society* 23 (1945): 166; James Gallagher, *The Western Sketch Book* (Boston: Crocker and Brewster, 1850), 32–33. See also Boles, *The Great Revival;* and Neils H. Sonne, *Liberal Kentucky, 1780–1825* (New York: Columbia Univ. Press, 1939).

21. Semple, *A History of the Rise and Progress of the Baptists in Virginia,* 35–36.

22. James Smith, ed., *The Posthumous Works of the Reverend and Pious James M'Gready, Late Minister of the Gospel, in Henderson, Kentucky,* 2 vols. (Louisville: W. W. Worsley, 1831), vol. 1: 165.

23. Young, ed., *Baptists on the American Frontier,* 163.

24. Francis Asbury, 25 Apr. 1796, in Elmer T. Clark, ed., *Journal and Letters of Francis Asbury,* 3 vols. (Nashville: Abingdon Press, 1958), vol. 2: 83. See also the entry dated 26 Mar. 1797, in *Asbury,* 125.

25. Spencer, *A History of Kentucky Baptists* 2: 49, 67, 83, and 85; Lewis Garrett, *Recollections of the West* (Nashville: Western Methodist Office, 1834), 11.

26. David Rice to Ashbel Green, 4 Mar. 1796, Gratz Collection, Historical Society of Pennsylvania, quoted in Boles, *The Great Revival,* 18.

27. John Lyle, "A Narrative of John Lyle's Mission in the Bounds of Cumberland Presbytery," Lyle Family Papers, Special Collections and Archives Service Center, Univ. of Kentucky.

28. "Transylvania Presbytery Minutes" (microfilm), entry for 6 Oct. 1789, 27.

29. Toulmin, *Western Country in 1793*, 70.

30. Richard M'Nemar, *The Kentucky Revival, or A Short History of the Late Extraordinary Outpouring of the Spirit of God in the Western States of America* (rpt., New York: Edward O. Jenkins, 1846), 9.

31. David A. Johnson, "Beginnings of Universalism in Louisville," *FCHQ* 43 (1969): 173–75.

32. Harry Toulmin, a British emigrant and disciple of Joseph Priestly, was president of Transylvania Seminary from 1794 to 1796. After serving as Kentucky secretary of state, Toulmin was for many years a superior court judge for the Eastern Mississippi Territory (Alabama). Johnson and Malone, *Dictionary of American Biography* 18: 601–2.

33. Spencer, *A History of Kentucky Baptists* 1: 132.

34. Elkhorn Association minutes for 1804 show the expulsion of twelve members at Indian Creek, two at Union, and two at Flat Lick. All of Cooper's Run remained expelled, except for a small number of black members. Green Creek was investigated but not disciplined. Sweet, "Minutes of the Elkhorn Association," *The Baptists*, 495, 499–501, and 503–4.

35. Davidson, *Presbyterian Church in the State of Kentucky*, 94–98.

36. James Poage to Archibald Woods, 6 July 1793, Archibald Woods Papers; Andrew McClelland Jr. to Rev. James Welch, 3 July 1792, in Sweet, *The Presbyterians*, 717. See also Robert McAfee, "The History of the Rise and Progress of the First Settlements on Salt River, and Establishment of the New Providence Church," Draper Coll., 14CC136.

37. Davidson, *Presbyterian Church in the State of Kentucky*, 97; Ernest Trice Thompson, *Presbyterians in the South*, vol. 1: *1607–1861*, 3 vols. (Richmond: John Knox Press, 1963) 218–19; McAfee, "History," Draper Coll., 14CC102. Rankin remained in Lexington, leading his small band of devout followers into the ultra-conservative Associate Reformed Presbyterian Church. The psalmody issue caused division elsewhere as well. See, e.g., Joseph Smith, *Old Redstone, or Historical Sketches of Western Presbyterianism, Its Early Ministers, Its Perilous Times, and Its First Records* (Philadelphia: Lippincott, Grambo, 1854), 290–96.

38. Benjamin Snelling interview, 12CC111–12; W. P. Strickland, ed., *Sketches of Western Methodism: Biographical, Historical, and Miscellaneous, Illustrative of Pioneer Life. By Rev. James B. Finley* (Cincinnati: Methodist Book Concern, 1855), 70; Garrett, *Recollections of the West*, 18.

39. Sweet, "Minutes of the Elkhorn Association," *The Baptists*, 444–46, 500.

40. Sweet, "Minutes of the Transylvania Presbytery," *The Presbyterians*, 149, 154, 173, and 182.

41. Martzolff, "Reminiscences of a Pioneer [Thomas Rogers]," 196.

42. Sweet, "Minutes of the Transylvania Presbytery," *The Presbyterians*, 149–50.

43. Ibid., 153–61; Eslinger, "Some Notes on the History of Cane Ridge prior to the Great Revival."

44. "A Very Short Sketch of the State of Religion in the Several Quarters of the World," in *The Baptist Annual Register for 1794, 1795, 1796–97, including sketches of the state of Religion among Different Denominations of Good Men at Home and Abroad*, ed. John Rippon (London: 1791), 201.

45. Winthrop D. Jordan, *White over Black: American Attitudes toward the Negro, 1550–1812* (Baltimore: Pelican Books, 1969), 281–93; Davis, *The Problem of Slavery in the Age of the Revolution*; Wood, *Creation of the American Republic*.

46. Daniel, "Virginia Baptists and the Negro in the Early Republic," 60–69; Essig, *Bonds of Wickedness*, 26–51; Isaac, *Transformation of Virginia*, 161–67.

47. Virginia Baptist General Committee, 1789, quoted in Spencer, *A History of Kentucky Baptists* 1: 183. Daniel, "Virginia Baptists and the Negro," 65–67.

48. "Minutes of the General Conferences of the Methodist Episcopal Church," quoted in A. H. Redford, *A History of Methodists in Kentucky*, 2 vols. (Nashville: Southern Methodist Publishing House, 1868), vol. 1: 254–55.

49. Carlos R. Allen Jr., ed., "David Barrow's Circular Letter of 1798," *William and Mary Quarterly*, 3d ser., vol. 20 (1963): 44 n; David Barrow, *Involuntary, Unmerited, Perpetual, Absolute, Hereditary Slavery, Examined on the Principles of Nature, Reason, Justice, Policy, and Scripture* (Lexington: D. and C. Bradford, 1808), 22; David T. Bailey, *Shadow on the Church: Southwestern Evangelical Religion and the Issues of Slavery, 1783–1860* (Ithaca: Cornell Univ. Press, 1985); Essig, *Bonds of Wickedness*, 74–75.

50. Mathews, *Slavery and Methodism*, 10–19.

51. *Records of the Presbyterian Church in the United States of America, Embracing the Minutes of the General Assembly and General Synod, 1707–1788* (New York: Presbyterian Board of Publication, 1904), 540.

52. Virginia Baptist General Committee, quoted in Spencer, *A History of Kentucky Baptists* 1: 184.

53. Fred J. Hood, "The Restoration of Community: The Great Revival in Four Baptist Churches in Central Kentucky," *Baptist Quarterly Review* 39 (1978): 75–77; Ellen Eslinger, "The Beginnings of Afro-American Christianity among Kentucky Baptists," in *"The Buzzel about Kentucky": Interpretations of the Promised Land, 1750–1830*, ed. Craig Thompson Friend (Lexington: Univ. Press of Kentucky, forthcoming). As might be expected, a similar trend is discernible for Virginia Baptists. See Janet Moore Lindman, "A World of Baptists: Gender, Race, and Religious Community in Pennsylvania and Virginia, 1689–1825" (Ph.D. diss., Univ. of Minnesota, 1994).

54. "Minutes of Elkhorn Association at Cooper's Run," 27 Aug. 1791, Southern Baptist Theological Seminary, Louisville.

55. Cooper's Run Baptist Church Minute Book, John Fox Jr., Library, Duncan Tavern, Paris, Ky., entries dated 19 June 1795 and 11 Feb. 1798, 51 and 69.

56. Edna Talbott Whitley, "Footnotes to Local History," *Kentuckian-Citizen* (Paris), 21 June 1957.

57. "Methodist Rules Concerning Slavery," quoted in Mathews, *Slavery and Methodism*, 298–99.

58. Mathews, *Slavery and Methodism*, 10–19.

59. Sweet, "Minutes of the Transylvania Presbytery," *The Presbyterians*, entry for 13 Oct. 1794, 147.

60. "Minutes of the Transylvania Presbytery" (microfilm), entry dated 15 Apr. 1796, 102.

61. Sweet, "Minutes of the Transylvania Presbytery," *The Presbyterians*, 169–70.

62. Presbyterian Church, "West Lexington Presbytery Minutes, 1799–1804" (mi-

crofilm), Special Collections and Archives Service Center, Univ. of Kentucky, entry dated 6 Aug. 1800, 42–43; "Minutes of the Synod of Virginia" (Richmond: Microfilm Publications, n.d.), entry dated 27 Sept. 1800, 54–58.

63. Sweet, "Minutes of the Elkhorn Baptist Association," *The Baptists,* 508; Kentucky Society, Daughters of Colonial Wars, *Kentucky Pioneers and Their Descendants* (Frankfort: Daughters of Colonial Wars, 1951), 257.

64. Quoted in Ezra H. Gillett, *History of the Presbyterian Church,* 2 vols. (Philadelphia: Presbyterian Board of Publications, 1873), vol. 1: 285.

65. David Rice to unknown, 11 Dec. 1799, John D. Shane Collection, Presbyterian Church (U S. A.), Department of History and Records Management Services, Philadelphia. See also Jeffrey Brooke Allen, "Means and Ends in Kentucky Abolitionism, 1792–1823," *FCHQ* 57 (1983): 371–73.

66. Martzoff, "Reminiscences of a Pioneer [Thomas Rogers]," 194; Isaiah W. Irvin, *Biographical Sketches of Elder Isaiah W. Irvin, Together with a Condensed Biography of His Relatives* (Mouton, Iowa: J. B. King, Book and Job Printers, 1872), 2. See also Drake, *Pioneer Life,* 209; and Josiah Espy, "A Tour in Ohio, Kentucky and Indiana Territory in 1805," *Ohio Valley Historical Series, Miscellanies No. 1* (Cincinnati: Robert Clarke, 1870), 63.

67. See, for instance, G. Adolph Koch, *Republican Religion: The American Revolution and the Cult of Reason* (New York: Henry Holt, 1933); H. M. Morais, *Deism in Eighteenth-Century America* (New York: Columbia Univ. Press, 1934); Vernon Stauffer, *New England and the Bavarian Illuminati* (New York: Columbia Univ. Press, 1918); C. R. Keller, *The Second Great Awakening in Connecticut* (New Haven: Yale Univ. Press, 1942).

68. Devereaux Jarratt to John Coleman, 28 Jan. 1796, in Devereaux Jarratt, *The Life of the Reverend Devereaux Jarratt, rector of Bath Parish, Dinwiddie County, Virginia. Written by himself in a series of letters addressed to the Rev. John Coleman, one of the ministers of the Protestant Episcopal Church* (Baltimore: Warner and Hanna, 1806), 128.

69. William Warren Sweet, "Journal of Benjamin Lakin, 1794–1820," in *Religion on the American Frontier, 1783–1840,* vol. 4: *The Methodists: A Collection of Source Materials* (Chicago: Univ. of Chicago Press, 1946), 204–7. Hinkston Circuit lay in northeastern Kentucky, primarily in the counties of Bourbon, Harrison, Montgomery, and Clark.

70. Clark, *Journal and Letters of Francis Asbury* 2: 254.

71. Andrew McClellend Jr. to Rev. James Welch, 3 July 1792, in Sweet, *The Presbyterians,* 717; "Minutes of Transylvania Presbytery" (microfilm), 20 Feb. 1792, 25 Apr. 1794, 9 Oct. 1795 and 8 Oct. 1800, 61–62, 81–82, 120, 127–28, and 258; "West Lexington Presbytery Minutes, 1799–1805," entry dated 4 Oct. 1799, 12.

72. Sweet, "Minutes of the Elkhorn Association," *The Baptists,* 451–52 and 457; Rev. David Barrow journal, Draper Coll., 12CC180; Young, *Baptists on the American Frontier,* 163.

73. "To the Rev. Dr. Rippon, [a letter dated] Bourbon County, January 7, 1802," in Sweet, *The Baptists,* 613.

74. Bishop, "Memoirs of David Rice," 80.

75. Garrett, *Recollections of the West,* 8–10 and 21; Sweet, "Minutes of the Elkhorn

Association," *The Baptists,* 419, 421, 430, 436, 439, and 454; *Minutes of the Annual Conference of the Methodist Episcopal Church* ,vol. 1; Strickland, "Autobiography of Rev. William Burke," *Sketches of Western Methodism,* 73.

76. Boles, *The Great Revival,* 45; Thomas A. Cleland, *Memoirs of the Reverend Thomas Cleland: Compiled from His Private Papers* (Cincinnati: Moore, Wilstash, Key, printers, 1859), 37 (quotation).

77. Davidson, *Presbyterian Church in the State of Kentucky,* 104.

Chapter 8. Spiritual Awakening

1. The pattern of post-frontier revivalism was first noted by Cross, *The Burned-Over District.* See also P. Jeffrey Potash, *Vermont's Burned-Over District: Patterns of Community Development and Religious Activity, 1761–1850* (Brooklyn, N.Y.: Carlson, 1991).

2. Scholars of the Great Revival in Kentucky, and Southern evangelicalism generally, have readily noted the influence of colonial antecedents. See Davidson, *Presbyterian Church in the State of Kentucky*; Thompson, *Presbyterians in the South*; Boles, *The Great Revival*; Eslinger, "The Great Revival in Bourbon County." More recently, Leigh Eric Schmidt has demonstrated a continuity going back to the Scottish Reformation, in *Holy Fairs* (1989), as has Marilyn J. Westerkamp in *Triumph of the Laity: Scots-Irish Piety and the Great Awakening, 1625–1760* (New York: Oxford Univ. Press, 1988). Paul K. Conkin extends Schmidt's insights in *Cane Ridge: America's Pentecost* (1990).

3. Davidson, *Presbyterian Church in the State of Kentucky,* 42–45; Thompson, *Presbyterians in the South* 1: 149–50.

4. Here and elsewhere in the story of early camp meeting revivalism, tantalizing but scattered references point to important Methodist influences. On early Methodism see Russell Richey, *Early American Methodism* (Bloomington: Indiana Univ. Press, 1991); John Henry Wiggar, "Taking Heaven by Storm: Methodism and the Popularization of American Christianity, 1770–1820 (Ph.D. diss., Univ. of Notre Dame, 1994).

5. Smith came from a prominent Presbyterian heritage. His early education had been under his father, a Whitefield convert and a significant Great Awakening evangelist in his own right. After further studies at the College of New Jersey, Smith succeeded his brother as president at Hampden-Sydney, guiding the institution through the difficult wartime and postwar years. In 1783 he secured the institution's incorporation as a college. Charles Grier Sellers Jr., "John Blair Smith," *Journal of the Presbyterian Historical Society* 34 (1956): 201–25.

6. Letter of Robert Smith dated 22 Oct. 1788, in William Henry Foote, *Sketches of Virginia, Historical and Biographical,* 1st series (Philadelphia: William S. Martin, 1850), 422–24. This was John Blair Smith's father.

7. William Hill, quoted in Foote, *Sketches of Virginia,* 424–25.

8. Smith, *Old Redstone,* 359–63; Davidson, *Presbyterian Church in the State of Kentucky,* 132–33. See especially the recent study by John Thomas Scott, "James McGready: Son of Thunder, Father of the Great Revival" (Ph.D. diss., College of William and Mary, 1991).

9. John Rogers, ed., *The Biography of Elder Barton Warren Stone, Written by*

Himself with Additions and Reflections (Cincinnati: J. A. and U. P. James, 1847), 8. See also Conkin, *Cane Ridge*, 53.

10. Smith, *Posthumous Works of James M'Gready* 1: 316–17.

11. Davidson, *Presbyterian Church in the State of Kentucky*, 103–4; Smith, *Old Redstone*, 155–58; James S. Dalton, "The Kentucky Camp Meeting Revivals of 1797–1805 as Rites of Initiation" (Ph.D. diss., Univ. of Chicago, 1973), 17–19; Schmidt, *Holy Fairs*, 70–73.

12. Smith, *Old Redstone*, 155 (quotation); Schmidt, *Holy Fairs*, 95–96; Eslinger, "The Great Revival in Bourbon County," 309; Conkin, *Cane Ridge*, 85.

13. Rogers, *Stone*, 9.

14. Stuart, "Reminiscences," 167; Foote, *Sketches of Virginia*, 428–29; Davidson, *Presbyterian Church in the State of Kentucky*, 104–5. All of these young missionaries were active in the Kentucky revival except Cary Allen, who died in 1795, and William Calhoun and Robert Wilson, who left Kentucky before the revival commenced.

15. Cartwright, *Autobiography*, 30; John Rankin, "Autobiography of John Rankin Sr." (typescript), Durrett Coll., Codex 156, 31.

16. "Narrative of the Commencement and Progress of the Revival of 1800 by the late Rev. James M'Gready in a letter to a friend . . . dated Logan County, Kentucky, October 23, 1801," in Smith, *Posthumous Works of James M'Gready* 1: ix–xi.

17. Rankin, "Autobiography," 33.

18. Smith, *Posthumous Works of James M'Gready* 2: xi.

19. Rankin, "Autobiography," 36.

20. James Ross, *Life and Times of Elder Reuben Ross* (Philadelphia: Grant, Faires, and Rogers, 1882), 233; John McGee to Rev. Thomas L. Douglas, 23 June 1820, *Methodist Magazine* [New York], vol. 4 (1821): 190.

21. Rankin, "Autobiography," 36–37 (quotation); Garrett, *Recollections of the West*, 19. See also McGee to Douglas, *Methodist Magazine*, 189–91. Presbyterian sources are very quiet about the relationship with Methodists during this period, but for an explicit statement of the Methodist contribution see Davidson, *Presbyterian Church in the State of Kentucky*, 136 and 140–41. Conkin also acknowledges a Methodist role, yet perceives greater continuity with the Scottish communions. See Conkin, *Cane Ridge*, 60.

22. James McGready, "A Short Narrative of the Revival of Religion in Logan County, in the State of Kentucky, and the Adjacent Settlements in the State of Tennessee, from May 1797, until Sept. 1800," *Western Missionary Magazine and Repository of Religious Intelligence* 1 (1803): 49 and 52. The details differ slightly in later retellings: Smith, *Posthumous Works of James M'Gready* 1: xiii; Davidson, *Presbyterian Church in the State of Kentucky*, 134–35. See also Conkin, *Cane Ridge*, 60–62. The importance of lay participation in early American revivalism has been elucidated in greatest depth by Westerkamp, *Triumph of the Laity*.

23. McGee to Douglas, *Methodist Magazine*, 190.

24. Smith, *Posthumous Works of James M'Gready* 2: xiii.

25. Ibid., 1: 3.

26. Letter from George A. Baxter dated 1 Jan. 1802, *Connecticut Evangelical Magazine* 2 (Mar. 1802): 355.

27. "To the Rev. Dr. Rippon, Bourbon County, January 7, 1802," in Sweet, *The Baptists*, 613–16. Like the Presbyterian sacramental occasion as well as the Methodist conference, the annual associational meetings of Baptists were special religious events that usually had a more evangelical tone compared with regular Sunday worship. Walter B. Shurden, *Associationalism among Baptists in America: 1707–1814* (New York: Arno Press, 1980), 58–61. One account ascribes the beginnings of the Baptist revival to a "union meeting" with Methodists near Carrollton, but no date is given, nor is this confirmed elsewhere. The informant may have been unaware of developments in the Elkhorn Association. See Rev. John Taylor's account in Young, *Baptists on the American Frontier*, 131–34.

28. Bryant's [Bryan's] Station Church Minute Book (typescript), Kentucky Historical Society; Sweet, "Minutes of the Elkhorn Baptist Association," *The Baptists*, 487–88; "Extract of a Letter from the Rev. Mr. John Evans Findley, of Mason-County, Kentucky," *Methodist Magazine* [London] 26 (Mar. 1803): 126; "Extracts of a Letter from a Gentleman to His Friend at the City of Washington, Dated Lexington, Kentucky, March 8, 1801," in Sweet, *The Baptists*, 609.

29. See, for instance, "A letter from a Gentleman to his Friend, . . . dated Lexington, August 10, 1801," in Sweet, *The Baptists*, 611; "To the Rev. Dr. Rippon, Bourbon County, January 7, 1802" in Sweet, *The Baptists*, 613–16.

30. "Extract 38, of a letter from a gentleman in Kentucky to his friend in Philadelphia, dated June 3, 1801," in William W. Woodward, ed., *Increase of Piety, or The Revival of Religion in the United States of America, Containing Several Interesting Letters Not before Published, Together with Three Remarkable Dreams* (Newburyport, Mass.: Angier March, 1802), 94. These Baptist associations encompassed much the same geographical region as the presbyteries of Transylvania, West Lexington, and Washington.

31. "To the Rev. Dr. Rippon, Bourbon County, January 7, 1802," in Sweet, *The Baptists*, 613–16. See also Spencer, *A History of Kentucky Baptists* 1: 507.

32. Richard Collins quoted in J. N. Bradley, "History of Great Crossings Church, 1785–1877" (pamphlet, n.p., n.d), 4.

33. John Lyle, "Diary of Rev. John Lyle" (typescript), Reuben T. Durrett Collection, Department of Special Collections, Univ. of Chicago, 23–24 and 37; "Extract of a Letter from a Gentleman to His Sister in Philadelphia," in Sweet, *The Baptists*, 610; "To the Rev. Dr. Rippon, Bourbon County, January 7, 1802," in Sweet, *The Baptists*, 615; Spencer, *A History of Kentucky Baptists* 1: 615; Ira Earle Fowler, "Kentucky 150 Years Ago . . . Two Letters Written by Henry Alderson, dated September 10, 1801," *RKHS* 49 (1951): 55. See also Strickland, *Finley*, 363; McGee to Douglas, *Methodist Magazine*, 190; and Boles, *The Great Revival*, 99.

34. Rogers, *Stone*, 8, 25; Sweet, "Minutes of the Transylvania Presbytery," *The Presbyterians*, 180–81.

35. Barton Warren Stone, *History of the Christian Church in the West* (Lexington: College of the Bible, 1956), 1; "Minutes of West Lexington Presbytery," entry dated 15 Oct. 1800, 49.

36. Rogers, *Stone,* 34–35.

37. Ibid., 36. Stone remembered this moment as marking his departure from Calvinism, but he remained a Presbyterian in good standing until 1803.

38. Rogers, *Stone,* 36–37; Purviance, *Biography of Elder David Purviance,* 299.

39. Stone wrote to Rev. John Lyle, and probably other colleagues, describing "the wonderful work carrying on among them." See "Diary of Rev. John Lyle" (typescript), entry dated June 14 1801, 1. Lyle was impressed enough by this report to immediately begin a diary of the revival, the most extensive and immediate account of early camp meeting revivalism now extant. Sections of this work have been published in Cleveland, *The Great Revival in the West,* appendices IV and V.

40. M'Nemar, *Kentucky Revival,* 23–24; B. F. Ells, "The Great Kentucky Revival," *Western Miscellany* 1 (1840–49): 275; "Extract of a letter [dated Sept. 25, 1801] from Colonel Robert Patterson, of Lexington (Ken.) to the Rev. Doctor John King," in William W. Woodward, ed., *Surprising Accounts of the Revival of Religion in the United States of America, in Different Parts of the World, and among Different Denominations of Christians, with a Number of Interesting Occurrences of Divine Providence* (Philadelphia: privately printed, 1802), 34. Stone lived closer to these congregations than did most of the other ministers in Transylvania Presbytery. Also influential in the adoption of the new style of sacramental occasion was Rev. Richard M'Nemar, who had formerly lived in the Cane Ridge neighborhood.

41. "Letter from Patterson," in Woodward, *Surprising Accounts,* 35.

42. Purviance, *Biography of Elder David Purviance,* 299. See also "Extract of a Letter from a gentleman in Kentucky to his brother in Lower Virginia," *Conn. Evang. Mag.* 2 (Apr. 1802): 392.

43. "Letter from Patterson," in Woodward, *Surprising Accounts,* 35.

44. M'Nemar, *Kentucky Revival,* 24. See also Rogers, *Stone,* 37.

45. Strickland, "Autobiography of Rev. William Burke," *Sketches of Western Methodism,* 75. Motivated perhaps by interdenominational rivalry, Burke claimed that this event marked the "first appearance of the revival in the Presbyterian Church."

46. "Diary of Rev. John Lyle" (typescript), 2.

47. "Letter from Findley," *Methodist Magazine,* 126; M'Nemar, *Kentucky Revival,* 25; "Diary of Rev. John Lyle" (typescript), 3. Point Pleasant had been primarily under the care of Rev. Joseph P. Howe for several years. Howe also kept a diary, but entries are very brief: Rev. Joseph P. Howe journal, 4 Oct. 1798–7 Apr. 1816, John D. Shane Collection, Presbyterian Church (USA), Department of History and Records Management Services, Philadelphia.

48. "Letter from Patterson," in Woodward, *Surprising Accounts,* 35. Patterson was a militia officer, and his estimates of the crowds are probably fairly accurate, particularly for the number of communicants, who had to request a lead token in order to participate. His estimates have the added advantage that they include most of the large revival meetings held during 1801, providing good information at least on relative size.

49. Ibid., 35–36.

50. "Diary of Rev. John Lyle" (typescript), 5; "Letter from Patterson," in Woodward, *Surprising Accounts,* 35. Indian Creek was under the care of Rev. William Robertson and Lexington under the care of Rev. James Welch.

51. "Letter from Findley," *Methodist Magazine,* 126–27; M'Nemar, *Kentucky Revival,* 25–26.

52. "Minutes of Transylvania Presbytery" (microfilm), entry dated 4 Oct. 1791, 56; Alexander A. Mitchell, "Cane Ridge" (typescript), Bosworth Memorial Library, Lexington Theological Seminary, Lexington, Ky., 1–2; James R. Rogers, quoted in Edna Talbott Whitley, "Footnotes to Local History," *Kentuckian-Citizen* (Paris), 28 June 1957.

53. Rogers, *Stone,* 37; "Extract of a Letter from a Gentleman to His Sister in Philadelphia," in Sweet, *The Baptists,* 610.

54. "Extract 29, of a letter from a gentleman, to his friend in Baltimore, Bourbon-county, August 7, 1801," in Woodward, *Surprising Accounts,* 56.

55. Rogers, *Stone,* 37; Strickland, *Finley,* 363. For estimates of the size, see the following: Rogers, *Stone,* 37; M'Nemar, *Kentucky Revival,* 26; Rev. John Evans Findley letter dated 20 Sept. 1801, in Woodward, *Surprising Accounts,* 225; "Extract of a Letter from a Gentleman to his Sister in Philadelphia," in Sweet, *The Baptists,* 610; "Extract of a Letter from Colonel Robert Patterson," *Methodist Magazine* 26 (Feb. 1803): 85; Purviance, *Biography of Elder David Purviance,* 300.

56. Purviance, *Biography of Elder David Purviance,* 301.

57. "Letter from Findley," *Methodist Magazine,* 127; Sweet, "Minutes of the Elkhorn Baptist Association," *The Baptists,* 495–96 and 499. Elkhorn Baptist Association would finally exclude Garrard and the entire Cooper's Run congregation in 1803.

58. Robert McAfee interview, Draper Coll., 14CC138.

59. Rogers, *Stone,* 38; letter from George A. Baxter dated 1 Jan. 1802, *Conn. Evang. Mag.,* 356; Strickland, "Autobiography of Rev. William Burke," in *Sketches of Western Methodism,* 79; Robert McAfee interview, Draper Coll., 14CC138.

60. "Diary of Rev. John Lyle" (typescript), 12–18. Lyle was a native of Rockbridge County in the Valley of Virginia. He received his education at Liberty Hall Academy, after experiencing religious conversion during the revival that spread there from Hampden-Sydney. See Davidson, *Presbyterian Church in the State of Kentucky,* 117.

61. Strickland, "Autobiography of Rev. William Burke," *Sketches of Western Methodism,* 77–78.

62. "Diary of Rev. John Lyle" (typescript), 13–14.

63. Findley letter dated 20 Sept. 1801, in Woodward, *Surprising Accounts,* 226.

64. "Diary of Rev. John Lyle" (typescript), 13–14.

65. James B. Finley makes no mention in his autobiography of being accompanied by his father, although James was a youth at the time and far from home. Lyle's reference, on the other hand, sounds as though he recognized the man as the congregation's old pastor. See Strickland, *Finley,* and "Diary of Rev. John Lyle" (typescript), 16.

Chapter 9. The Social Significance of Camp Meeting Revivalism

1. The literature on religious revivalism as a product of social strain is extensive, but see Cross, *The Burned-Over District*; Paul E. Johnson, *A Shopkeeper's Millennium: Society and Revivals in Rochester, New York, 1815-1837* (New York: Hill and Wang, 1978); Ryan, *Cradle of the Middle Class*; Roth, *The Democratic Dilemma*. Although frontier interpretations of the Great Kentucky Revival might have drawn more upon this paradigm, Frederick Jackson Turner seems to have maintained an almost exclusive grip.

2. The body of literature on this is extensive, but see Nathan O. Hatch, *The Democratization of American Christianity* (New Haven: Yale Univ. Press, 1989).

3. Schmidt, *Holy Fairs*; Scott, "James McGready."

4. Rogers, *Biography of Elder Barton Warren Stone*, 12-14.

5. Ibid., 29-30. Blythe, a native of North Carolina, had been one of the students involved with the revival at Hampden-Sydney College. Marshall had participated in the revival at Liberty Hall Academy while a student there. The two ministers had shared a professional association since at least 1791, when they participated in a large revival meeting at Sandy River in Virginia (the same meeting at which Stone first partook of the sacrament). They moved to Kentucky soon afterwards.

6. Ibid., 30-33.

7. Smith, *Posthumous Works of James M'Gready* 1: 37 and 113; Stone, *History of the Christian Church*, 3.

8. "Extract of a Letter from a Gentleman in Washington, Kentucky, to His Son in Philadelphia, July 15, 1801," in *Methodist Magazine* [London] 26 (Mar. 1803): 130.

9. "Diary of Rev. John Lyle" (typescript), 56 and 63. Lyle also noted more orthodox Calvinist preaching at Cane Ridge by Rev. John Rankin and others.

10. Purviance, *Biography of Elder David Purviance*, 137-41; "Minutes of West Lexington Presbytery," entries dated 15 Oct. 1801 and 14 Apr. 1802, 62 and 75.

11. Rogers, *Stone*, 50-55; Stone, *History of the Christian Church*, 3; Thompson, *Presbyterians in the South* 1: 155-65; William Garrett West, *Barton Warren Stone, Early American Advocate of Christian Unity* (Nashville: Disciples of Christ Historical Society, 1954), 53-70; Boles, *The Great Revival*, 149-59.

12. John Opie Jr., "James McGready: Theologian of Frontier Revivalism," *Church History* 34 (1965): 445-56; Thompson, *Presbyterians in the South* 1: 144-55; Boles, *The Great Revival*, 159-64.

13. Conkin, *Cane Ridge*, 99; D. Newell Williams, "Barton W. Stone's Revivalist Theology," in *Cane Ridge in Context: Perspectives on Barton W. Stone and the Revival*, ed. Anthony L. Dunnavant (Nashville: Disciples of Christ Historical Society, 1992), 73-92.

14. A classic treatment of the rites of passage at early camp meetings is Bruce, *And They All Sang Hallelujah*. See also Dalton, "The Kentucky Camp Meeting Revivals of 1797-1805 as Rites of Initiation."

15. Rogers, *Stone*, 39-40; Strickland, *Finley*, 267; "Diary of Rev. John Lyle" (typescript), 3; "Letter from Patterson," in Woodward, *Surprising Accounts*, 36; "Extract 38, of a Letter from a Gentleman in Kentucky to his friend in Philadelphia, dated June 3, 1801," Woodward, *Increase of Piety*, 94-95.

16. Letter from George A. Baxter dated 1 Jan. 1802, *Conn. Evang. Mag.,* 358; "Diary of Rev. John Lyle" (typescript), 3, 11. See also "Extract 38," in Woodward, *Increase of Piety,* 94.

17. Descriptions of falling abound, but see the letter from George A. Baxter dated 1 Jan. 1802, *Conn. Evang. Mag.,* 358. See also "Letter from Patterson," in Woodward, *Surprising Accounts,* 36; "Extract 26. Of a letter from the Rev. Moses Hoge, of Shepherd's Town, to the Rev. Dr. Ashbel Green, of this city, dated September 10, 1801," in Woodward, *Surprising Accounts,* 53; Strickland, *Finley,* 367.

18. Strickland, *Finley,* 365; Davidson, *Presbyterian Church in the State of Kentucky,* 140. See also "Diary of Rev. John Lyle" (typescript), 70.

19. Conkin has argued most strongly for continuity, but only one contemporary account of the Kentucky revival attempts to compare the events of 1800 and 1801 with the extraordinary meeting at Cambuslang, Scotland, in 1742. See Conkin, *Cane Ridge,* 104–6. For a full description of Cambuslang and Scots-Irish revivalism see Schmidt, *Holy Fairs;* and Westerkamp, *Triumph of the Laity.*

20. "Letter from Findley," *Methodist Magazine,* 126; McGready, "A Short Narrative," 49; letter from George A. Baxter dated 1 Jan. 1802, *Conn. Evang. Mag.,* 355; "Letter from Patterson," in Woodward, *Surprising Accounts,* 35.

21. "To the Rev. Dr. Rippon, Bourbon County, January 7, 1802," in Sweet, *The Baptists,* 616. Historians have variously explained this phenomenon as common fainting or hysteria. An exception is Paul Conkin, *Cane Ridge,* 106.

22. "Diary of Rev. John Lyle" (typescript), 10; Purviance, *Biography of Elder David Purviance,* 300; M'Nemar, *Kentucky Revival,* 28. See also Ells, "Great Kentucky Revival," 277; Rogers, *Stone,* 36–37.

23. "Letter from Patterson," *Methodist Magazine* 26 (Feb. 1803): 86; M'Nemar, *Kentucky Revival,* 28; "Letter from Findley," *Methodist Magazine,* 126–27. See also Lyle in Cleveland, *The Great Revival in the West,* 174 and 187; Strickland, *Finley,* 365.

24. Strickland, *Finley,* 166–67.

25. "Diary of Rev. John Lyle" (typescript), 1, emphasis added; Rogers, *Stone,* 158 and 42.

26. Findley letter dated 20 Sept. 1801, in Woodward, *Surprising Accounts,* 225; David Thomas, *The Observer Trying the Great Reformation in This State and Proving It to Have Originally Been a Work of Divine Power* (Lexington: John Bradford, 1802), 22. See also letter from George A. Baxter dated 1 Jan. 1802, *Conn. Evang. Mag.* 2 (1802): 360.

27. McGready, "A Short Narrative," 3; letter from George A. Baxter dated 1 Jan. 1802, *Conn. Evang. Mag.,* 358; "To the Rev. Dr. Rippon, Bourbon County, January 7, 1802," in Sweet, *The Baptists,* 615.

28. "Diary of Rev. John Lyle" (typescript), 7; Findley letter dated 20 Sept. 1801, in Woodward, *Surprising Accounts,* 225.

29. George A. Baxter to Mr. Davis, 4 Sept. 1803, Univ. Archives, Leyburn Library, Washington and Lee Univ. Library.

30. "Letter from Patterson," in Woodward, *Surprising Accounts,* 35–37; "Extract of a Letter from a Gentleman to His Sister in Philadelphia," in Sweet, *The Baptists,* 611. Patterson had military experience, which probably aided his estimates of the crowd. The old practice of distributing lead or pewter tokens to qualified communicants also helped in estimating the number of participants, although at the sacramental revivals ministers could not always know who was eligible, and some gave a token simply upon request.

31. Strickland, *Finley,* 364 and 167; Stuart, "Reminiscences," 173; "Letter from Findley," *Methodist Magazine,* 126; Davidson, *Presbyterian Church in the State of Kentucky,* 134; M'Nemar, *Kentucky Revival,* 31. See also "Letter from Findley, *Methodist Magazine,* 127; "Letter from Patterson," in Woodward, *Surprising Accounts,* 35–39. Boles and others have emphasized the importance of camp meeting hymns in conveying theological information, but the integrative ritual experience of group song was also important. See Boles, *The Great Revival,* 111–24; Bruce, *And They All Sang Hallelujah.*

32. Rogers, *Stone,* 39–40; Purviance, *Biography of Elder David Purviance,* 301; M'Nemar, *Kentucky Revival,* 61–62; Stuart, "Reminiscences," 172–73.

33. "Extract 26. Of a letter from the Rev. Moses Hoge, . . . dated September 10, 1801," in Woodward, *Surprising Accounts,* 53–54; Strickland, *Finley,* 365–67; "Diary of Rev. John Lyle" (typescript), 16.

34. Purviance, *Biography of Elder David Purviance,* 301; Cartwright, *Autobiography,* 48; Strickland, *Finley,* 372; Lorenzo Dow, *The Dealings of God and the Devil as Exemplified in the Life, Experience, and Travels of Lorenzo Dow, in a Period of More than Half a Century,* 4th ed. (Norwich, Conn.: W. Falkner, 1833), 144, 155. The notion that these more extreme behaviors appeared by the time of Cane Ridge probably originates in the impressions of chaos and loss of control by observers, and particularly from Stone's autobiography, where he proceeds from a description of Cane Ridge abruptly into a new chapter describing the various bodily exercises. Nowhere, however, does he or any other witness explicitly claim that the jerks occurred at Cane Ridge or other early camp meetings. The vagueness of contemporary descriptions nonetheless does leave the question open.

35. M'Nemar, *Kentucky Revival,* 26.

36. Victor Turner, *The Ritual Process: Structure and Antistructure* (Chicago: Aldine, 1969). Turner's theory is succinctly summarized in Mathieu Deflem, "Religion: A Discussion of Victor Turner's Processual Symbolic Analysis," *Journal for the Scientific Study of Religion* 1 (1991): 14–15.

37. Strickland, *Finley,* 366.

38. Ibid., 166. See also letter from George A. Baxter dated 1 Jan. 1802, *Conn. Evang. Mag.,* 356; Purviance, *Biography of Elder David Purviance,* 300.

39. "Letter from Findley," *Methodist Magazine,* 127.

40. "Extract 26. Of a letter from the Rev. Moses Hoge, . . . dated September 10, 1801," in Woodward, *Surprising Accounts,* 53–54.

41. Strickland, *Finley,* 166–67. See also "Letter from Patterson," *Methodist Magazine* 26 (Feb. 1803): 86; Stuart, "Reminiscences," 173–74.

42. "Diary of Rev. John Lyle" (typescript), 30 (quotation) and 61.

43. Ibid., 16. Unfortunately, no lay exhortation was recorded in sufficient detail to explore the intriguing possibility that the laity contributed their own theological interpretations. On the significance of lay participants, see Bell, *Ritual Theory, Ritual Practice*, 213–21.

44. Rankin, "Autobiography," 35. See also Strickland, "Autobiography of Rev. William Burke," *Sketches of Western Methodism*, 76; Rogers, *Stone*, 37–38; Smith, "Tours into Kentucky," 372; Boles, *The Great Revival*, 143–48.

45. H. C. Northcott, ed., *Biography of Rev. Benjamin Northcott, a Pioneer Local Preacher of the Methodist Episcopal Church in Kentucky, and for More than Sixty-three Years in the Ministry* (Cincinnati: Western Methodist Book Concern, 1875), 35. See also George McIlvaine's comment in Willard Rouse Jillson, "Early Kentucky History in Manuscript: A Brief Account of the Draper and Shane Collections," *RKHS* 33 (1935): 147.

46. Strickland, "Autobiography of Rev. William Burke," *Sketches of Western Methodism*, 79. See also Rogers, *Stone*, 44–45.

47. "Diary of Rev. John Lyle" (typescript), 19; Rogers, *Stone*, 37–38. See also Stone, *History of the Christian Church*, 3.

48. Purviance, *Biography of Elder David Purviance*, 297; "Letter from Findley," *Methodist Magazine*, 127; "Extract 22. Of a letter from a gentleman in Washington (Ken.) to his son in this city, dated March 19, 1801," in Woodward, *Surprising Accounts*, 47; Garrett, *Recollections of the West*, 29.

49. Western Methodists experienced a similar change during this period. "The class meetings were free to all, the love-feasts open to all; and they were mixed up in such confusion that it was impossible to tell to what Church or denomination they [participants] belonged": Strickland, "Autobiography of Rev. William Burke," *Sketches of Western Methodism*, 80.

50. McGready, "A Short Narrative," 48; Findley letter dated 20 Sept. 1801, in Woodward, *Surprising Accounts*, 226; Fowler, "Kentucky 150 Years Ago [Henry Alderson letter, September 10, 1801]," 50; "To the Rev. Dr. Rippon, Bourbon County, January 7, 1802," in Sweet, *The Baptists*, 614.

51. McGready, "A Short Narrative," 50. See also Purviance, *Biography of Elder David Purviance*, 300.

52. Strickland, *Finley*, 366; M'Nemar, *Kentucky Revival*, 20. Another good example is found in McGready, "A Short Narrative," 100–101.

53. M'Nemar, *Kentucky Revival*, 25–26. Additional examples of exhortation by children are found in M'Nemar on pages 20–21 and "Letter from Patterson," in Woodward, *Surprising Accounts*, 36–37.

54. "Diary of Rev. John Lyle" (typescript), 25–26. On the reversal of status, see Beverly J. Stoeltje, "Festival in America," in *Handbook of American Folklore*, ed. Richard M. Dorson (Bloomington: Indiana Univ. Press, 1983), 243.

55. The literature on religion as a feminine activity is rich as well as extensive, but see: Ryan, *Cradle of the Middle Class*; Nancy A. Hewitt, *Women's Activism and Social Change: Rochester, New York, 1822–1872* (Ithaca: Cornell Univ. Press, 1984); Anne E. Carr, *Transforming Grace: Christian Tradition and Women's Experience* (San Francisco, Harper and Row, 1988); Curtis Johnson, *Islands of Holiness*; Ted Ownby, *Subduing Satan: Religion, Recreation, and Manhood in*

the Rural South, 1865–1920 (Chapel Hill: Univ. of North Carolina Press, 1990); Susan Juster, *Disorderly Women: Sexual Politics and Evangelicalism in Revolutionary New England* (Ithaca: Cornell Univ. Press, 1994); Randy J. Sparks, *On Jordan's Stormy Banks: Evangelicalism in Mississippi, 1773–1876* (Athens: Univ. of Georgia Press, 1994).

56. M'Nemar, *Kentucky Revival*, 35–36; "Diary of Rev. John Lyle" (typescript), 18 and 2. See also Strickland, *Finley*, 166–67.

57. Providence Baptist Church Minute Book (typescript), Kentucky Historical Society; Bryant's [Bryan's] Station Church Minute Book (photocopy), Kentucky Historical Society.

58. Fowler, "Kentucky 150 Years Ago [Henry Alderson letter, 10 Sept. 1801]," 55.

59. "Michaux's Travels," 249.

60. "Diary of Rev. John Lyle" (typescript), 5 and 69; McGready, "A Short Narrative, 102. The Great Revival was accompanied by a rise in emancipated slaves, at least at Cane Ridge and possibly other quarters as well. See Eslinger, "Some Notes on the History of Cane Ridge prior to the Great Revival," 18–20, and "The Great Revival in Bourbon County," 285–86.

61. McGready, "A Short Narrative," 51; "Diary of Rev. John Lyle" (typescript), 15; "Extract of a Letter from a Gentleman to his Sister in Philadelphia," in Sweet, *The Baptists*, 611; Robert Stuart Sanders, "Walnut Hill Presbyterian Church," *RKHS* 54 (1956): 114–16; "Diary of Rev. John Lyle" (typescript), 24–25.

62. Key works on Afro-American Christianity in eighteenth-century Virginia include Albert J. Raboteau, *Slave Religion: The "Invisible Institution" in the Antebellum South* (New York: Oxford Univ. Press, 1979); Sobel, *Trablin' On*; Sylvia R. Frey, *Water from the Rock: Black Resistance in a Revolutionary Age* (Princeton: Princeton Univ. Press, 1991); Isaac, *Transformation of Virginia*; Jon Butler, *Awash in a Sea of Faith: Christianizing the American People* (Cambridge: Harvard Univ. Press, 1990), chap. 5. For a closer consideration of race and religion in Kentucky during this period, see Eslinger, "Beginnings of Afro-American Christianity among Kentucky Baptists."

63. In two large Baptist congregations located in the Bluegrass region, blacks were not numerous before the Great Revival, but they constituted approximately 20 percent of the new converts. For western Methodists, on the other hand, only 3 percent of the new members gained between 1800 and 1806 were black. Leland Winfield Meyer, "The Great Crossings Church Records, 1795–1801," *RKHS* 34 (1930): 3–21, 171–95; Bryant's [Bryan's] Station Church Minute Book; *Minutes of the Methodist Conference*, 97 and 364; Eslinger, "Beginnings of Afro-American Christianity among Kentucky Baptists."

64. Hardly any Baptist congregation with black members escaped this issue. See, e.g., Bryant's [Bryan's] Station Church Minute Book, 27–28, 41, 49, 82, 84, and 102–3.

65. McGee to Douglas, *Methodist Magazine*, 190; "Diary of Rev. John Lyle" (typescript), 15.

66. Stone, *History of the Christian Church*, 2; "Recollections of Thomas Hamilton," in *Biographical Sketches of Living Old Men of the Cumberland Presbyterian Church*, ed. E. B. Crisman (St. Louis: A. F. Cox, 1877), vol. 1: 95; Strickland,

"Autobiography of Rev. William Burke," *Sketches of Western Methodism,* 78. Interestingly, however, the first reference to sexual misconduct was recorded by Lyle, the most critical and reliable contemporary source, shortly after the meeting at Cane Ridge—following a full summer of evangelical events. See "Diary of Rev. John Lyle" (typescript), 22.

67. Stuart, "Reminiscences," 174; Stone, *History of the Christian Church,* 2.
68. McGee to Douglas, *Methodist Magazine,* 190.
69. "Extract 40, Of a letter from a gentleman in Washington, Kentucky, to his Son in Philadelphia, dated July 28, 1801," in Woodward, *Increase of Piety,* 99–100.
70. Later in the nineteenth century, party politics and voluntary associations joined camp meetings as integrative mechanisms. See Don Harrison Doyle, *The Social Order of a Frontier Community: Jacksonville, Illinois, 1825–70* (Urbana: Univ. of Illinois Press, 1978).
71. Archibald Alexander letter dated 25 Jan. 1802, *Conn. Evang. Mag.* 2 (1802): 354. See also "Extract of a letter received by Mr. Joseph Magoffin, merchant, of Philadelphia, from his son, dated Salisbury N. Carolina, 26th June 1802," in Woodward, *Increase of Piety,* 108–9.
72. "[Minutes of the General Assembly—A.D. 1803]: General State of Religion in the Presbyterian Church of the United States," in *Western Missionary Magazine and Repository of Religious Intelligence* (Washington, Penn.) 1 (1803): 310. See also letter from George A. Baxter dated 1 Jan. 1802, *Conn. Evang. Mag.* 2 (1802): 354–60; "Letter from Patterson" in Woodward, *Surprising Accounts,* 34–39; "Letter from Findley," *Methodist Magazine,* 125–27; and various contributions published in the *Western Missionary Magazine* 1 (1803): 19–27, 48, 103, 139–47, 173–77, 180–84, 254–57, 287–95, 310, 456–62. Many of these letters and others were collected and published in a single volume by William W. Woodward, ed., *Surprising Accounts of the Revival of Religion in the United States of America, in Different Parts of the World, and among Different Denominations of Christians,* in 1802, and in a similar volume, *Increase of Piety, or The Revival of Religion in the United States of America, Containing Several Interesting Letters Not before Published, Together with Three Remarkable Dreams* (Newburyport, Mass.: Angier March, 1802).
73. Clark, *Journal and Letters of Francis Asbury* 3: 251 and 453.
74. Russell Richey, *Early American Methodism* (Bloomington: Indiana Univ. Press, 1991).
75. "Diary of Rev. John Lyle" (typescript), 22–24; letter from George A. Baxter dated 1 Jan. 1802, *Conn. Evang. Mag.,* 356–57. See also Stuart, "Reminiscences," 173. For the developmental nature of ritual, see Turner, *Ritual Process.*
76. Johnson, *Frontier Camp Meeting,* 43; Bruce, *And They All Sang Hallelujah,* 70–73; Ellen Weiss, *City in the Woods: The Life and Design of an American Camp Meeting on Martha's Vineyard* (New York: Oxford Univ. Press, 1987); Roger Robins, "Vernacular American Landscape: Methodists, Camp Meetings, and Social Respectability," *Religion and American Culture* 4 (1994): 165–91. For an example of instructions for organizing camp meetings, see B. W. Gorham, *Camp Meeting Manual: A Practical Guide for the Camp Ground* (Boston: H. V. Degen, 1854).

77. Turner distinguished between the "spontaneous" communitas of new rituals and the more common "normative" communitas of established rituals. See Turner, "Variations on a Theme of Liminality," 46; Mathieu Deflem, "Religion: A Discussion of Victor Turner's Processual Symbolic Analysis," *Journal for the Scientific Study of Religion* 30 (1991): 14–15. See also Victor Turner, *Ritual Process*, 131–40.

78. *Minutes of the Annual Conferences* 1: 92 and 129; "Minutes of the Elkhorn Association," *The Baptists*, 486 and 506; Henry S. Robinson, "History of the Green River Association of Baptists in the State of Kentucky" (typescript), Southern Baptist Theological Seminary, Louisville. (Since one congregation did not submit a report of members in 1800, figures for 1801 were adjusted accordingly.) See also Boles, *The Great Revival*, 185.

79. "Diary of Rev. John Lyle" (typescript), 47–48.

80. For examples of evangelical religion as a conservative social force, see Paul Johnson, *A Shopkeeper's Millennium*; and William Warren Sweet, "The Churches as Moral Courts of the Frontier," *Church History* 2 (1933): 3–21. See also the historiographical comments by Hatch, *Democratization of American Christianity*, 220–26.

81. Terah Templin to Joshua L. Wilson, 2 Feb. 1803, Joshua L. Wilson Papers, Durrett Coll.; McGready, *Western Missionary Magazine* 1 (May 1803): 177; letter from George A. Baxter dated 1 Jan. 1802, *Conn. Evang. Mag.* 2 (1802): 355; Thomas, *The Observer Trying the Great Reformation in This State* 1; Arthur Campbell to Rev. Charles Cummings, 25 Dec. 1802, Kings Mountain Papers, Draper Coll., 9DD76; Christopher Waldrep, "The Making of a Border State Society: James McGready, the Great Revival, and the Prosecution of Profanity in Kentucky," *American Historical Review* 99 (1994): 767–84. The latter work represents the most explicit attempt to connect the early camp meetings and subsequent morality, but I confess not being fully persuaded by the methodology.

82. The literature is extensive, but for recent works that consider evangelical Protestantism's sweeping effect, see Hatch, *Democratization of American Christianity*; Wood, *Radicalism of the American Revolution*; and Richard L. Bushman, *The Refinement of America: Persons, Houses, Cities* (New York: Alfred A. Knopf, 1992).

83. Gordon Wood, *Radicalism of the American Revolution*, argues that this was the Revolution's most radical aspect.

84. This term is drawn from Anderson, *Imagined Communities*.

85. Mathews, "The Second Great Awakening as an Organizing Process," 27 and 34.

86. Hatch, *Democratization of American Christianity*.

87. Watts, *The Republic Reborn*.

88. MacAloon, ed., *Rite, Drama, Festival, Spectacle*, 1–4.

89. Examples of this theory that ritual models or defines ideal relations and values may be found in the work of Clifford Geertz, Terence S. Turner, Mary Douglas, and Steven Lukes. See Bell, *Ritual Theory, Ritual Practice*, 175.

90. Hatch, *Democratization of American Christianity*, 68–81.

BIBLIOGRAPHIC ESSAY

Scholars of early Kentucky are fortunate in having available a rich body of archival material, much of which is fairly accessible.

The major manuscript collection, that of Lyman C. Draper, is housed at the Wisconsin State Historical Society, but copies of the microfilm are in practically every major research library. It is a massive, somewhat complex, but incredibly rich collection. A good point of departure is Josephine Harper, *Guide to the Draper Manuscripts* (Madison: State Historical Society of Wisconsin, 1983). Part of this collection, the John D. Shane Papers, includes the notes for numerous interviews with aging pioneers conducted by Shane circa 1840. Anyone interested in these interviews will want to consult Elizabeth A. Perkins, "Border Life: Experience and Perception in the Revolutionary Ohio Valley" (Ph.D. diss., Northwestern Univ., 1992). Other material collected by Shane is at the Presbyterian Historical Society in Philadelphia, where it is also available on microfilm. Many of the fuller interviews were published in the early years of the *Filson Club Historical Quarterly (FCHQ)*. Among these are the following interviews, edited by Lucien Beckner: "Reverend John D. Shane's Interview with Pioneer William Clinkenbeard," *FCHQ* 2 (1928): 95–128; "John D. Shane's Interview with Benjamin Allen, Clark County," *FCHQ* 5 (1931): 63–98; and "John D. Shane's Notes on an Interview with Jeptha Kemper of Montgomery County," *FCHQ* 12 (1938): 151–61. Published interviews edited by Otto A. Rothert include the following: "John D. Shane's Interview with Mrs. John McKinney and Her Son Harvey, Bourbon County," *FCHQ* 13 (1939): 157–78; and "John D. Shane's Interview with Pioneer John Hedge," *FCHQ* 14 (1940): 176–81.

Numerous other firsthand accounts of Kentucky settlement have been published. Only the short titles can be given here. Some of the best are as follows: Donald F. Carmody, ed., "Spencer Records' Memoir of the Ohio Valley Frontier, 1766–1795," *Indiana Magazine of History* 55 (1959): 323–77; Lucien Beckner, ed., "A Sketch of the Early Adventures of William Sudduth in Kentucky," *FCHQ* 2 (1928): 43–70; Levi Purviance, *The Biography of Elder David Purviance, with His Memoirs* (Dayton: published for the author by B. F. and G. W. Ells, 1848); James Smith, *An Account of the Remarkable Occurances in the Life and Travels of Colonel James Smith* (Lexington: John Bradford, 1799); W. P. Strickland, ed., *Autobiography of Rev. James B. Finley, or Pioneer Life in the West* (Cincinnati: printed at the Methodist Book Concern for the author, 1854); James Ross, *The Life and Times of Elder Reuben Ross* (Philadelphia: Grant, Faires, and Rogers,

1882); Charles Drake, ed., *Pioneer Life in Kentucky: A Series of Reminiscential Letters from Daniel Drake, M.D., of Cincinnati to His Children* (Cincinnati: Robert Clarke, 1870); John I. Rogers, ed., *Autobiography of Elder Samuel Rogers* (Cincinnati: Standard, 1881); and Chester Raymond Young, ed., *Westward into Kentucky: The Narrative of Daniel Trabue* (Lexington: Univ. Press of Kentucky, 1981).

Firsthand descriptions are also found in various travel and promotional material. These include James Nourse, "Journal to Kentucky in 1775," *Journal of American History* 19 (1925): 121–38; and James Smith, "Journey through Kentucky and into the Northwest Territory, 1795," *Ohio Archaeological and Historical Quarterly* 16 (1907): 348–401. English immigrant Harry Toulmin left two detailed accounts: *A Description of Kentucky in North America,* ed. Thomas D. Clark (Lexington: Univ. Press of Kentucky, 1945), and *The Western Country in 1793: Reports on Kentucky and Virginia,* ed. Marion Tinling and Godfrey Davis (San Marino: Henry E. Huntington Library, 1948). See also Gilbert Imlay, *A Topographical Description of the Western Territory of North America, Containing a Succinct Account of Its Climate, Natural History, Population, Agriculture, Manners and Customs, . . .* (London: printed for J. Debrett, 1792); J. F. D. Smyth, *A Tour in the United States of America Containing an Account of the Recent Situations of That Country; the Population, Agriculture, Commerce, Customs, and Manners of the Inhabitants,* 2 vols. (London: printed for G. Robinson, J. Robinson, and J. Sewell, 1784). The journals of André Michaux and his son, François-André Michaux, are reprinted in *Early Western Travels, 1748–1846,* 32 vols., edited by Reuben Gold Thwaites (Cleveland: Arthur H. Clark, 1904). See also the two journals of William Fleming in Newton D. Mereness, ed., *Travels in the American Colonies* (New York: Macmillan, 1916).

A great deal of primary source material is, of course, found in Kentucky. The three largest historical collections are at the Kentucky Historical Society in Frankfort, the Filson Club Historical Society in Louisville, and the Margaret I. King Library at the University of Kentucky in Lexington. In addition to extensive manuscript holdings, all three libraries offer much genealogical material useful to the historian. Microfilm copies of many county records are also available.

The other main manuscript collection on early Kentucky is that of Reuben T. Durrett at the University of Chicago. Many items in this collection are actually early-twentieth-century typescript copies of material available in manuscript in the Draper Collection or elsewhere. A huge portion consists of miscellaneous legal documents such as land titles and notes of hand. A significant portion is original manuscript and rich in content, especially when used in conjunction with other materials.

Other manuscript collections relevant to early Kentucky settlement may be found by tracing settlers either back to their origins or, less frequently, forward to where they spent their later years. In the special collections at the University of Virginia, early Kentucky material may be found the Terrell-Carr Family Papers, Isaac Davis Papers, and Carter-Smith Family Papers. At the Virginia Historical Society in Richmond, see the Hugh Blair Grigsby Papers; at Washington and Lee University in Lexington, Virginia, are the Zachariah Johnston Papers and the William Fleming Papers. Letters from Kentucky pioneers may also be found at the College of William and Mary's Swem Library, including the Skipwith Family Papers, Archibald Wood Papers, and Leven Powell Papers. The James McDowell Papers reside in the Southern Historical Collection at the University of North Carolina at Chapel Hill, and Duke University offers the William Bolling Papers. A few public figures have papers in manuscript at the Library of Congress, the largest collections being for Harry Innes, Isaac Shelby, and the Breckinridge family. See also scattered letters from Kentucky in the Peter Force Collection.

Other public records used in this study include various county tax lists, will books, and court order books. Nearly all have been microfilmed, with copies of many at the Kentucky Historical Society or Margaret I. King Library at the University of Kentucky. Some of these have also been published in early volumes of the *Register of the Kentucky Historical Society* or the *Filson Club History Quarterly*. For the period when Kentucky was part of Virginia, see William P. Palmer et al., *Calendar of Virginia State Papers*, 11 vols. (Richmond: Rush U. Derr, 1875–93); and James Rood Robertson, ed., *Petitions of the Early Inhabitants of Kentucky to the General Assembly of Virginia, 1769 to 1792*, Filson Club Publications, no. 27 (Louisville: John P. Morton, 1914). Since this latter work is not complete, see also John Frederick Dorman, comp., *Petitions from Kentucky to the Virginia Legislature, 1766–1791, A Supplement to "Petitions of the Early Inhabitants of Kentucky to the General Assembly of Virginia, 1769–1792"* (Easley, S.C.: Southern Historical Press, 1981). For two secondary works on the process to Kentucky statehood, see Patricia Watlington, *The Partisan Spirit: Kentucky Politics, 1779–1792* (Chapel Hill: Univ. of North Carolina Press for the Institute of Early American History and Culture, 1972); and Joan Wells Coward, *Kentucky in the New Republic: The Process of Constitution Making* (Lexington: Univ. Press of Kentucky, 1979). The best study of Kentucky's relationship with the new national government may still be Mary K. Bonsteel Tachau, *Federal Courts in the Early Republic: Kentucky, 1789–1816* (Princeton: Princeton Univ. Press, 1978).

The literature on early camp meeting revivalism is very large, but an excellent place to start because of the extensive use of primary sources is with John B. Boles, *The Great Revival, 1797–1805: The Origins of the Southern Evangelical Mind* (Lexington: Univ. Press of Kentucky, 1972). Early camp meeting revivalism had some superb contemporary chroniclers. The fullest account is the diary kept by Presbyterian minister John Lyle. For this book, I consulted the typewritten transcript in the Durrett Collection, but extensive passages have been published as appendixes IV and V in Catherine C. Cleveland, *The Great Revival in the West, 1797–1805* (Chicago: Univ. of Chicago Press, 1916). Another early account was kept by a colleague who soon joined the Shakers: Richard M'Nemar, *The Kentucky Revival, or A Short History of the Late Extraordinary Outpouring of the Spirit of God in the Western States of America* (rpt., New York: Edward O. Jenkins, 1846). Other key figures leaving firsthand accounts include James Smith, ed., *The Posthumous Works of the Reverend and Pious James M'Gready, Late Minister of the Gospel, in Henderson, Kentucky,* 2 vols. (Louisville: W. W. Worsley, 1931); Barton Warren Stone, *History of the Christian Church in the West* (Lexington: College of the Bible, 1956); and Rev. James B. Finley in his *Sketches of Western Methodism: Biographical, Historical, and Miscellaneous, Illustrative of Pioneer Life,* ed. W. P. Strickland (Cincinnati: printed at the Methodist Book Concern for the author, 1855). Detailed letters by Robert Patterson, George A. Baxter, and John E. Findley describing the early camp meetings were reprinted in numerous religious publications. These, plus a number of others, were collected in two rare volumes edited by William W. Woodward of Philadelphia: *Surprising Accounts of the Revival of Religion in the United States of America, in Different Parts of the World, and among Different Denominations of Christians, with a Number of Interesting Occurrences of Divine Providence* (Philadelphia: privately printed, 1802), and *Increase of Piety, or The Revival of Religion in the United States of America, Containing Several Interesting Letters Not before Published, Together with Three Remarkable Dreams* (Newburyport, Mass.: Angier March, 1802). See also the documentary material collected by William Warren Sweet in his four-volume treatment of religion's westward expansion in the nineteenth century, *Religion on the American Frontier.*

Other useful sources for early western religion include Robert Davidson, *A History of the Presbyterian Church in the State of Kentucky with a Preliminary Sketch of the Churches in the Valley of Virginia* (New York: Robert Carter, 1847); Robert H. Bishop, *An Outline of the History of the Church in the State of Kentucky during a Period of Forty Years* (Lexington: Thomas Skillman, 1824); J. H. Spencer, *A History of Kentucky Baptists from 1769 to 1885, Including More than Eight Hundred Biographical Sketches,* 2 vols. (Cincinnati: J. R. Baumes, 1885); Ernest Trice Thompson, *Presbyterians in the South,* vol. 1: *1607–1861* (Richmond: John Knox Press, 1963); and the professional memoirs of preacher John Taylor, most recently available in a volume edited by Chester Raymond Young, *Baptists on the American Frontier: A History of Ten Baptist Churches of Which the Author Has Been Alternately a Member*, by John Taylor (Macon: Mercer Univ. Press, 1995).

My interpretation of early camp meeting revivalism was informed by a number of theoretical works, including the following: Michael Banton, ed., *Anthropological Approaches to the Study of Religion* (London: Tavistock, 1966); Victor Turner, *The Ritual Process: Structure and Antistructure* (Chicago: Aldine, 1969); and *Dramas, Fields, and Metaphors: Symbolic Action in Human Society* (Ithaca: Cornell Univ. Press, 1974); Sally Falk Moore and Barbara G. Myerhoff, eds., *Secular Ritual* (Amsterdam: Van Gorcum, Assen, 1977) and *Symbol and Politics in Communal Ideology* (Ithaca: Cornell Univ. Press, 1975); John J. MacAloon, ed., *Rite, Drama, Festival, Spectacle: Rehearsals toward a Theory of Cultural Performance* (Philadelphia: Institute for the Study of Human Issues, 1984); Catherine Bell, *Ritual Theory, Ritual Practice* (New York: Oxford Univ. Press, 1992).

Many more general works are helpful in understanding the broad contours of the early camp meeting era. These include Joyce Appleby, *Capitalism and a New Social Order* (New York: New York Univ. Press, 1984); Robert H. Wiebe, *The Opening of American Society: From the Adoption of the Constitution to the Eve of Disunion* (New York: Alfred A. Knopf, 1984); Stanley Elkins and Eric McKitrick, *The Age of Federalism* (New York: Oxford Univ. Press, 1993); Malcolm J. Rohrbough, *The Trans-Appalachian Frontier: People, Societies, and Institutions, 1775–1850* (New York: Oxford Univ. Press, 1978); Richard R. Beeman, *The Evolution of the Southern Backcountry: A Case Study of Lunenburg County, Virginia, 1746–1832* (Philadelphia: Univ. of Pennsylvania Press, 1984); John Mack Faragher, *Sugar Creek: Life on the Illinois Prairie* (New Haven: Yale Univ. Press, 1986); Don Harrison Doyle, *The Social Order of a Frontier Community: Jacksonville, Illinois, 1825–70* (Urbana: Univ. of Illinois Press, 1978); Richard White, *The Middle Ground: Indians, Empires, and Republics in the Great Lakes Region, 1650–1815* (Cambridge: Cambridge Univ. Press, 1991); Gordon S. Wood, *The Creation of the American Republic, 1776–1787* (Chapel Hill: Univ. of North Carolina Press, 1969); Nathan O. Hatch, *The Democratization of American Christianity* (New Haven: Yale Univ. Press, 1989).

The works recommended here are but a selection of the more prominent materials pertaining to early Kentucky settlement and religion.

INDEX